ZIONISM AND ARABISM
IN PALESTINE AND ISRAEL

ZIONISM AND ARABISM IN PALESTINE AND ISRAEL

Edited by
ELIE KEDOURIE
and
SYLVIA G. HAIM

FRANK CASS

First published 1982 in Great Britain by
FRANK CASS AND COMPANY LIMITED
Gainsborough House, 11 Gainsborough Road,
London, E11 1RS, England

and in the United States of America by
FRANK CASS AND COMPANY LIMITED
c/o Biblio Distribution Centre
81 Adams Drive, P.O. Box 327, Totowa, N.J. 07511

Copyright © 1982 Frank Cass & Co. Ltd.

British Library Cataloguing in Publication Data

Zionism and Arabism in Palestine and Israel.
 1. Palestine – Politics and government
 I. Kedourie, Elie
 II. Haim, Sylvia G
 956.94'04   DS126

ISBN 0-7146-3169-8

All rights reserved. No part of this publication may be reproduced, stored in a retrieval system, or transmitted in any form, or by any means, electronic, mechanical, photocopying, recording, or otherwise, without the prior permission of Frank Cass and Company Ltd.

Typeset by Computacomp (UK) Ltd, Fort William, Scotland
Printed in Great Britain by
Bourne Press Limited, 3-11 Spring Road, Bournemouth

Contents

PREFACE		vii
NOTES ON CONTRIBUTORS		ix
THE YISHUV, SIR HERBERT SAMUEL, AND THE ARAB QUESTION IN PALESTINE, 1921–25	Neil Caplan	1
ARAB REBELLION AND TERRORISM IN PALESTINE 1929–39: THE CASE OF SHEIKH IZZ AL-DIN AL-QASSAM AND HIS MOVEMENT	Shai Lachman	52
THE MILITARY FORCE OF ISLAM: THE SOCIETY OF THE MUSLIM BRETHREN AND THE PALESTINE QUESTION, 1945–48	Thomas Mayer	100
THE ARAB STATES AND PALESTINE	Aaron S. Klieman	118
THE ANGLO-AMERICAN COMMISSION OF INQUIRY ON PALESTINE 1945–46: THE ZIONIST REACTION RECONSIDERED	Joseph Heller	137
HUSNI AL-BARAZI ON ARAB NATIONALISM IN PALESTINE	Allen H. Podet	171
'WITHDRAWAL WITHOUT RECOMMENDATIONS': BRITAIN'S DECISION TO RELINQUISH THE PALESTINE MANDATE, 1947	Amitzur Ilan	183
JEWISH EMIGRATION AND SOVIET-ARAB RELATIONS, 1954–67	Yaacov Ro'i	210
THE DEVELOPMENT OF AFRICAN-ISRAELI RELATIONS TO THE YOM KIPPUR WAR: NIGERIA AS A CASE STUDY	Ibrahim A. Gambari	228
INTEGRATION OF ARABS IN AN ISRAELI PARTY: THE CASE OF MAPAM, 1948–54	Yael Yishai	240

Preface

The ten studies published in this volume were submitted, and accepted, for publication in *Middle Eastern Studies*. But it has seemed to the Editors that these studies, tackling as they do various issues stemming from the long drawn out conflict between Arabism and Zionism before and after the establishment of Israel, form a coherent collection and could, with advantage, be published together – hence the present volume. The studies fall into a number of well-defined groups. The first three chapters reconsider aspects of Arab-Jewish relations and the Arab struggle against Zionism from the arrival of Sir Herbert Samuel in Palestine until the end of the Mandate. New light is here thrown on Zionist attitudes to the Arab question, on the beginnings of the Arab armed struggle against the Mandate and Jewish settlement, and on the character of the intervention by the Muslim Brethren in the affairs of Palestine during the last years of the Mandate.

The next four chapters are concerned with the diplomatic events and the political decisions leading to the abandonment of the Mandate by Great Britain. Here, too, issues are raised and questions posed which stimulate thought and give rise to further questions.

Chapters eight and nine relate to the diplomatic history of Israel and of the Arab-Israeli conflict. They illustrate how the Palestine question, from being a relatively local and minor question at its beginnings, now has multifarious and world-wide ramifications.

Finally, the last chapter deals with an aspect of the political and economic life of town Arabs of Palestine who, through the accident of war, now find themselves Israeli citizens.

E.K.

S.G.H.

Due to the high cost of printing, it has been decided to eliminate diacritical marks in transliteration, except in a few cases where ambiguity could arise.

Notes on Contributors

Neil Caplan, author of *Palestine Jewry and the Arab Question, 1917–1925* (Cass, 1978) and *Futile Diplomacy: A Documentary Study of Arab-Zionist Negotiation Attempts* (forthcoming), teaches Humanities at Vanier College, Montréal.

Shai Lachman teaches at the Department of Middle Eastern History of the University of Haifa. From 1972 to 1975 he was Coordinator of the Middle East Research Unit in the Harry S. Truman Research Institute, the Hebrew University of Jerusalem. At present he is preparing his Ph.D. thesis.

Thomas Mayer has studied Modern History of the Muslim Countries at the Hebrew University of Jerusalem, and is currently a Ph.D. student at the London School of Economics.

Aaron S. Klieman is senior lecturer in International Relations and former chairman, Department of Political Science, Tel-Aviv University. Visiting professor at Georgetown University (1979–80), he is author of *Foundations of British Policy in the Arab World*.

Joseph Heller is senior lecturer in the Departments of International Relations and Jewish History at the Hebrew University of Jerusalem. His book on *British Policy towards the Ottoman Empire, 1908–1914* is soon to appear, and he is currently completing another book on *The Emergence of the State of Israel, 1945–1948*.

Allen Podet is Associate Professor of Philosophy and Religious Studies at New York State University College, Buffalo, New York. He has done primary research at the U.S. Department of State and the Foreign and Colonial Offices, and has lectured extensively in the United States, England and Germany. He is producing a book on post-war Palestine.

Amitzur Ilan is a Research Fellow at the Institute for Zionist Research of Tel-Aviv University, and a Senior Associate Member of St Antony's

College, Oxford. He is the author of *America, Britain and Palestine* (Jerusalem 1979).

Yaacov Ro'i is Head of the Russian and East European Research Center at Tel Aviv University and Senior Lecturer in Russian History there. He is the author of *From Encroachment to Involvement* (John Wiley and Israel Universities Press, 1974) and *Soviet Decision Making in Practice: Soviet-Israeli Relations, 1947–1954* (Transaction, forthcoming), and editor of *The Limits to Power* (Croom Helm and St Martin's, 1979).

Ibrahim A. Gambari, formerly an Assistant Professor at State University of New York, Albany, is now Senior Lecturer in Political Science, Ahmadu Bello University, Zaria, Nigeria. He is editor of *Nigerian Journal of Political Science*, and his book, *Party Politics and Foreign Policy: Nigeria 1960–65*, has just been published by Ahmadu Bello University Press.

Yael Yishai is a graduate of the Hebrew University of Jerusalem where she received her PhD in Political Science (1976). She is currently a Senior Lecturer in Political Science at the University of Haifa. Her publications include a book and numerous articles on interest groups and political parties in Palestine and Israel.

The Yishuv, Sir Herbert Samuel, and the Arab Question in Palestine, 1921-25

Neil Caplan

In recent years, the use of unpublished British and Zionist archive material has produced a number of interesting and detailed studies of British Palestine policy and the early development of the Zionist-Arab conflict. Sir Herbert Samuel, first High Commissioner to Palestine (1920-25) and a Jew, has been the subject of scholarly articles by Elie Kedourie and Bernard Wasserstein.[1] The present article seeks to complement the existing literature on Samuel by exploring in more detail the reactions of the Yishuv (Jewish community of Palestine) to his chosen style and methods of governing Palestine during his term of office.

While Herbert Samuel often differed with official Zionist spokesmen, like Chaim Weizmann, the clash between him and local Palestinian Jews was more pronounced. Jews on the spot were hardly as subtle or sophisticated as either Samuel or Zionist leaders from England, Europe or America. Showing little patience for diplomatic niceties, Yishuv leaders preferred a direct approach to most questions, perceiving and advancing their political and communal interests with single-minded tenacity. The Jews of Palestine saw themselves as a beleaguered minority endowed with historic rights, but without the strength to protect those rights from a hostile native population. Hence, during the period of the mandate they persisted in demanding from British rulers of the country a degree of active sympathy which went far beyond the latter's proclaimed 'equality of obligation' to both Jews and Arabs.[2]

In a sense, the differences between the Yishuv and Sir Herbert Samuel were not unlike today's gap between local Israeli attitudes and those of influential Jewish friends from abroad who would suggest solutions to the Arab-Israeli dispute. The Yishuv disagreed sharply with those who, like Samuel, sought 'liberal' solutions to the Palestine conflict. Although approaches to the 'Arab question' varied among the diverse elements within the Yishuv, Samuel's policies which aimed at conciliating and reassuring the Arabs of Palestine were contrary to almost all of the 'local wisdom' on the question of how to deal with Arab hostility to the Jewish National Home.

Samuel's recognition of the legitimacy and the seriousness of an 'Arab national movement' led him to make various proposals aimed at removing grievances and satisfying Arab 'national sentiment' in a way that would not have impaired the growth of the Jewish National Home in

Palestine. Professor Kedourie has discerned three major efforts in this direction: (a) the appointment of al-Hajj Amin al-Husaini as 'Grand Mufti' and the creation of the Supreme Muslim Council, (b) proposals for controlled representative institutions as a step towards self-government, and (c) proposals for the inclusion of Palestine within a confederation of Arab states. Immediately below we shall be examining differences between Samuel and the Yishuv on the 'Arab question' generally, while their specific differences on the question of self-governing institutions for Palestine will be dealt with further on.

I

SAMUEL'S APPOINTMENT AND HIS 'HONEYMOON PERIOD' IN OFFICE

Much of local Yishuv feeling towards Sir Herbert Samuel was influenced by the fact of his being a Jew. At first the appointment of a Jew as first High Commissioner for Palestine was considered a positive indication of British support for Zionism; but it was not long before this fact was seen as an enormous drawback. For Samuel's Jewishness undoubtedly reinforced his studied impartiality, which was far from what the Yishuv expected from a Jewish High Commissioner. Within the short space of a year, Yishuv emotions were to swing from jubilation to despair.

The timing of the announcement of Samuel's appointment was crucial for the Yishuv. Following the Jerusalem riots of April 1920, the Jews were in a near-hysterical state. There had been a complete breakdown of Jewish trust in the British military administration, whose officers were being denounced for having allowed and encouraged a 'pogrom' to take place in the Holy City. The news of the San Remo decision, awarding the British a mandate over Palestine under the terms of the Balfour Declaration, had not really dissipated Yishuv anger, which was still focused on the imprisonment of Vladimir Jabotinsky and nineteen other *hagana* (self-defence) activists who had been sentenced by a military tribunal, along with a handful of Arabs convicted of rape and rioting.[3]

Local Jewish feeling improved somewhat on learning of Samuel's appointment. 'Could there be anything better', asked Haifa Jewish leaders, 'than to have one of our own at the head of the Palestine Government? A Nehemiah! A liberator!' Dr M. D. Eder of the Zionist Commission [hereafter: ZC] felt that the appointment was sure to be 'enthusiastically welcomed' by the entire Yishuv.[4] But, aware of the local mood, Dr Weizmann in London was worried:

> If when Mr Samuel arrives they [Yishuv leaders] are going to besiege him with all their 'demands, protestations and requests' Mr Samuel will be utterly

disgusted and will turn his back on the Jewish community just as the others [i.e., military administrators] did, and our best chance will have gone.[5]

Weizmann feared very much that on his arrival Samuel would encounter not only 'difficulties with the Arabs' and the 'legacy' of the old régime, but also 'the bad spirit amongst our own people, and that will be fatal. ...' It was only during the last week before Samuel's arrival that Eder was able to report an increase of 'good sense' and calm among the Jewish population.[6]

The Yishuv attached great hopes to the arrival of the 'Jewish High Commissioner'. But these hopes were bound up with specific expectations, against which Samuel's achievements would be measured. To what extent would his new administration restore their lost confidence in British good faith? Would Samuel begin an era of truly 'sympathetic' British rule, and would he share the Yishuv's particular understanding of how to deal with Arab agitation against the Jewish National Home policy?

The arrival on 30 June 1920 of Sir Herbert Samuel seemed to bring about a near-miraculous change in the bad spirit and uneasiness which had been evident in the Yishuv even two weeks previously. The ceremonial beginnings of the new régime were particularly effective in winning the heart of the Jews, and the Yishuv soon hailed Herbert Samuel as 'their' High Commissioner ('*netzivenu*'), almost forgetting that he was, first and foremost, a servant of H.M. the King.[7] On 7 July Samuel received a deputation of the *Vaad Zmani* [Provisional Council of Palestine Jews; hereafter VZ] headed by Dr Yaakov Thon, who expressed his appreciation of the 'difficulties' of the High Commissioner's task, and pledged that the Yishuv was 'ready, as one man, to help him to the utmost'. At the same time, the VZ also declared its desire for 'peace with the Arab people and co-operation in the reconstruction of the country.'[8]

In his first week in office Samuel set about cleaning up part of the legacy of the former administration. He decreed an amnesty for all those convicted of crimes during the Jerusalem riots, and informed the War Office of his view that the results of the military inquiry into the riots would best be buried. The *hagana* prisoners accepted their amnesty, but not without registering a warning about the likely effect of this general amnesty on the 'Arab mind'.[9]

Nevertheless, even Jabotinsky began encouraging Jews to place 'great hopes' in Samuel, and that an appropriate '*situation nette*' was at last being created in Palestine.[10] During the coming months Samuel consolidated the good impression which he had created on the Jewish community, to the extent that in late November Dr Thon felt as though he were dealing with 'a brother' at Government House. Even though local Jews still saw room for improvement in the attitude of Government officials, there was a noticeable change for the better in the spirit of

Yishuv-British relations and in the tranquillity which returned to the country in the second half of 1920.[11]

As far as the Yishuv was concerned, one of the most welcome changes which occurred during Samuel's 'honeymoon period' was the apparent improvement in the Arab attitude towards the Jews. Following the French advance on Damascus and Faisal's flight from Syria, there was a temporary lull in the anti-Zionist propaganda emanating from that source.[12] From July until November 1920 the Zionist press pointed enthusiastically to the decline in Arab agitation. In many reports destined for external consumption, this happy state of affairs was attributed directly to the respect which Samuel had won for himself and his administration from all sections of the population.[13] Repeated references were made to previous Arab opposition as having been artificial. While it was admitted that a few 'extremists' stubbornly refused to accept the *fait accompli* of San Remo, it was pointed out that there were also many 'moderates' who were now prepared to co-operate with the new régime and the Zionist programme it implied. Several instances of superficial intercourse between Arab and Jewish notables on ceremonial occasions seemed to justify this impression.[14]

In this new atmosphere of Yishuv-Samuel confidence, Jewish leaders were anxious to begin the 'real' work of Zionism: immigration, land-acquisition, settlement and economic development. 'Our neighbours', wrote the influential labour publicist Berl Katznelson, 'judge us only by our deeds, and the sole act which changes our position for the better in the country is *immigration*'.[15] From the outset Samuel showed himself to be truly sympathetic in assisting practical Zionist work. He approved the first immigration schedule of 16,500 certificates, and granted a generous share of the new public works projects to organised Jewish labour. Samuel also granted one of the Yishuv's 'national demands' by making Hebrew an official working language of his administration.[16]

But, as hinted publicly in his first proclamation to the people of Palestine,[17] Samuel's approach was to be a 'gradualist' one. Sir Wyndham Deedes, Samuel's first Chief Secretary, explained this quite frankly in a letter to Dr Weizmann in November 1920:[18]

> We go slowly perhaps but I think surely – and good foundations are being laid.
>   *Secure* – particularly because I think I can say that, so far, no susceptibilities have been hurt among those very elements, the gaining of whose confidence is so essential to our success. ...
>   H. E. [Samuel] himself has gone further than anyone to allay [exaggerated, etc.] fears, and we shall go further still. ...

The practical effects of this philosophy were soon felt by the Yishuv. When, for example, the ZC was eager to begin negotiations for the purchase of Trans-Jordanian lands from willing sellers, the High Commissioner recommended postponing any action until such time as public security in that region was improved. Similarly, when Jewish attempts to open a school for Samaritans in Nablus met with hostility and intimidation on the part of the Mayor and other local notables, Samuel rejected Zionist requests for strong Government intervention, preferring 'tact and patience in the matter of Jewish infiltration into that city'.[19] While Yishuv leaders were disappointed, especially about Nablus, they were not bitter against Samuel.

But Samuel's approach, which attempted to keep the confidence of Arabs and Jews simultaneously, was already showing its first signs of strain at the close of 1920. Berl Katznelson, who was less enthusiastic than most people about symbolic victories, noted that the good effects of the Samuel appointment had already worn off by late November.[20] Despite the 'new era', he felt that the Jews were 'still living in a country atop a volcano. True, it is in a quiet state at the moment, but the political intrigue around us will not sleep nor slumber.' Following several months of relative quiet, Damascus once again became a centre for anti-Zionist propaganda, and by spring 1921 both British and Zionist observers looked apprehensively at a wider 'pan-Islamic revival' in the surrounding countries.[21]

In Palestine itself, Arab jealousy became aroused by alleged Government favouritism to Zionist practical work. As the Arab Executive's memorandum to Mr Churchill (see below) complained,

> the Government, in spite of the poverty of the people, ... has opened up new unnecessary roads, repaired old ones which fully served their purposes, widened some railway lines, and created new gardens ... more in order to give employment to the thousands of Jewish immigrants than because they are immediate necessities. The Jewish labourer is paid double the amount given to the native, though he does less work.[22]

These kinds of complaints did have their effect on Samuel and Deedes, who were sensitive to the accusation that the Government was 'all Jewish'. Both were anxious to minimise the spread of such accusations, and in late December the High Commissioner expressed his reluctance to proceed with any further practical steps until after the ratification of the Mandate.[23]

The central event marking the revival of Arab unrest in Palestine was the Third Palestine Arab Congress, which met in Haifa in mid-December 1920 (the 'Haifa Congress').[24] Thirty-seven delegates attended, representing several local Muslim-Christian Association [hereafter: MCA] branches, and passed resolutions calling for such things as a rejection of the Balfour Declaration as being contrary to the 'Laws of God and Man'; the establishment of national self-government (but without explicitly rejecting the British presence in Palestine); and a revocation of the visible signs of favour already conferred on the Jews. The Congress elected Musa Kazim Pasha al-Husaini to head its Executive Committee [or 'Arab

Executive'; hereafter: AE], which was to continue the struggle on behalf of the Arabs of Palestine. The first organised protest demonstration under the Civil Administration took place in Nablus shortly after the Congress, and by the end of February 1921 the League of Nations was receiving a flood of challenges to the validity of the Balfour Declaration.[25]

At first, this renewal of anti-Zionist cries caused only mild concern in British circles. The unrepresentativeness of the Haifa Congress provided the main justification for Samuel's unperturbed analysis. The delegates (which he numbered at only 25) could hardly be considered representative of the population as a whole, and the administration initially stood firm in refusing to deal 'officially' with the AE, not wishing to grant recognition to 'a committee' which openly rejected the Government's Jewish National Home policy.[26] On the other hand, Samuel had to recognise that the Haifa Congress did reflect a 'considerable body of latent opinion in the country', which would require proper handling. In order to disarm this potentially hostile segment of the population, Samuel affirmed his readiness to apply a wise, firm, but not aggressive policy.[27] For its part, the Yishuv reacted with relatively more concern to the change in the outward attitude of the Arabs. On the eve of the Haifa Congress, Tel Aviv mayor Meir Dizengoff considered the Arab question as one which was 'still unpleasant and still unresolved': a movement 'against us and against the High Commissioner' had been aroused, and it was, he felt, 'very important for us to do something about it'.[28]

CHURCHILL'S VISIT TO PALESTINE

The visit to Palestine of the new Secretary of State for the Colonies, Winston Churchill, marked the peak of British and Zionist optimism during Samuel's 'honeymoon period'. On 28 March 1921 Mr Churchill received Arab and Jewish deputations at Government House in Jerusalem. The memorandum read by the Haifa Congress deputation[29] was a lengthy document, dotted with scurrilous warnings against the 'Jewish Peril' and obviously inspired by a recent edition of the 'Protocols of the Elders of Zion'. The Arabs presented detailed illustrations of how this 'Peril' menaced all the nations, but especially Great Britain and Palestine. The Balfour Declaration was 'an act of modern Bolshevism, pure and simple'. From the legal, historical, moral and economic points of view, the Jews had absolutely no rights to Palestine and the Arabs resented and would fight 'the idea of transforming Palestine into a home for the Jewish people'. The memorandum concluded with five demands: (1) abolition of the Jewish National Home policy; (2) establishment of a 'National Government'; (3) stoppage of Jewish immigration; (4) return to the legal *status quo* prior to the British occupation; and (5) an end to the enforced separation between Palestine and her 'sister states'.

If the Arab memorandum was an hysterical warning, the submission of the *Vaad Leumi* [National Council of the Jews of Palestine, successor to the VZ; hereafter VL] was a joyous vote of gratitude and confidence.[30] The Jews of Palestine thanked Great Britain for having been the first Power to recognise and support Jewish aspirations to return to and rebuild the ancient homeland. The appointment of Sir Herbert Samuel, 'a brother Jew', as first High Commissioner was hailed as 'the first concrete step' towards the implementation of the Balfour Declaration and the San Remo decision. Very kind words were said about Samuel's first eight months in office, both in his capacity as governor of the country and also as one who appreciated his historic task in relation to the Jewish people. 'In safeguarding the rights of all the inhabitants, and in caring for their interests', the memorandum stated, 'the High Commissioner is fulfilling the Balfour Declaration in its full meaning.' The Yishuv also used this opportunity to reaffirm its earlier pledges 'to assist the High Commissioner in establishing cordial relations between all sections of the population'.

A prominent place in the VL memorandum was accorded to the Arab question. The Yishuv was overflowing with optimism about the prospects for Jewish-Arab understanding, for the cultural and economic revival of the whole Middle East, and for the increasing benefits which the Arab population of Palestine – and the British administration as well – would enjoy as a result of Zionist prosperity and development. Even though the Arab world in March 1921 may not have been satisfied with the results of the peace settlement, the VL nevertheless felt justified in invoking the fulfilment of Arab national aspirations outside of Palestine:

> *The Jewish people treat the national aspirations of the Arabs with complete understanding* [the memorandum underlined]. But we know that by our efforts to rebuild the Jewish national home in Palestine – which is but a small area in comparison with all the Arab lands – we do not deprive them of their legitimate rights. On the contrary, we are convinced that a Jewish renaissance in this country can only have a strong and invigorating effect on the Arab nation.

The memorandum ended optimistically:

> Under the guidance of Great Britain, the Jewish and the Arab peoples will work hand in hand to establish a country of glorious past and of ever-promising future.

Mr Churchill's reply to the AE memorandum was seen as a real political victory for the Yishuv. Regarding the principal Arab demand for a repudiation of the Balfour Declaration, the Secretary of State said: 'It is not in my power to do so, nor, if it were in my power, would it be my wish.'[31] He told the Arabs plainly that the creation of a Jewish National Home in Palestine was 'manifestly right':

> We think it will be good for the world, good for the Jews and good for the British Empire. But we also think it will be good for the Arabs, and we intend that it shall be good for them. ...

Mr Churchill was convinced that Zionism meant progress and prosperity, and not ruin, for the Arabs, and he urged the Arab leaders, in the interests of their own people, to take 'a wise and tolerant view' of Zionism and to give it 'a fair chance'. If they did so, they would see for themselves how the success of Zionism would be 'accompanied by a general diffusion of wealth and well being ... and by an advance in the social, scientific and cultural life of the people as a whole.' Sir Herbert Samuel supplemented Mr Churchill's remarks with a brief statement conveying his sincere conviction that the fears expressed in the AE memorandum were 'unfounded', and he reaffirmed his faith in a policy which sought to promote 'good-will among the three sections of the community'.

RIOTS AND ATTACKS OF MAY 1921: IMMEDIATE REACTIONS

The net result of the Churchill visit left the Yishuv elated. Not since 2 November 1917 had the hopes for a Jewish National Home in Palestine received such firm and unambiguous official endorsement. But, if the appointment of Sir Herbert Samuel and his first months in office had given many Jews the luxury of believing that Arab attacks and 'pogroms' were a thing of the past, then the events of May and June came as a profound shock. Sharp disillusionment quickly replaced the optimism which had been bound up in the Yishuv's reliance on 'its' High Commissioner.

Although the actual rioting which broke out in Jaffa on 1 May 1921 was almost totally unexpected,[32] it is still possible to see signs of a build-up in tension during the month of April. From the tone of the Arabic press, as from subsequent events, it appears that Mr Churchill's outspoken affirmation of the Zionist policy angered, rather than pacified, Arab spirits.[33] In the aftermath of the forceful Government suppression of an illegal demonstration in Haifa during Mr Churchill's visit, tension rose in that town, and British police brutality was denounced in the press. Following complaints from Haifa Jews, the VL took up the matter with Samuel, and complained that no exemplary punishment had yet been meted out to the organisers of the illegal demonstration.[34] The Jews warned that Government inaction would leave the impression of weakness on the Arab mind; without a forceful display of authority, the inhabitants of the town would not have the feeling of 'public security so badly needed' for 'the required atmosphere of friendship and goodwill'.

Two other incidents in April added to Yishuv anxiety. In Jaffa, citrus-owner Samuel Tolkowsky complained that Government permission for the reappearance of *Falastin*, which had been closed down by the Turks for incitement to race-hatred in April 1914, could only be a source of discouragement to 'moderate' Arabs and an official invitation to 'extremists' to oppose the Jewish National Home policy.[35] Secondly, in the north, the High Commissioner paid a visit to Beisan, 'with a view to allaying anxieties felt by the inhabitants of the Jordan valley about the future of their lands'.³⁶ Although the visit was relatively successful from the administration's point of view, the Yishuv regarded the accompanying Arab demonstrations as 'wild' and the Arab speeches as hostile. Worst of all, Samuel gave the Jews the impression of giving in to protesting shaikhs who were denouncing all Zionist claims to a share in the distribution of these lands.³⁷

Arab rioting was sparked off in Jaffa by a clash between authorised and unauthorised Jewish May-day parades; this led to the spread of rumours and to Arab attacks on several Jewish settlements in the coastal plain. At the end of six days, these attacks had resulted in almost fifty Jewish deaths and 150 wounded, with thousands of pounds of property damaged or stolen. The general picture left in the Yishuv mind after 6 May was that the British had once more been ineffective, on the whole, in protecting Jewish life and property. Once order was restored, Yishuv leaders waited in vain for direct responsibility to be cast upon Arab politicians and Arab policemen, and the guilt of the MCA was, for some Jews, obvious enough to merit immediate closure and prohibition.³⁸

But, instead of the expected punitive action against the 'criminals', District Governors and military advisers appeared to the Yishuv to be submitting deliberately exaggerated accounts of Arab strength and restiveness, thereby 'forcing' Sir Herbert Samuel to embark upon a policy of conciliating the forces of disorder at the expense of Jewish interests. Zionists hoped in vain for a purge of all Arab and British anti-Zionist elements in Palestine during the subsequent legal proceedings, while at one point Nahum Sokolow of the Zionist Executive was even planning to arouse world-wide publicity on a scale similar to the Beiliss trial.³⁹ During these weeks of continued Jewish insecurity and an Arab boycott, Yishuv leaders grew increasingly frustrated at the administration's demonstrated 'weakness' and its conciliatory attitude to the Arabs. Only a forced self-restraint prevented the Yishuv from giving loud public expression to its true feelings of bitterness against Sir Herbert Samuel and his administration.

As far as the Yishuv was concerned, the most depressing sequel to the actual rioting was Samuel's announcement of a temporary stoppage of Jewish immigration.⁴⁰ For the Jews, immigration was sacred. As Dr Thon declared during an interview with the Chief Secretary, 'If we had to choose between an important political declaration with restrictions on immigration, and no declaration but complete freedom to immigrate – we would choose the latter.'⁴¹ The dangers of conceding, even temporarily, to the forces of violence what they considered to be an elementary Zionist right haunted Yishuv leaders. If control over immigration were not left enshrined as an 'untouchable' right of Zionists, and Zionists alone – then, given the tendencies of the Arabs *and* the administration, the net result of 'British' control would be that 'a visa from the Government would be of no use' to the Jewish immigrant 'unless he also had a visa from Musa

Kazim Pasha [President of the AE]'.⁴² This long-term possibility that the Arabs would, in practice, have the ultimate say in controlling Jewish immigration was one of the most dreaded consequences of Samuel's reactions to the May riots. It was at this point that some labour leaders began to contemplate organising illegal immigration as a necessary answer to the administration's power to turn immigration on and off at will.⁴³

Towards the end of May, all sections of the population anxiously awaited a statement which the High Commissioner was scheduled to deliver on the King's birthday, 3 June. The Jews, in particular, were awaiting that statement with some apprehension, but also

> with the expectation that it would guarantee security of Jewish life and property, that it would resolutely assert the authority of the Government against violence and crime, and that it would maintain and proclaim the rights of the Jewish people to their National Home in Palestine.⁴⁴

But – as the Yishuv could not fail to notice – the main thrust of the Statement of 3 June was in another direction altogether: namely to reassure an anxious *Arab* population that HMG would take all necessary steps to ensure that the realisation of the National Home would result in no injustice to their interests. Arab fears, which only two months earlier Samuel had lightly dismissed as 'unfounded', now received the High Commissioner's primary attention:⁴⁵

> If any measures are needed [Samuel announced] to convince the Moslem and Christian population ... that their rights are really safe, such measures will be taken. For the British Government, the trustee under the Mandate for the happiness of the people of Palestine, would never impose upon them a policy which the people had reason to think was contrary to their religious, their political, and their economic interests.

On the delicate question of immigration, Samuel laid down new guidelines and affirmed that 'it must be definitely recognised that the conditions of Palestine are such as do not permit anything in the nature of a mass immigration'. He also held out the prospect that the people of Palestine would be 'associated more closely with the Administration', and announced that London was studying the 'question of securing a free and authoritative expression of popular opinion' – i.e. some form of 'representative institution', but without using those words. Finally, on the immediate question of the Jaffa riots, Samuel wished to reserve judgment until after the report of the inquiry commission. Nevertheless, he felt that 'the thoughtful men of all sections' of the population would share his view that the 'flagrant crimes' of murder, assault and looting should be 'deplored and condemned'. Those found guilty would 'receive their due punishment', and to the families of the killed and wounded the High Commissioner offered his 'heart-felt sympathy'.

It is not difficult to imagine the alarm and despondency which this

Statement caused in Zionist and Yishuv circles. As he sat and listened to Samuel's address, the word 'Judas' came to Dr Eder's lips; he reported to London that the Zionists had just 'gone through the gravest crisis in our movement since the declaration of war in 1914'.[46] In his diary entry of 4 June 1921, Arthur Ruppin wrote: 'Herbert Samuel, who was sort of a god to the Jews in Palestine only yesterday, has now become a traitor to the Jewish cause in their eyes.'[47] Samuel's '*re-*'definition of the Balfour Declaration – namely,

> that the Jews, a people that are scattered throughout the world but whose hearts are always turned to Palestine, should be enabled to found here their home, and that some among them, within the limits that are fixed by the numbers and interests of the present population, should come to Palestine in order to help by their resources and efforts to develop the country, to the advantage of all the inhabitants

– was wholly at variance with Yishuv interpretations of the extent of British promises (see below). As Dr Weizmann phrased it, 'the Jewish National Home of the war-promise has now in peacetime been transformed into an Arab National Home.'[48] Samuel's stress on the duty of Zionists to improve the lot of the Arabs led one Jerusalem correspondent to re-word the High Commissioner's interpretation as follows: 'only on the condition that whatever we do is to enrich all the inhabitants are we to be tolerated at all.'[49] Finally, Samuel's allusions to the establishment of representative institutions came as a severe shock and disappointment to the Yishuv, and this set the stage for Samuel's 'constitutional solutions' to the Arab question in Palestine.

But worse than any specific injury to the Jews was the whole tone of the Statement, which left the impression that the administration was giving in to 'mob violence'. On 8 June, the VL formally replied to the Statement of Policy and deplored that, in 'form and spirit', the speech was

> an indictment not of those who have committed crimes and organised disorder, but of those who have been the victims of those crimes and that disorder. ... The general impression made by the Statement is that it is an endeavour to protect the Arabs from the 'Jewish Peril'. ...[50]

While the stoppage of immigration, which 'follow[ed] promptly upon the crimes' in May, had appeared to all sections of the population as 'the sequel to and the reward for violence and outrage', Samuel's references to immigration in the 3 June Statement were seen to 'confirm the victory of crime'. As *Hagana* founder and organiser, Eliahu Golomb, concluded at the time, 'not even in the Ukraine or in Russia was such remuneration given to rioters'.[51]

DIFFERING ATTITUDES AFTER JUNE 1921

Throughout May and June 1921 Yishuv leaders were overworked with daily meetings or interviews at Government House. At the end of June many differences still separated the Yishuv from 'its' High Commissioner, and a VL memorandum attempted to summarise these in 'a simple and undisguised manner' for Samuel's benefit.[52] After dealing with the questions of labour immigration and Zionist investment in Palestine, the VL went straight to the heart of the political question. Whereas, only two months earlier, the Yishuv had warmly praised Samuel in its memorandum to Churchill for 'fulfilling the Balfour Declaration in its full meaning', now, at the end of June, it rejected his recent definition of that Declaration and clung firmly to the 'true contents of the promise of the British Government'. These 'true contents', as the VL saw them, did

> not allow for any numbers or incidental interests of the present population of the country to affect the life and the historic aspirations of the Jewish people, whose return to the land of its fathers has been decided by historic justice and by the decision of the Nations.

As it had done before Mr Churchill, the VL again protested that the Jews had no wish 'to encroach upon the Arab people' which possessed 'the right and the opportunity to revive its homeland in its extensive historic lands'. But, the memorandum repeated, these lands did *not* include Palestine, that small 'corner' reserved by history, the League of Nations and the British Government as the homeland of the Jewish people. In no way would the 'individual rights' of the Arabs living in Palestine be denied, 'but the political right to erect a National Home should be given [only] to the Jewish people'. Before reaching its pessimistic general conclusion (see below), the memorandum presented complaints about the continuing lack of public security and levelled some basic criticisms of the methods of the administration. The Government had, on the one hand, 'rejected Turkish methods which in certain cases are suited to local conditions', while on the other hand it had failed to set up a truly efficient 'European' administration.

Thus, in mid-1921, many Palestinian Jews were convinced that they had been the victims of another 'pogrom' – but this time worse than Jerusalem and even, in Nahum Sokolow's words, worse than Kishinov.[53] What made Jaffa, 1921, tragically worse was the fact that this time 'it took place in the Jewish National Home in Palestine and under the rule of a British High Commissioner who is a son of the Jewish people.'[54] While Samuel's personal good faith was only rarely called into question, many in the Yishuv believed that the lower ranks of the administration were staffed by enemies of the Jewish National Home policy, especially officials of the previous military régime who should have been removed in July 1920. Some went further, arguing that Samuel was 'a prisoner' of those officials.[55] The conduct of the Jaffa police – considered by many as the ugliest aspect of the actual rioting – seemed to provide an authentic 'pogrom' character to the Arab attacks.

Nonetheless, high-level Government policy was considered to be the major contributing cause of the outbreaks. Prominent labour leader, Yitzhak Ben-Zvi, pointed to the immediate connection between the unpunished defiance of a Government ban (i.e. the illegal Haifa demonstration) and the Jaffa riots.[56] To many Yishuv leaders, the riots had been the inevitable outcome of Samuel's inopportune gentleness and misplaced liberalism in the face of mounting Arab arrogance. General Gouraud's handling of the Syrians was sometimes cited as the example to be emulated in Palestine.[57] When considering the amnesty of Hajj Amin al-Husaini (convicted for incitement in the April 1920 riots) and his subsequent appointment as 'Grand Mufti',[58] and when considering the *de facto* prominence enjoyed by Musa Kazim Pasha and the AE – it was not difficult for Jews to conclude that 'their' High Commissioner had 'elevated to the highest rank the lowest of our enemies', thereby dealing a blow to Jewish prestige in Arab eyes.[59] 'A little while ago', observed one labour spokesman, 'we had to deal with only a gang of agitators. But Samuel's weakness has changed this opposition into antagonism of the masses.'[60] E. Golomb took this point one step further. In his view, the absence of Zionist activity and 'the Government's methods' were *jointly* responsible for

> planting among the Arab masses the idea that the Government is not with us, that strength is on their side, and that they can easily remove us from their path. The High Commissioner strengthens this [view] in everything he says and does, and it is he who is driving the Arab masses under the banner of the MCA. He greatly exaggerates the strength of the Arab movement, and by so doing, and by his fear, he is strengthening it until one day it may justify the extent of his fears.[61]

This, then, was how many Yishuv leaders came to view Samuel's approach and its negative effects upon Jewish-Arab relations. But we must note that almost every word of the bitter and despairing criticism thus far described was kept behind closed doors, or was directed privately to Samuel. If 'their' High Commissioner, however noble his intentions, had so undermined their political and security position in the country, why, then, did the Jews of Palestine not declare 'open war' on him, as they had done to the military administration after the Jerusalem 'pogrom'?

In May and June of 1921, Yishuv leaders were acutely aware of the fact that they were no longer dealing with suspected anti-semites like General Bols and Ronald Storrs, and their avenues of protest were limited. Instinctive first reaction to Samuel's stoppage of immigration in May and to his Statement of 3 June had been to demand redress on the threat of mass resignations from all Jewish public bodies in Palestine. But, after sober reflection, most leaders were forced to realise that such a show-down would prove either ineffective or else harmful.[62] Only Ben-Zvi gave up his seat on the Government Advisory Council on 11 May in protest against Samuel's handling of the riots, and he resisted strong pressure from many quarters to reconsider his resignation.[63]

There were several considerations which effectively robbed the Jews of the luxury of being able to cry out their full anguish and bitterness against Samuel and his administration. The most powerful argument for not taking any drastic step which might weaken the position of the High Commissioner or cause his resignation was, of course, Samuel's Jewishness. Most Yishuv leaders were fully sensitive to the fact that Samuel's downfall could seriously harm the Zionist position. Ben-Zvi observed that the situation was more serious than it had been in 1920 'because the Government is ours and its fall will be our downfall'.[64] The departure of a *Jewish* High Commissioner, following *Arab* riots, would inevitably be interpreted as an Arab victory, and the Yishuv could not lend its hand to this. What might be even worse, some argued, would be the effect on public opinion abroad if it appeared that the Jewish High Commissioner was being forced to resign because his *own* people refused to co-operate with him.[65] Finally, the stand adopted by Dr Weizmann and the Zionist Executive was to support Samuel through the crisis, and any Yishuv elements disagreeing with the wisdom of self-restraint were faced with the prospect of acting in open defiance of the official Zionist line.[66]

Those who did dissent from this self-imposed restraint came mainly from the labour ranks. Berl Katznelson and others argued forcefully that, above all else, Samuel was unable to handle Arab unrest and was too willing to concede Jewish interests; hence, the Yishuv might actually be better off if England were to send in Samuel's place a strong non-Jewish 'general' who could do the 'job' properly. Samuel's Jewishness had proved a decided disadvantage: someone like Bols might 'at least be a little afraid of the Jewish people', whereas Samuel knew 'only how to fear the Arabs'.[67] Spokesmen for this view were able to add to their argument that it had been precisely the official Zionist policy of 'not embarrassing Samuel' in May that allowed him to lean so heavily towards the Arab side in his 3 June Statement. Yet, whenever it came to a vote in the VL, the counsels of caution prevailed, and Samuel was not to be challenged in public.

Although the VL decided to keep its frankest and most vigorous criticism of Samuel out of the public domain, it was nevertheless forced, as authorised spokesman for the organised Yishuv, to take a public stand on the riots. Even in the public proclamation issued on 23 May we are able to see self-restraint operating between the lines.[68] Despite the widespread conviction that a 'pogrom' had indeed taken place in Jaffa, this emotive word did not appear in the proclamation. Instead, the guilt of Arab agitators was violently denounced, and in place of any harsh criticism directed against Samuel's leniency and weakness, we find the following:

The Jewish population of Palestine affirms that the irresponsible haughtiness of the politicians of Eastern lands is not capable of appreciating either the humane and easy-going policy of the Jewish High Commissioner or the seasoned moderation of Western politics. ...

The proclamation called for the speedy ratification of the Mandate, lodged a protest against the temporary stoppage of immigration, and summoned world Jewry to unite in contributing men and means for sustained immigration and development of the Jewish National Home. The VL reaffirmed solemnly that the Jews were determined never to abandon the peaceful and constructive enterprise of building their National Home:

> Even now, after the bitter experiences which recent days have bequeathed to us, we proclaim that a spirit of peace moves us, and that it is our desire to live together with the Arab people in fraternal peace on this land which is in such need of work and energy.

THE XIITH ZIONIST CONGRESS (SEPTEMBER 1921)

In the second half of 1921, Samuel continued to impress Zionists with his views of the seriousness of Arab opposition, and by so doing he did little to win back the shattered confidence of the Yishuv. From Jerusalem, he pressed Arab and Zionist representatives in London to meet to attempt to resolve their differences.[69] Samuel also urged the XIIth Zionist Congress, meeting in Carlsbad in September, that two things, above all, were needed: (a) immediate constructive activity, to prove to the Arabs that 'the success of Zionism will be to their benefit and not result in their destruction', and (b) an official Zionist declaration to reassure the Arabs in the same sense.[70]

To some extent, the fifth resolution passed by the Congress can be seen as a response to Samuel's pressure. Indeed, the resolution was soon labelled historic and parts of it were subsequently quoted on numerous occasions to demonstrate Zionist 'moderation' and concern for the Arabs. The full text of that resolution deserves quoting here, so that we may better appreciate just how far Zionists were willing to go in Samuel's direction:

V. The Arab People

> With sorrow and indignation the Jewish people have lived through the recent events in Palestine. The hostile attitude of the Arab population, incited by unscrupulous elements to commit deeds of violence, can neither weaken our resolve for the establishment of the Jewish National Home nor our determination to live with the Arab people on terms of concord and mutual respect, and together with them to make the common home into a flourishing Commonwealth, the upbuilding of which may assure to each of its peoples an undisturbed national development. The two great Semitic peoples united of yore by the bonds of common creative civilisation will not fail in the hour of their national regeneration to comprehend the need of combining their vital interests in a common endeavour.

> The Congress calls upon the Executive to redouble its efforts to secure an honourable entente with the Arab people on the basis of this Declaration and in strict accordance with the Balfour Declaration. The Congress emphatically declares that the progress of Jewish colonisation will not affect the rights and needs of the working Arab nation.[71]

If this resolution succeeded, in its conciliatory phrases, in evoking satisfaction from British quarters, we cannot overlook the anger and determination which are intermixed with the call to peace. Indeed, if we view the resolution in the context of the Congress atmosphere, it would appear that concern for Yishuv security was a paramount consideration, ahead of the desirable, but distant, 'honourable entente with the Arab people'. Dr Weizmann set the tone of the Congress by affirming in his opening address that Zionists clung firmly to 'the rights guaranteed to us by the Balfour Declaration':[72]

> [R]ecognition of this fact by the Arabs is an essential preliminary to the establishment of satisfactory relations between Jew and Arab. Their temporary refusal to recognise that fact compels us to give thought to the means by which we can best safeguard our Yishub against aggression. Self-protection is an elementary duty. ...

The Yishuv took its own security no less seriously than the Zionist leader. On the eve of the Congress a telegram from the VL spoke of the Yishuv's desire for 'unity and brotherhood with the Arab people', 'in spite of the depressing events of recent months'.[73] But, the message went on, it was the duty of the Palestine administration to guarantee complete security of life and property and to afford 'the possibility for Jewish inhabitants to protect themselves against theft and murder' (i.e. with the *Hagana*). At the Congress itself, Berl Katznelson spoke even more forcefully for the Yishuv. Hardly in a spirit of conciliation, Katznelson expressed annoyance with those who were arguing that the Jews had a moral duty to improve relations with the Arabs. As far as he was concerned, there was no doubt as to who was attacking whom: 'During the forty years of the New Yishuv, Jews have yet to attack an Arab village and there has yet to occur a case where a Jew has attacked an Arab.'[74] The labour movement, in whose name he spoke, had always preached 'deep words of brotherhood and peace' in the framework of national autonomy for both peoples. And yet, great was 'the distance between us and the Arabs. ... We must guarantee the security of our own lives; only then will there be a basis for negotiations. We cannot concede our aspiration to become a majority in the country.' It was, Katznelson concluded,

> obvious to everyone that our most crucial political activity must be: to renew our immigration; to strengthen our pioneering spirit; to reinforce our *hagana*; and to fortify our position in the country.

One final indication of the true tone of the 1921 Zionist Congress may be found in the less-quoted fourth resolution on the May riots, in which the Congress protested bitterly against the outrages and the stoppage of immigration, declaring 'before the entire world that the free immigration to Erez Israel is an uncontestable right of the Jewish people, of which in no circumstances it may be deprived.'[75]

> The Congress expresses its firm conviction that only a just policy of equal rights and equal duties for all sections of the population in Erez Israel, only a strict and inexorable enforcement of justice and the protection of life and property, only an honest and consistent policy based upon the Balfour Declaration, can give peace to the country. ...

Thus, while Samuel was pressing Zionists for words of compromise and conciliation in the fall and winter of 1921, Zionists both in Palestine and abroad were preoccupied with re-establishing a sense of security in the Yishuv and strengthening the Zionist position.

LOOSENING THE SENTIMENTAL BONDS

The parting of the ways between Samuel and the Yishuv over how to deal with Arab hostility in 1921 involved a heavy emotional price for the latter: the painful 'undoing' of a sentimental bond which the Yishuv had created by looking on Sir Herbert Samuel as 'the *Jewish* High Commissioner'. Dr Weizmann captured the essence of this problem during one of his remarks to the XIIth Zionist Congress:

> Erez Israel [he reminded his audience] and Palestine are not identical and will not be identical for a long time to come. Sir Herbert Samuel is High Commissioner for Palestine, and we are the High Commissioners for Erez Israel. And a time may perhaps come when these two High Commissioners may have difficulties with one another.[76]

This problem of identification with Samuel as the Jewish High Commissioner comes out even more clearly from Yishuv sources. While the VL was observing its self-imposed restraint in June 1921, Berl Katznelson let loose a scathing attack on the administration, in the course of which he also heaped sarcasm on those Jews who had been taken in by the symbolism of having a Jewish High Commissioner.[77] Just as the 'Jerusalem pogrom' had unmasked the machinations of the hostile military régime, so too, he wrote, had the 'Jaffa pogrom' exposed the true nature of 'the friendly government of the Jewish High Commissioner, Herbert Samuel'.

> Having a Jewish High Commissioner has become a worthless decoration. The naive joy of the masses has become an empty joy; the expectations, disappointment. We are left with mourning. The people mourn for its dead sons, the immigrants, the workers, the creative people, the irreplaceable [popular poet] Brenner. ...[78]

Although it was not given public expression, the same dejection prevailed among the official Yishuv leadership. The VL memorandum addressed to Samuel privately on 27 June went through its list of grievances and outstanding points of disagreement, and concluded gloomily by recalling the optimism and the pledges of co-operation which had marked the beginning of the Samuel administration. In the name of that pledge, the Yishuv felt it had restrained itself and had 'endured the edicts and the blows of the past two months almost silently and without reaction'.

> We did not imagine [the memorandum continued] that a non-Jewish High Commissioner could have cast upon us blows such as those which we have taken from Your Excellency. We cannot imagine that such a [non-Jewish] High Commissioner could have found the strength, as Your Excellency has done, to influence the central Government to nullify the contents of the Mandate.

As the price of its self-restraint, the Yishuv felt that it was losing 'all the political advantages which [it] had gained during the past year'. But, the memorandum solemnly concluded, the Jews would persevere in the upbuilding of their National Home 'with much greater stubbornness' now that they knew that they had 'nothing to expect in the way of assistance from Your Excellency or from the British Government'.

It would be wrong to discount these words simply as rhetoric uttered in a passing moment of despair. This deep-rooted Yishuv disappointment was to be reinforced by other episodes during the remainder of Samuel's term of office. The Jerusalem disturbances of 2 November 1921, as David Ben-Gurion interpreted them, constituted just one more step in the retreat from the sentimentalism and optimism which had been based on the Yishuv's identification with the 'Jewish High Commissioner'.

> With the coming of the *Jewish* High Commissioner, we were permitted to hope and to be consoled that the first pogrom [Jerusalem, April 1920] would also be the last. ... The Yishuv did not complain or protest [against Samuel's general amnesty of the rioters]. ... With the coming of the Jewish High Commissioner, the Yishuv imagined that its rightful demands had been fulfilled. We imagined that the country would be rid of officials who believed in '*divide et impera*' and who intrigued and spread hatred between one people and another. We imagined [all this], but we were mistaken.[79]

Samuel's 'constitutional approaches' to the Arabs during 1921–23 further confirmed Yishuv insecurity and discontent with the High Commissioner.

In addition to this loosening of sentimental bonds, the events of 1921 revealed the wide gap that existed between Samuel and the Yishuv on the question of how to handle the 'Arab question'. Memories of the temporary optimism of Samuel's 'honeymoon period' quickly faded, as Yishuv and Zionist leaders were reminded of earlier evidence of his tendency to take the Arabs, and Arab nationalism, 'too' seriously. A Yishuv delegation in Europe during the Peace Conference in 1919 had encountered Samuel as one of the 'important personalities' who had transmitted warnings against 'irritating' the Arabs.[80] During his visit to Palestine in early 1920 on behalf of the Foreign Office, Samuel had left no doubt with the ZC that his 'main consideration' was 'the Arab problem'. 'Over and over again', Israel Sieff had complained to Dr Weizmann, 'he would turn to this question.'[81] At that time Samuel had roundly criticised the ZC for (among other things) not making use of 'Jews familiar with Arab language and ways' and for not having 'recognised the force and value of the Arab nationalist movement', which was 'very real and no bluff'.[82] Dr Eder had been very 'depressed' at having to listen to Samuel repeating 'en bloc the view of the [military] Administration', to the point where Eder accused Samuel of having 'no (Jewish) backbone'.[83] Yishuv leader Eliahu Berligne had also reacted negatively in spring 1920 to Samuel's criticism of the Yishuv's 'exaggerated' demands, and the VZ was urged to ignore his suggestions, 'even though he was an important man'.[84]

Following the May 1921 riots Yishuv leaders were reminded that Sir Herbert Samuel, 'their' High Commissioner, still took a far more serious view of Arab hostility than they did – to the point of his regarding anti-Zionist agitation as the expression of a 'deep national movement'.[85] Dr Yitzhak Levi, Sephardi community leader and a director of the Anglo-Palestine Bank, expressed the Yishuv's instinctive fears of the consequences of Samuel's 'fostering the idea of their [i.e., Arab] nationalism': 'He will return to England and be re-instated as a Minister, but *we* shall remain here – in danger.'[86]

As irresponsible as Samuel's attitude may have seemed to local Jews, Samuel himself took the matter very seriously indeed. On 8 May he reported his conviction that there were 'deep-seated causes at work' behind Arab hostility, and that the situation called for political correctives: 'It would be folly', he wrote, 'to rest content with the re-establishment of order and the punishment of offenders. The trouble would recur.'[87] During the course of the next month he reached the firm conclusion that a 'serious attempt' had to be made

> to arrive at an understanding with the opposition to the Zionist policy, even at the cost of considerable sacrifices. The only alternative is a policy of coercion which is wrong in principle and likely to prove unsuccessful in practice.[88]

Having received, only six weeks before the May riots, the Yishuv's repeated pledge to assist him 'in establishing cordial relations between all sections of the population', as well as official and public Zionist pledges of 'unshakable confidence' in early May,[89] Samuel was indeed expecting all Zionists to brace themselves for the 'considerable sacrifices' which he felt the situation required. He was

> quite aware that this Policy [of conciliation] must inevitably disappoint many,

indeed most, of my Zionist friends, and seriously diminish the satisfaction which was so cordially expressed at the time of my appointment.[90]

But he was determined that his course was the right one – indeed, the 'only one' – for Zionism in Palestine: 'Unless there is very careful steering', he warned Weizmann, 'it is upon the Arab rock that the Zionist ship may be wrecked.'

The fundamental opposition of local people to the attitude adopted by Samuel was in many respects part of their larger resentment against the advice offered by well-meaning outsiders on how they ought to behave towards the Arabs. They firmly believed that their experience living beside their 'neighbours' made them better 'experts' than any outsider.[91] As we have seen, this local 'expertise' usually amounted to the call for government with a firm hand. Perceiving Samuel's chosen course, Golomb protested:[92]

> We are all peace-loving people, and there is not a man among us who believes that it is possible to subdue a popular movement with a strong hand; but is this the way to peace – to add to the power of inciters and rioters?

What was needed was

> a tough stand, one which will prove to friends and foes that no evil-doing will shake our rights and that attacks on the peaceable way of life of the inhabitants will be punished by the full force of the law. ...

But, as resolutely as the Yishuv stressed the *criminal* aspect of the riots, Samuel searched for a way to relieve underlying *political* discontents; as firmly as the Yishuv believed that the key to a solution lay in Samuel's adoption of a firmer attitude, the latter sought a conciliatory attitude on the part of the Jews. In the ensuing debates with VL leaders, Samuel displayed increasing annoyance and gave frank expression to his strong doubts and misgivings about the Yishuv attitude to the Arabs. He warned VL spokesmen that it was *they* who were 'courting disaster' by their attitude which appeared to ignore the existence of a powerful Arab movement. Yishuv representatives, reporting on interviews with the High Commissioner, quoted Samuel as saying:[93]

> You yourselves are inviting a massacre, which will come as long as you disregard the Arabs. You pass over them in silence. ... You have done nothing to come to an understanding. ... You know only how to protest against the Government.

> There is only one way, and that is an agreement with the inhabitants. Zionism has not yet done a thing to obtain the consent of the inhabitants, and without this consent immigration will not be possible.

Typical of the main stream of Yishuv reactions to this kind of advice was Ben-Zvi's view that 'in times of stern rule over the Arabs, it is possible to negotiate, but not when the Jews feel themselves beaten'.[94] For those who shared this view, only a change on Samuel's part could create the necessary prerequisites for a peace agreement with the Arabs. And, since such a change appeared remote,[95] the Arabs would have to remain for the Yishuv first and foremost a threat to be held in check. Even if reluctantly some were forced to agree with Samuel, local Jews were not prepared to go as far as Samuel did in deferring to the power of Arab hostility.

SAMUEL AND THE 'CHURCHILL' WHITE PAPER (JUNE 1922)

To complete our picture of Samuel's determined attempt to get the Zionists to conform to his chosen policy of conciliation in the wake of the May riots, let us look at the Statement of Policy, written by Samuel,[96] but bearing Mr Churchill's name. While not neglecting to improve security in Palestine after May 1921, Samuel still attached great importance to the political gains that he hoped would be achieved if the Colonial Office could oversee a constitutional break-through and an Arab-Zionist compromise in London.[97] At the same time, Samuel specifically expected the Zionists to come round to endorsing the principles laid down in his 3 June Statement of Policy. While he took appreciative note of the 'common home' resolution of the XIIth Zionist Congress, he could not fail to notice how little its 'moderate' spirit was being applied in Palestine and in the Anglo-Jewish press. He felt he still needed something more explicit from the Zionists to help 'clear up the political atmosphere' in the country.[98]

But the hopes which Samuel was pinning on London were not to be realised. Dr Weizmann refused to endorse the 3 June Statement, while meetings between Zionist and Arab representatives in London in late 1921 proved fruitless.[99] In order to bypass this deadlock, the Colonial Office sought Zionist and Arab endorsement of a dictated policy which it hoped would cause neither 'alarm to the Arab population' nor 'disappointment to the Jews'.[100] A 'Statement of British Policy in Palestine' was presented to the Zionist Organisation and to the Palestine Arab Delegation. Subsequently known as the 'Churchill White Paper', the document in effect combined the Colonial Secretary's previous encouragement of the Jews (March 1921) with the High Commissioner's assurances to the Arabs (June 1921).

On the assumption that most Arab 'apprehensions' stemmed from 'exaggerated interpretations' of the Balfour Declaration, the White Paper opened with the statement that HMG had never intended for Palestine 'to become "as Jewish as England is English" ', or for the whole country to be 'converted into a Jewish National Home'. The Statement quoted approvingly from the 'common home' resolution of the Zionist Congress in an attempt to illustrate that Zionist aims were not unreasonable.

Turning to the Jews, the Statement sought to allay fears of any reversal of British policy by solemnly affirming that the Balfour Declaration was 'not susceptible of change'. Tribute was paid to the Yishuv for its growth, autonomous life, and 'national' characteristics. In this light, the meaning of the words 'development of the Jewish National Home' was given to be

> not the imposition of a Jewish nationality upon the inhabitants of Palestine as a whole, but the further development of the existing Jewish community ... in order that it may become a centre in which the Jewish people as a whole may take, on grounds of religion and race, an interest and a pride.

The Jews, the White Paper proclaimed, were in Palestine 'as of right and not on sufferance'; this right was based upon 'ancient historic connection', would be internationally guaranteed, and presupposed the further right to increase the numbers of the Jewish community by immigration. Such immigration, however, would not be allowed to strain the economic absorptive capacity of the country. The constitutional development of the country would proceed gradually in accordance with the terms of the draft Constitution of Palestine, which provided for a partly-elected Legislative Council.

The Arabs rejected the White Paper, while the Zionist Organisation felt compelled to provide the 'formal assurance' specifically requested by the Colonial Office that it 'accept[ed] the policy as set out in the ... statement' and was 'prepared to conduct its ... activities in conformity therewith'. Thus, Dr Weizmann, who had adamantly refused to endorse the 3 June 1921 Statement, was now forced to accept the June 1922 White Paper, boldly framed in the same spirit and also a product of Samuel's thinking.[101]

SAMUEL LEAVES PALESTINE

Zionist official endorsement of the Churchill White Paper and the subsequent ratification of the Mandate for Palestine by the League of Nations in July 1922 marked a certain détente in Zionist-British relations. Outwardly, the last three years of Samuel's tenure as High Commissioner seemed peaceful and successful from all points of view.

Yet, below the surface, two issues kept alive Yishuv uneasiness and dissatisfaction with the Jewish High Commissioner. In the area of Zionist political work among the Arabs, the approach taken by Samuel and his administration seemed to thwart Yishuv efforts at winning the sympathy of 'moderate' Arabs, while appearing to encourage the boldness of 'extremist' elements.[102] And, as previously mentioned, in the constitutional domain the Yishuv felt its position undermined by Samuel's efforts at winning Arab co-operation in the setting up of various self-governing institutions (see below).

Nevertheless, as Samuel's term of office was coming to a close, all signs seemed to point to a tendency for both Jews and Arabs to be 'tiring of politics'. 'Equilibrium' was a word often used to describe the new situation, and the 'Arab problem' was declared by some Zionists to be 'in process of solution'.[103] Tension had indeed decreased, security had improved, and economic prosperity was beginning to be felt. Few could dispute the fact that Samuel had been an outstanding administrator, and that he would be leaving the country in far better shape than he had found it.

But, despite the outward expressions of official Zionist satisfaction at the improvements in the situation in Palestine, the local Jewish community remained bitter and critical of what they still considered the insufficiently sympathetic administration of Sir Herbert Samuel. The Yishuv continued to complain about the lack of government sympathy in such matters as support for education and the low proportion of Jews in administrative posts and in the police.[104] This Yishuv disappointment in the Samuel administration was often accompanied by a lingering and primitive suspicion of British intentions, and some local leaders found no reason to cease their public and private accusations against the hostile or conspiratorial behaviour of certain British officials. Yishuv spokesmen still invoked unfavourable comparisons between British 'liberalism' and the methods of the Turks, who, whatever their faults, nevertheless 'knew how to demand respect from one race and religion to another'.[105]

Preparing for the visit of Colonial Secretary Amery in 1925, Yishuv leaders were anxious to avoid a repetition of their audience with Mr Churchill in March 1921. Yitzhak Ben-Zvi warned the VL not to allow the impression 'that we explicitly agree to the British administration without any modifications: we cannot agree to this because, in fact, we have no confidence in the British administration'.[106] And when the Palestinian Jews returned from their audience with Mr Amery, they were confirmed in the conclusion they had bitterly reached in the dark days of June 1921 – namely, that 'the Government is not thinking of actively helping in the creation of the Jewish National Home' and that 'we ourselves will have to build up our own National Home'.[107] This disillusionment, which dated back to the parting of the ways between the Yishuv and 'its' High Commissioner over the Arab question in 1921, was accompanied by the Jews' continuing frustration at knowing that loyalty to the 'Jewish High Commissioner' operated to their disadvantage – by allowing Samuel to ignore his positive obligations to the National Home policy and to concentrate instead on giving satisfaction to Arab grievances.

It was precisely Samuel's rôle as the 'Jewish' High Commissioner which complicated Zionist and Yishuv reactions to his scheduled departure from Palestine. When local Jews were first confronted with the prospect of Samuel's leaving Palestine, and his likely replacement by a non-Jew, Yishuv leaders pressed him to stay on.[108] The dilemma caused by the many specific grievances against Sir Herbert Samuel, on the one hand, and the fact of having the post of High Commissioner filled by a Jew, on the other, was evident at a February 1925 meeting of the VL, where the 'general view' was summarised in the following words:[109]

> despite Jewish public opinion which does not agree with the political methods of the High Commissioner, and despite the fact that, until we forced it to, the Government did not take any steps to fulfil the Balfour Declaration ..., especially in the matter of opening the gates of the country to the Jews wishing to return to their homeland – in spite of all this, the Jewish public ... sees the need, for the sake of its national honour, to request the High Commissioner to remain in the country.

In March 1925, the VL clearly placed the symbolic value of having a Jewish High Commissioner ahead of all the specific faults of Sir Herbert Samuel by openly defying instructions from Dr Weizmann and the advice of other Zionist leaders and circulating a memorandum to ZE members and the Zionist federations in various countries.[110] This VL campaign to mobilise world Zionist support to press for an extension of Samuel's term of office met with little success, however, perhaps because the world Zionist leadership was motivated by more rational and practical considerations. Despite the glowing public tributes paid to Samuel by Dr Weizmann, the ZE and the XIVth Zionist Congress, most Zionist leaders seem to have concluded that the Samuel appointment, on balance, had been a mistake, and they were anxious to welcome a new High Commissioner.[111]

On 30 June 1925, Sir Herbert Samuel left Palestine much as he had come: in simple dignity and modest ceremony, and amid words of touching sentiment from his 'brother Jews'.[112] The High Commissioner's final *Report* on his administration of Palestine[113] both reflected and stimulated the public optimism which was then prevalent in many circles. The survey of Samuel's five years in office included a long and sympathetic description of the Zionist enterprise in Palestine. In his concluding passage on the development of the Jewish National Home, Samuel contrasted the Arab accusations that his administration had favoured the Jews unduly with the Jewish complaints that his Government had not done enough. So far as there was any truth in these criticisms, Samuel admitted that 'the latter ... has the most substance', and he proceeded to summarise the evidence to prove that the Jews were, in fact, being forced to become 'self-dependent' in the absence of active assistance from the administration. His final words on the subject were no doubt intended as a flattering tribute to 'the Jewish movement':

> if it has been able to rely on the Government of Palestine to maintain order and to impose no unnecessary obstacles, for all the rest it has had to rely on its own internal resources, on its own enthusiasm, its own sacrifices, its own men. ... But this one factor, at least, is propitious: that the building of the National Home has not been the work of any Government; it is not the artificial

construction of laws and official fostering. It is the outcome of the energy and enterprise of the Jewish people themselves.

Among those Yishuv elements who had come to appreciate the overall negative results of having a liberal British Jew as High Commissioner, there was a decidedly hostile reaction to the *Report* which Samuel had left behind. Labour leaders Berl Katznelson and David Ben-Gurion were particularly unmoved by Samuel's 'kind words'.[114] Katznelson saw absolutely no reason why the Yishuv should accept as either complimentary or 'propitious' the fact that all Zionist achievement had been '*in spite of* the methods of the Government which was appointed to execute the Mandate'. In his dissection of Samuel's *Report*, Katznelson stated plainly that the High Commissioner's words of 'affection' were not good enough, and he urged his readers to note that *words* were all that the administration had been prepared to pay to the Yishuv:

> Every reader must not allow himself to be bought off by the tender words of sympathy, but should dwell on the political methods of the Mandatory administration and its spokesman in order to appreciate the realities ... in which we must operate.

The *Report*, Katznelson went on, would have 'most dangerous consequences' if, by its flattery, it were to succeed in

> teaching us to go along with the violation of our rights and the lowering of our stature, and to accept the injustice against us *with love*. ...
>
> One gets the incorrect picture [from the *Report*] that the Yishuv has accepted the infringement of its rights and the injustice against it willingly and submissively. Why is the political character of the Yishuv distorted to such an extent? And what right has the High Commissioner to brush aside all the claims of the Yishuv, even in the hour of his departure, at a time when he himself admits that all our complaints have some substance to them?

One final passage from Katznelson's critique of Samuel's *Report* deserves quotation here as reflecting a real fear of the effect which this official 'apologia' for Zionism might have on the Arab mind. Despite its 'good intentions' and its more than obvious aim of pacifying the Arabs, Katznelson felt that Samuel's *Report* had presented a dangerous image of 'the Jew' to the Arab reader. Which Arab, he asked,

> who fears the ultimate aim of Zionism will be calmed when it becomes clear to him that, instead of methods of aggressive political conquest, we have adopted a system of political infiltration; that we have replaced an upright approach by a clandestine one? Is not the true story, as told in the *Report*, that despite the absence of any assistance from the Government; despite restrictions on immigration; despite the declarations weakening the contents of the Balfour Declaration; despite the balancing of [the Declaration] in favour of others – [in spite of all this,] *our numbers have doubled in five years*? Does this not confirm that the 'Zionist danger' is greater than all the exercises of maximalist

declamation and extremist political positions? In this sense, Samuel has hardened the mystical fears of the Arab patriot.

On the basis of the evidence we have seen above, it would seem that former Palestine Attorney-General Norman Bentwich (who was married to Samuel's niece) was as guilty as Sir Herbert of 'distorting the political character of the Yishuv' when he wrote in his *Mandate Memories* (to contradict another author's appraisal) that 'Most Jews felt a deep gratitude for what he [Samuel] did to found the [National] Home, whatever the disappointment of their Messianic expectations. The greatest tribute to his fairness, his statesmanship and his devotion to all the inhabitants was the peacefulness of his last two years.'[115] Almost no local Jew in the 1920s would have argued that the period of relative peace from 1922 to 1928 might, in part at least, be credited to Samuel's conciliatory approach; only a few Israelis would so argue today. In most Yishuv and Israeli analyses, the failure of British attempts to co-opt al-Hajj Amin al-Husaini, to set up controlled representative institutions, and to solve the Palestine problem by promoting pan-Arab unity schemes[116] only proves the futility of 'liberal' or 'statesman-like' approaches to the conflict.[117] Although many still respect and admire him for his qualities, few Israelis today would place Sir Herbert Samuel high on their list of the best British High Commissioners in Palestine.[118]

II

During the period of the British Mandate (1920–48), the population of Palestine, both Arab and Jewish, carried on without the opportunity of learning the art of representative self-government from its British rulers. Each community developed separately, and had its own recognised patterns of leadership and political rivalry in matters of national-communal concern. Leaders of varying abilities mobilised their masses, with varying degrees of success, in response to the challenges and crises of the period.

While the Jewish community of Mandatory Palestine had its own fairly well-developed Elected Assembly, National Council (*Vaad Leumi*) and political parties, politics in the Arab community revolved largely around traditional family loyalties and rivalries, and the religion-based power wielded by al-Hajj Amin al-Husaini, from 1921 to 1937 Mufti of Jerusalem, 'Grand Mufti' of Palestine and President of the Supreme Muslim Council.[119]

During the 1920s, the Muslim-Christian Association formed in response to the Zionist threat, became the main vehicle for the nationalist struggle. Several Palestine Arab Congresses were held between 1919 and

1928, but with decreasing frequency. Each of these congresses elected an Executive Committee (each time headed by Musa Kazim Pasha al-Husaini) to represent Arab interests. This 'Arab Executive' was dissolved following the upheavals of October 1933 and the death of Musa Kazim. The outbreak of the general strike and rebellion of 1936 saw the formation of the Arab Higher Committee, a coalition of still-rudimentary political 'parties' which continued to reflect factional splits within the Arab community.[120]

But apart from local Jewish and Arab community politics, the real power to make decisions affecting the day-to-day administration and the future status of Palestine remained outside Jewish or Arab hands. With the exception of a brief period in 1920–21, the Government of Palestine was conducted throughout the Mandatory period in true 'colonial' style, without even the semblance of consultative or representative democracy. Several abortive attempts were made, but the worsening Zionist-Arab struggle made it impossible for British administrators to implement that part of their Mandatory obligations to foster the 'development of self-governing institutions' in Palestine.[121]

Much is already known about Palestinian Arab rejection of British attempts to introduce limited forms of self-government.[122] In what follows we deal with a different dimension of these British initiatives: Yishuv reactions to Sir Herbert Samuel's successive proposals to set up (1) a partly-elected Legislative Council, (2) an appointed Advisory Committee and (3) an 'Arab Agency'.

SAMUEL'S CONSTITUTIONAL APPROACH

We have attempted above to show how Samuel's liberal approach to the Zionist-Arab conflict differed sharply from that of the Yishuv. Samuel's general belief in a solution which could be brought about by greater flexibility, reasonableness and good faith on both sides was accompanied by a sustained attempt to improve the situation by offering to introduce democratic constitutionalism in Palestine. As a liberal, Samuel felt that it was right in principle that the will of the local population should find expression in representative governmental institutions; in practice, he hoped that this would reduce native suspicion of foreign rule in Palestine. In the years 1921–23, a large part of Sir Herbert Samuel's energies was devoted to finding a constitutional formula by which Arab representatives would agree to participate in the administration of the country, and, by implication, tacitly acquiesce in the Mandate and its Jewish National Home provisions. Not only was Samuel unsuccessful with the Arabs, but here, as elsewhere, he found the Yishuv strongly opposed to his constitutional proposals, and the gap separating the two following the May 1921 riots became deeper and wider.

Samuel's approach seemed a direct answer to the political-legal arguments being raised by Palestinian Arab spokesmen. If after 1921 the latter appeared to abandon violence as an effective political instrument in their fight against Zionism,[123] they continued to reject the Balfour Declaration and refused to recognise the Mandate or the Constitution which were based on that declaration. In a positive way, they insisted on the fullest interpretation of the injunction against 'prejudicing' their rights, while pressing their demands (made repeatedly since 1919)[124] for some form of 'native national government'. Since a part of Britain's mandatory obligation was to promote self-governing institutions in Palestine, Arab constitutional grievances appeared quite legitimate from certain points of view. The constitutional issue reached its peak during 1923, when Sir Herbert Samuel successively offered to establish three constitutional organs in the hope of inducing Arab representatives to co-operate in the administration of the country.

At an early stage, Zionists realised that the constitutional demands of the Arabs were almost totally irreconcilable with their own demands and needs, and would have to be considered a 'threat' to be resisted. Yet, it was occasionally asked whether there were some modifications in the constitutional arrangements for Palestine on which Zionists and Arabs might agree, as a first step to an overall accommodation.[125] Once the Mandate was ratified, however, Zionists preferred not to re-open any constitutional issues in their discussions with Arab representatives.[126] According to the analysis of Col. Kisch of the Palestine Zionist Executive [hereafter: PZE], there was indeed little room for manoeuvre on this question in mid-1923:

> so long as we need the Mandate at all, it is clearly impossible to contemplate any modification of those guarantees which it affords to our national aspirations. It is also clear that we do emphatically need the Mandate today, while we number only 11 per cent of the population of which the remainder are ranged almost to the last man behind the banner of a hostile organisation [the MCA].
>
> For these reasons it appears that we cannot to-day join the Arabs in demanding a change in the Constitution which would weaken the English control of the situation, a control which the English Government has introduced into the constitution in order to be able to carry out the pledges contained in the Mandate.[127]

Neither was L. Stein, Secretary of the Zionist Executive (ZE) in London, able to conceive of any Arab demands which the Jews could support, apart from an extremely careful 'liberalisation' of the admittedly autocratic form of government in Palestine by allowing native Palestinians greater participation in 'non-political' areas of the administration.[128]

For the British, the problem was to strike a balance between the Jewish National Home policy, on the one hand, and the Mandatory obligation to introduce democratic forms of government, on the other, in such a way that the full implementation of the latter would not – as was likely to be the case – make it impossible to fulfil the former, equally valid, obligation.[129] 'Gradualness' became the catchword for both Zionism and self-government under the British Mandate. During his first year as High Commissioner, Samuel easily put off Arab demands for the immediate introduction of representative institutions with the vague argument that conditions in the country (security, economic growth, etc.) were not yet favourable.[130] While visiting Palestine in March 1921, Secretary of State Winston Churchill added his weight to these attempts to side-step early Arab demands for self-rule. In his reply to the AE's memorandum,[131] Churchill made it quite clear that the present form of government would 'continue for many years' and that only 'step by step' would Britain 'develop representative institutions leading up to full self-government'. As an indication of just how gradual the process was to be, Mr Churchill went on: 'All of us here today will have passed away from the earth and also our children and our children's children before it is achieved.'

However, like so many other cherished notions, the idea of the extremely gradual development of self-government in Palestine did not stand up to the May 1921 riots. On 8 May Samuel wrote to Churchill suggesting 'the very early establishment of representative institutions'.[132] The Secretary of State was most reluctant to 'make such a concession under pressure', which would be, in his view, 'to rob it of half its value'; he informed Samuel that he was decidedly 'not of opinion that the morrow of the Jaffa riots was the best moment for such a concession'. But Samuel was not pressing so much for *full* self-government, as for a speedy way to restore Arab confidence in his administration by offering a channel for expressing public opinion. Thus, Samuel was asking for authority to issue an official declaration to the effect that HMG were 'considering [the] constitutional question and that opinions will be taken into account of all sections' of the population. Mr Churchill gave his authorisation for a statement, but with the strong recommendation not to use 'any such words as "elected" or "representative" '. Samuel's Statement of Policy on 3 June 1921 therefore contained the circuitously-worded, but very real, assurance that representative institutions for Palestine were under consideration. Over the next two and a half years, Samuel displayed great determination to introduce constitutional organs which would satisfy the Arabs as adequately responsive to their interests and opinions.

ZIONIST ATTITUDES TOWARDS SELF-RULE IN PALESTINE

On the question of developing self-governing institutions in Palestine, Samuel and the Zionists were necessarily at odds. General Zionist fears of representative institutions while the Jews formed only a small minority of the population are almost too obvious to require elaboration. Even before there were any concrete plans for such institutions, experience under the military administration (1917–20) had led Zionists to appreciate the dangers of allowing 'only the brutal numbers to speak' in Palestine. In 1918 and 1919 Dr Weizmann was urging the British to recognise 'the fundamental difference in quality of Jew and Arab', and that the latter would not be 'fit for self-government for a very long time to come'.[133] Zionist publicists, as well, sought tactful ways of presenting arguments against the introduction of democratic institutions in Palestine in the foreseeable future.[134]

As it developed into the 1920s, the basic Zionist stand was that, while the Jews did not oppose the *gradual* development of self-governing institutions, it had to be recognised that Palestine would not be 'ripe' for self-rule for many years to come. They realised that it was impossible to say publicly that the proper time might come only once the Jews formed a majority (or near-majority) of the population. But it was not difficult for them to appeal to the general European view that – quite apart from the question of Zionism – to grant self-government to the Arabs of Palestine, with their primitive 'standard of education and political experience', 'would clearly be to run the risk of consigning Palestine to chaos'. If any practical argument was needed against representative institutions, Zionists would point to the state of Arab feeling in Palestine and the control of the 'agitators' over the illiterate masses to show that democracy would merely be perverted into an effective tool in 'extremist' hands for 'the abolition of the Palestine Mandate and the withdrawal of the Balfour Declaration altogether'.[135]

For many, the riots of May 1921 seemed to strengthen the argument that the Arab majority was quite 'unripe for civic responsibilities',[136] and it was thus with particular distress that Zionists saw Samuel apparently discarding all the recent pronouncements on 'gradualness'. Samuel's attempt 'to deal with the Arab movement as a constitutional opposition'[137] became as unwelcome to them as his general tendency to take the Arabs 'too' seriously. The Weizmann-Samuel correspondence of summer 1921[138] contained earnest and eloquent restatements of the two conflicting basic positions on the question of representative institutions. In the end, Zionists were powerless to deflect Samuel from his chosen course, and they were forced to appreciate that, however 'premature and in some ways artificial' Arab demands for self-government may have been, they could not be 'indefinitely resisted' or deferred 'until the day, necessarily far distant, when there is a Jewish majority'.[139] In the wake of the 3 June Statement, Zionist leaders reluctantly accepted Samuel's determined lead on this question (as on the White Paper policy as a whole) but not without stressing constantly the need for adequate safeguards for the inviolability of the Balfour Declaration and the Mandate.

YISHUV ATTITUDES AND REACTIONS

It is useful to distinguish the particular attitudes of the Yishuv from the general Zionist reactions described above. The acute fears of the former on this question should be viewed in the context of the peculiar constitutional arrangements which Palestinian Jews had expected to emerge from the Paris Peace Conference. The Jaffa 'Eretz-Israel Conference' of December 1918 had envisaged a post-war Palestine under predominantly Jewish and European governing bodies, with only token representation for Arabs.[140] Yishuv leaders had immediately recognised the contradiction between 'pure' national self-determination, on the one hand, and the type of régime which would be required for the development of the Jewish National Home, on the other. However much they wished to consider themselves 'democrats' by temperament or upbringing, they realised that, as a minority, the Jews could not *afford* to be democrats with regard to their own claim to Palestine.

> We are afraid, [confessed Jabotinsky before the Conference] and we don't want to have a normal constitution here, since the Palestine situation is not normal. The majority of its 'electors' have not yet returned to the country. If there is a normal constitution here, responsible to the 'majority', then the majority of *us* would never enter, and even you – with all due respect – they [Arabs of Palestine] would expel from the country.[141]

In 1918 the Yishuv had put forward the demand for a system of 'national-communal autonomy' for all groups as a legitimate alternative to numerical or parliamentary democracy. This concept was in the tradition of the *millet* system, where ethnic-religious communal autonomy was enjoyed under the Turks.[142] But this 'national-communal autonomy', as the Yishuv understood it, was never enshrined in the constitutional framework of the British Mandate; it became relegated to the status of a cherished internal goal of the Yishuv.

It is interesting that the *Vaad Leumi* never forcefully challenged Samuel's plans for a western-style elective institution by suggesting an alternative system based on this 'national-communal autonomy'. Only Berl Katznelson, the influential labour spokesman, brought out the contrast between these two forms, in a 1923 article which criticised Samuel for trying to force western liberal democracy on the unwilling Arab and Jewish communities.[143] Why, he wondered, had Samuel not chosen to implement the Mandatory obligation for the 'development of self-governing institutions' in another way – namely, by 'recognising the existing natural institutions of national autonomy, the correct and most appropriate form for a country like ours, with its various races, languages and cultures'?

Whatever the merits of such a counter-proposal, the typical reaction of organised Yishuv bodies to Samuel's constitutional plans was simple fear and rejection. After Samuel alluded to the dreaded subject in his 3 June 1921 speech, he summoned Yishuv leaders to give them an informal indication of the composition and functions of the intended Legislative

Council. During the interview, the members of the VL Executive took the opportunity of making clear their opposition to any form of elective institution, not so much 'because of our desire to deny the rights of others', but rather because 'in this case an elective institution makes difficult the realisation of the promises given to us by the League of Nations and the British Government'.[144]

In the prevailing atmosphere of Yishuv-Samuel relations during those weeks, it is little wonder that local leaders were hardly impressed by Samuel's assurances that the special position of the Jews would not be endangered under any council schemes. The feeling that an elective institution constituted a grave threat to Yishuv interests dominated the VL meeting (28–30 June 1921) which heard the report of the interview with the High Commissioner. Only Y. Radler-Feldman (later to be, under the name 'Rabbi Binyamin', one of the bi-nationalist leaders) was optimistic enough to suggest that there might perhaps be 'some party combinations among the Arabs favourable to us', and he urged the VL to adopt a 'positive attitude' to the idea of an elected council.[145] Another speaker suggested that the Yishuv might agree to participate in the council only if the proportion of seats allotted to the Jews would reflect the ratio of the *world* Jewish population to the Palestine Arab population, while VL chairman, Dr Yaakov Thon, was prepared to accept a guaranteed quota of one-third Jewish seats. But, apart from these exceptions, the discussion focused on what steps might prove most effective in averting the proposed Legislative Council. The general view was that the Yishuv would be quite foolish to lend its hand to a scheme from which no good could possibly come, and the resolution finally adopted by the VL was unanimous in stating that

> as long as the Mandate, which fixes the political status of the country, the rôle of the Government and the rights of the Jewish people and the inhabitants of Palestine is not signed, the step of creating an elected council in the country is illegal and the *Vaad Leumi* has no need whatsoever to concern itself with the idea.[146]

The Yishuv stand happened, in any case, to conform with the procedure which the British chose to follow, and the delay in the ratification of the Mandate provided the Jews with a postponement of the dreaded scheme for representative institutions. In the interim, a draft constitution for Palestine, with provisions for a Legislative Council, was among the subjects of the correspondence between the Palestine Arab Delegation in London and the Colonial Office. The White Paper of June 1922 offered some slight modifications to the original proposals for the Council, in the hope of making the constitution less objectionable to the Arabs. But the delegation remained firm in rejecting *any* constitution based on the Balfour Declaration and the draft Mandate.[147] The long-awaited ratification of the Mandate on 24 July 1922 was duly followed by the promulgation of Orders-in-Council for the Palestine Constitution (10 August) and for elections to a Legislative Council (1 September). Within six months a Council – composed of 12 elected Palestinians (eight Muslims, two Christians and two Jews) and ten Government officials, under the presidency of the High Commissioner – was to come into being.[148]

The weighted composition of the Council illustrated Sir Herbert Samuel's belief that the time was not yet ripe for *full* self-government. Although many Yishuv leaders were slow to appreciate Samuel's position, the High Commissioner was well aware (as he admitted to Dr Weizmann) that it was 'undoubtedly somewhat early in the new stage of development of Palestine to introduce an elective element into the Constitution'; nevertheless, he did feel that this had to be done:[149]

> So long as the people have no elected representatives to keep in touch with the measures of the Government, they will remain suspicious and will probably become hostile.

The 'risks and dangers' of an elective element were, in Samuel's opinion, 'outweighed by its advantages'. These 'risks and dangers' were felt to be minimised by the British-Jewish majority of 13–10, but at the same time Samuel was hoping that the Council would 'go some way to satisfy [Arab] opinion as a further stage on the road to self-government.'[150]

But all this optimistic constitutionalism and risk/advantage balancing were really beside the point. The Vth Palestine Arab Congress, meeting in Nablus on 22 August 1922, firmly rejected the new Constitution based on the Balfour Declaration policy, and resolved to boycott any elections to the proposed Council.[151]

YISHUV PARTICIPATION IN THE LEGISLATIVE COUNCIL ELECTIONS

In the months immediately following the boycott decision of the Nablus Congress, the attitude of the Yishuv was unclear. The VL had taken no new official position on the Council, but a number of its leaders appear to have been assuming that Jewish participation would be inescapable. No one in the Yishuv relished the prospect of this Council, in itself, but when it became a matter of a battle between the Government and the 'extremists', Yishuv representatives had little choice. They noted with satisfaction that Sir Herbert Samuel was – initially – not intimidated by the threatened Arab boycott, and that he was prepared to suppress any anti-election activity 'as constituting an act against the Government'.[152] Some local Jews assisted the PZE and the administration by encouraging 'moderate' Arabs to defy the Nablus Congress boycott.

But Samuel's apparent resoluteness, and Yishuv satisfaction with it, were very short-lived. Almost within a month of the promulgation of the Elections Ordinance and increasingly thereafter, Samuel appeared to display pathetic weakness and inactivity in the face of a boycott campaign which mounted in intensity and boldness. Beginning in late September 1922, Zionist complaints grew steadily, and Col. Kisch ended one of his reports in March 1923 with the opinion that 'the present lamentable situation' was 'the direct result of the application of the methods of English liberal administration to the government of an Eastern and backward people accustomed to the strong hand of Turkish misrule!'[153] Initial optimism among the Jews that the elections would succeed, with the resultant boost to Government and (by extension) Zionist prestige, progressively faded.

By the time detailed instructions for election procedures were issued on 7 February 1923, the difficulties of the situation and the Yishuv's own ambiguous attitude were becoming unbearable for local Jewish leaders. Most did not deny the basic principle that the Yishuv would be far better off if the Council never came into being; but the Jews were equally conscious of the fact that it was tactically impossible to reject the Council out-of-hand, by following only their 'healthy and simple instincts'. With only one week remaining before the voting was to begin, the VL held a meeting (14–15 February 1923) to resolve the lingering uncertainty over Yishuv participation.[154]

The theme of the first day's debate was: how to make the best of a bad thing. Interspersed throughout the discussions were hypothetical questions revealing the continuing anxieties of the Yishuv with regard to the proposed constitutional innovation: How would the Jews react if the Arab members on the Council immediately demanded its dissolution and elections for a fully democratic body? How would the Jews react to Arab attempts to use the Council to interfere in internal Yishuv matters? Were there two Yishuv personalities of sufficient weight and dignity to hold their own against twenty Arabs and officials?

On the immediate question of participating in the elections, only Meir Dizengoff stated categorically that he would not place himself in the absurd position of casting his vote for a 'fictitious' mock-parliament which was, at the same time, visibly dangerous to Jewish interests. But most other speakers adduced a variety of tactical considerations to justify a decision in favour of participating in the unwanted council. Col. Kisch and M. Ussishkin of the PZE presented the 'official' Zionist reasoning for Jewish participation. Kisch reminded the VL that a successful election with substantial Arab participation would be a welcome defeat for the 'extremists', and would amount to Arab recognition of the Constitution and the Mandate. He argued further that, even if the elections were to be called off owing to lack of *Arab* participation, a co-operative and 'loyal' Yishuv stood only to gain from the subsequent gratitude of the administration. Ussishkin brought up the well-tried argument that only harm could come from Samuel's humiliation and likely resignation after a combined Jewish-Arab rejection of his constitutional proposals.

At the end of the debate, a motion was passed in favour of participation by 10 votes to one, but with abstentions from all the labour representatives. It was clearly less out of love for Samuel than out of fear of Musa Kazim and the AE that the Yishuv leaders were prepared to participate in the elections; at this particular meeting and elsewhere, the refusal to make common cause with Musa Kazim was the most frequently and strongly argued justification used by the local Jews.

But the matter did not end there. On the following day, the VL decided to vote again on a new motion, drafted to conform with the more stringent position adopted by the powerful *Histadrut* (General Federation of Jewish Workers). Since the proposed Legislative Council was seen to endanger, in particular, Jewish autonomous development, the labour movement announced it would participate in the elections only on condition that the Government speed up its study and approval of the much-delayed 'Communities Ordinance'.[155] The new VL resolution which was finally passed at 2 a.m. read (somewhat incoherently):

> The *Vaad Leumi* regards as a prior condition to its participation in the elections the sanction of the Communities Ordinance and its autonomous rights before the convening of a Legislative Council; otherwise, it is certain that there will not be the desired participation in the elections, the abstention of important sections is to be feared, and the necessary moral prestige for Jewish participation in the elections will be lacking.

A delegation was chosen to bring the matter to the attention of the High Commissioner.

It is not too much to say that the Yishuv's hesitancy with regard to the Legislative Council elections was a direct reflection of its declining confidence in Sir Herbert Samuel's ability to remain faithful to the interests of the Jewish National Home in the course of his attempts to develop self-governing institutions in Palestine. We have only to look back to the previous VL session of 2–3 January 1923 to feel the intensity of the bitterness and frustration in the Yishuv with regard to Samuel's record on a number of issues. Quite apart from the Yishuv's obvious disillusionment at the glaring evidence of Government timidity in the face of the boycott campaign, its dissatisfaction with the administration on the questions of immigration and land-acquisition facilities had mounted steadily since the ratification of the Mandate.[156] The fear that Zionists abroad might be receiving a false and rosy picture that 'all's well in Palestine' prompted the drafting of a blunt VL memorandum addressed to the Zionist Actions Committee in Berlin.[157] From this sombre memorandum and the debates of 2–3 January, we can see that, despite the external appearance that the Yishuv was content with 'its' High Commissioner, the disappointment caused by Samuel's reactions to the May 1921 riots had not yet been erased. A remark by Hebron native David Avissar evoked some discussion on whether the position of the

Jews, *vis-à-vis* the authorities, had not been better under the Turks. Several spokesmen – this time not exclusively from labour ranks – displayed irritation at the prevailing tactic of dealing gently with the 'Jewish' High Commissioner so as not to play into the hands of his critics in the Arab camp. The idea of an inevitable confrontation with Samuel was already brewing then, as Yitzhak Ben-Zvi reflected the growing feeling that Samuel's 'whole policy' was 'based on the belief and the assumption that the MCA is the power and that we are not; if we don't show our strength, we won't be able to influence him.'

The same undercurrent of discontent with Samuel permeated the February debates on the question of Yishuv participation in the elections. David Ben-Gurion noted drily that he and his party were 'responsible neither for Samuel's appointment, nor for his resignation', and that there was therefore no need to weigh the merits of any Yishuv decision against the possibility of Samuel resigning.[158] Even more pointed was another speaker's suggestion that the VL ought to address Samuel frankly in the following terms:

> 'Two years ago, when you decided on the Council, you saw no need to consult us. We told you that this matter was dangerous for us, the country and the Mandate. Without taking this into consideration, you did what you did, and we are unable to go along with it. ... We shall not declare a boycott, but neither shall we call our people out to vote. You have placed yourself in this ridiculous position and you must find your own way out of it. ...'

Although the actual words addressed to the High Commissioner during his interview with the VL delegation on 16 February were somewhat milder in tone, Samuel was nevertheless taken aback by the bitterness and dissatisfaction expressed by the Yishuv representatives.[159] No doubt preoccupied in recent months with the Arab campaign of boycott and non-co-operation, Samuel had been taking for granted that the Palestinian Jews would appreciate that they shared a common interest with him for the success of the elections. The VL delegation, fed up at precisely this point – being taken for granted – now took the opportunity to make clear its disappointment with the Government's recent record and, in particular, the delegation insisted on receiving some assurance that the Communities Ordinance would be approved in exchange for organised participation in the elections. The Yishuv spokesmen stressed that any VL support would, in any event, be forthcoming against the better judgment of the Yishuv and only owing to force of circumstance. Although he perhaps knew better, Ben-Gurion spoke of the proposed council as though it were deliberately structured to set 'two Jews against 20 Arabs and officials.'

In his reply to the Yishuv delegation, Samuel attempted to convince it of the political wisdom of Yishuv participation in the elections mainly by pointing to the strong anti-Zionist and anti-Mandate lobbies in England, which would use a combined Jewish-Arab boycott as ready ammunition in the campaign for complete abandonment of the Palestine 'burden'. He hinted further that, in the event of a joint boycott, he and Attorney-General Norman Bentwich (another British Jew) would see little point in continuing 'to sacrifice the best of their forces here'. On the other hand, Samuel showed much sympathy for the Yishuv position. Although he was unable to give a definite assurance that the Communities Ordinance would be sanctioned before the Legislative Council was convened, Samuel did succeed in convincing the VL delegation that he was energetically supporting the Ordinance in its difficult passage through the Colonial Office.[160]

The crisis over Yishuv participation in the elections passed as the VL reconvened two days later to learn the results of the interview. The feeling was unanimous that the Yishuv had been as successful as could have been expected in having its position understood at Government House. In the short time remaining, Yishuv leaders devoted their energies to preparing the population to participate in the elections. The primary elections held between 20 and 28 February returned more than the required number of Jewish and Druze secondary electors. But, despite an extension of the deadline, only 126 of the 722 places allotted to Muslim and Christian Arabs were filled, testifying to the success of the boycott. On 4 May 1923, an Order-in-Council in London declared the elections 'null and void', and on 29 May Samuel announced this officially to the people of Palestine, who had not 'fully availed themselves of the opportunity afforded to participate in the Government of the country through elected representatives'.[161]

To the extent that the elections had been a battle between boycotting 'extremists' and co-operative 'moderates', the resounding victory of the former was obvious well before Samuel's official announcement. Although the 'extremist' victory was to be regretted as such, many Palestinian Jews were clearly relieved that the unwanted council would not be created, and were satisfied that they could not be reproached for having failed to do their duty by supporting Samuel.[162]

THE ADVISORY COUNCIL PROPOSAL

The offer of a Legislative Council in 1921–23 represented Sir Herbert Samuel's major effort in the direction of self-governing institutions for Palestine. Even after the failure of this project, Samuel persisted in his search for some other appropriate constitutional apparatus which would allow the Arab population to feel that the administration was indeed interested in taking its views into account. But Samuel's initial optimism was now somewhat diminished, and in mid-1923 he admitted that it would be very difficult to find any solution which the Arabs will accept short of the transfer of the government to their own hands, with the purpose and the result – whatever paper guarantees might be given – that the Jewish enterprise will be destroyed.[163]

In his proclamation of 29 May, Samuel appeared to be taking one step backward on the road to self-government when he announced the proposed formation of a nominated Advisory Council.[164] Before making this announcement, Samuel had taken the trouble to consult members of the AE and had been informed that the Executive would see nothing objectionable in an appointed advisory body to co-operate with the Government on administrative matters only, leaving the sensitive political questions aside. Samuel then waited until he had obtained the acceptances of ten suitable and apparently co-operative Arab notables before publicly disclosing his plan for a new Advisory Council. With all this careful preparation, the High Commissioner was hoping that the country might soon return to its 'normal business', with the thorny constitutional question temporarily resolved and the battered prestige of the Government somewhat restored. Zionists, too, welcomed the Advisory Council announcement and predicted a 'favourable change' in the political situation.[165]

But the AE soon had second thoughts about allowing the administration so easy a victory. It now saw reason to condemn the Council because Arab participation on it might well be construed as satisfaction with 'representative' institutions under the Constitution, since (a) the structure of the new Council was identical to that of the recently aborted Legislative Council, and (b) the Jewish community was allowed to *elect* its two allotted representatives. Strong pressure was exerted on the Arab nominees to withdraw their acceptances, or to demand 'conditions' to their participation.[166] The AE was supported in its campaign by fresh resolutions and demands voted by the VIth Palestine Arab Congress, which met in Jaffa on 16–20 June 1923.[167] Negotiations between the Arab nominees and the Government – accompanied throughout by vigorous public and private reminders of the proper patriotic attitude – continued unresolved through the summer of 1923.

While this was going on, Yishuv representatives, for their part, expressed only mild disappointment over the fact that the distribution of seats gave them only two, compared with three on the 1920–21 Advisory Council.[168] But David Yellin and H. M. Kalvaryski, the two Jews elected by the Yishuv to sit on the Council, were on the whole quite satisfied with the new arrangements. They considered only one of the ten Arab nominees an 'extreme opponent', and expressed the hope that the Council might provide a useful stimulus to informal Jewish-Arab contacts. But the real constitutional tug-of-war over the Advisory Council centred on the Government-Arab negotiations, and this left Yishuv leaders with little active rôle to play.

The PZE, however, did take a more active interest in a Government victory over 'extremist' attempts to obstruct the operation of the Advisory Council. 'It seems to me essential', wrote Col. Kisch, 'that it should not be possible for the Government in London and the League of Nations to say that no Arabs of importance or authority are ready to take a share in the administration of Palestine on the present Zionist basis.'[169] Both he and Kalvaryski held several private meetings with some of the Arab nominees, but in the end Zionists were unsuccessful in their attempts to convince the Arabs to resist the campaign which was being mounted against their participation in the Council.[170] By early August, the Government gave up trying to find willing appointees.

THE 'ARAB AGENCY' PROPOSAL

After Samuel's two successive failures at having the Arabs 'play the constitutional game' and channel their opposition through their participation in Government organs, Zionists were beginning to feel that the limit had been reached. They had loyally, but reluctantly, endorsed the June 1922 White Paper policy; likewise, they had gone along with the Legislative Council scheme at Samuel's insistence, but against their own better judgment. The fact that Samuel had still not succeeded in winning Arab confidence was, in their view, no Zionist fault, and should not entail any further futile concessions which could only be at Zionist expense. True, the Balfour Declaration policy itself had not been overturned by these constitutional offers, but the very process of trying to conciliate the Arab non-co-operation movement was doing only harm: it threatened to diminish the major Zionist diplomatic victories of recent years; it did nothing to enhance Government prestige in Arab eyes; and it had already decreased Jewish confidence in Samuel's administration.

Such was the Zionist feeling in July 1923, as a special Cabinet Committee on Palestine began meeting in London. This feeling was transmitted officially and unofficially to British policy-makers in the form of warnings that any 'new concessions to the Arabs would not only be of no value as a means of conciliating the Arab extremists, but would ... give an impression of weakening which would have a most disheartening effect on Zionist opinion'.[171] In the Yishuv, as well, many were hoping that, after the lessons of the Legislative and Advisory Council offers, the British would now resume direct, 'efficient, if not representative' rule.[172] Yishuv confidence in Sir Herbert Samuel had not improved since early 1923, and in July the Jerusalem weekly, *ha-Tor*, looked uneasily to London, where both Samuel and a delegation of the VIth Arab Congress were then visiting:[173]

> Both London and Jerusalem have adopted a policy of keeping peace at the highest price – compromising on everything and listening to the threats of the

Arabs. Who will protect Jewish interests against the intrigues of Musa Kazim and Co.? The High Commissioner ...? Why, it is due to his policy and leniency that these people now speak in the name of the Arab people. It was he who allowed the Arab leaders to boycott the elections. He has allowed the Arab extremist movement to grow by trying suddenly to introduce British liberalism into the country of Jemal Pasha's scaffolds. Will he be able to protect Jewish interests now?

Nor was this suspicion and insecurity confined to 'unsophisticated' local elements in Palestine. Col. Kisch of the PZE gave his candid views to Dr Weizmann in a secret letter several months later:

> I have always been terrified of any attempt *by the Government* to come to an understanding with the Arabs. The CO and HC have both shown themselves so ready to make concessions on our policy while getting nothing in return, that I have ever dreaded what they might be tempted to do against some possible advantage ...[174]

Notwithstanding all the Zionist hopes and suggestions that no new concessions be offered to the Arabs, the Cabinet Committee was indeed contemplating a third 'palliative' to induce the Arabs to adopt a more positive attitude to the Constitution and administration of Palestine. This was the idea of inserting a 'counter-poise' to the Jewish Agency provision (art.4) in the Mandate, an idea which had first suggested itself to Samuel under the impact of the May 1921 crisis, but which had been rejected by the then Secretary of State, Winston Churchill.[175] When the proposal was resurrected in July 1923, Dr Weizmann was informed in strict confidence at the Colonial Office, and he reacted almost hysterically, venting all his anger on the 'Ghetto' mentality of Sir Herbert Samuel.[176] But, as in the case of Samuel's previous initiatives, Zionists were powerless to avert this latest intended offer to the Arabs.

On 4 October 1923 the Secretary of State, the Duke of Devonshire, wrote to Samuel to inform him of the final outcome of the recent deliberations on Palestine policy.[177] While reaffirming the policy embodied in the Balfour Declaration and endorsed by the League of Nations, the Government was nevertheless anxious to find some way to put an end to the continuing Arab resentment towards the 'supposed preferential treatment' of the Jews. Acknowledging that the most frequently cited of all Arab constitutional grievances was the privileged position of the Zionists under article 4 of the Mandate — which recognised 'an appropriate Jewish Agency' (in practice, the PZE) as a 'public body for the purpose of advising and co-operating with the Administration' on matters affecting the Jewish National Home and the Palestine Jewish population — the British Government was now prepared to accord 'similar privileges to an Arab Agency', which was to enjoy 'a position exactly analogous to that accorded to the Jewish Agency'. On the questions of immigration (art.6) and public works (art.11), the Arab Agency would also enjoy the parallel right to be consulted with regard to the 'rights and position of the other (i.e. non-Jewish) sections of the population'.

One week later, the High Commissioner convened a 'fully representative' assembly of Arab notables and read a statement containing the gist of the Secretary of State's letter. Samuel invited those present to accept, on behalf of the Arab population, this 'opportunity ... to share in the conduct of the country's affairs'. Samuel added that, contrary to recent misrepresentations in the press, HMG were definitely not considering any constitutional modifications beyond the present proposal. This take-it-or-leave-it offer was rejected by the assembly as not satisfying 'the aspirations of the Arab people'. Musa Kazim al-Husaini, on behalf of the assembly, 'added that the Arabs, having never recognised the status of the Jewish Agency, have no desire for the establishment of an Arab Agency on the same basis'.

In London, the Duke of Devonshire received the Arab decision 'with great regret' and informed Samuel on 9 November that HMG were 'reluctantly driven to the conclusion that further efforts on similar lines would be useless' and had 'accordingly decided not to repeat the attempt'. He authorised Samuel to resume the administration of Palestine with an Advisory Council or according to his statutory discretion. In December it was announced that the High Commissioner would be governing henceforth with an 'Executive Council' composed of senior Government officials.[178] Practical consideration of any new proposals for the 'development of self-governing institutions' would be resumed only when the Arabs themselves took the initiative and expressed their 'readiness to participate'.[179]

Owing to the circumstances in which the offer was made and rejected, Zionist and Yishuv reactions to the Arab Agency proposal were entirely theoretical and after the event. If the proposal had not amounted to a real danger, its contents were felt to be far more disturbing than either of the previous Council schemes. The fact that the Arab Agency became very quickly a dead issue did not detract from the serious and unambiguous Zionist denunciation of the proposal. The Yishuv and the ZE took separate but similar *post facto* stands on the Arab Agency scheme;[180] two main reasons were given for the severe displeasure of both bodies. The first was the very fact that the British could have contemplated 'tampering' with the Mandate (and, worse still, so soon after its coming into effect on 29 September 1923); this threatened to undermine the sanctity and authority of that 'unalterable and solid international document' and the Zionist position enshrined in it. Secondly, the offer made to create an Arab body 'exactly analogous' to the Jewish Agency had apparently overlooked the 'distinctive characteristics' of the Jewish Agency as a body representing the interests of *world* Jewry with regard to Palestine; this 'oversight', Zionists feared, might lead to the disastrous conclusion that Britain recognised that the *Arab world* had a parallel right to be consulted on internal Palestinian matters (a result which was to come about in the wake of the 1936 Arab general strike in Palestine).[181] A third anxiety, expressed particularly in Yishuv circles, was that immigration – 'the most elementary of the Jewish rights' – should have been specifically mentioned among the subjects on which the Arabs were to have a right to be consulted.

But, counterbalancing all these negative reactions, the Arab Agency episode nevertheless left in its wake some compensating features for the Zionists. Samuel's reaffirmation of the inviolability of the Balfour Declaration and his overall tone of firmness on 11 October were welcome and refreshing to the Jewish public. The Declaration and the Mandate had now survived three successive offers of 'constitutional palliatives', and the British appeared for the time being to have realised the futility of further concessions.[182]

Despite the noticeable relief of Zionists following a difficult constitutional struggle, the Arab demand for representative 'national' government was to remain a permanent feature of Arab-Jewish relations in Palestine. In the years after 1923, Yishuv leaders would look only with dread on the recurring possibility that the British might resurrect proposals aimed at satisfying Arab constitutional demands. Such demands were often in the air, but in 1924 and 1925 no Arabs were willing to take responsibility for approaching Sir Herbert Samuel with the direct overture which the High Commissioner now insisted had to come from the Arab side.[183]

By 1925 Sir Herbert Samuel was a changed man, and no longer the constitutional optimist of 1921–23. Although Yishuv leaders may not have abandoned their impression of Samuel as one who was all too willing to appease the Arabs at their expense, the High Commissioner was to leave Palestine with the firm conclusion that there was no immediate prospect of a workable Zionist-Arab accommodation based on the development of self-governing institutions.[184] Although proposals for a Legislative Council were to be reconsidered on several future occasions (notably 1928–29 and 1935–36),[185] the Mandate for Palestine would end without the population being given the opportunity to learn the fine art of parliamentary democracy at the hands of its British rulers.

NOTES

The present article is an expansion of sections of the author's *Palestine Jewry and the Arab Question, 1917–1925* (London: Frank Cass, 1978). I would like to thank the Directors and Staffs of the following archives for their kindness and helpfulness: Central Zionist Archives [hereafter: CZA], Jerusalem; Israel State Archives [hereafter: ISA], Jerusalem; Weizmann Archive [hereafter: WA], Rehovot; Public Record Office [hereafter: PRO], London. Crown Copyright records appear by permission of the Controller, Her Majesty's Stationery Office.

1. E. Kedourie, 'Sir Herbert Samuel and the Government of Palestine', in *The Chatham House Version and Other Middle Eastern Studies* (London, Cass, 1970), pp. 52–81; B. Wasserstein, 'Herbert Samuel and the Palestine Problem', *English Historical Review* XCI (October 1976), 753–75.
2. Christopher Sykes, *Crossroads to Israel: Palestine from Balfour to Bevin* (London: Mentor NEL, 1967), pp. 34, 50, 63.
3. See Caplan, *Palestine Jewry*, pp. 53–61, 66 f.
4. Eder to Weizmann, 5.5.1920, CZA, Z4/16033; Elias Gilner, *War and Hope: A History of the Jewish Legion* (New York, 1969), p. 383; Esco Foundation for Palestine, Inc., *Palestine: A Study of Jewish, Arab, and British Policies*, Vol. I (New Haven, 1947), p. 259.
5. Weizmann to Eder, 8.6.1920, *The Letters and Papers of Chaim Weizmann* [hereafter: *LPCW*], Series A: Letters, Vol. IX, ed. Jehuda Reinharz (Jerusalem/New Brunswick, NJ, 1977), p. 355.
6. Eder to Weizmann, 28.6.1920, CZA, Z4/16033. See also: S. Landman report on visit to Palestine (Aug. 1920), PRO, FO 371/5122, file E11996/85/44.
7. See: Hemda Ben-Yehuda, *Nosseh ha-Degel* [The Standard Bearer: The Life of Ittamar Ben-Avi] (Jerusalem, 1944), pp. 193 f; H. L. Samuel, *Memoirs* (London, 1945), pp. 168, 176; I. Ben-Avi, *Im Shahar Atzma'utenu* [With the Dawning of our Independence] (Tel Aviv?, 1961), pp. 373 f; David Ben-Gurion, *Zikhronot* [Memoirs], Vol. I (Tel Aviv, 1971), p. 144 f; Gad Frumkin, *Derekh Shofet B'Irushalayim* [The Way of a Jerusalem Judge] (Tel Aviv, 1954), pp. 233 f; Arthur Ruppin, *Memoirs, Diaries, Letters*, ed. Alex Bein, translated from the German by K. Gershon (London/Jerusalem, 1970), p. 186; Norman and Helen Bentwich, *Mandate Memories* (New York, 1965), pp. 59 f, 100 f; Sykes, *Crossroads*, pp. 50 f.
8. *Zionist Bulletin* (London), 6.8.1920, p. 1.
9. Creedy to Under-Secretary of State, FO, 14.8.1920, PRO, FO 371/5121, file E9379/85/44; Jabotinsky to Zionist Executive (ZE), London, 10.7.1920, CZA, Z4/1213; Jabotinsky *et al.*, petition to Samuel [n.d.], PRO, FO 371/5122, file E10893/85/44; Ben-Gurion, *Zikhronot* I, 179; Berl Katznelson, *Kitvei Berl Katznelson* [Writings], Vol. I (3rd ed.), (Tel Aviv, 1946), p. 283.
10. *Zionist Bulletin*, 21.7.1920, p. 5; Z. Jabotinsky, *Ne'umin* [Speeches] *1905–1926* (Tel Aviv, 1940), p. 178; Esco, *Palestine* I, 260; VZ meeting, 27.7.1920, CZA, J1/8799; *The Times*, 2.9.1920, p. 9. For Jabotinsky's less optimistic *private* views, see: Gilner, *War and Hope*, p. 383; Jabotinsky to ZE, 10.7.1920 (n. 9).
11. Thon speech, *Vaad Leumi* [National Council of the Jews of Palestine, successor to the VZ]. Executive (VLE) meeting, 24.11.1920, CZA, J1/139; Landman report on visit to Palestine [Aug. 1920], n. 6; Stein to Lattes, 31.8.1920, CZA, L3/278.
12. Yehoshua Porath, *The Emergence of the Palestinian-Arab National Movement, 1918–1929* (London, Cass, 1974), pp. 103 f; Jabotinsky, *Ne'umin*, p. 188.
13. Jabotinsky interview, *The Times*, 2.9.1920, p. 9; Landman report (n. 6) and

interview with Scott, 3.8.1920, CZA, Z4/25004; Eder to Weizmann, 21.7.1920, L3/289; Thon speech, 24.11.1920 (n. 11); Bentwich, *Mandate Memories*, pp. 72, 101; Wasserstein, 'Herbert Samuel', pp. 762 f.

14. For details, see: *Zionist Review* (London), Aug. 1920, p. 69; *Zionist Bulletin*, 13.8 (p. 6), 17.9 (p. 3) and 15.10.1920 (p. 1); *The Times*, 29.12.1920, p. 7; Michael Assaf, *ha-Yihasim ben Aravim ve-Yehudim be-Eretz-Yisrael, 1860–1948* [Arab-Jewish Relations in Palestine] (Tel Aviv, 1970), p. 88; Ussishkin-Samuel interview, 15.11.1920. CZA, L3/222; Sokolow to Weizmann, 25.2.1921, Z4/16055.
15. *Igrot* [Letters] *1919–1922*, Vol. I (Tel Aviv, 1970), p. 173 (30.11.1920).
16. *Sefer Toldot ha-Hagana* [History of the Hagana; hereafter *STH*], Vol. II part 1 (Tel Aviv, 1964), pp. 15, 57; Alex Bein, *The Return to the Soil* (Jerusalem, 1952), pp. 241 f; *Political Report of the Executive to the XIIth Zionist Congress (1921)*, p. 56; Katznelson, *Igrot* I, 160, 169, 173, 175.
17. Esco, *Palestine* I, 262 f; Ben-Gurion, *Zikhronot* I, 145 f; John Bowle, *Viscount Samuel* (London, 1957), pp. 199 f; Samuel, *Memoirs*, p. 156.
18. Deedes to Weizmann, 7.11.1920, CZA, Z4/16073. Cf. Samuel, *Memoirs*, pp. 151, 156, 167; Wasserstein, 'Herbert Samuel', p. 774.
19. Ussishkin-Samuel interviews, 20.9, 19.10, 15.11 and 24.11.1920, CZA, L3/222.
20. See note 15. Cf. Wasserstein, 'Herbert Samuel', p. 764.
21. See Caplan, *Palestine Jewry*, pp. 74, 169 f, and sources cited on p. 230.
22. 28.3.1921, enclosed in Polit. Rpt. for March 1921, PRO, CO 733/2, file 21698; reproduced in Aaron S. Klieman, *Foundations of British Policy in the Arab World: The Cairo Conference of 1921* (Baltimore/London, 1970), pp. 259–67.
23. Weizmann report, VL meeting, 28.12.1920, CZA, J1/7224.
24. Following Porath, *Emergence*, pp. 108 f; Esco, *Palestine* I, 283 f, 474 f; Moshe Medzini, *Esser Shanim shel Midiniut Eretzyisraelit* [Ten Years of Palestine Politics] (Tel Aviv, 1928), p. 154.
25. For details, see: Sokolow to Weizmann, 25.2.1921, CZA, Z4/16055; VLE interview with the High Commissioner [hereafter: HC], 24.1.1921, J1/138; VL memorandum, 7.2.1921, J1/6282; *STH* II(1), 61; Brunton to GSI (HQ), 28.2.1921, ISA 2/163.
26. Correspondence and meetings with Musa Kazim Pasha 'and his Committee', Dec. 1920–Feb. 1921, in ISA 2/244. Cf. Porath, *Emergence*, pp. 125 f; Medzini, *Esser Shanim*, p. 167; *STH*, *loc. cit.*
27. Samuel to Curzon, 19.12.1920, ISA 100/7; Samuel to Baron Edmond de Rothschild, 31.12.1920, *loc. cit.*
28. VLE meeting, 7.12.1920, CZA, J1/139; cf. Ruppin, *Memoirs*, p. 189.
29. See note 22.
30. Following the Hebrew version in M. Attias, ed., *Sefer ha-Te'udot shel ha-Vaad ha-Leumi le-Knesset-Yisrael be-Eretz-Yisrael, 1918–1948* [Documents of the VL], 2nd enlarged ed. (Jerusalem, 1963), pp. 47 f. Cf. government translation of memo enclosed in Polit. Rpt. for March 1921 (n. 22), reproduced in Klieman, *Foundations*, pp. 275 f.
31. Churchill Reply to AE Memorandum, 29.3.1921, enclosed in Polit. Rpt. for March 1921 (n. 22); reproduced in Klieman, *op. cit.*, pp. 269–73.
32. VL meeting, 3.5.1921, CZA, J1/7224; Colonial Office, *Palestine: Disturbances in May 1921*, October 1921 (cmd. 1540) ['*Haycraft Report*'], p. 47. See also: Yosef Sprinzak, *Igrot* [Letters] Vol. I (1910–29), (Tel Aviv, 1965), p. 214; Golomb, *Hevion Oz* I, 210 f; *S.T.H.* II(1), 95, 105.
33. Sprinzak, *op. cit.*, p. 216; VL meeting, 16.5.1921, CZA, J1/7224; *ha-Aretz*, 4.4, 7.4 and 8.4.1921, following the Arabic press, cuttings in J1/300; Klieman, *Foundations*, pp. 177 f; Porath, *Emergence*, pp. 128 f; Michael Assaf, *Hitorirut ha-Aravim be-Eretz-Yisrael u-Vrihatam* [The Arab Awakening in and Flight from Palestine], (Tel Aviv, 1967), p. 98; Polit. Rpt. for April 1921, PRO, CO 733/3, file 24596.

34. VL to HC, 4.4.1921, CZA, J1/300; *Sefer ha-Te'udot*, pp. 51 f.
35. Tolkowsky to Samuel, 28.3.1921, quoted in *STH* II(1), 78; Assaf, *Hitorirut*, p. 254; Neville J. Mandel, *The Arabs and Zionism Before World War I* (London/Berkeley, 1976), pp. 180 f.
36. Polit. Rpt. for April 1921 (n. 33). Cf. Colonial Office, Palestine: *Report of the High Commissioner on the Administration of Palestine, 1920–1925*, Colonial No. 15, pp. 41 f; Esco, *Palestine* I, 309 f.
37. L. Stein, 'Situation in Palestine, August 1921', PRO, CO 733/16, file 52260; *STH* II(1), 64; Porath, *Emergence*, p. 135; Chaim Weizmann, *Trial and Error* (London, 1949), pp. 342 f.
38. See, e.g.: VL meetings of 3.5 and 16.5.1921, CZA, J1/7224; Ben-Zvi, at Government Advisory Council meeting, 3.5.1921, PRO, CO 733/3, file 24594; Ben-Zvi-HC interview, 5.5.1921, CZA, J1/138; Ben-Zvi to HC, 11.5.1921, in *Sefer ha-Te'udot*, pp. 58 f; Caplan, *Palestine Jewry*, pp. 86 f.
39. For details, see: VL meeting, 16–17.5.1921, CZA, J1/7224; Dizengoff to Thon, 26.5.1921, J1/300; Golomb, *Hevion Oz* I, 212 f, 314; *STH* II(1), 93 f.
40. See: Moshe Mossek, *Palestine Immigration Policy under Sir Herbert Samuel: British, Zionist and Arab Attitudes* (London: Cass, 1978), ch. 3; Wasserstein, 'Herbert Samuel', pp. 766 f.
41. Interview of 7.5.1921, CZA, J1/138.
42. *STH* II(1), 92; VLE meetings, 8.5 and 9.5.1921, CZA, J1/139; VLE interviews at Government House, 5.5 and 7.5.1921, J1/138; *Kitvei Berl Katznelson* I, 273.
43. Katznelson, *Igrot* I, 246; E. Blumenfeld, at VL meeting, 16.5.1921, CZA, J1/7224.
44. VL Statement to HC (private), 8.6.1921, CZA, J1/7224. Cf. *Sefer ha-Te'udot*, pp. 63 f, 66 f; VLE meetings, 21.5 (J1/139), 22.5 (J1/138) and 31.5.1921 (J1/300); Katznelson, *op. cit.* 235 f.; Mibashan to V.L.E., 29.5.1921, J1/300; Golomb, *Hevion Oz* I, 215.
45. The following discussion is based on Samuel's policy statement as forwarded to Churchill, 6.6.1921, PRO, CO 733/3, file 30263. Extracts quoted are from this source. Cf. Wasserstein, 'Herbert Samuel', pp. 767 f.
46. Eder to ZE, 4.6.1921, CZA, Z4/16151. Cf. Ronald Storrs, *Orientations* definitive ed. (London, 1943), p. 383; Stein, 'Situation in Palestine, August 1921' (n. 37), para. 23; VL to ZE, 3.6.1921, Z4/16151; *Sefer ha-Te'udot*, p. 63.
47. *Memoirs*, p. 192. Cf. Bentwich, *Mandate Memories*, p. 81.
48. Weizmann to Churchill [July 1921; draft not sent], quoted in Richard Crossman, *A Nation Reborn* (London/Rehovot, 1960), p. 127. Cf. VL Statement to Samuel, 8.6.1921 (n. 44); Golomb, *Hevion Oz* I, 314.
49. *Zionist Review*, Aug. 1921, p. 69. Cf. *Sefer ha-Te'udot*, pp. 66 f.
50. VL Statement to Samuel, 8.6.1921 (n. 44). Cf. Eder to ZE, 4.6.1921 (n. 46); *Kitvei Berl Katznelson* I, 274; Weizmann memorandum to Churchill, 'The Situation in Palestine', 21.7.1921, PRO, CO 733/16, file 38128; Crossman, *Nation Reborn*, pp. 127 f; Medzini, *Esser Shanim*, pp. 189 f.
51. *Hevion Oz* I, 314.
52. VL to HC, 27.6.1921, CZA, J1/6282.
53. VL meeting, 16.5.1921, CZA, J1/7224. Cf. *Report of the XIIth Zionist Congress, 1921* (London, 1922), pp. 44, 65; *Kitvei Berl Katznelson* I, 273 f; Sprinzak, *Igrot* I, 214; *Sefer ha-Te'udot*, pp. 58, 61; Weizmann, *Trial and Error*, p. 343.
54. *STH* II(1), 81.
55. Golomb, *Hevion Oz* I, 218; *Kitvei Berl Katznelson* I, 275.
56. VL meeting, 3.5.1921, CZA, J1/7224; *Sefer ha-Te'udot*, p. 58. Cf. 'Ben-Ha-Aretz' to HC, 3.5.1921, ISA 2/144.
57. 'Ben ha-Aretz' to HC, 3.5.1921 (n. 56); Ben-Zvi, VLE meeting, 5.5.1921, CZA, J1/138; Petah Tiqva Ctee. to VLE, 9.5.1921, J1/300, VL meetings, 3.5 and 16.5.1921, J1/7224; Ruppin, *Memoirs*, p. 191.

58. See Kedourie, 'Sir Herbert Samuel', pp. 60–69.
59. Dr Y. Levi, VLE meeting, 9.5.1921, CZA, J1/139; *Sefer ha-Te'udot*, p. 59; Golomb, *Hevion Oz* I, 219, 313; Katznelson and Tabenkin speeches, VL meeting, 16.5.1921, J1/7224; joint VLE-ZC meeting, 23.3.1921, J1/6282.
60. VL meeting, 16.5.1921, CZA, J1/7224. Cf. Ben-Zvi, VLE meeting, 5.5.1921, J1/138; Golomb, *op. cit.*, p. 213.
61. *Op. cit.*, p. 218; cf. *ibid.*, pp. 220, 313 f.
62. VLE meetings, 8.5 and 9.5.1921, CZA, J1/139; VL meetings, 16.5 and 6.6.1921, J1/7224; Eder to Cowen, 9.5.1921, Z4/16151; Golomb, *op. cit.*, pp. 216 f; Ruppin, *Memoirs*, p. 192; Samuel to Churchill, 12.5.1921 (tgm.), PRO, CO 733/3, file 23678. There is *no* evidence to support the claim made by Esco (*Palestine* I, 274) that Jewish bodies did in fact resign *en masse*.
63. *Sefer ha-Te'udot*, pp. 57 f and 66 f; joint VLE-*Ahdut ha-Avoda* meeting, 13.6.1921, CZA, J1/138; Eder to ZE, 13.6.1921, Z4/16151; VL meetings, 6.6 and 29.6.1921, J1/7224. On 4 June, Dr Eder had also submitted his resignation, but was prevailed upon to withdraw it.
64. VL meeting, 3.5.1921, CZA, J1/7224.
65. Yellin and Ben-Zvi, *loc. cit.*; Sokolow and Thon speeches, joint VLE–ZC meeting, 9.5.1921, J1/139; Yellin, VL meeting, 16.5.1921, J1/7224.
66. 'The Jaffa Riots: Statement of the Executive', 4.5.1921, CZA, J1/300; VL meeting, 16.5.1921, J1/7224; Weizmann to Eder, 13.6.1921 (tgm.), *loc. cit.*; Klieman, *Foundations*, pp. 185 f.
67. Katznelson, *Igrot* I, 235. Cf. VL meetings, 16.5 and 6.6.1921, CZA, J1/7224.
68. *Sefer ha-Te'udot*, pp. 54 f.
69. Samuel to Churchill, 8.5 (PRO, CO 733/3, file 24660), 13.6 (*loc. cit.*, file 31760) and 14.10.1921 (CO 733/6, file 52954); Samuel to Weizmann, 1.7 and 10.8.1921, CZA, Z4/16151; VL-HC interview, 10.6.1921, J1/138; Klieman, *Foundations*, pp. 191 f.
70. Samuel to Weizmann, 17.8.1921, CZA, Z4/16151.
71. *Report of the XIIth Zionist Congress*, p. 150. Cf. Esco, *Palestine* I, 276 f; Susan Lee Hattis, *The Bi-National Idea in Palestine During Mandatory Times* (Haifa, 1970), pp. 29 f, n. 13 and 43 f, n. 35.
72. *Report*, pp. 15 f. Cf. Esco, *op. cit.*, pp. 414–7; Landman to Young, 19.8.1921, PRO, CO 733/16, file 41952.
73. *Sefer ha-Te'udot*, pp. 72 f.
74. *Kitvei Berl Katznelson* I, 284.
75. *Report*, pp. 149 f.
76. *Ibid.*, p. 70. Cf. Wasserstein, 'Herbert Samuel', p. 769.
77. *Kitvei Berl Katznelson* I, 273–6.
78. On the second day of the rioting in Jaffa, the labour poet Y. H. Brenner was found bound and murdered in an outlying house. See Katznelson, *Igrot* I, 233 f and *STH* II(1), 82.
79. *Zikhronot* I, 179 f.
80. Caplan, *Palestine Jewry*, pp. 30 f.
81. Sieff to Weizmann, 29.1.1920, CZA, Z4/16033. Cf. Wasserstein, 'Herbert Samuel', pp. 758 f.
82. Eder to Weizmann, 14.3.1920, CZA, Z4/16078. In his letters to Weizmann dated 20.6.1920 (ISA 2/143) and 10.8.1921 (CZA, Z4/16151), Samuel reminded Zionists of these warnings, and stressed that it was their duty to remove Arab apprehensions. See also *Documents on British Foreign Policy*, First Series, Vol. XIII, ed. R. Butler and J. P. T. Bury (London 1963), p. 243; Wasserstein, 'Herbert Samuel', p. 759.
83. Eder to Weizmann, 14.3.1920 (n. 83).
84. VZ meeting, 17.3.1920, CZA, J1/140.
85. Interviews with HC, reported at VLE meetings, 8.5 and 9.5.1921, CZA, J1/139;

VLE confidential circular, 27.5.1921, J1/300; VLE-HC interview, 10.6.1921, J1/138; Golomb, *Hevion Oz* I, 217 f; Ruppin, *Memoirs*, p. 191.
86. VLE meeting, 9.6.1921, J1/139 (emphasis mine – NC).
87. Samuel to Churchill, 8.5.1921, PRO, CO 733/3, file 24660. Cf. same to same, 20.5.1921 (tgm.), *loc. cit.*, file 25095.
88. Same to same, 13.6.1921, *loc. cit.*, file 31760. Cf. Samuel's private letters to Weizmann, 1.7 and 10.8.1921, CZA, Z4/16151.
89. 'The Jaffa Riots: Statement of the Executive', 4.5.1921 (n. 66); *The Times*, 14.5.1921, p. 6; Weizmann to Samuel, 12.6.1921 (tgm.), WA.
90. Samuel to Weizmann, 10.8.1921 (n. 88). Cf. Klieman, *Foundations*, pp. 186 f.
91. E.g., Meyuhas, VL meeting, 3.5.1921, CZA, J1/7224; Avissar, VL meeting, 10.7.1922, J1/7225.
92. *Hevion Oz* I, 314.
93. Taken from accounts of interviews of 10.6 (J1/138) and 5.6.1921 (Golomb, *op. cit.*, p. 217).
94. Interview of 10.6.1921 (n. 93).
95. See, e.g., Samuel's Interim Report, June 1921 (cmd. 1499).
96. See: Shuckburgh minute, 19.6.1922, PRO, CO 733/36, file 29270; Sykes, *Crossroads*, p. 77; Weizmann, *Trial and Error*, p. 360. Many sections of Samuel's despatches of 8.5 (n. 87), 13.6 (n. 88) and 14.10.1921 (PRO, CO 733/6, file 52954) appear verbatim in the White Paper.
97. Rose Deedes [mother of Samuel's Chief Secretary] to Weizmann, 7.8.1921, CZA, Z4/16055; Samuel to Churchill, 14.10.1921 (n. 96); Deedes to Weizmann, 14.1.1922, Z4/16146; Samuel to Weizmann, 22.1.1922, *loc. cit.*; Deedes to Weizmann, 17.2.1922, WA.
98. Samuel to Churchill, 14.10.1921 (n. 96); Thon-Samuel interview, 23.9.1921, CZA, J1/138; Eder to Weizmann, 30.10.1921, Z4/16151; Deedes to Shuckburgh, 22.11.1921, PRO, CO 537/852; Deedes to Weizmann, 26.11.1921, CZA, Z4/16151; Shuckburgh to Weizmann, 16.1.1922, *loc. cit.*
99. A meeting between Weizmann and Musa Kazim al-Husaini at the Colonial Office, 29.11.1921, is recorded in PRO, CO 733/855. For details of this and other meetings at this time, see: Porath, *Emergence*, pp. 64 f; Klieman, *Foundations*, pp. 196 f; Caplan, *Futile Diplomacy* (forthcoming).
100. Colonial Office, *Palestine: Correspondence with the Palestine Arab Delegation and the Zionist Organisation*, June 1922 (cmd. 1700); reproduced in Walter Laqueur, ed., *The Israel-Arab Reader: A documentary history of the Middle East Conflict*, revised Pelican ed. (Harmondsworth, 1970), pp. 67–72. Unless otherwise indicated, quotations in the following paragraphs are from this source.
101. Weizmann-Shuckburgh interview, 10.1.1922, CZA, Z4/16145; Weizmann to Deedes, 12.11 and 13.12.1921, *LPCW*, Vol. X, ed. Bernard Wasserstein (Jerusalem/New Brunswick, NJ, 1977), pp. 282 f & 329 f; Samuel to Devonshire, 8.12.1922, PRO, CO 733/28, file 62328; *Report of the HC ... 1920–1925* (n. 36), pp. 5, 27 f.
102. For details, see the author's 'Arab-Jewish Contacts in Palestine After the First World War', *Jnl. of Contemporary History* XII (October 1977), 641–7; *Palestine Jewry*, pp. 142–5; and esp. 'Britain, Zionism and the Arabs, 1917–1925', *Wiener Library Bulletin* XXXI (1978), new series Nos. 45/46, 10–13.
103. See, e.g., F. H. Kisch to Landau, 27.10.1924, CZA, Z4/16071; *New Judaea* (London, 27.11.1924, pp. 78 f. Cf. Caplan, *Palestine Jewry*, pp. 185 f.
104. VLE meeting, 16.4.1925, CZA, A153/152(a); VL meeting, 13.5.1925, J1/7228.
105. Levin to Kisch, 1.5.1924, CZA, Z4/4112. Cf. F. H. Kisch, *Palestine Diary* (London, 1938), p. 177; Jacobs to Under-Secretary of State, CO, 29.4.1924, PRO, CO 733/84, file 20555; David Ben-Gurion, *Anahnu u-Shkhenenu* [We and Our Neighbours] (Tel Aviv, 1931), p. 91; *Kitvei Berl Katznelson* II, 159.

106. VLE meeting, 16.4.1925 (n. 104). Cf. Ben-Gurion, *loc. cit.*
107. VL meeting, 13.5.1925 (n. 104). Cf. *New Judaea*, 8.5.1925, pp. 279 f.
108. VLE-Samuel interview, 22.6.1924, CZA, J1/72.
109. VL meeting, 17.2.1925, CZA, J1/7228. Cf. Kisch, *Palestine Diary*, p. 115; *Sefer ha-Te'udot*, pp. 105 f.
110. Memorandum reproduced in *Sefer ha-Te'udot*, pp. 104 f. Cf. Weizmann to PZE, 19.2.1925 and van Vriesland to VL, 1.3.1925, in CZA, J1/78.
111. See: Esco, *Palestine* I, 291; Samuel, *Memoirs*, pp. 178 f; Kisch, *Palestine Diary*, p. 134; Eder to Weizmann, 22.8.1923, CZA, Z4/16132; Israel Sieff, *Memoirs* (London, 1970), p. 126; Bernard Wasserstein, *The British in Palestine* (London, 1978), pp. 149–50; Humphrey Bowman Diary, entry of 26.10.1924, Middle East Centre, St. Antony's College, Oxford.
112. See, e.g., Ruppin, *Memoirs*, p. 218; Kisch, *Palestine Diary*, p. 190; M. Dizengoff, farewell speech for Samuel (n.d.), CZA, J1/78; Bentwich, *Mandate Memories*, pp. 100 f, 104 f.
113. *Report ... 1920–1925* (n. 36). Pages 24–40 deal with the Jewish National Home; extracts quoted here are from pp. 32 & 40. Cf. Bentwich, *op. cit.*, pp. 103 f; Wasserstein, 'Herbert Samuel', p. 763.
114. Katznelson's critique reproduced in *Kitvei Berl Katznelson* II, 153–61 (discussed below). Ben-Gurion's critique reproduced in *Anahnu u-Shkhenenu*, pp. 84–94.
115. *Mandate Memories*, p. 100.
116. See: Kedourie, 'Sir Herbert Samuel', pp. 77 f.
117. For a recent critique of modern-day versions of this approach, see Gil Carl AlRoy, *Behind the Middle East Conflict* (New York, 1975), ch. 4 ('Mirage in the Desert – Diplomats, Journalists and other Strangers').
118. See, e.g., David Ben-Gurion, *Ben-Gurion Looks Back in Talks with Moshe Pearlman* (New York, 1965), ch. 7; Sykes, *Crossroads to Israel*, p. 51.
119. Even after 1937, al-Hajj Amin continued his *de facto* leadership of the Palestinian Arab community through the illegal Arab Higher Committee. On his rise to power, see Porath, *Emergence*, ch. 4.
120. On the political organisation of the Arab community, see: J. C. Hurewitz, *The Struggle for Palestine* (New York, 1950), ch. 4; Y. Porath, 'The Political Organization of the Palestinian Arabs Under the British Mandate', in *Palestinian Arab Politics*, ed. M. Maoz (Jerusalem, 1975), pp. 1–20; Ann Mosely Lesch, 'The Palestine Arab National Movement under the Mandate', in *The Politics of Palestinian Nationalism*, Wm. B. Quandt *et al.* (Berkeley/London, 1973), pp. 14–22.
121. Under article 2 of the Mandate, the British were responsible 'for placing the country under such political, administrative and economic conditions as will secure the establishment of the Jewish national home ... *and* [my emphasis, NC] the development of self-governing institutions ...' For the text of the Mandate, see *The Israel-Arab Reader*, ed. Walter Laqueur.
122. See, e.g., Porath, *Emergence*, pp. 147–58, 169–83; Y. Porath, *The Palestinian Arab National Movement, 1929–1939* (Vol. II – *From Riots to Rebellion*) (London: Cass, 1977), pp. 143–59; Wasserstein, *British in Palestine*, ch. 6.
123. See, e.g., Porath, *Emergence*, pp. 133 f.
124. Porath, *op. cit.*, pp. 108, 224; Jamal al-Husaini to High Commissioner (HC), 9.7.1921, ISA 2/244; Palestine Arab Delegation, Statement submitted to the President of the League of Nations, Sept. 1921, copy in CZA, Z4/1250.
125. E.g. F. H. Kisch, 'Palestine Political Report: Internal Policy', 31.5.1923, CZA, Z4/16061; Kisch to Stein, 22.6.1923, Z4/16050.
126. Stein to Kalvaryski, 31.1.1923, CZA, S25/10296.
127. 'Palestine Political Report', 31.5.1923 (n. 125).
128. Stein to Kisch, 12.6.1923, CZA, Z4/16061.
129. See, e.g.: W. Churchill, *H. of C. Deb.* (Vth Ser.), Vol. 143, col. 284 (14.6.1921);

Samuel, quoted below, page 38; Samuel interview with Sulaiman Bey Nassif, 1.6.1924, ISA 2/142(2); *Report ... 1920–1925* (n. 36), p. 45; Samuel, *Memoirs*, p. 171.
130. Notes of meetings between HC and 'an Arab Committee', 16.1.1921, ISA 2/244.
131. 29.3.1921, (see note 31, above).
132. Samuel to Churchill, 8.5.1921 (n. 69). The remainder of this section is based on telegraphic correspondence between Samuel and Churchill, May–June 1921, CO 733/3, files 23678, 25095, 25349 and 27792. Cf. Wasserstein, 'Herbert Samuel', pp. 769 f.
133. Weizmann to Money, 26.1.1919, *LPCW* IX, 109. Cf. same to Ormsby-Gore, 16.4.1918, *LPCW* VIII, ed. Dvorah Barzilai and Barnet Litvinoff (Jerusalem/New Brunswick, NJ, 1977), p. 130; same to Balfour, 30.5.1918, *op. cit.*, pp. 201 f.
134. E.g., *Zionist Review*, Dec. 1919, p. 124.
135. S. Landman to Under-Secretary of State, CO, 1.6.1921, PRO, CO 733/16, file 27373; Stein to Kisch, 12.6.1923 (n. 128); Weizmann to Samuel, 19.7.1921, *LPCW* X, 221; Medzini, *Esser Shanim*, p. 197.
136. Jabotinsky, in *The Times*, 14.5.1921, p. 6; ZE to HC, 6.5.1921, ISA 2/144.
137. Stein, 'Situation in Palestine, August 1921' (n. 37), para. 14.
138. Esp. Samuel to Weizmann, 1.7.1921, CZA, Z4/16151; Weizmann to Samuel, 19.7.1921 (n. 135).
139. Stein, 'Situation in Palestine' (n. 37), para. 27. Cf. Ben-Zvi, VL meeting, 14.2.1923, CZA, J1/7226.
140. For a detailed discussion of these debates, see Caplan, *Palestine Jewry*, pp. 23–9 and Appendix I.
141. Minutes of Conference, CZA, J1/8766/I (22.12.1918).
142. On the '*millet*' system, see Bernard Lewis, *The Emergence of Modern Turkey* (London, 1961), pp. 328 f.
143. *Kitvei Berl Katznelson* II, p. 47. Cf. *Zionist Bulletin*, 18.9.1922, p. 46; Ben-Gurion, *Anahnu u-Shkhenenu*, pp. 72 f; Moshé Burstein, *Self-Government of the Jews in Palestine since 1900* (Tel Aviv, 1934), pp. 283 f.
144. Report of interview, VLE meeting, 23.6.1921, CZA, J1/138.
145. VL meeting, 28–30.6.1921, CZA, J1/7224.
146. *Sefer ha-Te'udot*, p. 70.
147. Cmd. 1700 (n. 100).
148. Colonial Office, *Palestine: Papers Relating to the Elections for the Palestine Legislative Council, 1923*, June 1923 (cmd. 1889).
149. Samuel to Weizmann, 1.7.1921 (n. 138). Cf. Samuel to Churchill, 8.5.1921 (n. 69).
150. Samuel to Churchill, 8.5.1921 (n. 69). Cf. Samuel to Weizmann, 22.1.1922, CZA, Z4/16146.
151. See Porath, *Emergence*, pp. 148 f, and ISA file 2/168.
152. VLE-HC interview, 1.9.1922, CZA, J1/76. Cf. Ben-Zvi, VL meeting, 11.9.1922, J1/7225; van Vriesland to Stein, 3.9.1922, Z4/1053.
153. Kisch to Stein, 13.3.1923, CZA, Z4/16035. For details on the boycott see: Kisch, *Palestine Diary*, p. 35; Porath, *Emergence*, pp. 152 f.; Kedourie, 'Sir Herbert Samuel', pp. 74 f.
154. Minutes in CZA, J1/7226. Cf. Kisch to Stein, 18.2.1923, Z4/16035; Kisch, *Palestine Diary*, pp. 32 f.
155. Since early 1921, the VL had been active in presenting proposals for such an ordinance (which was to grant it statutory authority to levy taxes, etc.), but this was not to be sanctioned by the British until late 1927. For details, see Burstein, *Self-Government*, pp. 157–70; *Sefer ha-Te'udot*, pp. 39, 75, 77–80, 81, 207–9; Kisch, *op. cit.*, pp. 126, 177 f; Yellin-Shuckburgh interview, 20.7.1924, CZA, J1/76.
156. VL meeting, 2–3.1.1923, CZA, J1/7226. See also: 'Declaration of the 3rd of June 1921: Its Consequences and Interpreters', 29.4.1922, J1/75.

157. Cf. memorandum addressed to HC, 28.1.1923, *Sefer ha-Te'udot*, pp. 80–4; *Zionist Review*, July 1923, p. 38; Kisch, *Palestine Diary*, p. 47.
158. VL meeting, 15.2.1923, CZA, J1/7226.
159. For details of this interview, see: Political Report for Feb. 1923, PRO, CO 733/43, file 14202; Kisch to Stein, 18.2.1923, CZA, Z4/16035; Mossinsohn and Kisch reports, VL meeting, 18.2.1923, J1/7226.
160. See Samuel to Devonshire, two letters (one before, one after, the interview with VL representatives) dated 16.2.1923, PRO, CO 733/42, files 10140 and 10141.
161. Cmd. 1889 (n. 148), pp. 7–12.
162. See VL meetings, 26.3 and 9.5.1923, CZA, J1/7226.
163. Samuel comment, 18.7.1923, PRO, CO 733/47, file 35674.
164. Cmd. 1889 (n. 148), pp. 9 f. The following account is based on Porath, *Emergence*, pp. 169 f.
165. Kisch to Weizmann, 3.6.1923 (tgm.), CZA, Z4/16035.
166. Details in: Kisch interview with Sulaiman Bey Nassif, 8.6.1923, W.A.; Kalvaryski to Political Dept., ZE, 11.6.1923, CZA, S25/10296; Kisch to Stein, 13.6.1923, Z4/16035.
167. *The Times*, 17.7.1923, p. 11; Porath, *Emergence*, p. 172; Kisch report on the congress (sent to Clayton, 25.6.1923), PRO, CO 733/46, file 34366; Kalvaryski to Political Dept., ZE, 26.6.1923, CZA, Z4/2421.
168. Yellin-Thon-Kalvaryski-Samuel interview, 8.6.1923, CZA, J1/76.
169. Kisch to Weizmann, 20.6.1923, CZA, Z4/16050. Cf. Kisch, *Palestine Diary*, pp. 65 f.
170. For details, see Caplan, 'Arab-Jewish Contacts', p. 655.
171. Stein to Mond, 19.7.1923, CZA, Z4/16050. Cf. Weizmann to Devonshire, 26.7.1923, *LPCW* XI, ed. Bernard Wasserstein (Jerusalem/New Brunswick, NJ, 1977), pp. 345 f.
172. Y. H. Castel, *ha-Aretz*, 25.7.1923.
173. *Ha-Tor*, 13.7.1923. Cf. *Zionist Review*, Aug. 1923, pp. 42 f; Wasserstein, 'Herbert Samuel', pp. 771 f.
174. Kisch to Weizmann, 5.10.1923, CZA, Z4/16050. Cf. Weizmann to Kisch, 14.11.1923, *loc. cit.*
175. Samuel to Churchill, 24.5.1921 (tgm.), PRO, CO 733/3, file 26134. Cf. same to same, 31.5.1921, *ibid.*, file 27262; Churchill to Samuel, 2.6.1921 (tgm.), *loc. cit.*
176. Weizmann-Shuckburgh interview, 25.7.1923, CZA, Z4/16050. Samuel was, in Weizmann's words, 'a man who has not lost the shackles of the Ghetto. He would let his friends down in order to placate his enemies' etc. Cf. Medzini, *Esser Shanim*, p. 244.
177. Colonial Office, *Palestine: Proposed Formation of an Arab Agency*, Nov. 1923 (cmd. 1989). Subsequent quotations are from this source unless otherwise indicated.
178. *Official Gazette*, 1.12.1923, quoted in *The Times*, 4.12.1923, p. 12. Cf. *ibid.*, 24.12.1923, p. 9.
179. Cmd. 1989 (n. 177), p. 10. Cf. Kisch to Weizmann, 16.11.1923, CZA, Z4/16050; Kisch, *Palestine Diary*, p. 128.
180. Weizmann to Under-Secretary of State, CO, 15.11.1923, *LPCW* XII, ed. Joshua Freundlich (Jerusalem/New Brunswick, NJ, 1977), pp. 34 f; resolutions of VL meeting, 6–7.11.1923, *Sefer ha-Te'udot*, p. 91; press clippings in PRO, CO 733/51, file 57864; VL meeting, 6–7.11.1923, CZA, J1/7227; VLE-HC interview, 21.11.1923, J1/76.
181. Cf. Kedourie, 'Sir Herbert Samuel', pp. 79 f.
182. See, e.g., Kalvaryski to James de Rothschild, 12.10.1923, CZA, S25/1180; Weizmann to U.S.S., CO, 15.11.1923 (n. 180); Kisch to Weizmann, 19.10.1923, Z4/16050; Kisch to Franck, 12.11.1923, *loc. cit.*; Kisch to Weizmann, 16.11.1923 (n. 179); Kisch, *Palestine Diary*, p. 75.

183. For details, see Caplan, 'Arab-Jewish Contacts', pp. 658 f.
184. Samuel, note of conversations with Kalvaryski and Sulaiman Bey Nassif, 17.3.1925, ISA 100/10; cf. Caplan, *op. cit.*, p. 659.
185. See Wasserstein, *British in Palestine*, pp. 152–7; Porath, *Emergence*, pp. 247, 272–3, 308–9; Porath, *Palestinian Arab National Movement*, pp. 143–59.

Arab Rebellion and Terrorism in Palestine 1929–39
The Case of Sheikh Izz al-Din al-Qassam and his Movement*

Shai Lachman

THE RADICALISATION PROCESS AND THE CONCEPT OF ARMED STRUGGLE, 1929–35

The early 1930s was a decisive period in the development of the Palestinian Arab national movement which was undergoing at this time a process of political and organisational reform. While the Arab Executive Committee (AEC) headed by Musa Kazim al-Husayni was losing power and gradually disintegrating, new nationalist groups subscribing to more radical and militant ideas were emerging. This development, which took place against the background of the 1929 riots and the subsequent awakening of national awareness among the Arabs of Palestine, was the result of a growing conviction that the political struggle for Arab self-determination had failed, and that the national leadership was incapable of bringing about a change in Britain's policy vis-à-vis the Jewish National Home. While the White Paper of October 1930 was a prominent achievement, perhaps the most significant of Arab politics until that time, the nullification of its promises and the new interpretation of Britain's policy in the MacDonald Letter of February 1931 (dubbed the 'Black Letter' by the Arabs) was regarded as a major setback to the Arab cause and a complete bankruptcy of the AEC's moderate tactics.

The growing disillusionment among Arab circles found its expression in two conferences which took place in Nablus in the summer of 1931. The conferences met in protest against what the Arabs called 'the Government's arming of the Jews', and in the course of their discussions, which were very extreme in tone, the idea of armed struggle as the only means of preventing the realisation of the Zionist enterprise, and implementing the national aspirations of Palestinian Arabs, was publicly propounded for the first time.[1] These gatherings, and various events which followed in their wake, brought to the fore a new cadre of Arab activists. These were members of the younger generation and the first graduates of the Mandatory educational system. Influenced by the role played by Nazi and Fascist youth movements in Europe, they challenged the AEC and its policy, and called for new, more radical lines of action. In January 1932 the first National Congress of the Arab Youth met in Jaffa. It adopted a radical pan-Arab platform, and several resolutions with

* This article is a revised and expanded version of a seminar paper presented in 1976 to Prof. N. Levtzion. For his useful comments I wish to express my sincerest thanks.

regard to promoting national products, assisting the activities of the National Fund and working towards organisation of Arab youth. An executive body was elected to supervise the implementation of these resolutions, and local branches were established throughout the country. Although its activities met with little success, the Congress of the Youth was a conspicuous expression of the growing national awareness among Arab youth and their gradual emergence as an independent and more radical political force.

The radicalisation process was first and foremost the result of the accelerated evolution of the Zionist enterprise. During the early thirties, Jewish immigration, mainly from Nazi Germany, reached unprecedented proportions. Whereas in 1928 emigrants still outnumbered immigrants, in 1932 the number of newcomers totalled 9,500, and in 1934, 42,359. The demographic change was accompanied by marked economic development of the Yishuv, which enjoyed a steadily increasing flow of private capital and investment. This was expressed, among other things, in the renewal of large-scale land purchasing by Jews (1932 – 18,895 dunams; 1933 – 36,991; 1934 – 62,114), and the establishment of dozens of new settlements throughout the country.

The Arabs thus had cause for grave concern, as they saw entire regions of the country rapidly changing face. Exaggerated rumours about large-scale illegal Jewish immigration intensified the tension, convincing the Arabs that there were many more Jews in the country than the official estimates. At a secret meeting of Arab activists from Safed and the vicinity held on 26 February 1933, Rashid al-Hajj Ibrahim, of Haifa, declared: 'The Jews are advancing on all fronts. They keep buying land, they bring in immigrants both legally and illegally, and they have even invaded Transjordan. If we cannot demonstrate to them convincingly enough that all their efforts are in vain and that we are capable of destroying them at one stroke, then we shall have to lose our holy land or resign ourselves to being wretched second-rate citizens in a Jewish state.' When asked how the Jews could be made to see the point, he replied: 'By doing what we did in 1929, but using more efficient methods. We have learned from our mistakes and they will not recur.'[2]

Unfortunately for the Arab movement, it was precisely at this time that the AEC was exposed in all its weakness and ineffectiveness. Not only was it unable to cope with the growing Zionist challenge and to prevent land transfers, but even its own members were accused of selling land to the Jews. The prestige of the AEC declined precipitously, it lost its capacity to act, and it gradually fell apart. The October 1933 demonstrations were its swan song. With the death in March 1934 of Musa Kazim al-Husayni, the last justification for its existence disappeared, and within a few months it had completely passed from the political scene. The disappearance of the AEC put an end to the last vestiges of unity in the Arab camp. This framework, which for over a dozen years had held the various rival factions together, was now replaced by five different 'parties' who began to compete for control of the national movement, thereby emphasising the internal divisions all the more. In this atmosphere of confusion and frustration, the voice of the Arab extremists preaching the intensification of the struggle against the Yishuv grew ever stronger.

The call for armed struggle came mainly from two sources: radical elements supporting the pan-Arab movement, and groups of clergy and fanatic Muslim youth who drew their inspiration from the Mufti of Jerusalem, al-Hajj Amin al-Husayni.

The pan-Arab element gave rise in 1932 to the *Istiqlal* (Independence) Party, founded by the veteran leader Awni Abd al-Hadi. This new party marked the first attempt by Palestinian Arabs to set up a modern political organisation based not on family-regional affiliations or on factional interests, as was the tradition, but on an agreed ideological platform and individual membership. The party's founders and activists were mostly of the urban intelligentsia, and either did not belong to or had dissociated themselves from the traditional leading Arab families.[3] Another important feature was the fact that many of them came from northern cities, especially Haifa and Nablus, rather than Jerusalem. This phenomenon corresponded with the party's declared aversion to the deep-rooted family disputes which had been so characteristic of the Jerusalem leadership and its desire 'to avoid local, personal and family politics entirely'.[4]

The party platform was saliently pan-Arab. Based on the principles of the Arab Covenant (*al-Mithaq al-Arabi*) signed in a special meeting of Arab delegates to the Pan-Islamic Congress held in Jerusalem in December 1931,[5] it demanded independence within the framework of comprehensive Arab unity, the abolition of the Mandate and the Balfour Declaration, and the establishment of parliamentary Arab rule in Palestine.[6] The party's leaders launched a full-scale campaign of political activities. They were engaged in abortive attempts to convene a popular pan-Arab congress in Baghdad chaired by Amir Faysal, which would work towards advancing Arab nationalist goals, while internally they waged a vigorous anti-British campaign and urged the public to refrain from paying taxes and co-operating with the government. The British Mandate was likened by the Istiqlalists to a tree – cutting it down would do away with its Zionist branch, too. The new propaganda style and the stress on anti-British activities came as a total innovation to the Arab community, which was accustomed to the Mufti's anti-Jewish stance, and had tremendous influence especially on the educated and the new youth organisations. The March 1933 non-co-operation policy and the October 1933 demonstrations, both directed principally against the British authorities, were very much the consequence of *Istiqlal* propaganda.

However, the *Istiqlal* Party proved very short-lived. Its limited political base which, in the absence of wide popular urban and rural support, never extended beyond a small circle of intellectuals and professionals; its inevitable involvement in personal and factional rivalries – especially with the Mufti and his adherents who were not at all enthusiastic about the appearance of this new rival party; its lack of financial resources; the growing antagonism between the pro-Hashemites and the pro-Saudis which divided the Pan-Arab movement in the thirties – all these weakened the party and caused its rapid disintegration and erosion amid the frictions of traditional Palestinian politics.[7] In less than two years the *Istiqlal* Party had ceased to exist as an organised body, leaving behind on the political scene no more than a handful of active extremists.

The impact of the militant Muslim elements was far more important. This movement, which in effect generated the 1936–39 revolt, grew and crystallised in the context of two parallel processes: the decline, from the end of the twenties, and eventual disintegration of the Muslim-Christian front of the national movement;[8] and the concomitant increase in power of the Supreme Muslim Council (SMC), and the rise to pre-eminence of its president, the Mufti al-Hajj Amin al-Husayni. Particular importance was attached to the latter development; even though the Mufti had so far refrained from openly defying the authority of the Mandatory Government, his very rise to power encouraged and lent impetus to the Arab militants. Furthermore, so as not to tarnish his image as a 'nationalist' and to ward off his rivals' accusations that he was co-operating with the British, Amin al-Husayni allowed his fellow extremists to join the radical trend, while his mouthpiece, *al-jami'ah al-Arabiyya*, stood out in its continuous anti-British propaganda. He himself, as we shall see later, secretly encouraged militant groups and helped to lay the organisational infrastructure for the underground movement.

The developments on the socio-political plane were accompanied by important changes in the patterns of organisation and activity. The Muslim-Christian Associations gradually declined and disappeared in the course of the thirties, giving way to new communal formations focusing on the idea of defending Muslim holy places in Palestine and on mobilising the Arab people for the coming struggle by means of Islamic symbols. Such were the Young Men's Muslim Associations (*Jam'iyyat al-shubban al-muslimin*), which, towards the end of the twenties, began forming on a strictly communal basis and which included in their programme pronounced anti-Jewish propaganda. Another movement of a definite Muslim-communal character was the Arab Boy Scout troops which first appeared in Palestine in the early thirties. Independent of the official Baden-Powell scouting organisation, this new movement stressed radical nationalist attitudes and was assiduously fostered by the Congress of the Arab Youth and the YMMA. All these frameworks were a hot-house for extremist nationalist activity, and, as such, contributed significantly to the process of radicalisation undergone by Arab youth in the period preceding the 1936 revolt.

The militant Muslim movement gave rise at the beginning of the thirties to a number of clandestine organisations which emblazoned on their banner the slogan of an armed struggle against the Yishuv. From a chronological point of view, it is customary to connect the emergence of these groups with the tense atmosphere prevailing in the country following the 1929 riots and the MacDonald Letter. An early manifestation of this trend was a small armed gang which appeared in the Safed and Upper Galilee regions at the beginning of October 1929.[9] Called the 'Green Hand' gang (*al-kaff al-khadra*), it was mainly composed of rioters and wanted criminals who had fled from Safed after the bloody riots there. The gang leader, Ahmad Tafish, was wanted on murder charges. Later they were joined by several Druze who had participated in the Syrian-Druse uprising in 1925 and were being sought by the Syrian authorities. The gang members, numbering about twenty-five, regarded themselves as *mujahidun*. They wandered from village to village collecting money for the 'national cause', and alongside attempts at highway robbery, they also opened fire on the Jewish Quarter of Safed and attacked police patrols in the Safed-Nazareth area. The gang was formed and subsidised by extremist circles in the North, especially the YMMAs, and was supported by local *fellahin*.[10] Police investigation later showed that Subhi al-Khadra (himself from Safed and active in the 1929 riots in the city), as well as several other radicals, were associated with the gang and assisted it in secret.[11] The aim of the gang organisers was to stir up the population and create a tense atmosphere in the North, thereby encouraging the establishment of similar gangs in other parts of the country, particularly in the Nablus, Jerusalem and Hebron regions. At one point envoys were sent to Jaffa to further this aim and collect contributions, but these were caught by the police and the information extracted from them helped the security forces to locate the gang and liquidate it by means of a combined military and police operation in January 1931. However, the four-month existence of the 'Green Hand' gang was not without influence. It left a powerful impression on the local population and was a portent of things to come. Assessing the gang's activity, the High Commissioner expressed the following opinion: 'It may be anticipated that in the event of a recrudescence of disturbances in Palestine, this method of embarrassing the Government would be resorted to on a considerable scale.'[12] Indeed, from that time, the organisation of armed bands has never been dropped from the agenda of the Arab extremists. During the first Nablus conference on 31 July 1931, one of the Hebron representatives, probably Sheikh Sabri Abidin, proposed the establishment of armed bands to fight the British and the Jews. One of the important, non-publicised decisions of the conference was the appointment of a three-man committee to deal with purchasing and stockpiling arms.[13] Although this and other decisions were apparently never implemented, the idea of armed struggle was given a powerful

ARAB REBELLION AND TERRORISM

incentive and a web of secret contacts began to evolve for the purpose of carrying out clandestine activities as proposed. Referring to the 1931 Nablus conferences, Izzat Darwaza states that one of their main results was the 'formation of a number of secret fighting societies (*Jam'iyyat sirriyyah jihadiyyah*) which displayed considerable ability before and during the 1936 revolt'.[14] Although Darwaza neither elaborates nor specifies these societies by name, their very existence and activities are generally confirmed by other sources pertaining to this period.

It emerges that at this time three centres of clandestine activity had developed in the Arab sector: one in the Jerusalem-Ramallah area; another in the Tulkarm-Qalqilya area; and a third in the Haifa-Galilee region. These centres operated independently, and as far as is known there was no co-operative link between them. There was, however, a common denominator: all were at some time connected in one way or another with the Mufti and his camp.

The principal source of information concerning the first organisation is Emil al-Ghawri's *Palestine through Sixty Years*. This partisan, semi-autobiographical book, based according to the author on memoirs and personal diaries,[15] contains some interesting and probably authentic revelations about Amin al-Husayni's behind-the-scene activities in the years preceding the revolt. According to this source, a clandestine organisation made up of some of the Mufti's young Muslim adherents was active in the Jerusalem area from the beginning of the thirties, stockpiling arms and training in their use for The Day.

This organisation, of which al-Ghawri claimed to be one of the leaders, was at first called *Munazamat al-muqawamah wa al-jihad* (The Resistance and Jihad Organisation), the name being later changed to *al-jihad al-muqaddas* (The Holy War).[16] Its founder and commander was Abd al-Qadir al-Husayni, son of the late president of the AEC and the Mufti's nephew. The organisation was formed as early as 1931, but it did not become really cohesive until 1934, after the October 1933 demonstrations and the paralysis which took hold of the national movement following the collapse of the AEC. The plan of action was drawn up in a secret meeting in Jericho on 25 March 1934. The make-up of participants, 27 in number, provides us with the geographical-regional cross-section of the organisation at this time: Jerusalem – 6, Ramallah – 5, Hebron – 3, Nablus – 2, Jaffa – 2, Lod – 2, Gaza – 2, Beisan – 2, Nazareth – 2, Beersheba – 1.[17]

Among the resolutions at this meeting was the decision to reorganise into independent, five-man secret cells, to increase training and arming activities among the youth, and to appoint a five-member 'organisational higher committee' to assist Abd al-Qadir al-Husayni in the on-going management of the organisation.[18] During the next few months, the organisation developed rapidly. New cells were set up, contributions were collected, 122 rifles and pistols were acquired, and seven regional training centres were established. The training was supervised by junior officers who had infiltrated into the country from Syria and Iraq, as well as several Palestinian police officers recruited for this purpose by Abd al-Qadir. By the end of 1934 the organisation comprised, according to al-Ghawri, no less than 63 secret cells, with close to 400 youngsters undergoing training.[19] All these activities were carried out in secret. None of the leaders of the national movement knew about them, and even the Mufti, the organisation's spiritual father, was held outside the picture. When he was finally informed about the organisation, Amin al-Husayni welcomed the news. Meeting with the leaders of the organisation on 12 July 1934, he expressed his satisfaction with its activities and promised his assistance – on condition that it be kept secret. He made it clear, however, that the time had not yet come for openly fighting the British, and that all the necessary preparations had to be completed first. His final remark was that the leaders of the organisation might one day soon be asked to cooperate with other elements 'which had not ceased working – and perhaps had worked even harder – to achieve the same goal'.[20] A year later, in the summer of 1935, the Mufti assumed personal command of *al-jihad al-muqaddas*.[21]

On the whole, al-Gharwi's book abounds in errors, exaggerations and distortions. One must also take into account its tendentious nature, which comes to extol the achievements of Amin al-Husayni, the author being one of his long-standing right-hand men. Nevertheless the essence of his account may be considered reliable, if only because of the numerous details and names he cites and his personal involvement in the events described. In any event, the very existence of this clandestine organisation is not in doubt. Salih al-Rimawi, a national movement activist referred to by al-Ghawri as one of the founders of *al-jihad al-muqaddas*,[22] confirms in a short memoir about Abd al-Qadir al-Husayni that an Arab underground did, in fact, operate in the Jerusalem region at this time.[23] *Al-jihad al-muqaddas* continued to operate underground and with the outbreak of the 1936 revolt its members joined the Arab struggle, some as agitators and members of National Committees in the towns, others as commanders of armed bands in the mountains. Abd al-Qadir al-Husayni himself became one of the major commanders in the Jerusalem-Hebron area during the first stage of the revolt.

Similar underground activity, though on a smaller scale, took place in the Tulkarm-Qalqilya area.[24] The active element here was the local Arab Boy Scout troops, particularly those of Tulkarm – the Abu Ubayda and Umayyah troops. These incited the local youth, agitated among the villagers and underwent para-military training. Politically, they were affiliated with the Congress of the Arab Youth headed by Ya'qub al-Ghusayn, and through it with the Husaynis, whose support they enjoyed.

The Abu Ubayda troop gave rise in the beginning of 1935 to a secret society called 'The Rebellious Youth Association' (*jam'iyyat al-shabab al-*

tha'ir) whose aim was 'to take revenge in secret ways' on the Jews, the British and on Arab traitors.[25] Numbering no more than 20–25 persons, this association engaged in distributing anti-Jewish fly-sheets in Tulkarm and Qalqilya, and sending threatening letters to Arab government officials. Members were also required to carry firearms and to undergo military training. The Rebellious Youth Association was supported by local radical leaders such as Salim Abd al-Rahman al-Hajj Ibrahim, son of the mayor of Tulkarm and head of the local 'Congress of Youth' organisation, and Hashim al-Sabu', an Istiqlalist and son of the mayor of Qalqilya, and its heads maintained secret ties with Husayni's leaders, especially with Jamal al-Husayni and Emil al-Ghawri.[26] Its activity, however, did not go on for long. The discovery of a clandestine printing press in Jaffa, in July 1935, led to the arrest of several members of the organisation's Qalqilya branch, and thus to its disintegration.[27]

The two organisations described above, though committed to militant methods, never actually resorted to violence. The first attempt in the Arab camp to put into practice the idea of armed struggle is firmly connected with the figure of Sheikh Izz al-Din al-Qassam, founder and leader of the third clandestine organisation, which operated in Haifa and the Lower Galilee area.

SHEIKH IZZ AL-DIN AL-QASSAM – A BRIEF BIOGRAPHY

Izz al-Din Abd al-Qadir al-Qassam was born in 1871 or in 1882 in the small village of Jablah, near Ladhikiyyah in Syria. His father, Sheikh Abd al-Qadir al-Qassam, was a poor man who taught Qur'an in the local *kuttab*, and, according to one source, headed the al-Qadiriyyah Sufi order in the area.[28] Upon completing his village school, Izz al-Din was sent by his father to the Al-Azhar University in Cairo, where he studied under the well-known Muslim thinker Muhammad Abdu.[29] After graduating as *alim* al-Qassam spent a short time in Turkey as a religious teacher.[30] He then returned to his native village and was appointed preacher at the local mosque.

However, al-Qassam appears not to have confined his interests solely to religion, already turning his mind at a relatively early stage to political matters. During his stay in Egypt he came under the influence of the local national movement and, according to one source, even participated in anti-British demonstrations in Cairo.[31] Later, in 1912, when Italy attacked Libya, al-Qassam took an active part in the anti-Italian campaign in Syria. He called the people to *jihad* and, assisted by the local Ottoman authorities, recruited some 250 volunteers to go to Libya. His efforts, however, proved unsuccessful. The volunteers concentrated in Alexandretta waited in vain for a vessel, and after forty days returned home.[32] The defeat of the Ottoman Empire in World War I, the 'Arab

Revolt' in the desert and above all, the establishment of an Arab regime in Damascus under Amir Faysal – all these events left their mark on the Syrian *alim* and further honed his political awareness.

Al-Qassam's debut in the Arab national movement took place in the years 1919–20, when Faysal was leading the struggle for Syrian independence. He first joined an armed band which operated in the Ladhikiyyah area under Umar al-Bitar, and later took part in an anti-French uprising in Jabal Sahyun in the Alawi region under Sheikh Salih al-Ali. For this activity he was sentenced to death by a French military court and, with the collapse of Faysal's Damascus regime, he was forced to flee Syria.[33] At the beginning of 1921, al-Qassam, now over fifty, arrived in Palestine and settled in Haifa.[34]

In Haifa, Izz al-Din al-Qassam was warmly welcomed by local leaders and quickly became active in Arab community life. At first he taught at a Muslim school, but he was very soon appointed *imam* of the new *al-Istiqlal* mosque established by the SMC in January 1922.[35] As *imam* al-Qassam proved to be an outstanding figure – his impressive personality, his resounding success as orator and preacher, his original ideas and unique manner of expounding them, his reputation as a freedom-fighter against the French – all these attracted many adherents and helped him consolidate his position among the clergy and in his immediate circle. Indeed, within a brief span of time he was able to gather around him a small coterie of disciples and loyal followers who regarded him as their leader and were prepared to do his bidding.

Al-Qassam's activities were not confined to the mosque. He turned his attention to improving the lot of the poorer classes, brought about the establishment of a night school for illiterate adults,[36] and constantly worked for the rehabilitation of fringe elements alienated from religion, some of whom had taken to crime. After his death many young people confessed that it was thanks to his efforts that they managed to stay away from brothels, drink and gambling.[37] This educational activity proved of great importance, as it enabled him to take advantage of the religious aura that surrounded him and his influence upon the common people, for whom religion was the most cohesive and catalysing force. Indeed, it was from this social stratum that his movement drew its main strength.

Al-Qassam's standing as a religious and public figure steadily consolidated during the late twenties. In May 1928, he participated in the establishment of the Young Men's Muslim Association in Haifa together with Rashid al-Hajj Ibrahim, manager of the Arab Bank in the city.[38] This association paved the way for new activities on al-Qassam's part, especially on the political level. Through it, he was able to establish ties with national movement circles and to promote close cooperation with several of its prominent members in the North – particularly Rashid al-Hajj Ibrahim, Subhi al-Khadra, Mu'in al-Madi (all three of them founding members of the *Istiqlal* Party), 'Atif Nuralah, local Scout commander, and

Hikmat al-Namli, the secretary of the Muslim Association in Haifa. These people helped to make al-Qassam known among Arab youth and Boy Scout organisations in Haifa and its environs.[39] Al-Qassam's standing in the Haifa YMMA soon rose to such heights that in 1932 he was elected acting president of the national conference of the YMMAs in Palestine.[40]

Al-Qassam's religious activity also took on a new dimension. In 1929 he was appointed marriage Registrar (Ma'dhun) of the sharia court in Haifa, and from that time on he circulated amongst the villages of Haifa and the Galilee performing wedding ceremonies and registering them by law.[41] This going out to the villages signified a new phase in Al-Qassam's activities: until then he had concentrated on the townspeople, and even with all his success had been able to reach only a comparatively small portion of the Arab community; now he was to turn more and more to the rural population in an attempt to win over the *fellahin* and get them to implement his ideas.

So it was that on the eve of the 1929 riots, Sheikh Izz al-Din al-Qassam held the three important and influential positions of *imam*, Sharia Registrar of the northern area, and prominent member of the Haifa YMMA. These functions brought him into contact with wide segments of the Arab population in the North and afforded him the most favourable conditions for dissemination of his militant ideas. A central motif in al-Qassam's sermons was the threat inherent in the Zionist enterprise and the necessity of intensifying the struggle against it. His politico-religious ideas were absorbed by the many disciples and followers who flocked to his mosque as well as by the members of the Haifa YMMA, which under his leadership (1934) became the most extreme and militant branch of this association in the country.

Al-Qassam actually put his preaching into practice. In the early thirties he formed a secret terrorist society which operated against Jews and Jewish settlements in the North, but the band's activity was to be of brief duration. In November 1935 it was surrounded in the Jenin hills, resulting in the death of al-Qassam and several of his followers.

AL-QASSAM'S DOCTRINE

Al-Qassam's *Weltanschauung* was wholly rooted in Islam, which constituted the nexus of all his ideas and deeds. Al-Qassam was an orthodox Muslim, whose supreme ideal was to fulfil the precepts of his faith and do the Creator's will, and whose conviction it was that Islam must be defended and its orthodox form preserved. This was to be accomplished by defending Islam internally against infidelity and heresy; and politically against external enemies, namely the West — with which Islam was in political and ideological conflict — and the Zionist enterprise. In al-Qassam's view, the solution to the inner weaknesses of Islam lay in religious restoration based on *salafiyyah* tenets from the school of

Muhammad Abdu. In his sermons he preached for the purification of Islam, for a return to the principles and values of the original, fundamentalist faith, and for a decent and puritan way of life in the spirit of the Hanbali school of Islamic jurisprudence.[42]

The call to rid Islam of the absurdities and superfluities which had come to encrust it in the course of time is an important element in al-Qassam's doctrine. He condemned various customs originating in popular religion, such as grave-visiting, the worship of saints, the indiscriminate repetition of the name of God and of certain religious formulas (*dhikr, tahlil, takbir*) at funerals and religious ceremonies, making a living from reading the Qur'an, and the like, defining them as manifest *bid'a*, and contending that they had nothing in common with original Islam.[43] A true Muslim upbringing, he believed, could only be achieved by bringing people together, strengthening Muslim solidarity and fraternity, and working systematically for the betterment of the individual in accordance with the precepts of pure Islam. This conception underlay al-Qassam's educational activity in Haifa. For him the rehabilitation of individuals and groups estranged from religion was not only a moral and religious obligation but also a valuable social contribution, as he believed that society would be the gainer when these people had been reformed.[44] It is noteworthy that al-Qassam's doctrine and activist militant approach were not far removed from the school established in Cairo by Rashid Rida. We do not know of any contacts between the two, but it is not impossible that during his sojourn in al-Azhar, al-Qassam came under his influence.

Al-Qassam's *salafiyyah* tenets, his contacts with fringe elements and his growing popularity with the common people were a thorn in the flesh of certain Muslim circles in Haifa. In the mid-1920s sharp differences arose between al-Qassam and several local *ulama* who accused him of distorting certain religious matters and sowing dissension among the faithful.[45] When the dispute grew more acute, al-Qassam's antagonists attempted to hamper his activities and even tried — unsuccessfully — to have him removed from the post of *imam*.[46]

Al-Qassam's religious fanaticism was manifested, inter alia, in a pronounced xenophobic and anti-Jewish militant stance. He preached the preservation of the country's Muslim-Arab character and urged an uncompromising and intensified struggle against the British Mandate and the Jewish National Home in Palestine. Palestine could be freed from the danger of Jewish domination, he believed, not by sporadic protests, demonstrations or riots which were soon forgotten, but by an organised and methodical armed struggle. In his sermons he often quoted verses from the Qur'an referring to *jihad*, linking them with topical matters and his own political ideas. The militant nature of his sermons and his unorthodox interpretation of passages from the Qur'an not only incensed local Muslims,[47] but also gradually attracted the attention of local British intelligence.[48]

After the 1929 riots, al-Qassam intensified his anti-Jewish agitation. He justified on religious grounds the excesses committed during the riots, and in 1930, even managed to obtain a *fatwa* from the Mufti of Damascus, Sheikh Badr al-Din al-Taji al-Hasani, authorising the use of violence against the British and the Jews. He made a practice of reading this *fatwa* in mosques and in secret meetings with his disciples and followers.[49] Al-Qassam's devotion to the idea of an armed struggle brought him, according to one source, into conflict with the Supreme Muslim Council and its leaders. He criticised the way the *awqaf* funds were being spent, arguing that large sums were being wasted on edifices and the restoration of mosques (including al-Aqsa mosque), instead of being mobilised to arm the people and prepare them for the coming struggle.[50]

It should be pointed out that ideologically it is no easy task to distinguish between Arabism and Islam in al-Qassam's doctrine; indeed, the two are tightly interwoven. His Arabism was of a saliently religious character and inseparable from Islam, which in its militant-political manifestations, was consonant with the nationalistic sphere. His views coincided to a large extent with those held by the Muslim Brethren (who, like him, were influenced by Rashid Rida), i.e., that Arabism was the cradle of Islam, and that as its standard-bearers, the Arabs were the purest and most faithful believers. In other words, the bases of religious and racial-linguistic identity are virtually indistinguishable. Although we have no written or oral proof of this, one may surmise that if al-Qassam thought in political terms at all, he undoubtedly envisaged a Muslim community or an independent Muslim nation – Arabic-speaking, true – but not an Arab state in the modern national sense we know. The synthesis of religion and political militancy was thus organic and indivisible. The national endeavour of the Arabs of Palestine was indeed a political struggle with political aims, but it was definitely religious in origin, its ultimate goal being the preservation of Islam's holy places in Palestine and the demonstration of the faith's superiority.

CLANDESTINE ORGANISATION AND THE FIRST ACTS OF TERROR

Sheikh Izz al-Din al-Qassam was not content with words alone, and in the early 1930s proceeded to establish a secret association, called 'The Black Hand' (*al-kaff al-aswad*),[51] whose aim was to kill Jews and generally to terrorise the Jewish population in the North.[52] We do not know exactly when al-Qassam arrived at this decision, but the idea seems to have come to him towards the end of the 1920s and to have finally crystallised in the course of the 1929 riots and their aftermath. One of the leaders of the Qassamite movement recalls that the decision was taken following the Day of Atonement incident at the Wailing Wall in September 1928, which paved the way for the 1929 riots. It was then resolved that agitation and speeches were not enough and that concrete action was required.

According to this version, the foundations for the secret association, with a command staff of five, headed by al-Qassam were laid at this time.[53]

The nucleus of the clandestine association was composed of al-Qassam's close friends and adherents. Members were carefully selected. It is related that while preaching at the mosque, al-Qassam would scrutinise the worshippers and invite those who seemed the most zealous and the most suitable to his home, where he would address them on the need to act in order to save Palestine.[54] Gradually, the organisation grew and expanded beyond the bounds of Haifa. The YMMA, with branches in most of the surrounding villages, served as cover for its clandestine activity.[55] The principal strongholds were the YMMA branches in Haifa and in Safuriyyah, near Nazareth. The latter, headed by Muhammad Sa'id Abd al-Mu'ti, leagued itself with al-Qassam and his organisation from the outset and served as the main departure base for operations against neighbouring Jewish settlements.[56] The organisation ran an elaborate network of cells in the Arab villages of Nazareth, Nablus and Jenin regions,[57] and apparently also had a small branch in Tulkarm.[58]

The clandestine organisation was of an extremist-religious character and in some ways resembled a dervish order; its members grew their beards wild, called themselves 'sheikhs', and upon initiation to the secret society, took a stringent religious oath before al-Qassam to guard closely its secrets and to devote their lives to the war against the Jews.[59] At meetings held in mosques and secret places around Haifa, al-Qassam would preach to the society's members to prepare themselves for the eventual *jihad* and self-sacrifice. They were also trained in the use of arms. As one of the Qassamite leaders recalls: 'We purchased a rifle and we brought an instructor by the name of Abu al-Uyun. The meetings would commence with religious instruction by the Sheikh, who would then turn to preaching for the *jihad*. Finally the instructor would take each member of the audience in turn and teach him the handling of the rifle.'[60] In time, the society's activities extended in scope to include reconnaissance and information-gathering.[61] Members had to acquire arms at their own expense. They recruited collaborators and sympathisers among the quarry workers in the Haifa suburbs, who supplied them with explosives, and were taught how to manufacture primitive home-made bombs.[62]

Financially, the organisation relied mainly on monthly membership dues (not less than 10 piastres) and on contributions from members and sympathisers.[63] Among the latter were several wealthy Haifa residents who had close connections with al-Qassam.[64]

In structure, nature and objectives, the organisation was al-Qassam's own creation. Formed and moulded in the spirit of his doctrine, it evolved around his personality and religious authority, and followed the plans he drew up for it.[65] The salient points of this plan, according to Subhi Yasin, were as follows:[66]

(a) The abolition of British rule in Palestine. If this were achieved, the Zionist enterprise, being entirely dependent on it, would also be annulled.
(b) The resignation of the current leadership of the national movement in view of its inability to lead the people in its struggle. An organised uprising would be the only means of averting the establishment of a Jewish state in part of Palestine.
(c) Preparing the people for the coming revolt by training hundreds of fighters, stockpiling arms and providing for adequate financial resources.
(d) Forming alliances with the enemies of Britain in order to obtain aid and support for the organisation.

Shortly after publication of the MacDonald Letter, this clandestine organisation launched a campaign of murderous attacks on Jewish settlements in the North. The terror campaign opened with the murder of three members of Kibbutz Yagur, who were ambushed near the gate of the settlement on 5 April 1931. The perpetrators of this crime were never found. Analysing the murder, Mr Barker, Deputy District Superintendent of the CID, concluded in a memorandum dated 9 May 1931, that 'the killers were determined men, intent on the business of killing Jews, who belonged to a gang acting under the direction of a political organisation as did the Green Hand Gang which — as had been definitely established — was organised by political extremists'.[67] After a lull of several months the band renewed its activity, and at the beginning of 1932, several bombs were thrown into outlying homes in the Jewish suburbs around Haifa; these, however, failed to explode and the band returned, for the time being, to the tactic of ambushing its victims. Four members of northern settlements were killed or wounded this way in several operations.[68]

The terror campaign came to a climax on 22 December 1932 with the deaths of two Jews, father and son, when a bomb was thrown into their Nahalal home. This act shocked the Yishuv and spurred the police to action. A special investigation team was formed and a monetary reward offered to anyone aiding in the apprehension of the murderers. For six months police and 'Haganah' members worked together until one of the murderers was finally discovered in Safuriyyah with a bomb similar to the one employed in Nahalal found in his house. With him were arrested several Arab youths from Haifa and Safuriyyah, all members of the YMMA.

In the course of police investigation, a large amount of information was compiled about the activities of Sheikh Izz al-Din al-Qassam and his group of 'bearded sheikhs', but for reasons still unclear, and in spite of testimony by police agents who had been keeping the secret organisation under surveillance, their information was not utilised and the police confined themselves to a limited number of arrests.[69] Of the accused brought to trial at the end of 1933, one was sentenced to death and hanged, and two others received prison terms; a fourth defendant, Khalil Muhammad Isa, known also as Abu Ibrahim al-Kabir, was acquitted for lack of evidence.[70]

This last[71] was connected with an interesting controversial episode. In his important book, which contains valuable, often unique, information on the Qassamite movement, Subhi Yasin[72] tells of a split which occurred in the ranks of the movement after 1929, and led to the secession of a group of militant youths headed by Abu Ibrahim. The falling out was over tactics. The extremists demanded that an armed revolt be launched forthwith to be financed by a massive drive for contributions employing all possible means, while al-Qassam and the upper ranks of his organisation thought the time was not yet ripe for such an action, and urged the continuation of clandestine preparations and avoidance of any moves liable to disclose the organisation's intentions or cause internal dissension.[73] The acts of terrorism perpetrated in the northern areas, including the Nahalal murder, were, according to Subhi Yasin, carried out by members of the dissident group acting in disregard of Qassam's view and authority.[74]

Abu Ibrahim categorically denies these allegations. In an interview given in 1969 he maintains that he never seceded from al-Qassam's organisation, either in the period in question or at any later stage. On the contrary, until his arrest on suspicion of participation in the Nahalal murder – in which he denies having had a hand – he operated in close collaboration with al-Qassam and carried out his orders. True, at a later stage they had some differences of opinion, but this was in another context, and even then there was no secession or rift.[75]

It is difficult to establish which version is closer to the truth. Arab sources do not shed much light on this issue; most do not refer to it at all, while others are content to quote Subhi Yasin without comment. Nevertheless, the little we have been able to glean on this problem inclines us to give more weight to Abu Ibrahim's version. The reasons are as follows:

(a) Material collected by Jewish intelligence on the Nahalal murder indicates that Abu Ibrahim and his associates were not acting on their own initiative, but rather that the entire operation was organised and planned in Qassamite headquarters. Under cross-examination, one of the murderers, Mustafa Ali al-Ahmad, of Safuriyyah, testified that the decision to act was made by a restricted meeting in Haifa, at which al-Qassam was also present.[76] Furthermore, the fact that al-Qassam rushed to Safuriyyah immediately after the arrests[77] is not without significance and may point to some measure of involvement in the murders.

(b) Abu Ibrahim's activities, so far as they are known to us, hardly correspond with his description as a 'dissident' who 'rebelled' against the movement and its leader. Not only did he continue to be active in the movement after his release from detention, but his standing there grew even greater and after al-Qassam's death he became one of its most

prominent leaders. As we shall see, he took an active part in the events which preceded the outbreak of the 1936 revolt and became one of its principal commanders.
(c) Additional corroboration may be found in a short memoir published several years ago by a veteran of the Qassamite movement. The writer, Ibrahim al-Shaykh Khalil, firmly denies Yasin's 'rift' story and upholds Abu Ibrahim's explanation concerning the difference of opinion with al-Qassam and its date.[78]

If our assessment is correct, then we have before us a relatively common case of reversing the order of events. Subhi Yasin was probably referring to an internal controversy over whether or not to take to the mountains. This actually took place in 1935,[79] but for one reason or another he placed it in his memoirs in an earlier period.

THE BATTLE OF YA'BAD; AL-QASSAM'S DEATH AND ITS EFFECT ON THE PALESTINIAN ARAB NATIONAL MOVEMENT

The capture of the Nahalal murderers and the unmasking of the terrorist organisation brought the activities of Izz al-Din al-Qassam to a standstill – but not for long. Towards the end of 1934, after the public storm had abated and the police had ceased their inquiries, the Sheikh renewed his clandestine activities in the North.[80] This time, emphasis was laid on thorough and adequate preparations. The association was reorganised into five-man cells and subcommittees were set up to deal with such matters as acquisition and storage of arms, military training, intelligence, religious propaganda and political contacts.[81] Steps were also taken to increase membership and to improve the operational efficiency of the organisation. In all this, al-Qassam was actively assisted by both Subhi al-Khadra, who carried out subversive activities in northern villages, and by Rashid al-Hajj Ibrahim, who that year gave up the presidency of the Haifa YMMA in favour of al-Qassam. Agents of the British police reported about secret meetings of these three leaders which were frequently held under the guise of social-financial dealings in the Arab Bank of Haifa.[82]

While al-Qassam was preparing to resume his violent activity, the political climate of the country had changed for the worse. The year 1935 was critical for the Arabs of Palestine: that year, Jewish immigration reached a record high of some 62,000 persons. In fact, the Yishuv more than doubled in size in the span of four years. While at the end of 1931 there had been some 175,000 Jews in Palestine, accounting for 17 per cent of the population, by the spring of 1936 their number approached 400,000, or some 31 per cent of the total. The Arab community was very apprehensive. It was not difficult to visualise a day in the not too distant future when, if immigration continued at the same rate, the Jews would become a majority, and consequently assume hegemony in the country.

The upshot was rapid growth of intercommunal tension. Accusations were hurled regarding illegal Jewish immigration, the alleged dispossession of Arab *fellahin*, and the 'arming' of Jewish settlements by the British authorities, while the public campaign – headed by the SMC – against sale of land to Jews steadily intensified, extending to areas which hitherto had taken virtually no part in the national struggle. All this was accompanied by mounting religious incitement which gained even greater momentum following the First Ulama Congress organised by the Mufti and held in Jerusalem on 25 January 1935, and the formation of the extremist religious association *al-amr bi al-ma'ruf wa al-nahy 'an al-munkar* ('To Commend Virtue and Condemn Vice'), whose main aim was to combat land-selling to Jews.[83]

Certain developments in the international sphere further increased the ferment in the Arab community. The Italo-Abyssinian war which broke out in the autumn of 1935 shook the entire region and exposed Britain's startling impotence. At the same time, the rise of Nazi Germany and the mounting crisis in Europe aroused great hopes among the Arabs. It was widely held that the tense political situation would lead to a global war which, in turn, would free the Arabs of Palestine from the Mandatory Government. 'There is not a single Arab who does not fervently pray for the coming war which will free us of the yoke of the Western Powers', declared one of the Arab newspapers. 'The Muslim East in its entirety is awaiting this opportunity and is doing what it can to hasten its arrival ... in the belief that war is the only means whereby the Arabs could achieve their national aspirations and put an end to the Zionist threat.'[84]

The Palestinian leaders hoped to benefit from Britain's desire to maintain peace in the Middle East, and averred that more concessions could be extorted with appropriate pressure. This was coupled with an intense feeling of frustration and envy at the political achievements of the other Arab countries: Saudi Arabia and Iraq were already independent or about to become so, Syria and Egypt were in revolt, fighting for their freedom, and even humble Transjordan was by degrees attaining a greater measure of independence. Only the Palestinian Arabs remained inactive, and were content to keep on submitting futile protests and petitions. In national circles there was growing conviction that the hour of decision had come and that more drastic and violent action needed to be taken before the Arab community missed its last opportunity to seize hegemony in the country.

All these developments, and the rising political tension they led to, lent a strong impetus to al-Qassam's ideas and spurred him on to more intense activity. In the course of 1935, he continued his religious incitement, stirred up Bedouin in the Haifa Bay region whose lands had been purchased by the Jews,[85] and worked towards recruiting more youth to his clandestine organisation. The size of the organisation, it should be pointed out, is a source of controversy, and there is a variety of conflicting estimates. Darwaza says it consisted of fifty members;[86] Subhi Yasin, who was a junior member of the organisation, claims there were about 200 in 1935;[87] while other Arab sources place the total number in the hundreds and even thousands.[88] Darwaza's estimate seems closest to the truth. From various testimonies and on the basis of a membership list of the Qassamite movement compiled for the purpose of this study using all available sources, it seems that the active nucleus of the organisation consisted of only 30–35 persons, most of them from Haifa and its environs, while the entire movement, including supporters and collaborators in the villages, probably comprised no more than 50–60 persons at this time.

Besides engaging in clandestine activity and organisational efforts, al-Qassam tried to establish contacts with foreign elements he hoped would assist him in his struggle. The first attempt of this kind took place in the fall of 1935, against the backdrop of the Abyssinian war. At this time, his emissaries secretly approached Italian representatives, among them the Italian consul in Jerusalem, and requested arms for their organisation.[89] Similar overtures were made to the Turkish consul in Jerusalem.[90] We do not know the outcome of these attempts, or whether any agreement was ever reached between the various sides, but in the absence of proof to the contrary, it may be assumed that nothing concrete came of them.

In mid-October 1935, political tension rose to a new peak with the seizure of an arms shipment, hidden in barrels of cement, in the Port of Jaffa.[91] This incident aroused Arab public opinion and a wave of protests and incitement swept the country, the agitators contending that the Jews were secretly stockpiling arms for use against the Arabs. At a meeting of the heads of the Arab parties, which convened under public pressure, it was decided to submit a joint protest to the Government, and a general strike was declared on 26 October 1935.[92] These events considerably strengthened the Arab militants. At mass gatherings and through the press they preached an intensified campaign against the Government and openly called on the Arab population to arm itself against the Zionist threat.[93] Nor did extremism confine itself to words. Reviewing the agitation in the Arab camp, a Jewish intelligence report stated that 'the activity of the Arab youth organisations, whether clandestine or not, has intensified greatly following the "cement incident" ... traffic in and stockpiling of arms among the Arabs are on the rise'.[94]

It was at this juncture that Sheikh Izz al-Din al-Qassam decided to resume his military activity. When, precisely, he came to this decision is not clear, but it is generally assumed that the discovery of the arms shipment at Jaffa and the consequent public storm were major inducements for advancing his timetable.[95] At all events, towards the end of October 1935, al-Qassam approached his followers and members of his organisation and put before them his plan to take up arms. Not everyone was in favour of such action. Some of his close adherents, with Rashid al-Hajj Ibrahim at their head, rejected the plan and suggested that it be postponed at least until the High Commissioner's reply with regard to the contraband arms affair had been received.[96] The attitude of the Safuriyyah YMMA was also negative, their opinion being that the time was not ripe for such action.[97] Opponents of al-Qassam's plan could also be found among the members of the secret organisation. Abu Ibrahim states that he was against both the proposed method of operation and its timing, and that he tried to dissuade al-Qassam from carrying out his plan. He stressed the shortage of arms and money, warned that the organisation was still incapable of facing the British openly, and proposed instead that underground activity continue until all necessary preparations were completed.[98]

Al-Qassam, however, would not be swayed. He appears to have reached the conclusion that the time was ripe for action, and was firmly resolved to take advantage of the political opportunity to shock both the British and the Jews, and rouse the Arabs to take to arms in accordance with his doctrine.

On 6 November 1935, al-Qassam left Haifa for the Jenin area, accompanied by about 25 of his men.[99] Prior to setting out, the members of the band had sold their private effects and their wives' jewellery, and had equipped themselves with arms and hand grenades.[100] Their object was to work among the villagers and enlist their support, or, in al-Qassam's words: 'We do not wish to declare a revolt, but we want to equip ourselves with arms and go to the villages to rouse them to the *jihad*.'[101] Subhi Yasin asserts that there was a further objective. The group, he claims, planned as its first military operation, after having secured its base, to take over Haifa and to occupy government offices there for three days.[102] This claim can hardly be taken seriously. Quite apart from the fact that such an operation was not consistent with the limited aims the band had set itself, one cannot impute to al-Qassam such irresponsibility as would be implied by a plan to take over an important seaport teeming with police and military without ensuring adequate manpower and supplies, without having made adequate preparations, and with only a handful of inexperienced and ill-equipped men under his command.[103] The band's speedy liquidation by the British can only underscore the absurdity of such a plan, if indeed it ever existed.

Al-Qassam's first stop was the village of Kafr Dan, near Jenin. From there the group headed north and reached the vicinity of Beit Alpha and the Gilboa, where they encamped in caves and groves, and began making the rounds of the villages to disseminate their message and recruit supporters.[104] The local population seems to have been fairly responsive and hospitable; al-Qassam was well known in the area from his sermons at the *Istiqlal* mosque and from his attendance at village weddings and other festivities, and when word spread that he had arrived in the area, local *fellahin* were found who volunteered to supply his men with food and drink.[105]

The group's brief sojourn in the Jenin mountains constitutes an important chapter in the history of the Qassamite movement and is the source of many of its myths. It was then that the Islamic-fanatic spirit of the movement became fully manifest. The members of the group generally kept together, hardly ever parting company. Local villagers relate that they spent their days in prayer and self-mortification, with the Sheikh reading to them from the Qur'an and preaching *jihad* and self-sacrifice. At nightfall they would go into the villages, or would build fires and continue prayer by their light. They imagined themselves as the *mujahidun* of Muhammad's days and later periods, who consecrated themselves to the Holy War.[106]

However, the group managed to operate only for a very short time. On 7 November, in the vicinity of Faqu'ah, two of al-Qassam's men encountered a police patrol on the lookout for persons who had been stealing citrus fruit from the groves of Ein Harod. They killed the Jewish sergeant, Moshe Rosenfeld, but let the two Arab policemen go free.[107] This premature incident upset al-Qassam's plans and robbed him of the element of surprise. Henceforth, he became a hunted man. The police managed to lay their hands on a notebook with the names of several of his men, and reinforced patrols began to comb the area, aided by local Arab informers and collaborators. On 17 November, the band was discovered near Beit Qad, east of Jenin. In the exchange of fire, one of the Qassamites, a *fellah* from Halhul (Hebron area) who had been a vendor of beverages in Haifa, was killed, but the others managed to escape and split into two groups. In the meantime a rumour spread in the area that the hunted band was not made up of highwaymen, as the authorities claimed, but was a political body aimed at killing Jews and Englishmen. This stirred up the population and the police began to receive reports of growing sympathy for the band and of locals who were joining its ranks.[108]

On 20 November 1935, the police located part of the band near the village of Ya'bad, west of Jenin. The cave in which al-Qassam and eight of his men were hiding was surrounded, and they were called upon to surrender. But the Sheikh refused and commanded his men to fight to the end. The exchange of fire lasted for over four hours. After al-Qassam and three others had been killed, the rest, including Sheikh Nimr al-Sa'di, who was severely wounded, surrendered to the police.[109] Hidden in the folds of al-Qassam's turban, a talisman with the following verses was found:[110]

> O God save me from the terrible armoury of the infidel
> O God let your religion win and go victorious
> O God protect me in my coming adventure.

The Ya'bad clash had strong repercussions in the Arab camp. What most impressed the populace was the very resort to arms, and the fact that al-Qassam and his comrades had been prepared to fight to the end for their ideals. The band's heroic stand was a stirring new phenomenon which fired the imagination of the youth and posed a challenge to the Arab leadership, with its obsolete methods of struggle. It is no wonder that the *Istiqlalis* and other extremist groups hastened to extol the fallen and their deeds. Akram Zu'aytir, of Nablus, was the first to proclaim that the battle of the Sheikh and his comrades had been a holy war for the sake of the people and the fatherland, and he called on all the leaders to attend the funeral and pay their last respects.[111] The funeral cortege which left Haifa for the Muslim cemetery at Balad al-Shaykh became an impressive national demonstration. Shops and schools closed and thousands of persons walked behind the biers, which were draped with flags and national emblems. In a fervent oration in the mosque, Sheikh Yunis al-Khatib said: 'Dear and sainted friend, I heard you preaching from this lectern, leaning on your sword; now that you have left us you have become, by God, a greater preacher than you ever were in your lifetime.'[112] Several policemen were wounded when the mob began stoning the police during the burial ceremony.[113]

Virtually overnight, Izz al-Din al-Qassam became the object of a full-fledged cult. The bearded Sheikh's picture appeared in all the Arabic-language papers accompanied by banner headlines and inflammatory articles; memorial prayers were held in mosques throughout the country. He was proclaimed a martyr who had sacrificed himself for the fatherland, his grave at Balad al-Shaykh became a place of pilgrimage, and his deeds were extolled as an illustrious example to be followed by all. In addition, a countrywide fund-raising campaign was launched in aid of families of the fallen,[114] and leading Arab lawyers volunteered to defend the members of the band who were put on trial.[115]

It is noteworthy that the figure of al-Qassam was also esteemed and respected outside the Arab camp. Some of the Yishuv leaders were quick to grasp the significance of the phenomenon and its implications. Moshe Beilinson wrote: 'These people are not bandits. To that, the names of some of them, their social standing, their political position, bear unequivocal witness. Mosque preachers, school directors, chairmen of Young Men's Muslim Association do not engage in banditry. Not a gang of thieves but a body of political terrorists has lately confronted the authorities in Palestine.'[116] David Ben-Gurion, in one of his speeches, commented on the Ya'bad battle as follows: 'This is the first time the Arabs have a sort of Tel-Hai of their own ... This is the first time the Arabs have seen that a man could be found ready to give his life for an idea, and this will undoubtedly be a very important educational factor for the Arab masses, and at all events for their youth ... There is no doubt that this episode will now bring about further attempts at terrorism.'[117] The events of the next few months more than bore out Ben-Gurion's assessment and apprehensions.

The Ya'bad clash set the Arab movement on new lines of struggle, politically and militarily. The al-Qassam cult was assiduously nourished by the militants, who never ceased extolling him and calling upon the youth to follow in his footsteps. 'We are in need of more deeds like al-Qassam's ... each and every one of us should be an al-Qassam', declared Akram Zu'aytir at a meeting in Tulkarm.[118] At another public meeting held in Jaffa on 9 December 1935 to mark the anniversary of Allenby's capture of Jerusalem, militant youth leaders attacked the Arab leadership and its methods and called for a struggle 'with rifles and not with words'. The meeting opened with two minutes of silence in memory of al-Qassam, whose picture was distributed to the audience.[119] In Jenin, speakers at the unveiling of the tombstone of one of al-Qassam's followers declared that the fallen 'had done more for the Arab cause than anything so far undertaken by the Arab leaders'.[120]

The public storm and the agitation carried out by extremists put the Arab leaders in a difficult position. On the one hand, they clung to their traditional methods of conducting political campaigns, and as far as can be judged they had marked reservations regarding al-Qassam's acts of violence;[121] Arab writers usually point out that the parties' leaders, the Husaynis included, were absent from the funeral of the Ya'bad dead, and stress the cool and neutral tone of their condolence telegrams.[122] On the other hand, the storm unleashed by al-Qassam and his associates could not be ignored. Pressured by public opinion, and in order to remain in control of the situation, the Arab parties – excluding the *Istiqlal* – decided to set up an inter-party coordinating committee and publish a joint appeal for national unity.[123]

On 25 November 1935, five days after al-Qassam's death, the leaders of the five Arab parties appeared before the High Commissioner and presented him with a memorandum demanding a halt to Jewish immigration, the prohibition of land sales to Jews and the establishment of self-rule for the Arabs of Palestine. This was accompanied by a warning that if a satisfactory reply were not received within a month, the parties would consider other ways of achieving their demands.[124] This was in fact the first time that the Arab parties, forever at odds, had succeeded in setting aside their differences even for a short while and forming a united front on a major issue. Moreover, the various parties now began to vie with each other in putting forward extreme demands in order to outmanoeuvre the others and gain support of the youth.[125]

The change of attitude was clearly manifested in the full participation of the Arab leaders in memorial assemblies held in Haifa on 5 January 1936, forty days after al-Qassam's death. Because of dissension within the national movement, two separate services were held: the first, under the auspices of the Youth Congress, was supported by the 'Coalition' parties and attended by some 500 persons; the second, with twice the number of participants, was organised by the YMMA of Haifa in conjunction with the *Istiqlalis*, and was marked by inflammatory speeches against the British and the 'Coalition' parties.[126] After the service, the *Istiqlalis* met to discuss the reorganisation and future activity of their party.[127]

A further important result of the Ya'bad battle was the emergence of a new cult of armed bands in the Arab community. Throughout the country, and in the North in particular, it became the fashion to organise secretly for terrorist activity after the model of al-Qassam. Reports to this effect started coming in from various parts of the country at the beginning of 1936. In Hebron, an extremist religious society appeared whose members carried out *dhikr* ceremonies and were resolved to conduct themselves according to al-Qassam's tenets.[128] Arms traffic and the manufacture of bombs were reported from villages in the North,[129] while nuclei of armed bands appeared in the areas of Jerusalem, the Huleh, Safed and Mount Carmel.[130]

The campaign of subversion and incitement was headed by the leaders of the extremist youth, most of them *Istiqlalis*: Akram Zu'aytir in Nablus; Salim Abd al-Rahman al-Hajj Ibrahim and Boy Scout commanders in Tulkarm; Farid Fakhr al-Din in Beisan; Hamdi al-Husayni and Hashim al-Sabu' in Jaffa; Subhi al-Khadra, 'Atif Nurallah and Rashid al-Hajj Ibrahim in Haifa. The latter assumed presidency of the Haifa YMMA in succession to al-Qassam in mid-January 1936 and began to revive the activities of its branches in the area.[131] All these figures were much in evidence in the villages, where they incited the *fellahin* and forged connections with relatives of the fallen Qassamites as well as those killed in the course of the land sale clashes in Tiv'on and elsewhere, urging them to acts of revenge.[132] Nor did the Arab parties lag far behind. At the beginning of 1936, the Palestinian Arab Party, under Jamal al-Husayni, began to organise youth squads bearing the name of *al-futuwwah*, modelled after the Hitlerjugend; while the Nashashibi Defence Party attempted to set up a rival 'Blackshirt' organisation modelled on the Italian Facist youth movement. Particularly notable for their increasing militant activity were the Boy Scout troops and Arab Workers Associations, which were being exploited for political ends by the various parties.

These developments markedly aggravated the situation and boded ill for the future. A British intelligence report, referring to the appearance of al-Qassam's band in the Jenin mountains, held that 'these and the growing Youth and Scout movements must be regarded as the most probable factors for disturbances of the peace in Palestine in the future'.[133]

In summing up the al-Qassam episode, it will be instructive to dwell on two important aspects of this movement. The first concerns the question of al-Qassam's political affiliation and his relations with the national movement. Arab sources are at odds on this issue, and with good reason. With the growth of the al-Qassam cult, open rivalry developed among national circles as to which should assume the mantle of the fallen, each party attempting to take the movement and its leader under its wing and to demonstrate its affinity to al-Qassam politically and ideologically, in order to share in his glory. Whereas Izzat Darwaza writes that al-Qassam was a member of the *Istiqlal* Party and one of the leaders of its Haifa branch,[134] Al-Ghawri and Husayni sources assert that he joined the Palestinian Arab Party, which was founded in the spring of 1935, and served as a Haifa delegate in its executive committee;[135] while Qassamite sources, and also the *Istiqlali* leader 'Ajaj Nuwayhid, contend that al-Qassam acted independently and did not belong to any of the existing parties.[136] A careful study of the sources shows that these seemingly conflicting versions are not necessarily contradictory. All have some basis in reality, reflecting various aspects and phases in al-Qassam's political activity and relations with the national movement and its leadership. Al-Qassam's connections with *Istiqlal* circles need no proof; they grew out of his close ties with Rashid al-Hajj Ibrahim, Subhi al-Khadra and Mu'in al-Madi. As propagandists and extremist agitators, these *Istiqlalis* found a common language with the fanatical sheikh and supported his clandestine organisation. However, the *Istiqlal* party, as we have seen, was not long-lived, and by the end of 1933 it was no longer in existence. Moreover, the boundaries between it and the Husayni faction were gradually blurred. *Istiqlali* leaders, among them al-Qassam's personal associates, had close ties with Amin al-Husayni and filled senior positions in the SMC administration. Subhi al-Khadra, for example, was director of the *awqaf* in Galilee,[137] Izzat Darwaza served as general-director of the *awqaf* in the 1930s,[138] and for a while, 'Ajaj Nuwayhid was secretary of the SMC.[139] Articles by other figures such as Akram Zu'aytir and Hamdi al-Husayni, appeared regularly in *al-Liwa*, the Husaynis' mouthpiece.[140] Under these circumstances, it would not have been impossible for al-Qassam to maintain simultaneous close connections with *Istiqlal* party leaders and those of the Husayni camp. Evidence of his association with the latter may be found in Jewish intelligence reports from the beginning of 1935.[141] The process of *Istiqlal* assimilation in the Husayni camp steadily accelerated until it reached a peak during the rebellion of 1936–39.

Even more controversial and interesting is the question of the relationship between Amin al-Husayni and al-Qassam. Subhi Yasin, whose book is emphatically anti-Mufti in tone, describes al-Qassam as one who had cast off the Mufti's authority and had raised the banner of the revolt in defiance of the latter's opinion. Yasin claims that al-Qassam, at quite an early stage, asked to be appointed 'roving preacher' (*wa'iz 'amm mutanaqil*) so that he could prepare the people for revolt, but his request was turned down by the Mufti. Subsequently, in 1935, several months before his departure for the Jenin hills, al-Qassam again approached the Mufti through a special emissary, informed him of his intention to go into action, and proposed that Hajj Amin join him in proclaiming a general revolt in the country. The Mufti, however, refused, arguing that 'the time had not yet come for such action, and the political efforts now being made are sufficient to secure the rights of Palestinian Arabs'.[142]

Husayni sources categorically reject Yasin's version. According to al-Ghawri, al-Qassam's clandestine organisation was established with the knowledge and wholehearted encouragement of the Mufti as part of the general effort of the national movement under his leadership. Al-Qassam, he asserts, maintained close contacts with Amin al-Husayni and acted in full co-operation with him. Their go-between was Sheikh Kamil al-Qassab of Haifa,[143] who travelled back and forth to Jerusalem with instructions and money from the Mufti. Furthermore, according to his version, al-Qassam's ill-fated move in 1935 was planned in advance with the Mufti, who gave him his blessing and promised to supply arms, money and even men for this purpose.[144]

The historical truth, it would seem, lies somewhere in the middle. The relations between al-Hajj Amin al-Husayni and al-Qassam were, as far as we can conclude, quite complex and uneven. During the twenties, both were on good terms, their understanding probably based on identity of views and mutual esteem. It was then that al-Qassam was appointed *imam* of *al-Istiqlal* mosque and sharia registrar – appointments which required the Mufti's prior consent and approval and were financed by the *awqaf* administration.[145] The co-operation between them may well have increased as a result of the 1929 riots. One source claims that al-Qassam's men took an active part in the bloody riots.[146] This is not confirmed in other sources, but it is known that al-Qassam himself was involved in anti-Jewish agitation and was even detained for questioning by the Haifa police.[147] Later, towards the mid-1930s, there was a falling-out between the two men. The reason for this is unknown, but it seems to have been closely related to al-Qassam's independent activity and his decision to put his militant theories into practice. As long as the terrorist activity was directed only at Jewish targets, the Mufti saw nothing wrong with this. On the contrary, it fell in line with his own anti-Jewish policy; he secretly encouraged it and apparently extended financial aid to al-Qassam and his organisation.[148] His attitude changed only when there was a change in al-Qassam's tactics. When the Mufti saw that al-Qassam was turning toward open defiance of the Government's authority, he withdrew his support and, according to one source, even ordered his dismissal from the Palestinian Arab party.[149] Another version has it that al-Qassam was dismissed from his position as sharia registrar.[150]

The ties between the two men may not have been severed completely, and sporadic contact may have continued for some time afterwards by means of intermediaries. The rift, however, was never healed. Al-Qassam's retreat to the Jenin mountains in November 1935 showed all signs of being a personal decision and of not being co-ordinated in advance with the Mufti. The Palestinian Arab Party's undemonstrative reaction after the Ya'bad battle, the fact that al-Hajj Amin al-Husayni, in his book *Truths regarding the Palestine Problem*, does not mention al-Qassam and his movement at all, and most decisive, the testimony of the

Qassamites themselves — all these go to support this conclusion. Furthermore, even in his latest memoirs as compiled by Zuhayr al-Mardini (see note 28) in which al-Qassam and his deeds are highly extolled, the Mufti does not claim any complicity in Qassamite clandestine activity or in the preparation preceding the Y'abad incident.

The second particularly noteworthy aspect of the al-Qassam episode concerns the social composition of his movement. Apart from a few sheikhs and men of religion, the majority of the secret society members came from the lower classes of Arab society, which until then had hardly taken any part in political and national activity. Some were peasants and Bedouins,[151] but most came from the fringes of urban society: porters, hawkers, apprentices, kerosene vendors, railway labourers, quarry workers and also former criminals rehabilitated through al-Qassam's influence. Many of them were *fellahin* who, for economic reasons, had migrated to Haifa. The opening of the Haifa Port in November 1933, the laying of the oil pipeline to the Haifa refineries, the formation of railway maintenance units, large-scale road construction, increased building activity and the economic boom of the following two years — all these attracted to Haifa a growing stream of employment-seeking villagers from Galilee and Samaria. Already in 1935, workers of rural origin formed the majority of the Haifa proletariat.[152] They were crowded in slummy tin shacks (*harat al-tanak*) on the outskirts of town and subsisted on casual labour. Uprooted from their natural environment, strangers to the Arab urban society which had failed to absorb them — these people, susceptible to religious and political incitement, were fertile ground for the formation of local groups and societies as a substitute for the organised social life to which they had been accustomed in their villages.[153]

Al-Qassam's society offered these people the niche they were looking for — a social and organisational framework of markedly national character, based on familiar symbols of Muslim self-identification. Al-Qassam's social and educational activity, and the fact that as *fellahin*, they were well aware of the threat of spreading Jewish colonisation, no doubt contributed to their successful absorption into the movement. According to one source, most of the members of the secret society were former illiterates who had learned to read and write at the night school which al-Qassam had established at the Haifa YMMA.[154] Al-Qassam, on his part, knew how to utilise this element of urbanised *fellahin* for his own purposes. These people and their relatives in the villages were instrumental in enabling him to travel freely in the northern areas and to find friends and collaborators almost everywhere.

Al-Qassam's reliance on popular elements was certainly a thoroughgoing innovation. Arab sources note that he avoided operating among the intelligentsia and middle classes which had always been the mainstay of the national movement, and preferred to concentrate instead on enlisting and organising the lower classes, whom he found loyal and more prepared for sacrifices.[155] After al-Qassam's death, the process of enlisting the lower strata of society in the national cause was accelerated and reached impressive proportions. In the course of the 1936–39 revolt, urban leadership rapidly declined and disintegrated and hegemony in large areas of the country passed into the hands of the armed bands movement, made up almost exclusively of *fellahin*, from the rural hill population.

QASSAMITES IN THE ARAB REVOLT, 1936–39

Sheikh 'Izz al-Din al-Qassam's death did not put an end to his clandestine organisation. Under Sheikh Farhan al-Sa'di, the remnants of the band scattered at Ya'bad managed to evade the police forces and took refuge in the Nablus mountains, where they reorganised.[156] Other Qassamites in the Haifa and Safuriyyah regions rallied around Abu Ibrahim al-Kabir and formed a new band called *al-Darawish* (the Dervishes),[157] while the leadership of the Haifa society passed to Sheikh Kamil al-Qassab.[158] An incendiary element among the rural population, the Qassamite groups in Galilee and the Samarian hills maintained close co-operation.[159] They established contacts with extremist leaders in the towns, and were in large measure responsible for the deterioration of the situation in the North in the months preceding the outbreak of the Arab strike of April 1936.[160] Certain Arab sources attribute to them the Nur al-Shams incident, which triggered off the bloody riots in Jaffa. According to this version, the murderers of the two Jews on the Tulkarm-Nablus road on 15 April 1936 were not just highwaymen, as some other sources suggest,[161] but were members of *Ikhwan al-Qassam* (Al-Qassam Brethren) under Sheikh Farhan al-Sa'di, who for political and nationalist motives[162] committed the robbery in order to obtain arms with which to avenge their fallen leader.[163] It was clear from the behaviour of the bandits that they were not common highwaymen. They neither demanded money from the passengers nor checked their pockets, but merely asked for contributions. When offered the sum of £10 by one of the Arab passengers, a rich merchant from Tulkarm, they contented themselves with only 50 pence.[163] This and the brutal, cold-blooded murder of the two Jews – one of them a seventy-year-old man – indicate that this incident was indeed a well-conceived act of terror which probably had as its purpose the intensification of tension and the instigation of inter-communal riots between Arabs and Jews.

In any event, Qassamite involvement in the first incidents of the 1936 revolt is not in dispute. Qassamites were among the vanguard in the incitement campaign in the villages after the declaration of the general strike.[164] They took part in the outbreaks of violence at the end of May 1936 which marked the transition from strike to revolt, and they actively participated in the armed struggle. Qassamite leaders were zealous organisers and key commanders of bands in the North. Sheikh Farhan al-Sa'di, al-Qassam's spiritual heir, captained an armed band near the village of Nuris. On Fawzi al-Qawuqji's arrival in Palestine at the end of August, he joined the latter's force, but very soon fell out with him and went on operating independently in the Jenin area.[165] Abu Ibrahim al-Kabir was one of the major commanders in upper Galilee, while Sheikh Atiyyah Ahmad 'Awad from Balad al-Shaykh led an armed band in the Mount Carmel area.

When the strike was called off in October 1936, most of the rebels dispersed to their homes and, together with the rest of the country, awaited publication of the Royal Commission's conclusions. Several commanders, headed by Fakhri Abd al-Hadi, joined Qawuqji and left the country for Iraq, while others preferred to cross into Syria. The hard core of the band's movement, however, remained intact. Those who preferred to stay in the mountains were, in the main, wanted criminals who feared returning to their villages with no amnesty in the offing, but there were also some who were motivated by patriotism. These included Sheikh Farhan al-Sa'di and Sheikh Atiyyah 'Awad, who declined Qawuqji's invitation to join him in Iraq[166] and continued roving in the Haifa-Jenin area in close mutual co-operation.[167]

At the beginning of 1937 the situation in Palestine deteriorated rapidly. Conditions were particularly serious in the Northern Districts, where the relentless Qassamites were operating. The 1936 disturbances seemed to rejuvenate the 'Black Hand' band and infuse it with new vigour. With the proclamation of the strike the Qassamites launched a campaign of terror and revenge against Arab police officers and other persons who had been involved in one way or another in the arrest and interrogation of members of the secret society in the period prior to the revolt.[168] Ahmad Naif, a police officer who had taken an active part in the capture and interrogation of the Nahalal murderers, was shot and killed in Haifa on 2 August 1936. All the mosques in town closed down and midday prayers were cancelled in order to avoid giving the 'traitor' religious burial.[169] About two months later, on 13 October 1936, an attempt was made on the life of Mahmud Habab, a Jenin police officer, while Halim Basta, head of the Haifa police investigation department, who had already escaped one attempt on his life, was shot and killed together with his bodyguard on 15 April 1937.[170] The campaign of terror increased after the strike. The Qassamites, who, according to one report, then numbered some fifty men, intimidated all of Haifa. Operating in groups of four, they carried out numerous acts of murder and extortion. The monthly pay was LP 6, and their expenses covered by local national associations. Payment for murder was LP 15.[171] This is how a CID report describes the methods employed by the Qassamite assassination band:

Following a decision to assassinate an individual, a message was sent to Sheikh

Farhan al-Sa'di or one of the Sheikhs in Damascus and the latter obtained from Sheikh Muhammad al-Ashmar a *fatwa* condoning the murder. The *fatwa* was brought by messenger from Damascus to Sheikh Farhan al-Sa'di or Sheikh Yusuf Abu Durrah. These two sheikhs then arranged for the followers to draw lots to decide who was to carry out the assassinations. Whoever was to commit the act was assured that – should he meet his death whilst performing the act or be caught and hanged – his soul would go to heaven as a reward for his services in the name of the Prophet. The would-be assassin was always accompanied by two, three or four persons to cover his escape. Arms to be used in the commission of the act were supplied by Sheikh Yusuf Abu Durrah or Sheikh Saleh Abu Hishmeh.[172]

Qassamite terror was aimed at moderate Arabs disposed towards making peace with the Jews, such as Hasan Shukri, Mayor of Haifa, who escaped a second attempt on his life on 22 January 1937; at politicians who were not considered nationalistic enough or who were at odds with the extremists, such as Hajj Khalil Taha, head of the National Committee in Haifa during the strike, and his son, Dr Ali Taha, who were murdered in swift succession, and at those who were suspected of trading with or selling land to Jews.[173] Christian Arabs, whom the Qassamites accused of secession and treason, were also a target when the terror intensified.[174]

In the course of 1937, the Qassamites gradually shook off the last vestiges of subordination to the national movement and began to threaten the members of the Arab Higher Committee themselves. In April of that year the Mufti received two threatening letters with the society's seal, accusing him of following a barren policy and of nepotism and self-interest; one of these letters stated that it had been decided to outlaw him and to execute him at the first opportunity. Similar letters were sent to Ragheb Bey al-Nashashibi and Ya'qub al-Ghusayn, as well as to the extremist *Istiqlali* Akram Zu'aytir, who was accused of feigning patriotism while selling himself to a foreign power (he was suspected of connections with the Italians – SL).[175]

As the terrorist campaign intensified, moderate Arabs began to speak of the need to organise for self-defence, and many applied for a licence to carry arms. On 11 February 1937 a delegation of six Haifa notables came to the District Commissioner with a proposal to make available to the authorities units of young men who would aid the police in their tasks,[176] warning at the same time that if the terror continued they would have no option but to organise a 'private police force' of their own.[177] It seems that the warning did nothing to improve the situation, as a short time later an anti-terrorist unit was formed in Haifa which helped the police and supplied it with information about local terrorists.[178]

Qassamite activities were not confined to Palestine. In the first half of 1937, a small Qassamite group called 'The Black Hand' was formed in Damascus. Headed by Sheikh Atiyyah Ahmad 'Awad, who, together with Sheikh Farhan al-Sa'di, had crossed over to Syria, this group planned terrorist activities in Palestine and was considered responsible for several murders which took place at that time in the Northern Districts.[179] Its members also attempted to intimidate the British Consul in Damascus, Colonel G. MacKereth, who was very active in combating Arab terrorists operating from Syria. He received several threatening letters warning him to stop interfering in matters concerning the revolt, under the pain of death.[180]

The *Ikhwan al-Qassam* were among the principal forces behind the resumption of the armed struggle at the end of 1937, in reaction to the British partition plan. As early as mid-July, reports began arriving from Galilee about incitement among the *fellahin*, the reorganising of armed bands, and a brisk traffic in arms – all these being infallible signs of imminent eruptions of violence. Abdullah al-Asbah, one of the rebel commanders, reappeared in the Safed area, toured the villages, and instructed the inhabitants to prepare for the coming struggle. Similar instructions were dispatched by Sheikh Farhan al-Sa'di from Damascus.[181] In Haifa, the Qassamite organisation intensified its activity and opened 'branches' in Beisan, Tulkarm and Nablus, which were intended to act mainly on the internal front, namely to liquidate traitors and moderates.[182] It should be pointed out that the spread of terrorism was in large measure made possible by the weakness and ineffectiveness of the British security forces. In spite of their efforts, the CID and the police forces failed to control the Qassamites, and for months at a time did not manage to apprehend a single member of the secret organisation.[183]

The Arab terror reached a climax on 26 September 1937, with the assassination in Nazareth of Lewis Andrews, the Acting District Commissioner of Galilee. The four murderers, who were dressed as *fellahin*, fled the scene without trace. The murder of the Commissioner shocked the British authorities and the entire population, as this was the first time since the riots had begun that such a high-ranking British official had fallen victim to Arab terrorism. The Government's reaction was swift and drastic. The Arab Higher Committee and all the National Committees were outlawed and the Mufti removed from his office as President of the SMC, while the SMC itself was disbanded and its property placed under the management of an appointed committee of Government officials. Hundreds of Arab leaders and notables were arrested and five of the most prominent were exiled to the Seychelles. The Mufti himself found refuge on the *Haram al-Sharif* but a fortnight later, on the night of 14 October 1937 he managed to slip out and flee to the Lebanon. His escape was accompanied by an organised outbreak of violence throughout the country. The second stage of the Arab revolt had begun.

The Andrews assassination was carried out by members of the *Ikhwan al-Qassam*. Subhi Yasin states that it was a premeditated and planned operation which had as its aim the raising anew of the banner of the revolt.[184] British and Jewish sources tend to accept this view, pointing to

Sheikh Farhan al-Sa'di, who had returned from Syria a short while previously,[185] as the brains behind the murder.[186] The threads of police investigation also led to the underground organisation. It emerged that the cartridge cases found at the scene of the murder had been fired from the same weapon used in the murder of Halim Basta, the Haifa police officer.[187] Finally, a month later, police arrested a young man from Qabatiyyah (Jenin area), who was suspected of terrorist activities. This youth, Muhammad Naji Abu Rob, a suspected Qassamite,[188] at first denied all connection with the terrorists, but as further evidence accumulated against him, he broke down and confessed to complicity in the Andrews murder.[189]

On 22 November 1937, after an intensive comb-out, Sheikh Farhan al-Sa'di was caught by the police in his village of al-Mazar. His arrest was made possible through the help of the influential 'Abushi family of Jenin, one of whose sons had been murdered by him.[190] Five days later, the seventy-five-year-old Sheikh was sentenced to death by a military court and hanged. His execution stirred up Arab public opinion. He was declared a martyr like his teacher al-Qassam, and the people were called upon to follow in his footsteps and to continue the struggle.[191] Some forty of his men, including collaborators in the villages, were arrested; the remainder dispersed or joined other bands.[192]

With the resumption of hostilities, the centre of activity shifted to Damascus, where the 'Central Committee of the National Jihad in Palestine' was established. Through this committee, which was designed to serve as the supreme directing body of the revolt, the Mufti and his associates sought to organise and control the rebels' movement in Palestine. In practice, however, their influence over events in the country was very slight. Each of the leaders of the armed bands, most of them of rural origin and with undeveloped political consciousness, set up his own camp and competed for hegemony among the rebels, in growing disregard of the Central Committee and its instructions. Thus, in the summer of 1938, at the height of the revolt, absolute anarchy descended upon the Arab community, expressing itself in a total collapse of civilian authority and public services, in the takeover of large areas and several towns by lawless rebels, and in an unprecedented campaign of terror and violence. Of particularly serious consequence was the internal terror. The brunt of the attack was directed against the Nashashibis and their allies throughout the country. After a short period of co-operation during 1936, the old antagonism between the Husaynis and the Nashashibis reappeared and rapidly intensified following the termination of the strike. The National Defence Party's withdrawal from the Higher Arab Committee in July 1937 (as a result of the attempted assassination of Fakhri al-Nashashibi), the Opposition's initial support of the Partition Plan and its disapproval of renewed violence – all these factors worsened the relations and deepened the gap between the two rival factions. With the resumption of violent acts in the fall of 1937, a systematic campaign of terror was launched by the Husaynis against members of the Opposition. There was no limit to the violence used by the Mufti and his followers in their endeavour to take revenge on their opponents and eliminate their strongholds throughout the country. Prominent Opposition leaders were a permanent target for assassins' bullets. Their families and possessions were left defenceless, and dozens of their supporters, in towns and villages, fell victim to acts of terror, extortion and intimidation.[193]

As terror intensified the Nashashibis and their allies looked for means of defence and finally managed to organise an armed force of their own – the Peace Bands – which, in co-operation with the British Army, fought the rebels and the Husayni faction and brought about their final defeat in 1939.

Parallel to the anti-Nashashibi terror, a systematic campaign of murder was conducted against people accused of 'disloyalty to the Arab cause': informers, loyal Arab policemen, and civil servants and moderates suspected of supporting Partition. Many of these 'traitors' were murdered in broad daylight. Others were kidnapped and taken to the mountains where they were brought before one of the rebel courts, tried and usually sentenced to death. The reign of terror was so effective that corpses of the murdered were sometimes left in the streets for days, their relatives afraid to bury them.[194] Many murders were arbitrary, executed without rhyme or reason. In the anarchical atmosphere of the Revolt, many people, some with criminal backgrounds, took advantage of the situation and, pretending to be rebels, committed numerous acts of violence, robbery and extortion.

The *Ikhwan al-Qassam*, who grew stronger and bolder during the second phase of the Revolt, played a leading part in all these events. Their leaders ranked high in the Rebels' movement and held key positions in both the local and general command of the Revolt. The most prominent among them were

(1) Abu Ibrahim al-Kabir – member of the 'Central Committee of the Jihad' in Damascus and the only active commander on this body. We do not know what his exact function was, but he may have dealt with matters of finance and co-ordination. Once every few months he would infiltrate into Palestine to look over the situation for himself and to pay the bands' wages.[195] In October 1938, he led the murderous attack on Tiberias, in which nineteen Jews were killed.

(2) Sheikh Atiyyah Ahmad 'Awad – leader of the 'Black Hand' in Damascus. In January 1938 he was sent to reorganise the bands in Samaria which had been badly defeated by the army a month previously. After a brief period of reorganisation, Sheikh Atiyyah went into action, his band attacking a British army unit near Umm al-Fahm on 31 January. A month later he attempted to break into Tirat Zvi. Both attacks failed. On

3 March 1938, a major encounter occurred near the village of al-Yamun in the Jenin area. The band was surrounded by an army force, and Sheikh 'Atiyyah and several dozen of his men were killed.[196]

(3) Tawfiq al-Ibrahim (Abu Ibrahim 'the Lesser') – a cigarette seller from the village of Indur, near Nazareth. Abu Ibrahim al-Kabir's successor as leader of the Dervishes group and one of the leading figures of the Qassamite terror in Haifa and Galilee. His headquarters were in Kafr Manda, some 15 kms north of Nazareth. This was also the location of his 'court', which sentenced to death and executed a large number of persons.[197]

(4) Yusuf Sa'id Abu Durrah (Abu al-Abd) – from the village of Silat al-Harithiyyah, in the Jenin sub-district. A porter at the Zikhron Ya'aqov railway station and later a day labourer in Haifa, he was not particularly prominent during the first phase of the revolt, but after Sheikh Atiyyah 'Awad's death he succeeded him as commander of the Jenin and Mount Carmel area and, using terrorism and blackmail,[198] he rapidly became one of the major commanders of bands in Palestine. Towards the end of 1938, he was appointed one of the four directors of the 'Bureau of the Arab Revolt in Palestine' (*Diwan al-thawrah al-arabiyyah fi filastin*), which was established by the Central Committee in Damascus in order to co-ordinate the operations of the rebels in the country.[199] At the peak of his career he controlled 17 sub-bands (*fasa'il*, sing. *fasil*) which totalled about 250 men, and also led a separate terrorist band in Haifa.[200]

(5) Yusuf Hamdan – from Umm al-Fahm; Abu Durrah's lieutenant. He led a small but highly organised and strictly disciplined band, and levied a fixed tax on his village and the vicinity. Moffat, the Deputy Commissioner of the Jenin sub-district, once described him as the most intelligent of the rebel leaders in the country.[201]

(6) Sheikh Muhammad al-Salih (Abu Khalid) – from Silat al-Zahr, near Nablus. Formerly a porter in Haifa, he was considered a dangerous terrorist after he joined the Qassamites. He did not stand out during the first phase of the revolt, but after its resumption in 1938 he became a band commander in the Jordan Valley and Tubas area. Known for his honesty and uprightness and for his complete devotion to the rebellion, he organised the Dayr Ghassanah meeting in September 1938, which was intended to make peace between the rival rebel commanders. The gathering was bombed from the air and al-Salih and many others were killed.[202]

The major contributions of *Ikhwan al-Qassam* to the 1936–39 revolt, as well as its geographical extent, are clearly reflected in the following two tables. These are based on a membership list and the biographical data of 153 members of the Qassamite movement:

Qassamites: Roles in the Revolt

Regional commanders	3
Band/Sub-band commanders	28
Members of bands	41
Rebels' court judges	2
Urban terrorists	46
Agitators	11
	131

Qassamites, by Place of Origin

I. *Galilee District*	(40)		Umm al-Fahm	3
Nazareth Area			Jenin	2
Safuriyyah	13		Qabatiyyah	2
Sulim	10		'Arrabah	2
Al-Mujaydal	2		Burqin	2
Indur	1		Kafr Ra'i	2
Kawkab Abu al-Hayja	1		Al-Mazar	2
			Dayr Abu Za'if	2
Safed Area			Zar'in	1
Amqah	1		Kafr Dan	1
Rihaniyyah	1		Anza	1
			'Anin	1
Besian Area	11		Fahma	1
II. *Haifa Area*	(51)	IV.	*Nablus Area*	(5)
Haifa	31		Nablus	4
Balad al-Shaykh	7		Qabalan	1
Al-Tirah	6			
Ijzim	2	V.	*Tulkarm Area*	(4)
Shafa 'Amr	2		Tulkarm	1
'Ar'arah	1		Anabta	2
'Ibillin	1		Baqah al-Gharbiyyah	1
Umm al-Zinat	1			
		VI.	*Ramallah Area*	(2)
III. *Jenin Area*	(38)		Al-Mazra'a	2
Silat al-Zahr	4			
Silat al-Harithiyyah	3	VII.	*Other Places*	(6)
Ya'bad	3			
Nuris	3		TOTAL	146
Maythalun	3			

The Qassamites and their allies played a prominent role in spreading terror in the northern regions. Dozens of Arabs of Haifa and Galilee were murdered by them during the years 1938–39,[203] while many others fell victim to violent attacks and extortion practiced in the name of this terrorist organisation.[204] At the peak of the revolt, a panic-stricken flight from the country greatly increased; almost all the wealthy Christians and many of Haifa's Muslim notables, together with their families, found refuge in neighbouring countries, and many of the lower classes followed suit.[205]

The decline and disintegration of the Arab revolt brought with it the end of the Qassamite movement. Many of its members were killed in the fighting; others, like Abu Ibrahim al-Kabir, Tawfiq al-Ibrahim and Yusuf Abu Durrah — who escaped with thousands of pounds he had extorted from the population[206] — fled the country, while the remainder were arrested or went underground. In later years, several attempts were made to revive Qassamite activity in the North. Thus, towards the end of 1942, two societies of distinctly Qassamite character were organised in Haifa: *Usbat Fityan Muhammad* (The Mohammedan Youth League), led by Sheikh Abdullah al-Ma'ani,[207] and *Nadi Ansar al-Fadilah* (The Upholders of Virtue Club). The latter, founded by Sheikh Nimr al-Khatib, *imam* of *al-Istiqlal* mosque, was characterised by religious extremism in the spirit of al-Qassam's doctrine, and some of its members, mostly divines, grew their beards wild.[208] Another association was founded at al-Mazar, Sheikh Farhan al-Sa'di's village. It was called *Ansar al-haqq ala al-batil* (The Champions of Justice against Iniquity), and its reported aim was to avenge the old Sheikh.[209] Another interesting figure who emerged at that time was Sheikh Muhammad Mahmud Ali al-Khadr, a *khatib* from al-Ramin, Tulkarm sub-district. Known as 'the new al-Qassam' (*al-Qassam al-jadid*), he headed a group of about fifteen bearded men, some of them from Ya'bad, and during 1942–43 he conducted religious propaganda modelled on al-Qassam's doctrine, in the Tulkarm-Jenin area.[210] Some attempts were also made at this time to revive Qassamite activity in Nablus and vicinity.[211] However, all these were no more than transient phenomena; the Qassamite movement as a whole emerged from the Revolt torn and in disarray, and within a short while it virtually disappeared from the local political scene.

CONCLUSION

The story of Sheikh Izz al-Din al-Qassam and his movement is one of the most fascinating episodes in the history of the Palestinian Arabs' struggle against the Zionist enterprise. It was in the context of deteriorating intercommunal relations during the first half of the 1930s and against the background of the ineffective and divided traditional Arab leadership, that the refugee Sheikh from Syria appeared and by personal example showed the Arab community a new, more radical and more satisfying way of action. He thought to solve the problems of the country by returning to the pristine sources of Islam, and the ideology he preached was one of armed struggle and war to the end against the Jewish community. To implement his ideas, he founded, at the beginning of the 1930s, a clandestine association — the first Arab terrorist movement in Palestine —

which was of an extremist religious character, and was based in the main on the lower classes of Arab society.

For his disciples and adherents, al-Qassam's attraction lay mainly in his synthesis of Muslim erudition and militant nationalist attitudes, traits embodied in his own personality. The identity between the man and the goals of his movement was thus a key factor in his popularity and his success, but, above all, it was his religious devotion which drew the veneration of villagers and common people. These saw in him the sheikh and the preaching *imam* and they joined his secret society as if it were a new religious sect, its members being known as *Ikhwan al-Qassam* or *Qassamiyun*. As a socio-ideological phenomenon this organisation can be classified as one of the 'Islam-as-protest' movements, which used religion as a catharsis for nationalistic and social pressure in Arab society. To al-Qassam's image as preacher, leader and religious teacher was added his austerity and unpretentiousness. Throughout his stay in Haifa he lived in poverty and left behind no property or estate.[212] And as if all this were not enough, the battle of Ya'bad served overnight to make him into a martyr and a symbol.

A summing up of al-Qassam's achievements will reveal that he did not succeed in attaining his goals. The acts of terrorism neither deterred the Jewish population nor prevented the founding of more settlements in the North; the organisation he formed was limited in size and lacked true operational effectiveness, and he himself was killed before he could carry out the plan for the sake of which he had taken to the mountains. Nevertheless, al-Qassam's deeds had a tremendous impact. He became the standard-bearer of the Arab armed struggle, and his actions, which were a source of inspiration and emulation, served as a catalyst in the coming revolt. In many ways, the battle of Ya'bad may be defined as the effectual starting point of the Arab revolt of 1936-39.

Various characteristic aspects of al-Qassam's activity – militant religious incitement, reliance on popular elements as an expression of the necessity to enlist the masses (and not only the educated elite) for the national endeavour, organising the militant forces as armed bands and transferring the main effort to the rural areas – became after his death accepted principles of action and were widely employed in the course of the 1936-39 revolt.

Al-Qassam's disciples and followers constituted one of the pillars of the revolt. It was they who by their actions triggered off the two stages of the revolt, who were the elite of the armed bands movement; and who stood at the head of the internal terrorism campaign in the North. As their strength grew, however, they gradually threw off all sense of responsibility. Qassamite terror was particularly bloodthirsty. From an organisation committed to fight the Jews and the British, the Qassamites became one of the most anarchical and destructive forces ever to arise in the Palestinian Arab community. Their campaign of terror and the indiscriminate murders they committed contributed heavily to the rebellion's distintegration from within, and caused the accumulation of a terrible blood-debt in the Arab community, a phenomenon which had serious future consequences for the strength and coherence of the Palestinian Arab national movement.[213]

Nevertheless, the Qassamite myth has not died, and continues to be revered to this very day. Sheikh Izz al-Din al-Qassam's deeds and personality are highly extolled by the Palestinian *fedayeen* organisations, including the most radical leftist and secular ones such as the Popular Front for the Liberation of Palestine (Habash) and the Popular Democratic Front for the Liberation of Palestine (Hawatmah). Publications of the Palestinian organisations describe him as the pioneer of the Palestinian armed struggle (*al-Fatah* dubs him 'the first commander of the Palestinian Revolution'),[214] as a model of personal sacrifice and endeavour – in utter contrast to the traditional leadership which had clung to old tactics and non-violence – and as one who by his very deeds ignited the torch of the 'heroic revolt of 1936–1939'. His organisational ability and the novel methods of action formulated by him are particularly emphasised.[215] Up to this day, military units named after Sheikh Izz al-Din al-Qassam may be found in almost all Palestinian organisations. Al-Qassam's major contribution to the Palestinian armed struggle was clearly defined by Leila Khaled. 'The Popular Front for the Liberation of Palestine', she wrote, 'begins where Qassam left off: his generation started the revolution; my generation intends to finish it.'[216]

List of Abbreviations
Central Zionist Archives. Jerusalem – CZA
Israel State Archives, Jerusalem – ISA
Haganah Archives, Tel-Aviv – HA
   Intelligence Services – IS
Public Record Office, London – PRO
   Colonial Office – CO
   Foreign Office – FO

NOTES

1. For a detailed description of the two conferences held on 31.7.1931 and on 20.9.1931 and the resolutions, see *Al-jami'a al-'arabiyya*, 2.8.1931, 23.9.1931; CZA, S 25/4108; CID, Daily Intelligence Summary No. 221, 21.9.1931; 'Nablus Congress of 20th September, 1931', FO 371/15333.
2. HA, Intelligence Service (IS) file No. 1508; also quoted in Y. Slutsky and others, *Sefer Toldot ha-Haganah* (The History Book of the Haganah; Vol. II, Tel-Aviv, 1959) Part 3, p. 1173, note to p. 451. (infra: STH).
3. Muhammad Izzat Darwaza, *Hawla al-harakah al-arabiyya al-hadithah* (On the Modern Arab Movement), III (Saida, 1950), pp. 103–4; Y. Shim'oni, *'Arvey Eretz Israel* (The Arabs of Palestine; Tel Aviv, 1947), pp. 288–9; Y. Porath, 'The Political

Organization of the Palestinian Arabs under the British Mandate', in M. Ma'oz (ed.), *Palestine Arab Politics* (Jerusalem, 1975), p. 16.
4. Darwaza, III, pp. 104–5.
5. The meeting was held at the initiative of Awni Abd al-Hadi and among the participants were some 40 former members of the *al-Fatah* organisation and active supporters of Faysal's Damascus regime. For a summary of the discussions and for the covenant, see *Al-Fath*, Vol. VI (14 Sha'ban 1350/1931), p. 10; and also Darwaza, III, p. 104.
6. *Al-jami'a al-'arabiyya*, 4.8.1932, Darwaza, III, pp. 309–10.
7. Darwaza, pp. 108–10; Kamil Mahmud Khila, *Filastin wa al-intidab al-baritani 1922–1939* (Palestine and the British Mandate 1922–1939; Beirut, 1974), pp. 334–8; Shim'oni, p. 288; Porath, Political Organisation, p. 16.
8. Y. Porath, *The Emergence of the Palestinian Arab National Movement 1918–1929* (London, 1974), pp. 300–3; S. Lachman, 'Christians and Druze in the Arab Revolt in Palestine, 1936–1939' (Seminar Paper, Hebrew University, Jerusalem, 1975), pp. 1–8.
9. For a detailed account of the band and its activity, see High Commissioner to the Colonial Secretary, Secret Dispatch, 22.2.1930, CO 733/190/77171. Where no other source is quoted, the information is derived from this report.
10. (CID) 'Terrorism, 1930–1937', HA 41/14.
11. *Doar Ha-Yom*, 29.8.1930.
12. The source in note 9.
13. *Al-Jami'a al-'Arabiyya*, 4.8.1932. STH, II, Part 1, p. 448.
14. Darwaza, III, p. 76.
15. Emil al-Ghawri, *Filastin 'ibra sittin 'amm(an)* Part I (Beirut, 1972), p. 9.
16. This was also the name of the Arab military organisation which operated during the 1948 war in the Judean mountains under the command of Abd al-Qadir al-Husayni.
17. Al-Ghawri, I, p. 232.
18. *Ibid.*, p. 233.
19. *Ibid.*, pp. 186, 228–34.
20. *Ibid.*, pp. 238–9.
21. *Ibid.*, p. 244.
22. *Ibid.*, p. 157.
23. 'Fi dhikra ma'rakat al-qastal', *Filastin al-Thawrah*, No. 138, 13.4.1975, p. 24.
24. The following description is based on material found in CZA, S 25/3875.
25. Najib (Khalil al-Khuri) to the Jewish Agency, Reports from Tulkarm, 14.4.1935; 16.4.1935; 28.4.1935, *ibid.*; for details on the organisation and its aims, see report of 26.6.1935, *ibid.*
26. Najib to the Jewish Agency, 16.4.1935, 28.4.1935, *ibid.*
27. Najib's reports from Tulkarm, 11.7.1935, 27.9.1935, 30.10.1935, *ibid.*; CID Report No. 12/35, 5.8.1935, FO 371/18957.
28. Zuhayr al-Mardini, *Alf yawm ma'a al-Hajj Amin* (Thousand Days with al-Hajj Amin; Beirut, 1977), p. 81; see also E.S. (Eliahu Sasson), 'Report on the Leader of the Assassin Group', 27.11.1935, CZA, S 25/3473.
29. Ibrahim Isa al-Misri, *Majma' al-athar al-'arabiyya wa-rijal al-nahdah al-fikriyya* (A Miscellany of Arabic Traditions and of Figures of the Intellectual Renaissance, Part I; Damascus, 1963), pp. 151–2; Khayr al-Din al-Zirikli, *Al-A'lam* (Distinguished Personalities, Vol. VII; Cairo, 1956), p. 142; Subhi Yasin, *al-Thawrah al-'arabiyyah al-kubra fi Filastin 1936–1939* (The Great Arab Revolt in Palestine, 1936–1939; Cairo, 1959), p. 19.
30. Al-Mardini, p. 82.
31. Subhi Yasin, *Harb al-'isabat fi Filastin* (Guerilla Warfare in Palestine; Cairo, 1967), p. 62 (infra: Yasin, Harb al-'isabat).
32. Al-Mardini, *ibid.*

33. Al-Misri, *ibid.*; 'Adil Hasan Ghunayyim, 'Thawrat al-shaykh Izz al-Din al-Qassam' (The Uprising of Sheikh Izz al-Din al-Qassam), *Shu'un filastiniyya*, No. 6, January 1972, p. 181. For a detailed description of the uprising led by Sheikh Salih al-Ali, see Abd al-Latif al-Yunis, *Thawrat al-shaykh Salih al-Ali* (Damascus, undated).
34. Yasin, pp. 19–20; al-Mardini, *ibid.*; *Filastin al-Thawrah*, No. 170, 23.11.1975. Other Syrian exiles reached Haifa together with al-Qassam. These continued with their subversive activities against the French and formed an inciting element among the local nationalist circles. On their activities and their attempt to convene a Syro-Palestinian congress in Jerusalem in May 1922, see Haut-Commissariat & Armée du Levant, Service de Renseignements, 'Bulletin Périodique No. 46, Renseignements du 1° au 20° Mai, 1922', Secret, Beirut, 20 May 1922, PRO, FO 684/1.
35. Ghunayyim, p. 181; Yasin, *Harb al-'isabat*, pp. 61–3; Khila, p. 375; al-Ghawri, p. 250.
36. Yasin, *Harb al-'isabat*, p. 64; Ghunayyim, *ibid.*
37. Yasin, p. 21; A. H. Cohen, 'The November Events in Northern Palestine' 20.1.1936, Secret, CZA, S 25/4224 (infra: 'The November Events').
38. Al-Karmil, 13.5.1928, *Al-Fath*, 9.7.1928; Yasin, p. 20.
39. Yasin, *Harb al-'isabat*, p. 63.
40. *Al-Jami'a al-'arabiyya*, 21.7.1932.
41. Yasin, p. 20; Ghunayyim, p. 182; CID Report on al-Qassam Movement, undated, Tegart Papers, Box I, File 3, St. Antony's Collge, Oxford (infra: CID Report on al-Qassam Movement, Tegart Papers).
42. Umar Abu al-Nasr *et al., Jihad Filastin al-'arabiyya 1936* (The Holy War of Arab Palestine, 1936; Jaffa, 1936), pp. 270–1; Ghunayyim, p. 182. On al-Qassam's connections with the *imam* and Sheikhs of the *Hanabila* mosque in Nablus, see Sheikh Radi al-Hanbali, Biographical Card, The Truman Research Institute, Hebrew University, Jerusalem; Sheikh Ahmad al-Hanbali, interviewed in Nablus, 19.6.1978, asserts that al-Qassam's followers in Nablus would regularly pray at the local *Hanabila* mosque, which was founded, and is to this day run, by the Sheikh's family.
43. 'Bayan haqiqa', letter sent by al-Qassam to the editor of *al-Karmil*, 6.6.1925, pp. 2–3. This letter was a reply to an attack on al-Qassam and his doctrines published in *al-Yarmuk*, 14.5.1925. For sharp criticism, supported by *fatwas*, concerning the raucous chanting of *tahlil* and *takbir* at funerals, see Muhammad Kamil al Qassab and Muhammad Izz al-Din al-Qassam, *al-Naqd wa al-bayan fi daf' awham Khuzayran* (Damascus, 1925). This book was published in reaction to a *fatwa* permitting such chanting, issued by Sheikh Muhammad Subhi al-Hanafi, President of the sharia Court in Acre.
44. Yasin, p. 21; Ghunayyim, p. 182.
45. *Al-Yarmuk*, 14.5.1925 (Editorial signed by Ibn 'Abbas); Yasin, p. 21; Yasin, Harb al-'isabat, pp. 62–3.
46. *Al-Karmil*, 6.6.1925.
47. Yasin, Harb al-'isabat, pp. 63–4; *al-Rabitah al-'Arabiyyah*, 16.9.1936; (CID) 'Terrorism 1936–1937', HA 41/14.
48. Al-Ghawri, I, p. 250; 'The November Events', 20.1.1936, CZA, S 25/4224.
49. (CID) 'Terrorism 1936–1937', HA, *ibid.*; CID Report on al-Qassam Movement, Tegart Papers.
50. Yasin, p. 22.
51. 'The Black Hand List', 5.3.1933, 6.3.1933; Memo, 2.3.1933, HA, IS 8/67; STH, II, p. 451.
52. 'Report to Shaul (Avigur)', 12.2.1933; Report by A.N. (? Police Officer Ahmad Naif), 2.7.1933, HA, *ibid.* 'The Sheikh Qassam Band – its origin and members', T/B 478, 2.6.1942, *ibid.*, IS 8/3. One of the Nahalal murderers, who was later executed, testified that 'The aim of this secret society is to defend our country from the Jews by

killing them and robbing them' – Central Police Station, Haifa, 'Statement of Mustapha Ali Ahmed of Safourieh', 29.5.1933, Tegart Papers, Box II, File 3, St. Antony's College, Oxford. An Arab who had been approached to enlist in the secret society testified at the Nahalal trial that he was told that the aim of the society was 'to avenge the blood of the heroes who had fallen in the (1929) riots against the Jews and of the martyrs who had been hanged at Acre' – Statement of Said Yusuf Abd al-Rahman, 6.12.1933, in 'The Nahalal Murder, the night of 22.12.1932', T/A2, HA, IS 8/2.

53. Abu Ibrahim al-Kabir, *al-Thawrah al-filastiniyya*, No. 19, 15.9.1969 (quoted by Khila, p. 376).
54. Yasin, p. 21; al-Ghawri, p. 251.
55. On the YMMA of Balad al-Shaykh and Yajur and its connections with al-Qassam, see Report from Yagur, 2.2.1933; 'The Black Hand List', 5.3.1933, HA, IS 8/67.
56. Report by Zvi Fein, Nahalal, 11.2.1933; 'The Young Men's Muslim Association at Safuriyyah', 23.4.1933; Report by A.N. (? Ahmad Naif), 2.7.1933, *ibid.*; 'The Nahalal Murder, the night of 22.12.1932', T/A 2, *ibid.*, IS 8/2; 'The Sheikh Qassam Band – its Origin and Members', T/B 478, 2.6.1942, *ibid.*, IS 8/3; 'The November Events', 20.1.1936, CZA, S 25/4224.
57. Zvi Shapira to S. Finklestein, 28.10.1936, CZA, S 25/10499; Report from Yagur, 2.2.1933, HA, IS, 8/67; (CID) 'Terrorism 1936–1937', *ibid.*, 41/14; 'Ajaj Nuwayhid, *al-Anwar*, 6.8.1961.
58. Written statement by Jamil Ramadan, 8.2.1933, HA, 8/67; Report of 1.2.1932, HA (quoted in STH, II, Part 3, note 451).
59. Central Police Station, Haifa, 'Statement of Mustapha Ali Ahmed of Saffourieh', 29.5.1933, Tegart Papers, Box II, File 3, St. Antony's College, Oxford; 'Report to Shaul (Avigur)', 12.2.1933, HA, IS 8/67; 'The Nahalal Murder, the night of 22.12.1932', T/A 2, *ibid.*, IS 8/2.
60. Abu Ibrahim al-Kabir, *al-Thawrah al-filastiniyya*, No. 19, 15.9.1969 (quoted by Khila, p. 376). See also written statement by Jamil Ramadan, 8.2.1933, HA, IS 8/67.
61. Muhammad Nimr al-Khatib, *Min athar al-nakba* (Some Results of the Disaster; Damascus, undated), pp. 87–8; Ghunayyim, p. 182.
62. 'Ajaj Nuwayhid, *al-Anwar*, 6.8.1961; Ghunayyim, p. 181; STH, II, p. 451.
63. Nuwayhid, *ibid.*; Yasin, pp. 22–3; Yasin, Harb al-'isabat, p. 68; Khila, p. 377; Ibrahim al-Shaykh Khalil, 'Risalah min mujahid qadim: dhikrayat 'an al-Qassam' (A letter from a Veteran Fighter; Reminiscences of al-Qassam), *Shu'un filastiniyya*, No. 7, March 1972, pp. 267–8 (infra: Khalil).
64. Khalil, p. 268; Zvi Shapira to S. Finklestein, 28.10.1936, CZA, S 25/10499.
65. According to al-Ghawri, p. 251, al-Qassam had formulated a 'national religious covenant' with a constitution and a set of regulations for the organisation.
66. Yasin, Harb al-'isabat, pp. 65–6.
67. See his report in CO 733/204/87156.
68. STH, II, p. 452; al-Ghawri, p. 252, lists, among the operations carried out by the organisation, attacks on army and police stations and the cutting of communication lines – an entirely unfounded claim.
69. CID, 'Note on the Terrorist Campaign', 17.12.1937, Tegart Papers, Box II, File 4, St. Antony's College, Oxford; the 'Nahalal File', HA, IS 8/67; STH, II, *ibid.*
70. Yasin, p. 26; Khila, p. 379; (CID) 'Terrorism 1936–1937', HA, 41/14.
71. From a peasant family in al-Mazra'a al-Sharqiyya, Ramallah sub-district. Worked as a labourer in Shafa 'Amr and then for 12 years as a porter at the Haifa post office, until dismissed. When arrested was employed as apprentice with Ahmad al-Ghalayni, a mender of 'primus' stoves, who had put together the bomb thrown at Nahalal. In his testimony at the trial he denied any complicity in the murder. He admitted to having been a member of the Haifa YMMA and to having visited Safuriyyah several times, but claimed to have left the association some time

previously owing to non-payment of membership dues – 'Statement of Khalil Mohammed Eissa, Acre', 12.1.1933, HA, IS 8/67.
72. Born at Shafa 'Amr, joined al-Qassam and was a junior member in his secret organisation. A member of *fasil* Shafa 'Amr during the second phase of the revolt. In mid-1950s he became an enthusiastic Nasserite and was employed as an agent by Egyptian intelligence. When the UAR dissolved he was imprisoned in Damascus. In March 1963, he founded, in Cairo, the organisation of 'Pioneers of Sacrifice for the Liberation of Palestine', which later merged with *al-Fatah*. A short time after the merger, in December 1968, Yasin was murdered in Amman by one of his men. In his book, Yasin presents al-Qassam as the father of the armed Palestinian struggle and considers himself and the 'Pioneers of Sacrifice' as the true successors of the Qassamite movement.
73. Yasin, pp. 23–4, 26; Yasin, Harb al-'isabat, pp. 68–9.
74. Yasin, Harb al-'isabat, *ibid*.
75. Abu Ibrahim al-Kabir, *al-Thawra al-filastiniyya*, No. 19, 15.9.1969 (quoted by Khila, p. 377).
76. 'The Rabbi Reports', 24.5.1933; Report by A.N. (? Police Officer Ahmad Naif), 2,7.1933, HA, IS 8/67. See also 'The Nahalal Murder, the night of 22.12.1932',: T/A 2, *ibid*., IS 8/2; 'The Sheikh Qassam Band – its origin and Members', T/B 478, 2.6.1942, *ibid*., 8/3.
77. 'An interview with Zimroni', 23.5.1933, HA, IS 8/67.
78. Khalil, p. 267.
79. On this dispute, see below.
80. STH, II, part I, p. 467. According to one source, al-Qassam had decided to organise a new terrorist band already in the middle of 1933 – 'The Zimroni Report', 5.5.1933, HA, IS 8/67; see also Abu Ibrahim al-Kabir, *al-Thawrah al-filastiniyya*, No. 19, 15.9.1969 (quoted by Khila, p. 380).
81. Yasin, pp. 22–3; Yasin, Harb al-'isabat, pp. 66–7.
82. A. H. Cohen, Arab Bureau News (through V.G.), Secret, 14.11.1934; from 'Oved', 2.12.1934, CZA, S 25/3542; and also 'The November Events', 20.1.1936, *ibid*., S 25/4224.
83. On the *'Ulama* Congress and its resolutions, see CID Reports Nos. 3/35, 30.1.1935; 4/35, 5.2.1935, Secret, FO 371/18957; on *al-Amr bi al-ma'ruf* association and its subversive activities, see CID Reports Nos. 6/35, 27.2.1935; 7/35, 9.3.1935, *ibid*.; M. Nisani and E. Sasson, 'Arab Problems' (from the Arabic press), undated, pp. 30–1, CZA, S 25/9326.
84. *al-Difa'*, 30.9.1935, and also the issues of 20.7.1935; 24.9.1935; 16.10.1935; *Filastin*, 28.8.1935; CID Reports No. 13/35, 24.8.1935; 14/35, 28.9.1935, FO 371/18957.
85. Report from Haifa, 24.1.1935, CZA, S 25/4127; 'The November Events', 20.1.1936, *ibid*., S 25/4224.
86. Darwaza, p. 120.
87. Yasin, p. 23.
88. Amin Sa'id, *al-Rabita al-'arabiyya*, 20.4.1938; Ghunayyim, p. 188; Khalil, p. 269; Abd al-Wahab al-Kayyali, *Ta'rikh Filastin al-hadith* (Modern History of Palestine; Beirut, 1970), p. 292; Naji 'Alush, *al-Muqawamah al-'arabiyya fi Filastin 1917–1948* (The Arab Resistance in Palestine 1917–1948; Beirut, 1969), p. 117. According to the last two sources, the society had 200 members and 800 supporters.
89. Yasin, p. 23; 'Alush, p. 116; al-Kayyali, p. 293; Zvi Shapira to S. Finklestein, 28.10.1936, CZA, S 25/10499. See also report on a resident of al-Yamun (Jenin sub-district), one of al-Qassam's men, who was in contact with the Italian Consul in Haifa and who spread fascist propaganda in the surrounding villages during the Revolt – 'Appreciation of Italian activities in Palestine for the Month of May 1937', PRO, Air 2/1813.

90. Yasin, *ibid.*; according to another source, a notorious terrorist from Turkey was brought over to serve as instructor to the secret society – 'The November Events', 20.1.1936, CZA S 25/4224.
91. For details on this episode, see STH, II, pp. 540–1.
92. CID Reports Nos. 16/35, 30.10.1935; 17/35, 16.11.1935, FO 371/18957; Survey for the period 15.10–8.11.1935, HA.
93. CID Reports cited in note 92 above; *Al-Difa'*, 22.10.1935, 5.11.1935.
94. Second source in note 92.
95. Khila, p. 381; Ghunayyim, p. 184; STH, II, p. 467.
96. 'The November Events' 20.1.1936, CZA, S 25/4224; D. Ben-Gurion, *Zikhronot* (Memoirs; Vol. II, Tel Aviv, 1972), p. 527.
97. 'The Sheikh Qassam Band – its Origin and Members', T/B 478, 2.6.1942, HA, IS 8/3.
98. Abu Ibrahim al-Kabir, *al-Thawra al-filastiniyya*, No. 19, 15.9.1969 (quoted by Khila, pp. 380–1); Khalil, p. 267.
99. Arab sources are divided as to the date of the departure for the mountains. Yasin, pp. 26–7, states that the band left Haifa on the night of 12.11.1935, at the conclusion of a secret meeting held at the house of one of the members (mentioned also by al-Kayyali, p. 295). This date cannot be accurate, as the first encounter with the police took place already on 7.11.1935 (see below). Khila, p. 381, contends that the departure had taken place on the night of 26–7 October, upon the end of the strike protesting at the contraband arms shipment seized at Jaffa, while 'Alush, p. 117, claims that the decision to take to the mountains was taken at a meeting of the leaders of the organisation held on 2.11.1935, the anniversary of the Balfour Declaration. Our date is taken from A. H. Cohen, 'The November Events', 20.1.1936, CZA S 25/4224.
100. Ghunayyim, p. 184; 'The November Events', *ibid.*; STH, II, p. 467.
101. As quoted by Abu Ibrahim al-Kabir, *al-Thawra al-filastiniyya*, No. 19, 15.9.1969 (Khila, p. 381). See also Yasin, pp. 26–7; 'Alush, p. 117; Ghasan Kanafani, 'Thawrat 1936–39 fi Filastin: Khilfiat wa-tafasil wa-tahlil' (The 1936–1939 Revolt in Palestine: Discrepancies, Details and Analysis), *Shu'un filastiniyya*, No. 6, January 1972, p. 62; Ihsan al-Nimr, *Tarikh jabal Nablus wa al-Balqa* (The History of Nablus Mountains and al-Balqa; III, Nablus, 1972), p. 215, note 1.
102. Yasin, pp. 27–8; Yasin, Harb al-'isabat, p. 70.
103. Among the Arab sources, Ghunayyim, p. 186, and Khila, p. 383, dispute Yasin's version, while others, as 'Alush, p. 118, and al-Kayyali, p. 295, accept it unreservedly.
104. Yasin, p. 27.
105. *Ibid.*; STH, II, p. 467; 'The November Events', 20.1.36, CZA S 25/4224.
106. *al-Rabita al-'arabiyya*, No. 17, 16.9.1936; Ghunayyim, p. 184; STH, *ibid.*; 'The November Events', *ibid.*
107. Yasin, p. 27; Zvi Shapira to S. Finklestein, 28.10.1936, CZA, S 25/10459; 'The November Events', *ibid.* According to the last two sources, the band had planned an attack on one of the Jewish settlements in the Emeq. By this version, the theft from the Ein Harod groves was carried out by al-Qassam's men, who sought to lure the settlers to the mountains in this way. See also Ben-Gurion, *Memoirs*, Vol. II, pp. 527, 561.
108. 'The November Events'; *ibid.*; Zvi Shapira to S. Finklestein, 28.10.1936, *ibid.*
109. Yasin, p. 28; Ghunayyim, p. 184; 'The November Events', *ibid.*; STH, II, p. 468; E.S. (Eliahu Sasson), 'The Clash with the Arab Terrorists, 21.11.1935', CZA, S 25/3473.
110. 'Terrorism in Islam and the Religious Motives', review in English, undated and unsigned, most probably of Jewish authorship, CZA, S 25/3473.
111. *Filastin*, 21.11.1935; 'Alush, p. 119.

112. Palestine Royal Commission Report (Cmd. 5479, 1937), pp. 88–9; STH, II, p. 468.
113. CID Report No. 18/35, 4.12.1935, FO 371/20018; 'The November Events', 20.1.1936, CZA, S 25/4224; STH, ibid. The Chief Secretary later asserted that the British authorities hesitated as to whether to permit the funeral to take place, but finally authorised it for fear of an Arab uprising and a repeat of the 1933 demonstrations – Ben-Gurion, Memoirs, II, p. 527.
114. Al-Qassam left a wife and three children.
115. These included Awni Abd al-Hadi from Jerusalem, Abd al-Latif Salah from Nablus, Mu'in al-Madi from Haifa and Ahmad al-Shuqayri from Acre.
116. Quoted in STH, II, pp. 468–9.
117. Ben-Gurion, Memoirs, II, p. 531. Tel Hai in upper Galilee, where Y. Trumpeldor and his associates were killed by Arabs in defence of their settlement in 1921, became the symbol of Jewish heroism and sacrifice.
118. Najib to JA, Report from Tulkarm, 7.12.1935, CZA, S 25/3875.
119. Najib's report from Jaffa, 9.12.1935, ibid.; Isa al-Sifri, Filastin al-'arabiyya bayna al-intidab wa al-sahyuniyya (Arab Palestine between the Mandate and Zionism; Jaffa, 1937), p. 239; 'Alush, p. 120.
120. CID Report No. 1/36, 22.1.1936, FO 371/20018.
121. CID Report No. 18/35, 4.12.1935, ibid.; 'Alush, p. 119, claims that al-Qassam had intended to come out openly against the Arab leaders and that he was even planning to assassinate some of them.
122. 'Alush, p. 119; al-Kayyali, p. 295; Ghunayyim, p. 187; Kanafani, p. 62; Khila, p. 382; see also CID Report of 4.12.1935, ibid.
123. Filastin, 23.10.1935; Mir'at al-sharq, 26.10.1935. The new body was known as the 'Coalition of the Parties' (I'tilaf al-ahzab).
124. HC to Colonial Secretary, Secret, 7.12.1935, CO 733/278/75156 Part II; CID Report, 30.10.1935, FO 371/18957.
125. It is noteworthy that the most extreme Arab spokesman at the meeting with the High Commissioner was none other than Ragheb al-Nashashibi, the Mufti's determined political adversary – Ben-Gurion, Memoirs, II, p. 530.
126. CID Report No. 1/36, 22.1.1936, FO 371/20018; RAF, Monthly Intelligence Summary, 31.12.1935, 31.1.1936, FO 371/20030; E.S. (Eliahu Sasson), 'The Memorial Meeting for the Terrorists in Haifa', 6.1.1936, CZA, S 25/3473.
127. RAF Monthly Intelligence Summary, 31.1.1936, ibid.
128. 'Armed Gangs' undated (British authorship), HA, IS 8/35; Y. Arnon, Fallahim ba-mered ha-'aravi be Eretz Israel, 1936–1939 (MA thesis, Hebrew University, Jerusalem, 1970), p. 5.
129. Arab Bureau News, 'Survey for March', 2.4.1936, CZA, S 25/10187.
130. On arms traffic and attempts to organise armed bands in the vicinity of Jerusalem, see unsigned letter, 13.3.1936, HA, IS 8/35; 'The forming of a band under the leadership of Amir Fa'ur' (Huleh); Survey for the period 8.1.1936–17.2.1936, Secret; Memos, Haifa, 17.2.1936, 25.2.1936, ibid. On secret meetings and attempts to form terrorist groups on the Qassamite model in the North, see Memos, Haifa, 12.2.1936, 10.3.1936, 17.3.1936, 19.4.1936, ibid.; RAF Intelligence summary for December, 31.12.1935, FO 371/20030.
131. RAF, Intelligence Summary for January, 31.1.1936, ibid.; CID Report No. 1/36, 22.1.1936, FO 371/20018.
132. Survey for the period 8.1.–17.2.1936, Secret, HA; Arab Bureau News, 'News from the North', Secret, 24.1.1936, CZA, S 25/10187.
133. CID Report No. 17/35, 16.11.1935, Secret, FO 371/18957.
134. Darwaza, p. 120; also al-Kayyali, p. 292; Ghunayyim, p. 188; Khila, p. 387.
135. Al-Ghawri, I, p. 250; Filastin (the mouthpiece of the 'Arab Higher Committee for Palestine', Beirut), No. 3, 15.4.1961 (quoted by Ghunayyim, p. 188).
136. Khalil, p. 269; 'Ajaj Nuwayhid, al-Anwar, 6.8.1961; Ghunayyim, p. 188.

137. 'The November Events', 20.1.1936, CZA, S 25/4224; A. H. Cohen, 'Interview with Sheikh Abdallah Khair at the Majestic Hotel', 12.4.1932, ibid., S 25/3501.
138. Porath, p. 191; Shim'oni, p. 289.
139. Khila, p. 335.
140. Al-Kayyali, p. 297.
141. Report from Haifa, 1.1.1935, 17.1.1935, CZA, S 25/3558. Report from Haifa, 25.1.1935, ibid., 4127.
142. Yasin, p. 21.
143. A Syrian man of religion and nationalist, who escaped to Palestine and settled in Haifa after the downfall of Faysal's Damascus regime. Was employed as director of the local Islamic school and was one of the founders of *al-Istiqlal* mosque, where al-Qassam was later appointed *imam*. He was al-Qassam's close friend and a member of his secret organisation, and at the same time one of the Mufti's close adherents. Khalil, p. 269, asserts his having been the go-between.
144. Al-Ghawri, I, pp. 250–2; Emil al-Ghawri, *Al-Shuqayri fi al-mizan* (Al-Shuqayri in the Balance; Beirut, 1972), pp. 54–5; *Filastin* (Beirut), No. 3, 15.4.1961; No. 94, 1.1.1969; No. 95, 1.2.1963 (quoted by Kanafani, p. 62).
145. See al-Mardini, pp. 79–80, 82.
146. Khila, p. 377.
147. Al-Mardini, p. 83.
148. A. H. Cohen's Report of 11.5.1932, CZA, S 25/3557.
149. Zvi Shapira to S. Finklestein, 28.10.1936, CZA, S 25/10499.
150. *al-Jihad* (Beirut), 30.1.1939.
151. Yasin, p. 21; (CID) 'Terrorism 1936–1937', HA, 41/14; Sheikh Farhan and Sheikh Nimr al-Sa'di were both of the Arab al-Sa'diyya, a small Bedouin tribe which used to camp around Tiv'on and on the lands of Ma'lul, near Nahalal. The tribesmen had contacts with the Safuriyyah YMMA and were sympathetic to al-Qassam and his movement –' Arab al-Sa'diyya and the Sheikh Qassam Band', T/B 433, 8.5.1933, *ibid.*, 8/67; on Bedouins from Arab al-Sakhna (Beisan) who enlisted in al-Qassam's band, see 'The Sheikh Qassam Band – its origin and members', 2.6.1942, *ibid.*, 8/3.
152. A. Agasi, 'The Activity among the Arab Labourers in Haifa', 31.7.1935, CZA, S 25/9360.
153. These tendencies were apparent in increased social and trade-unionist awareness and organisation. Thus, for example, *Jam'iyyat fityan al-jazira* (Al-Jazira Youth Association), which was active in Haifa in that period, was made up mostly of *fellahin* from the village of 'Asira al-Shimaliyya in the Nablus district, and some of its members came from rival clans in the village. During the IPC strike, and other strikes which occurred in Haifa in 1935, the *fellah*-labourers were as a rule better organised and more united than those of urban origin – *ibid*.; The phenomenon of internal migration considerably affected the village of Arabah, in the Jenin sub-district. From 1928 onwards, a good many of the villagers left their homes for Haifa. (In Arabah today, one can hear estimates that the migration during the Thirties and the first half of the Forties reached the very high rate of one half to two-thirds of the male population of the village at that time.) They earned their living mainly as unskilled labourers, peddlers and porters, though there were some who joined the local police. In the mid-Thirties a club, called *Jam'iyyat al-hilal* (The Crescent Society), all of whose members were of Arabah origin, was established in Haifa. Headed for some time by Abd al-Qadir Yusuf Abd al-Hadi – later 'Chief Justice' of the Revolt – the club operated for a few years, until it was closed down in 1938 – IS Files, HA; Interview with Shawqi Abd al-Hadi, Arabah, 1.8.1978; and also information given to me by Mr Jacob Firestone. Some of al-Qassam's followers were members of the 'Arab Workers' Union of Haifa – CID Report on al-Qassam movement, Tegart Papers.
154. Yasin, Harb al-'isabat, p. 63.

155. Amin Sa'id, *Thawrat al-arab fi al-qarn al-'ishrin* (Arab Revolts in the Twentieth Century; Cairo, undated), p. 117; Ghunayyim, p. 188; 'Alush, p. 117; al-Kayyali, p. 293.
156. Yasin, p. 29; 'The November Events', 20.1.1936, CZA S 25/4224; Survey for the period of 8.1.–17.2.1936, Secret, HA: (CID) 'Terrorism 1936–1937' *ibid.*, 41/14; STH, II, p. 468.
157. Yasin, p. 30; Report on Abu Ibrahim al-Kabir, T/A 72, 2.12.1938, HA, IS 8/2; Arab Bureau News, 'Survey for March', 2.4.1936, Secret, CZA, S 25/10187.
158. Yasin, p. 29. Another active Qassamite was Sheikh Husayn Hamdi Tamish who endeavoured to organise the Haifa *shabab* in two associations known as *Jam'iyyat fityan al-jazirah* (see note 153) and *Usbat fityan Muhammad* (The Muhammadan Youth League) – CID Report on al-Qassam movement, Tegart Papers.
159. Arab Bureau News, 'Survey for March', 2.4.1936, *ibid.*; al-Ghawri, II, p. 53; Arnon, p. 5.
160. Survey for the period, 8.1.–17.2.1936, Secret, HA; Arab Bureau News, 'News from the North', 24.1.1936; 'The November Events', 20.1.1936, CZA, S 25/4224; al-Ghawri, II, p. 50.
161. Darwaza, p. 121; Al-Sifri, II, p. 10. Yusuf Haikal, *al-Qadiyyah al-filastiniyya* (The Palestinian Problem; Jaffa, undated), p. 198; Najib Sadaqa, *Qadiyyat Filastin* (The Palestine Problem; Beirut, 1964) pp. 177–8; Al-Jami'ah al-islamiyya, *Thawrat Filastin 'Amm 1936* (The Palestine Revolt of 1936; Vol. I, Jaffa, 1937), p. 33; *al-Difa'*, 21.4.1936.
162. Yasin, pp. 30, 127; Yasin, Harb al-'Isabat, p. 71; Khalil Sakik, *Tarikh Filastin al-hadith mundhu al-fatr al-uthmani* (The Modern History of Palestine from the Ottoman Period; Gaza, 1964), p. 47.
163. *Filastin*, 17.4.1936;*Al-Difa'*, 17.4.1936; *al-Muqattam*, 18.4.1936; Khila, p. 393; also al-Ghawri, II, p. 50.
163a. Diary of Events, 18.4.1936; 'The Robbery and Murder in the Nur al-Shams-'Anabtah Road, 15.4.1936', HA, IS 8/36.
164. Memos from Haifa, 6.4.1936, 6.6.1936, 7.6.1936, HA, IS 8/38.
165. 'News on the Gangs and their Activities', Haifa, 12.10.1936, *ibid.*, IS 8/2; also 'News on the Arab Gangs in Palestine and their Activities', No. 2, 14.10.36, CZA, S 25/10539.
166. RAF, Weekly Intelligence Report, No. 23, 13.11.1936, FO 371/20031.
167. CID, 'Statement of Mohammed Naji Abu Rab (Abu Jab)', 30.11.1937, Tegart Papers, Box I, File 3, St. Antony's College, Oxford. According to this source, Farhan's group numbered 15 men after the strike while Sheikh Atiyya began with 30 but was finally left with 15 only.
168. Six of al-Qassam's men who had been captured at Ya'bad were brought to trial on 19.10.1936; four of them were sentenced to 14 years' imprisonment for the murder of Police Sergeants Rosenfeld and Mott.
169. STH, II, Part 2, p. 657; al-Sifri, II, p. 83; CID Report, Jerusalem, 11.12.1937, Tegart Papers, Box II, File 3, St. Antony's College, Oxford.
170. STH, II, pp. 657–8, 715; CID Report No. 18/36, 7.11.1936, FO 371/20018.
171. Report No. 6, 12.3.1937, HA, A. Hoshi File 8b/6; Survey for the period 15–22.1.1937, Secret, HA: CID Report, Tegart Papers (note 169).
172. CID Report on al-Qassam movement, Tegart Papers.
173. Arab Bureau News, 'An Appraisal of the situation among the Arabs, May 1937', 2.6.1937, HA.
174. See, for example, an anti-Christian leaflet, under the headline 'Raise al-Qassam's Banner', dated Shawwal 1335 (middle of December 1936–middle of January 1937), which was apparently distributed in Haifa by Qassamite circles – ISA, 65/3506. In the opinion of the CID, the murder of Michel Mitri, the Christian President of the Jaffa Arab Workers' Association, was instigated by the

'representative' of the Qassamite organisation in Jaffa, the lawyer Mustafa Rashid – CID Report on al-Qassam movement, Tegart Papers.
175. Last source in previous note. See also RAF Weekly Intelligence Report, 28.2.1937, FO 371/20824.
176. Chief Secretary to the Colonial Secretary, Cable No. 72, 12.2.1937, CO 733/311.
177. *Daily Herald*, 17.2.1937.
178. RAF, Weekly Intelligence Report, 28.2.1937, *ibid*.
179. G. MacKereth (Damascus) to A. Eden, Dispatch No. 74, 19.10.1937, FO 684/19, 2207/2; Battershill to Shackburgh, 12.10.37, Secret, FO 371/20819; CID Report, Tegart Papers (Note 169).
180. G. MacKereth to Eden, Dispatch No. 77, 30.10.1937 (enclosing translation of a threatening letter signed by 'The Black Hand', dated 23.10.1937), FO 371/20819.
181. Reports from Haifa, Nos. 1042, 4.7.1937; 1056, 19.7.1937, CZA, S 25/3292.
182. Arab News Bureau, 19.8.1937, Secret, HA, IS 8/103; the Qassamite group which formed in Nablus was led by Sheikh Ali al-Mufti and numbered some 140 men, including schoolboys from the *al-Najah* school – Arab News Bureau, 21.9.1937, *ibid*.
183. Battershill to Shackburgh, 12.10.1937, Secret, FO 371/20819. In this letter Battershill openly admits the failure of conventional methods and proposes new and more vigorous ways to deal with the Qassamite organisation.
184. Yasin, p. 92; Yasin, Harb al-'Isabat, p. 93; see also Ahmad al-Shuqayri, *Arba'un 'amm(an) fi al-hayat al-'arabiyya wa al-duwaliyya* (Forty years in Arab and International Life; Beirut, 1969), pp. 171–2.
185. He appeared in the Umm al-Fahm region in the middle of September 1937 at the head of 25 men – Report from Haifa, No. 1181, 21.9.1937, CZA, S 25/3292; Survey for the period 24–30.9.1937, Secret, HA.
186. Battershill to Downey, 5.5.1938, Secret, CO 733/370/57156/58; (CID) 'Terrorism 1936–1937', HA, 41/14; CID, 'Statement of Mohamed Naji Abu Rab (Abu Jab)', 30.11.1937, Tegart Papers, Box I, File 3, St. Antony's College, Oxford; STH, II, Part 2, pp. 761, 765; the day before he was murdered, Andrews showed Bergmann, the District Officer, a CID report warning him that three Arabs from Safuriyyah had been ordered to kill him at any price – Report from Haifa, No. 1197, 27.9.1937, CZA, S 25/3292; Survey for the period 24–30.9.1937, HA.
187. CID Report, 'Murder of Mr L. Y. Andrews and British Constable P. R. McEwan', 29.9.1939, Tegart Papers, Box II, File 3; *ibid*.; (CID) 'Terrorism 1935–1937', HA, 41/14.
188. Yasin, p. 25; 'The Sheikh Qassam Band – its origin and members', 2.6.1942, HA, IS 8/3.
189. CID, 'Statement of Mohamed Naji Abu Rab (Abu Jab)', 30.11.1937, Tegart Papers, Box I, file 3 *ibid*.; (CID) 'Terrorism 1936–1937', HA, 41/14.
190. CID, 'Statement of Ahmed Mohamed al-Sa'di of Nuris', 26.11.1937, Tegart Papers, *ibid*.; (CID) 'Terrorism 1936–1937', *ibid*.
191. See handbill *'Al-Shaykh al-Shahid'* (with Farhan's picture), undated and unsigned, CZA, S 25/9332; protest demonstrations took place in Damascus and in Baghdad and the Iraqi Foreign Minister expressed his Government's concern over the execution – A. Clark Kerr (Baghdad) to A. Eden, Cable of 29.11.1937, FO 141/676, 269 A/37; *Al-Ayyam* (Damascus), 28.11.1937; one of the heads of the Azhar, Sheikh Abd al-Rahman al-Sa'idi, cabled to the British Ambassador in Cairo: 'Today you executed in Palestine Sheikh Farhan al-Sa'di. We all of us are Farhan al-Sa'di' – see his cable of 30.11.1937, FO *ibid*.
192. Among those arrested were two Arab Government officials who had given financial support to the band in the North – (CID) 'Terrorism 1936–1937', HA, 41/14.
193. Various reports about the situation in the Arab camp, CZA S 25/3540; HC to Colonial Secretary, Secret despatches of December 1938 and early 1939, CO

733/398/75156/Part L.II. Interviews with Jamal Qasim Abd al Hadi, Jenin, 26.7.1978; Shawqi Abd al-Hadi, 1.8.1978, 7.8.1978 and Hafiz al-Hamdallah (ex-Peace Band Commander), Anabta, 1.8.1978.
194. Arab Bureau News, August 1937, CZA S 25/10097; News from Nablus, 25.7.1938, *ibid.*, 10098; Reuven (Zaslani) to Moshe (Shertok), 28.12.1938, *ibid.*, 3540. On the events in Jaffa, 3.10.1938, *ibid.*, 10098.
195. Report on Abu Ibrahim al-Kabir, T/A 72, 2.12.1938, HA, IS 8/2.
196. Yasin, pp. 73, 140; STH, II, Part 2, p. 769, 866–9; Arnon, p. 55.
197. Report on Abu Ibrahim al-Kabir, 2.12.1938; Report of 17.11.1938, T/A 69, HA, *ibid.*
198. He particularly harassed the Druze villages on Mount Carmel, Isfiyyah and Daliyat al-Karmil. On 27.11.1938 his band attacked Isfiyyah, beat up and held captive the village notables and desecrated the Holy Books of the Druze. A British army unit which hurried to the scene made contact with the band and killed several dozen terrorists, but Abu Durrah himself managed to escape – translation of letter from the Carmel Druze to Sultan al-Atrash, Amir Majid Arslan and As'ad Kanj, 4.12.1938, HA, A. Hoshi Files 8b/5; 'The Internal Arab Terror', 7.12.1938, *ibid.*, A. Hoshi Files 8b/6; The MAPAI Central Committee Newsletter, 'Latest Events in Palestine', No. 17, 12.12.1938, CZA, S 25/46.
199. (Ezra Danin et al.), *Te'udot u-Demyyot: mi-ginzey ha-kenufiyot ha-'arviyot bi-meora'ot 1936–1939* (Documents and Portraits, from the Arab Bands' Archives in the 1936–1939 Disturbances; Tel Aviv, 1944), pp. 148, 160, note 300 (infra: *Te'udot*); Yasin, *Harb al-'isabat*, pp. 95–6; Arnon, p. 68.
200. For details of the sub-bands and their strength, see translation of document found on Abu Durrah when captured on 24.7.1939 – Monthly Report of the Administration of the Transjordan Deserts, July 1939, FO 371/23296; Report of 17.11.1938, T/A 69, HA, IS 8/2.
201. *Te'udot*, p. 156; STH, II, part 2, p. 765.
202. *Te'udot*, pp. 48, 69; STH, *ibid.*; Yasin, *Harb al-'isabat*, p. 87.
203. Report of 17.11.1938, T/A 69, HA, IS 8/2; Survey for the period 24–30.11.1938, Secret, HA. At least a dozen Arabah villagers were murdered in Haifa by members of the 'Black Hand' organisation, during the campaign of terror directed against the Abd al-Hadis and rural families affiliated with them – Interviews with Shawqi Abd al-Hadi, Arabah, 1.8.1978, and with Hafiz Hamdallah, Anabtah, 1.8.1978, 7.8.1978.
204. al-Nimr, p. 215.
205. Letter to Moshe (Shertok), Haifa, 7.11.38, T/A 62, HA, IS 8/2; 'Terror', Haifa, 1.3.1939, T/A 129, *ibid.*
206. *Te'udot*, p. 148; STH, II, part 2, p. 778. A short time after his flight he was captured and executed.
207. Sheikh Radi al-Hanbali, Biographical Card, IS files, the Truman Research Institute, Hebrew University, Jerusalem. A copy of the constitution of the association can be found in CZA S 25/9350.
208. 'The Correspondent Reports: a new Club (Society) founded in Haifa', 27.10.1942; 'The Correspondent Reports', T/B 860, 13.11.1942; 'The Ansar al-Fadila Club in Haifa', T/B 432, 24.4.1942, *ibid.* In 1946, *Nadi ansar al-fadila* joined the Haifa branch of the Moslem Brethren movement which began operating in Palestine the same year – Ishaq Musa Husaini, *The Moslem Brethren* (Beirut, 1956), p. 80. My thanks to Mr A. Bar'am who drew my attention to this source.
209. 'Political Report' (by Lot), T/B 699, 7.9.1942, HA, *ibid.*
210. IS files, Truman Research Institute, Hebrew University, Jerusalem.
211. 'Activities of the Qassamites', T/B 544, 30.6.1942; T/B 558, July 1942, HA, *ibid.*; Sheikh Radi al-Hanbali, Biographical Card, IS files (Note 207).
212. 'The November Events', 20.1.1936, CZA, S 25/4224.
213. In discussing the lessons of the 1936–39 revolt, *al-Fatah* emphasises the destructive

effects of the internal terror: 'The pioneers of the revolutions should always hold fast the main road to the revolution, for the policy of assassinations which prevailed was a double-edged sword which played a negative role in the revolution and made of it a gang and brought about the destruction of its foundations' – *al-Fatah*, 'Study of the History of the Palestinian Revolution from the British Occupation', brochure from the series *Dirasat wa-tajarib thawriyya* ('Revolutionary studies and experiments'), undated, p. 63. Quoted also in Y. Harkabi, 'Trends in the attitude of radical Arab circles towards the history of the struggle in Palestine', in *Hartsa'ot be-kinsey ha-'iyun be-historiyah* (Lectures given at history seminars; the Israel Historical Society, Jerusalem, 1973), p. 321.

214. *al-Fatah*, 'Study of the Revolution', p. 54 (Harkabi, p. 320); see also *al-Fatah*, '*Aduw(un) qawiyy(un) wa-lakinahu laysa usturiy(an)* ('A Strong but not a Legendary Enemy'), from the series *Dirasat wa-tajarib thawriyah*, undated, p. 51; one of the names suggested for the military branch of al-Fatah when it was first established was '*al-Qassamiyyun*' – *Filastin al-thawra*, No. 67, 21.11.1973.
215. *al-Fatah*, 'Study of the Revolution', p. 52 (Harkabi, *ibid.*); *al-Fatah*, 'A strong Enemy', p. 52; *Filastin al-thawra*, No. 67, 21.11.1973; No. 74, 9.1.1974; No. 91, 5.5.1974. Kanafani, p. 62; 'Alush, p. 118.
216. Leila Khaled, *My People Shall Live* (Toronto, 1975), p. 23.

The Military Force of Islam
The Society of the Muslim Brethren and the Palestine Question, 1945–48

Thomas Mayer

The fascinating phenomenon of the Society of the Muslim Brethren (jam'iyat al-ikhwan al-muslimin) – the fundamentalist movement which was believed to have attracted millions of followers to its radical religious vision – has been carefully examined. Observers and scholars who have analysed the Society have paid special attention to its structure and, even more, to its ideology.[1]

The Society's success has been attributed to its ability to appeal, through the spell of Islam, to a growing number of believers who had abandoned all hope that current secular regimes would or could improve social and economic conditions. Equipped with a detailed programme for replacing existing secular constitutions by a radical Islamic doctrine which had been shaped according to the strict laws of the Shari'a (as explained and supervised by its religious divines), the Society reflected a grass-roots wish for 'the return of Islam' – the return of a period when Islam had been the major factor in the politics of the Orient.[2] In this respect the Society has been portrayed as one of the finest examples of the militant power of Islam.

Less attention has been paid to the Society's actual ability to carry out its programme, and to the real spectrum of its militancy. The Society's attitude regarding the Palestinian issue may illustrate the patterns and scope of this militancy, because it was over Palestine that the Society vowed time and again to fulfil its religious duty through military means. The Ikhwan regarded Palestine as an Arab and Islamic country, and the Jews – all of them taken to be Zionists – as enemies of Islam and pawns of Imperialism. To defeat these enemies and defend Palestinian Arab rights, the Society called for a Holy War (jihad) in Palestine.[3]

A. EARLY ACTIVITIES: THE IKHWAN AND THE PALESTINE QUESTION, 1936–39

Signs of the Society's special interest in, and sympathy for, the Palestinian Arab struggle were very evident even before the Second World War. With the eruption of the Arab revolt in Palestine in 1936, the Society formed special bodies to conduct the propaganda campaign for the Palestinian Arabs. A General Central Committee for the Aid of Palestine (al-lajna al-markaziya al-amma li-musa'adat filastin), headed by Hasan al-Banna, the Society's General Guide, issued protests against Britain's Palestinian policy, and sent emissaries throughout Egypt to advocate the Palestinian Arab cause.[4] Alongside this Committee, the Society formed another comprising student members of the Society who were responsible for advertising the Palestinian Arab cause within the universities.[5] Besides publishing numerous petitions for the Palestinian Arabs, these bodies also organised a fund-raising campaign and initiated several demonstrations in Egypt in support of the Palestinian Arabs.[6]

The Society also participated in the Young Men's Muslim Association's initiative which created the Supreme Committee of Relief for the Palestinian Casualties (al-lajna al-'ulya li-i'ana li-mankubi filastin).[7] The Society's representatives took part in the special sessions and fund-raising campaign for the Arab cause in Palestine which this Committee held.

In addition, the Society attempted to encourage active Egyptian involvement in Palestinian affairs. It praised politicians such as Ali Mahir and Abd al-Rahman Azzam, who represented Egypt at the 1939 London Conference which had been convened to discuss the Palestine conflict.[8] In contrast with this support the Society sharply criticised Muhammad Mahmud's Government (1938–39) for failing to fulfil the jihad obligation dictated by the Muslim-Arab struggle in Palestine, and pressed this Government to denounce the White Paper on Palestine (1939).[9]

However, the Society's own efforts to fulfil the jihad were remarkably ineffectual. It was accused, for example, of failing to transfer to the Palestinian Arabs all the money collected during its fund-raising campaigns.[10] Moreover, only a few volunteers belonging to the Society were reported to have taken part in armed raids against Jewish life and property during the Arab Revolt in Palestine.[11]

This should not be surprising since it was during this period (1936–39) that the Society's structure and ideology were actually determined. Other priorities dominated the Society's life, and its full participation in the jihad had to be postponed. When the Arab Revolt broke out in Palestine, the Society was still a small and insignificant religious group in Egypt. In May 1936, the number of its members was estimated at only 800.[12] Part of the money collected for the Palestinian Arabs might have therefore been used to assist the Society's growth. Although it grew quickly, and soon surpassed its biggest rival, the YMMA,[13] the Ikhwan suffered from internal splits and desertions. These difficulties were caused by frictions over the Society's ideological priorities and the fulfilment of its theoretical schemes.[14] Consequently, the Society failed to impress outside observers as late as September 1938. Hamdi Bey Mahbub, Egypt's Director General of Public Security at the time, belittled it as a society of 'limited influence', advocating 'sporadic ideas, that can cause no harm'.[15] Moreover, while a few Islamic tenets had already been advocated through special Calls (Rasa'il), a complete ideological doctrine, which revered Islam as a total and perfect way of life, was first adopted only in January 1939, during the Society's Fifth General Conference.[16] Only afterwards, in April 1939, did Britain's Ambassador to Egypt, Miles Lampson, first report that the Society was gaining popularity 'among both students and the people'.[17]

However, by this time the Arab Revolt in Palestine was already in its last death throes after being crushed by British troops. The Second World War prevented any further possibility of intervention in Palestinian affairs or exerting pressure over this issue. Consequently, the sacred mission of the jihad in Palestine remained unaccomplished; it had to wait for its execution until after the War.

B. THE ORGANISATION OF THE MUSLIM BRETHREN IN PALESTINE, 1945–48

The War did not affect the Ikhwan. Although the Society's leaders, al-Banna and his deputy Ahmad al-Sukkari, were imprisoned during the War for their anti-British pronouncements, they were not halted for long. Internal political considerations convinced various Egyptian Premiers to seek the Society's co-operation. Safe from Government persecution the Society grew very quickly. The flouting of Egyptian independence by British troops (the February 1942 incident), the influx of pleasure-seeking Allied troops to the big cities, British assistance to corrupt and inefficient regimes, and an impotent party system which failed to respond to Egypt's growing social and economic needs, encouraged the growth of the Society during the War.[18] By the end of 1945 the number of the Ikhwan was already estimated at between 100,000 and 500,000 members in more than 1,000 branches.[19] During the next two years these figures were believed to have doubled and even trebled.[20]

In light of this formidable growth combined with an uncompromising doctrine one would expect to find a serious upsurge in the Society's efforts to carry out its promised jihad in Palestine. But did such an upsurge really occur?

From the middle of 1944 several observers reported the Society's intentions to open branches and launch propaganda activities in Palestine.[21] However, it took the Society more than a year from that time to establish its first branch in Palestine. In September 1945, the General Assembly of the Society consented to authorise its Administrative Executive to send emissaries to Arab and Islamic countries 'in order to harmonise the collective work among the Arab and Islamic nations'.[22] Shortly afterwards the Society started its successful penetration into Palestine. During October 1945 special emissaries travelled through Arab towns in Palestine attempting to persuade people to form local branches of the Ikhwan.[23] According to one report, the Society's mediation ended a local dispute between Arab families of Jerusalem and Hebron. Subsequently, a senior official of the Society, Said Ramadan, arrived in

Palestine. On 26 October 1945, Ramadan opened in Jerusalem the first of the Ikhwan branches in Palestine.[24]

The Jerusalem branch did not remain alone for long. With the help and supervision of other emissaries from the Cairo centre of the Society, more branches were formed throughout the country.[25] The Society's reputation as a defender of Arab and Muslim interests attracted even local politicians to join it,[26] and it grew rather quickly. By 1947, there were already some 25 branches in Palestine, with a total membership estimated at between 12,000 and 20,000 active members.[27] Though these figures may have been somewhat exaggerated, they may indicate the direction of the Society's main efforts. In none of the other neighbouring Arab countries, such as Jordan or even the Sudan, did the Ikhwan succeed in building a system similar to the one created in Palestine.[28]

Theoretically, the local branches were subject to the control of the Cairo Centre of the Society. The local members had to swear an oath of allegiance to the General Guide,[29] and the first article of the branches' Code of Basic Regulations (al-qanun al-asasi) further confirmed their subordination to their Cairo Centre.[30]

Under the Centre's initiative, the deported Mufti, Hajj Amin al-Husayni, was nominated as the local leader of the Ikhwan in Palestine. Moreover, he was declared al-Banna's official representative and personal supervisor of the Society's activities in Palestine.[31] However, this nomination was largely a matter of propaganda because the Mufti, far from going to Palestine, never ventured out of his haven in Egypt.

It is, therefore, not surprising that no tension or differences of opinion occurred between the 'local' leader of the Palestinian Ikhwan and the Cairo Centre. In fact, both sides appeared to be rather satisfied with this arrangement. The Society's use of the Mufti's name undoubtedly helped its growth in Palestine. Through the network of the Mufti's followers, and with its emissaries' skills, the Society managed to form branches throughout Palestine. Neither did the Mufti suffer, since the Ikhwan helped to preserve his prestige in Palestine. By virtue of his nomination as the Society's local leader in Palestine, the Mufti continued to be recognised as the national leader by most of the Palestinian Arab population, including traditional opposition centres which now had Ikhwan branches.

The centre's main control over its local branches was established through its administrative apparatus. An Administrative Bureau (maktab idari) of 21 local representatives, selected by their local branches, was formed to monitor the daily activities. This Bureau was, in turn, subjected to the supervision of a Central Committee (al-hay'a al-markaziya li-l-maktab al-idari, or hay'at al-maktab al-idari). Ten out of the 17 committee members were appointed by the local branches (two each from Jerusalem, Jaffa, Haifa, Nablus and Gaza), and the rest by the Society's centre.[32] Theoretically, however, the centre's ability to dismiss or appoint these committee members was even greater than it appeared, because all members had to take the special oath of allegiance to the General Guide in Cairo. Al-Banna could, therefore, impose his will on the local committee at any time and over any issue. Furthermore, the centre's control over its Palestinian branches might also have been strengthened by the frequent visits of Palestinian Ikhwan to Cairo and by the almost constant presence of the centre's emissaries in the local branches. These emissaries organised and supervised the branches' general sessions, mediated in cases of dispute, and initiated future working agendas.[33]

However, all these efforts, which might have encouraged the branches' dependence on the Cairo centre, did little to promote the Society's vow to wage a Holy War in Palestine. Indeed, the Ikhwan attempted to emphasise the importance of Palestine by convening in Haifa a regional conference of the Society's branches in Syria, Lebanon, and Palestine.[34] From time to time the Palestinian branches also published petitions calling for the rescue of Arab lands, a boycott of Zionist goods, or the liberation of the country from Jewish domination.[35]

Nevertheless, an analysis of the branches' various Codes of Basic Regulations would show that the local branches were concentrated on the moral rather than the physical deliverance of their country. The local branch undertook to deliver Palestine from its oppression and to safeguard the unity of the Arab and Islamic State (article 2 in the Basic Regulations of the Jerusalem branch).[36] But these tasks were overshadowed by other undertakings to spread and teach the values of the Quran; to endeavour to achieve higher standards of living; to fight against poverty and illiteracy; and to participate in the construction of human civilization according to the spirit of Islam (article 2). In order to accomplish all these goals, the Society intended to hold lectures, to publish books and to establish social, economic and scientific institutions such as mosques, schools, and clinics (articles 3–4). Moreover, to emphasize the Society's a-political nature, its members were forbidden to engage in any political activity or to join any political party (article 5). This restriction did not prevent verbal attacks on both the Zionists and the British since the Society idolised the struggle for Palestine's liberation as a sacred mission imposed on all Muslims. However, this restriction appears to have influenced the branches' insulation from daily politics. Loyal to their Code of Basic Regulations, the Palestinian Ikhwan encouraged religious education in schools, sent lecturers to the mosques, initiated educational programmes for illiterate people, envisaged plans for raising the standard of living of the Islamic family, and built open clinics for the poor.[37]

The many attempts of the Society's emissaries to promote the branches' military capabilities were unsuccessful and in this field the Society suffered its most remarkable failure. Under apparent instructions from their Cairo centre, special emissaries took great pains to form the local Rover Bands (al-jawwala), and train them in para-military exercises. They also endeavoured to establish mutual training of the Rovers with other Palestinian Arab youth organisations.[38] The long hours spent in forming and training these units reflected the centre's aspirations to turn these bands into trained military units. Further evidence of this desire may be found in the Society's appointment of Mahmud Labib, the Ikhwan's commander of the military section, to mediate in the dispute between the local youth organisations of the *Najjada* and *Futuwwa*. After the Mufti had asked the Ikhwan to appease both sides, the Society authorised Labib to prepare and carry out plans for the unification of the youth movement.[39] These efforts might have been the most important attempt to unify all the Palestinian Arab youth organisations, the realization of which could have resulted in the creation of a local, well-trained force, which might have become the nucleus of an organised Palestinian Arab army. However, the whole project collapsed with the deportation of Labib from Palestine by the mandatory power.[40]

Labib's deportation caused a severe setback to the proposed union of the youth organisations. The local chief of the *Futuwwa* was appointed, instead of Labib, as head of the united youth organisation. But the *Najjada*, fearing that this nomination would lead to the Husaynis' control of the Palestinian Arab youth movements, refused to co-operate with the new leader of the organisation.[41] The failure to unite the youth movements badly affected Arab capabilities in Palestine during the 1948 war. By then, the main Palestinian Arab reserve forces – the youth – remained unequipped, untrained, undisciplined, and undermotivated. The poor resistance of the local Arab community resulted partly from these defects. The rapid dissolution of the local Arab units at the first stage of the 1948 war was mainly due to their lack of capable and motivated human reserves.

The military clashes that broke out in many parts of Palestine after the UN decision to partition (29 November 1947) hampered further efforts to unite the local Rover Bands. A plan to convene a special meeting of representatives of all the local branches of the Ikhwan to announce the formation of union,[42] was postponed and eventually cancelled because of the disturbances. There seems to be no evidence of any separate activity of even one of the Society's branches in Palestine after January 1948.[43] National Committees (lijan wataniya) had been formed in almost every town in Palestine. Several of the Ikhwan's local branches joined the local National Committee,[44] while others stopped their activity. Members of the Society's branches in Palestine took part in clashes with the Jewish population, but not as separate or independent units. Some of them joined the Ikhwan's volunteers from Egypt,[45] but many others fled to neighbouring Arab countries. Once there a number of these refugees formed new branches of the Ikhwan or joined existing ones.[46]

That a Society which succeeded in recruiting to its ranks many thousands of members in less than two years was incapable of organising even one military unit for the liberation of Palestine may indicate a basic inefficiency on the part of the Cairo Centre in the control of its Palestinian branches. It is remarkable that the deportation of only one official – admittedly the Society's chief military commander – was enough to jeopardise the Society's plans.

C. THE IKHWAN AND THE HOLY WAR IN PALESTINE, 1945–48

One may, of course, explain the Society's failure to promote the Palestinian Arabs' military potential by external rather than internal reasons. It may be argued that the Ikhwan had, after all, worked in Palestine just for a short period, and, therefore, their administrative apparatus had not enough time to successfully contend with the rapidly changing developments there. Moreover, as Egypt was the Ikhwan's centre, and it was from Egypt that the Society derived its manpower and financial resources, it is in Egypt, rather than in Palestine, that one would expect to find the greatest evidence of the Society's military efforts for the Palestinian Arab cause.

In Egypt the Ikhwan participated in the new anti-Jewish campaign which was renewed even before the end of the Second World War. In November 1944, the Society's representatives took part in a joint meeting, initiated by Fuad Abaza, the President of the small Arab Union Club (nadi al-ittihad al-arabi), and agreed to lay down 'the Front of the Arab and Islamic Organisations in Egypt'.[47] This Front (jabha), which was initially formed to protest against pro-Zionist declarations made by the two major political parties in the United States, was followed by other similar ad-hoc committees. Thus, for example, the Ikhwan invited the Popular Councils (al-hay'at al-sha'biya) – another form of the Front – to support the Palestinian Arab demands by convening a special conference.[48] On 2 November 1945, the Front's representatives, members of the Ikhwan, YMMA, Young Egypt, and the Arab Union organised a mass demonstration against Jewish immigration and settlement in Palestine and Britain's policy there. In the course of the demonstration, al-Banna led a rally of 10,000 to 20,000 demonstrators from al-Azhar to Abdeen Square where he delivered another speech condemning the Zionists and their British supporters. During and following the demonstration riots erupted against the Jewish and Christian communities in Cairo and Alexandria. Jewish property was looted, synagogues and churches were pillaged and desecrated, and a number of Jews and Christians were murdered.[49] Although al-Banna sharply denounced these riots, and urged his followers not to participate in them,[50] he did not stop the agitation that stimulated such incidents. Shortly afterwards, the Popular Councils, in which the Ikhwan played a leading part, asked the public to boycott Jewish merchants and merchandise. A special Committee of Boycott, formed by these Councils, labelled all the Jews in Egypt as Zionists, and, therefore, included all of them in the boycott.[51]

Public declarations, manifestos, fund-raising campaigns, and demonstrations became the major forms of expression of the various Fronts.[52] Representatives of the Front, heads of the Arab and Muslim organisations in Egypt, testified before the Anglo-American Committee when it visited Cairo (1946). They warned the Committee against taking any decisions which would favour the creation of a Jewish State in Palestine. They stated that such a decision would be strongly rejected by the Arabs and the Muslims, who would fight against it.[53] Upon the publication of the Committee's Report, the Front's representatives reconvened and decided to form another 'joint committee which would take necessary steps towards the establishment of an independent Palestinian Arab State'. The resolution was followed by a denunciation of the 'pro-Zionist report' of the Committee which was attributed to the pro-Zionist policy of Britain and the United States.[54]

In December 1947 the Front appeared to have reached the peak of its influence. Members of the Front, together with the major political parties, organised the biggest rally in Cairo's history in support of the Palestinian Arabs. About 100,000 people marched through the streets, and listened to speakers who expressed their hope of seeing Palestine liberated by blood and given its independence.[55] In the numerous petitions that the Ikhwan initiated, this motive of a liberation of Palestine through bloodshed was repeated time and again.[56] Al-Banna was so confident of the Arabs' ability to execute this mission that in February 1948 he sent a telegram to the Secretary General of the UN, warning him to remain neutral in the conflict, and not to meddle in it.[57]

As it turned out, the actual preparations of the Ikhwan for this liberation were not so impressive. In October 1947, the first bureaus to recruit volunteers for the liberation of Palestine were opened together with a substantial increase in the propaganda campaign for the jihad. According to the local Egyptian Press, the recruiting offices registered more than 2,000 volunteers during the first two days of their activities.[58]

However, if such a flow of volunteers really did occur – and not all observers agreed that it did[59] – it did not last long. The Government refused to assist the recruiting movement, fearing that the Ikhwan were exploiting the Palestinian problem in order to officially obtain arms, ammunition, and military training that would be used, in due course, to overthrow the regime and to set up a new Islamic order.[60]

The Government's refusal both to legalize the volunteer movement and train its members, did not seem visibly to deter the Ikhwan. The Society formed 'scientific' missions, whose ostensible task was to carry out explorations in Sinai. Once these 'scientists' arrived in Sinai, they threw off their academic cover, crossed the Palestinian frontier, and joined the Arab bands which were fighting there.[61] Other volunteers arrived via sea routes at the official recruiting camp of the Arab League in Qatna, near Damascus. The Society's propaganda apparatus manipulated these efforts, building up the impression that there was in Egypt a huge potential of eager volunteers who were impatiently waiting to seize the opportunity of taking part in the Holy War in Palestine. In a telegram to the Arab League's Council in 'Aley (Lebanon), al-Banna offered to place 10,000 volunteers at the League's disposal as 'a first detachment which is prepared to move at first signal'.[62] Some time later, in March 1948, al-Banna already claimed to have 1,500 Ikhwan fighters inside Palestine.[63]

It appears, however, that for the Ikhwan words spoke louder than action. The infiltration of the Palestinian borders, so praised and advocated by the Society, was, in fact, insignificant. While there is no evidence of mass infiltration of the Palestinian borders by the Ikhwan,[64] there is some evidence of the disappointing recruitment of Egyptian volunteers for the jihad in Palestine. An official report of the Arab League reveals that by February 1948, only fifty Egyptians, not necessarily the Society's members, reached the training camp of Qatna.[65] A certain amount of arms was indeed smuggled into Palestine, but the Ikhwan were not the only group to engage in arms-smuggling, which turned out to be a profitable business rather than a manifestation of altruistic patriotism.[66] The quick collapse of the Palestinian resistance indicates that the smuggling of both volunteers and arms into Palestine was of no special military significance. What made these activities look so formidable was not their large scope, but the impressive publicity that was given to them by the Ikhwan.

The Ikhwan also dealt with several clandestine groups concerning ways to overcome the Government's blockade of the Palestinian border. We are told that Hasan al-Banna himself held talks with representatives of the 'Free Officers', discussing ways of supplying arms and smuggling ammunition to the Arab fighters in Palestine.[67] However, although a few 'free officers' volunteered to join the fighting, no specific co-operation resulted from these talks.

If this failure of the Ikhwan could be attributed to the interference of the Government, then the Society must have been far weaker than claimed. Although its leaders overstated their ability to cause the downfall of any Cabinet,[68] the Society was not able to pose 'the most immediate threat to the establishment'.[69] If, on the other hand, the Government was not responsible for the Society's unimpressive military support of the Palestinian Arabs, then it must be concluded that the Ikhwan's actual ability to organise volunteering units was rather poor, and that the administrative apparatus built for this purpose was fairly inefficient.

This inefficiency, or weakness, which may explain the Society's failure to support the Palestinian Arab military efforts, may also explain the Society's unimpressive participation in the war. By March 1948, the

Egyptian Government reversed its decision, and announced its willingness to train volunteers and arm them for the Holy War in Palestine.[70] One may assume that by this decision the regime found a way to fulfil its moral obligation to the Palestinian Arabs, while at the same time assuaging the internal pressure in Egypt to train the volunteers. The huge arsenal of arms discovered in the Muqattam mountains in January 1948, after a small clash between the local police force and a Society's unit,[71] was perhaps sufficient warning of the form this recruitment of volunteers would take, should the Government fail to control it.

The Government opened two training camps for the volunteers. The first was at Hakstap, near the Suez Canal, and the second, which was smaller, was in Marsa Matruh, near the Libyan border.[72] Egyptian officers were appointed to supervise the camps and the military training, and they were assisted by the Ikhwan's chief military commander, Mahmud Labib.

Labib told a reporter that the Ikhwan had succeeded in recruiting 2,000 volunteers,[73] far less than al-Banna's promised 10,000. It is likely that even this number was exaggerated. The irregular volunteer forces from the various societies were combined into three battalions. The total number of this force, at its height, was estimated at 3,000.[74] From the Ikhwan's own sources it is clear that most of their volunteers joined the first battalion, the biggest one. Colonel Abd al-Aziz, a regular army officer, was appointed by the Egyptian War Minister to command this battalion, and was given the title of 'General Commander of the Volunteer Forces on the Southern Front of Palestine'.[75] Abd al-Aziz's personal diary reveals that 804 recruits served under his command, and of them only 344 were Egyptian volunteers; the rest were regular Egyptian soldiers and volunteers from other Arab countries.[76] Considering that not all the Egyptian volunteers belonged to the Ikhwan, it appears that the claim that the Ikhwan 'made the major contribution and greatest sacrifice in the struggle against the Jews in Palestine',[77] can be taken lightly. Moreover, from Arab sources it appears that not all the Society's volunteers who expressed a desire to take an active part in the fighting ever really fought. Many of them returned to Egypt after brief sabre-rattling in Arab towns near the Palestine border.[78]

If the number of the Society's members really reached hundreds of thousands, and even millions, of followers, then the Society's active participation in the military activities in Palestine was extremely small. The valour of the relatively few Ikhwan who took part in the fighting could not make up for their small number. This low participation is remarkable in view of the claim that Palestine was used by the Ikhwan as a training ground for guerrilla tactics which they were supposed to utilise later against the Egyptian regime.[79] However, even if the figures of the Society's membership have been exaggerated – a significant fact that may lead to unrealistic assumptions about the Society's power in Egypt – it is still remarkable that such a radical religious Society which regarded the war in Palestine as a sacred jihad could not recruit more Holy Warriors for the defence of that Islamic cause.

In view of their failure to organise mass recruitment for the sacred jihad which they advocated, it is clear that to maintain their militant reputation the Ikhwan relied on propaganda rather than on action. However, one should not underestimate the power of this propaganda. In Egypt, the Society's propaganda for a military solution of the Palestine problem created an atmosphere in which war seemed the only logical and natural process. In fact the very act of war was illusory, portrayed as a victorious march to Tel-Aviv aimed at wiping out the Zionist terrorist gangs ('isabat al-irhab) – a term used to describe the Zionist resistance movement – for their alleged atrocities against the Palestinian Arab population.

The Government's failure to suppress this propaganda encouraged the military intervention. Premier Nuqrashi's reluctance to involve the Egyptian army in a war with the Zionist State[80] was neutralised by his concession to open the training camps for the volunteers. By legalising the volunteer movement, and by providing military training and equipment to its members, the Government committed itself to a military solution of the Palestine problem. Once the Ikhwan were allowed to mix with regular soldiers, these soldiers were inevitably exposed to the Society's radical ideology. In fact, those soldiers who were camped near the Palestinian border had already been infected by the illusion of a quick victory, and revealed a keen desire to take part in the war.[81]

Significantly, this illusion also affected the Government's decision to invade Palestine. Had King Faruq respected the Zionist resistance, he might have been less concerned about Abdullah's aspirations, and consequently might not have ordered the army's invasion of Palestine. However, this was not the case. During the Senate's secret session (11 May 1948) which discussed the Government's decision to enter the war, one finds only the lone voice of Ismail Sidqi, Egypt's former Prime Minister, raised in opposition to the military intervention. It was Nuqrashi who stirred the Senate into believing that the war would be a relatively easy task which the Army, eager and ready, would successfully accomplish. The Senate, indeed, unanimously approved the Premier's decision and hailed it.[82]

It is therefore in the field of creating an atmosphere, preparing the groundwork, and stimulating public awareness, that the Ikhwan's contribution to the 1948 war lay. Once the Government adopted the volunteer movement, the prospects of a military intervention increased. Once regular Egyptian officers trained, equipped and commanded the volunteer units, the direct political and legal responsibility for their actions rested with the Egyptian Government. Egypt, therefore, bore the full responsibility for the military actions of the irregular forces. These operations started as early as April 1948 with two frontal attacks on a

Jewish settlement, Kfar Darom.[83] The invasion of Palestine by the Egyptian Army on 15 May 1948 was, in this respect, an escalation of a military intervention that already existed.

Thus, although the Ikhwan were never able to fulfil the duty of the jihad alone, the Society succeeded in drawing Egypt into a full scale military initiative in Palestine. By so doing it succeeded in realising its long propaganda campaign for a Holy War in Palestine.

NOTES

1. For some of the thorough studies on the Society, see: R. P. Mitchell, *The Society of the Muslim Brothers* (London, 1969); Ishak Musa al-Husaini, *The Muslim Brothers* (Beirut, 1956); Christina H. Harris, *Nationalism and Revolution in Egypt: the Role of the Muslim Brotherhood* (The Hague, 1964); J. Heyworth-Dunne, *Religious and Political Trends in Modern Egypt* (Washington 1950).
2. Bernard Lewis, 'The Return of Islam', *Commentary*, January 1976, pp. 39–49.
3. *Jaridat al-ikhwan al-muslimin*, 9, 16 June 1936, pp. 17–19 (218–216) 14–17 (227–231); *J.I.M.*, 5 Nov. 1937; *al-Nadhir*, 2 Sha'ban, 1357 (1938), 12 Jamadi al-Than, 1357, pp. 21–24; Mitchell, pp. 227–230; Muhammad Habib Ahmad, *Nahdat al-shu'ub al-islamiya* (Cairo, 1952/3), pp. 103–112; Anwar al-Jundi al-Banna, *Kifah al-dhabihayn filastin wa al-maghrib* (Rasa'il tarikh al-fikra al-islamiya, al-kitab al-thani, June 1946).
4. *J.I.M.*, 26 May 1936, p. 15 (148); 19 May 1936, pp. 19–20 (129–130); Hasan al-Banna, *Mudhakkirat al-da'wa wa al-da'iyya* (Cairo, n.d.), pp. 223–227; *al-Fath*, 13 Safar, 1357, p. 8 (1140); 8 Ramadan, 1358, pp. 21–22 (625–626); M. Lampson (Cairo) to Viscount Halifax (London) 19 Dec. 1938, FO 371/23219/E30.
5. *J.I.M.*, 26 May 1936, p. 15 (148); al-Banna, *Mudhakkirat*, p. 227; Lampson (Cairo) to London, 17 May 1938, FO 371/21877/E3172; Same to same, 8 June 1938, FO 371/21877/E3389; Bateman, Consul General (Alexandria) to London, 19 Dec. 1938, FO 371/21881/E5898.
6. Lampson (Cairo) to Wauchope, High Commissioner (Jerusalem), 3 July 1936, FO 371/20035/E4415, *J.I.M.*, 30 June 1936, p. 21 (286); *Al-Nudhir*, 12 Jamadi al-thani, 1357, pp. 21–24 (267–270); 12 Rabi'a al-thani, 1357.
7. *J.I.M.*, 2 June 1936, p. 17 (183); *al-Fath*, 14 Rabi'a al-Awal, 1355, pp. 5–6 (1193–94); *al-Nadhir*, 8 al-Muharram, 1358, p. 25; 15 al-Muharram, 1358, p. 15.
8. Al-Banna, *Mudhakkirat*, pp. 286–287; Heyworth-Dunne, pp. 23, 26–27; Harris, pp. 177–179.
9. *Al-Nadhir*, 10 Rabi'a al-thani, 1358, pp. 14–15.
10. Min mudhakkirat ahad al-ikhwan, *al-ikhwan al-muslimin, madihum wa hadiruhum* (n.p., n.d. [1954?]), p. 14; Heyworth-Dunne, pp. 22.
11. N. Lorch, *Korot Milhemet ha'Atzmaut* (Tel-Aviv, 1973), p. 238; Abd al-Hamid Fathi, *Qadiyat al-imam al-shahid Hasan al-Banna* (Cairo, n.d.), pt. I, p. 40; Kamil Isma'il al-Sharif, *al-Ikhwan al-muslimun fi harb filastin* (Cairo, n.d.), 2nd ed., Vol. I, p. 51.
12. Public Security Department's Note (Cairo), 18 May 1936, FO 141/536/403/12/36; A copy of this Note was enclosed in Lampson's Report to A. Eden (London), 28 May 1936, FO 371/19980/E3153.
13. Israel Gershoni, 'Religion and Nationalism in the Teachings of the Salafi Movements of Egypt', *Hamizrah he Hadash* (The New East) Vol. XXVI, 1976, Nos. 3–4 (103–104), p. 190, n. 35.
14. Al-Banna, *Mudhakkirat*, pp. 286–287; Heyworth-Dunne, p. 23; Note on the 'el-

Ikhwan el-muslimin', Enc. 'D', in FO 371/53251/J1324/24/16.
15. Bateman (Alexandria) to Halifax (London), 26 Sep. 1939, FO 371/21881/E5898.
16. Mitchell, p. 15.
17. Lampson (Cairo) to London, 1 April 1939, FO 371/23232/E2444. This growth was also demonstrated by an increase of the Society's branches in Egypt. In March 1948, Ahmad Sukkari, the Ikhwan ex-vice president, told an American writer, John Roy Carlson (Avedis Arthur Derounian), that by 1939 the Ikhwan already had 400 branches in Egypt. See, Carlson's Report, pp. 22–23 in Enc. No. 1 of S. Pinkney Tuck, American Ambassador (Cairo) to the Secretary of State (Washington, DC), 29 March, 1948, Recorded Group 59,883.00/3–2948.
18. For the socio-economic developments in Egypt during the War which encouraged the growth of the Ikhwan, see: H. A. R. Gibb's Report, 'The Political Forces in Egypt', 25 Feb. 1943 (Foreign Research and Press Service), FO 371/35530/J1407; Dr. J. Heyworth-Dunne's Report on Islamic organisations in Egypt, received in FO 18 Nov. 1943, FO 371/35539/J4741; Walter Smart's report (Cairo), 1 Nov. 1945, FO 371/45928/J3955; Ahmad al-Dasuqi, *Misr fi al-Harb al-'Alamiyya al-Thaniya, 1939–1945* (Cairo, 1976), pp. 183–266; Charles Issawi, *Egypt, at Mid-Century* (London, 1954), pp. 59–63, 141–143; Nadav Safran, *Egypt in search of Political Community* (London, 1961), pp. 180–205.
19. Abd al-Latif al-Baghdadi, *Mudhakkirat* (Cairo, 1977), pp. 13–14, estimated the number of the Ikhwan at the beginning of the 1940s as a quarter of a million members. A 'Security Summary', Middle East, no. 103, 10 Dec. 1942 (FO 371/35578/J245), could not ascertain absolute figures in its reconsideration of the Society. While British sources estimated that the Society comprised 100,000–200,000 members, a 'senior Egyptian Police official' put the estimate as high as 500,000. This confusion continued later: in April 1944, J. E. Jacobs, Chargé d'Affaires (American Legation, Cairo), reported to his Secretary of State that the admitted number of the Ikhwan members had reached 75,000, with branches in every Egyptian town (RG 59, 883.43/3). However, this moderate assessment differs significantly from other suggestions of the time. Sukkari, for example, claimed during his interview with Carlson (Carlson's Report, p. 23, *ibid.*), that the Society's membership grew up to half a million in 2,500 branches during the Wafdist regime (1942–44). Walter Smart, Oriental Secretary (British Embassy, Cairo), confirmed this figure in a report sent to London on 1 Nov. 1945 (FO 371/45928/J3955). The suggestion cited here was made by J. W. Robertson, Civil Secretary (Khartum) to all Governors (Sudan), 20 Feb. 1946, Enc. 'D', FO 371/53251/J1324. This suggestion seems to sum up the various assessments concerning the Ikhwan's number at the time.
20. In March 1948 al-Banna told Carlson that the Ikhwan had 1,500 centres in all Egypt and their membership reached nearly half a million (Carlson's Report, p. 32, *ibid*). However, the Ikhwan had never taken the trouble of establishing this 'moderate' figure, but tended instead to amplify bigger numbers. Thus, for example, basing himself on Ikhwan sources, Husaini, p. 18, tells us that in 1946 the Ikhwan had 500,000 members organised in between 1,700 and 2,000 branches. Tuck reported, on 24 Oct. 1947, an Ikhwan claim to possess a million adherents (RG 59, 867N.01/10–2447). With such a distortion of numbers, one should not be surprised to see higher figures mentioned. Harris, p. 159, and Tom Little, *Modern Egypt* (London, 1967), p. 103, speak about 2 million members organised into about 2,000 branches during late 1947 and early 1948. Bat Yeor, *Yehudei Mizraim* (Tel-Aviv, 1974), p. 112, even speaks about a movement of 2.5 million members in 1946/7.
21. Jacobs, American Legation (Cairo), to the Secretary of State (Washington, DC), Apr. 29, 1944, RG 59,883.43/3; Lord Kilearn [M. Lampson] (Cairo), to London, 8 Aug. 1944, FO 371/40137/E5287.
22. J. Bowker, British Embassy (Cairo) to E. Bevin (London), 3 Oct. 1945, FO 371/45926/J3402.

THE MILITARY FORCE OF ISLAM 113

23. See, for example, a 'Shay' (Sherut Yediot – Intelligence Service) Report on Qadri Hafiz Tuqan from Nablus, October 1945, *The Shay Archives* (Jerusalem), Set B, File No. 3. The Society's activity in Palestine in October 1945 was not, however, a new phenomenon. As early as August 1945 prominent members of the Cairo centre of the Society were already touring the country in an attempt to attract adherents to the Society's Calls. See: Jerusalem Secretariat (Government of Palestine) to the Chancery, British Embassy (Cairo), 20 Aug. 1945, FO 141/1011/32/204/45.

24. American Consulate's Report (Jerusalem), p. 2, File 02978 (Temp. number), Division 65, *Israel State Archives*. This report was apparently an internal Consulate report which helped Robert B. Macatee, American Consul General (Jerusalem) to send his own report on the Ikhwan in Palestine, on 18 March 1947, to the Secretary of State (Washington, DC), RG 59, 890B.00/3-1847. Macatee's report, though shorter and different in several details, is identical in its content to the Consulate's report. For the opening of the Jerusalem branch, see also: *al-Difa'* (Jaffa), 31 Oct. 1945; Husaini's version, *op. cit.*, p. 80, that the Jerusalem branch was opened only in May 1946 is, however, not wholly wrong. At that time the branch, which, of course, already existed, celebrated the inauguration of its club in a big ceremony. See: *al-Difa'*, 3, 6-7 May 1946.

25. See, for example, *al-Difa'*, 9, 11, 18, 19, 24, 30 Dec., 1945; *Sirat al-Mustaqim* (Jaffa), 20 Dec., 1945; *Filastin* (Jaffa), 17 Dec. 1945, for the various meetings and discussions that Ramadan held with different Palestinian Arab personalities in order to form Ikhwan branches in Jaffa, Haifa, Nablus, Be'er-Sheba, Ramla, Lud and Jericho.

26. Among the more distinguished members were Jamal al-Husayni (Jerusalem), Muhammad Ali al-Ja'bri (Hebron), Nimr al-Hatib (Haifa) and Zafir al-Dajani (Jaffa). See, for example, *al-Difa'*, 7 May 1946. An indication of the Society's increasing popularity may be seen by the British administration's regulations which forbade Arab clerks to join the Ikhwan. See: *al-Wahda*, (Jerusalem), 17 Dec. 1946; *Al-Difa'*, 17 Jan. 1947.

27. The first figure is Macatee's assessment from 18 March 1947, RG 59 890B.00/3-1847. The second is the estimation of the Consulate's report, *op. cit.*, pp. 4-5. The main branches were in Jerusalem, Haifa, Jaffa, Nablus, Jenin and Gaza.

28. In spite of Abdullah's sympathy with the Society, which he regarded as a benevolent religious movement attracting the youth and blocking the spread of communism, it remained a small and insignificant organisation. By May 1947 Samir Pasha, Abdullah's Prime Minister, estimated their number in Transjordan to be about six hundred. See A. Kirkbride (Amman) to E. Bevin (London), 20 May 1947, FO 371/62231/E4677. The Ikhwan activities in Sudan were controlled by British officials (See Robertson to all Governors, 20 Feb. 1946, FO 371/53251/J1324), and consequently the Society failed to build up in Sudan the same structure as in Palestine.

29. *Al-Difa'*, 31 Dec. 1945; the American Consulate's report, pp. 4-5.

30. *Al-Qanun al-Asasi li jamyat al-Ikhwan al-muslimin fi filastin* (Jerusalem, 1365/1946), p. 2.

31. The American Consulate's Report, *op. cit.*, pp. 4-5.

32. *Al-Wahda*, 29 Dec., 1946; *al-Difa'*, Filastin, 19 Jan. 1947. It is noteworthy that according to the American Consulate's Report, *op. cit.*, p. 3, the branches' dependency on the Cairo centre was even greater. According to this report the Committee was composed of 13 members, seven of whom were nominated by the Cairo centre.

33. *Al-Difa'*, 9, 14, 18-19, 21, 23, 30 Dec. 1946; 7 Aug. 1946; 16 May 1946 *Filastin*, 27 Dec. 1945; 4 Jan. 1946; 12, 20, 21, 25, 26 Dec. 1946; *al-Wahda*, 1 Nov. 1946; *al-Sha'b* (Jaffa), 17, 23, 30-31 Dec. 1946.

34. *Filastin*, 2, 17-20 Oct. 1946; *al-Difa'*, 16-19 Oct. 1946. It should, however, be noted that the Conference, which was held on 18 Oct. 1946, did not necessarily indicate the

subordination of the Syrian and Lebanese branches to the Egyptian Ikhwan. According to a memorandum on 'Youth Movements in the Middle East' (Research Department, Foreign Office), 12 Feb. 1947, FO 371/61542/E2130, the Lebanese branch was controlled by the Syrian Society. The latter was formed by a local Shaikh, Mustafa al-Siba'i, as an independent body without any Egyptian assistance or influence.

35. *Al-Difa'*, 20 Oct. 1946; 18 Dec. 1946; 7 July 1947; *al-Sha'b*, 17 Dec. 1946; *al-Wahda*, 2 Oct. 1946; 17 Dec. 1946; 22 April 1947; *Filastin*, 3 Feb. 1947; *Middle East Opinion* (Cairo), No. 20, 21 Oct. 1946, p. 11.
36. *Al-Qanum al-asasi*, pp. 2–4.
37. *Filastin*, 12 Jan. 1946; *al-Sha'b*, 30 Dec. 1946; *al-Wahda*, 18 Oct. 1946; 15, 17, 22 Dec. 1946; 7 Jan. 1947; 15 Feb. 1947; *al-Difa'*, 2, 3 Feb. 1946; 24, 30 June 1947; 1 July 1947. For a collection of lectures and magazines that the Jerusalem branch published and distributed, see: File 01763 (temp. no.), (F/352), Division 65, *I.S.A.*.
38. *Al-Difa'*, 12 June 1946; *al-Sha'b*, 17 Dec. 1946; *al-Wahda*, 18 Nov. 1946; 17, 22 Dec. 1946; *al-Sirāt al-Mustaqim*, 6 July 1946; File 03180 (temp. no.), (F/393), Division 65, *I.S.A.*, includes a report from 17 Jan. 1947. on the founding of al-Jawwala band in Jerusalem; *Eshnav* (Tel-Aviv), No. 135, 22 July 1946, p. 5; No. 149, 14 Jan. 1947, p. 5.
39. Subhi Yasin, *Tariq al-'awda ila filastin* (Cairo, 1961), p. 15; Y. Sluzki (ed.), *Sefer Toldot ha Hagana* (Tel-Aviv, 1972), Vol. III, p. 1200; Sharif, Vol. I, pp. 55–56; *al-Difa'*, 14 July 1947; 6, 12, 14 Aug. 1947.
40. *Al-Difa'*, 21 Aug. 1947; Macatee (Jerusalem) to Washington, 15 Aug. 1947, RG 59,867N.00/8–1547; same to same, 29 Aug. 1947, RG 59,867N.00/8–2947; Tuck to Washington, 23 Sept. 1947, RG 59,883.00/9–2347; Muhammad Izzat Darwaza, *Hawl al-qaraka al-arabiya al-qawmiya* (Sidon, 1951), Vol. IV, p. 96.
41. Macatee to Washington, 2 Sept. 1947, RG 59,867N.00/9–247; Sluzki, Vol. III, p. 1200. For an account of these organisations and their rivalry, see: Memoranda on the Najada and Futuwa, prepared by Major A. S. Eban, Arab Intelligence Service, Jewish Agency (London), in G. L. Jones, Second Secretary of Embassy (London) to Washington, 21 Nov. 1946, RG 59,890B.00/11–2146; Memorandum on Youth Movements in the Middle East (FORD), 12 Feb. 1947, FO 371/61542/E2130. It should, however, be noted that the reports differ considerably in their assessments of the organisations' power in Palestine.
42. For this intention, see *al-Difa'*, 29–30 Oct. 1947.
43. For the persisting cancellation of the local activities, see, for example, *al-Difa'*, 11 Dec. 1947.
44. For the union of the Gaza branch in the National Committee, *al-Difa'*, 11 Dec. 1947. For the union of the Nablus branch with the National Committee, *al-Difa'*, 28 Dec. 1947. The Jaffa branch, on the other hand, continued to keep its independence as late as January 1948 (*al-Difa'*, 5 Jan. 1948). The different attitude of the local branches to the National Committees points to the disintegration of the branches' administrative control which the Cairo centre was so anxious to build.
45. Arif al-Arif, *al-Nakba* (Beirut, 1956), pp. 389–390; Sharif, Vol. II, pp. 69–72, 75–76, Vol. III–IV.
46. Among the more distinguished refugees were Taqi al-Din al-Nabhani (Haifa), Subhi Zayd al-Gaylani (Haifa), and Nimr al-Misri (Ramla), *The 'Shai' Files*, Sets A, B. For lists of other Palestinian Arab refugees who joined local Jordanian branches, see: Files 345–7, 764–4, Division 114–2 (Nablus); Files 407–5, 426–2, 451–28, Division 114–18 (Jerusalem), The Jordanian Intelligence Service's Archives, *I.S.A.*
47. Fuad Abaza to Lampson (Cairo), 20 Nov. 1944, FO 371/40138/E7793.
48. *Filastin*, 30 Sept. 1945.
49. Bowker (Cairo) to London, 2 Nov. 1945, FO 371/45394/E8348, E8354; same to same, 3 Nov. 1945, FO 371/45394/E8418; Kellar (MI5) to Scrivener (FO, London), 9

Nov. 1945, FO 371/45928/J4008; Lord Killearn (Cairo) to London, 18 Nov. 1945, attaching T. W. Fitzpatrick's report (Cairo City Police) to Sir Thomas Russel (Cairo), 11 Nov. 1945, FO 371/45928/J4078; Cecil B. Lyon, Chargé d'Affaires ad interim, American Legation (Cairo) to Washington, 2 Nov. 1945, RG 59,883.00/11-245; same to same, 3 Nov. 1945, RG 59, 883.00/11-345; same to same, 10 Nov. 1945, RG 59,883.00/11-1045; Hooker A. Doolittle, Consul-General (Alexandria), to Washington, 3 Nov. 1945, RG 59,883.00/11-345; same to same, 5, 8 Nov. RG 59,883.00/11-545, 11-845; The Zionist Office Report (London), 3 Nov. 1945, Z4/14620, *The Central Zionist Archives* (Jerusalem).
50. A day before the demonstration Hasan Rifa't told Smart that the Ikhwan were co-operating with him to limit the manifestations regarding Palestine (Smart's report, 1 Nov. 1945, FO 371/45928/J3955). For al-Banna's efforts to prevent the riots during the demonstration, see Kellar's report, 9 Nov. 1945, FO 371/45928/J4008.
51. *Al-Ahram*, 5-9 Nov. 1945. For the Ikhwan responsibility of the anti-Jewish propaganda before, during and after the demonstrations, see Lyon to Washington, 14 Nov. 1945, RG 59,883.00/11-1445; Office of Strategic Services' analysis, American Legation (Cairo) to Washington, 27 Feb. 1946, RG 59, 883.00.
52. Defence Security Office's report (Cairo), 4 June 1945, FO 371/45922/J2096; Bowker (Cairo) to London, 27 Oct. 1945, FO 371/45927/J3694; CO 733/463/75872/13; *al-Difa'*; 2-3 May 1946; Tuck (Cairo) to Washington, 5 Sept. 1946, RG 59,883.00/9-546; Office of Strategic Services' analysis (Cairo) to Washington, *ibid.*; Tuck to Washington, 13 Jan. 1948, RG 59,883.00/1-1348.
53. Among those who gave evidence before the Committee were Sayyid Ahmad Murad al-Bakri, the Bakaria Order's President, Hasan al-Banna for the Ikhwan, Muhammad Ali Zaki Pasha, the Vice-President of the YMMA, and Dr. Mansur Fahmi from the Cairo University, one of the main pan-Arab activists in Egypt. *Al-Ahram*, 6 March 1946; S25/6386, *C.Z.A.*.
54. *Al-Difa'*, 2, 3, 5, 6, 8, 12, 13, 15 May 1946.
55. For the chain demonstrations which culminated in such a huge demonstration, see: *al-Ahram, al-Difa'*, 5-16 Dec. 1947; Tuck (Cairo) to Washington, 4, 5, 15 Dec. 1947, RG 59,883.00/12-447, 12-547, 12-1547; Robert L. Buell, Consul-General (Alexandria), to Washington, 3 Dec. 1947, RG 59,883.00/12-347; Muhammad Nimr al-Hawari, *Sirr al-Nakba* (Nazaret, 1955), pp. 57-58.
56. See, for example, *al-Ikhwan al-muslimin*, 4 Oct. 5, 10 Dec. 1947 which have headlines such as 'the door to paradise lies through death for Palestine', and 'only red blood can wipe out the black shame of partition'; For similar expressions, see also: *al-Ahram*, 6 Aug. 1944; *al-Difa'*, 16 Dec. 1946; *al-Wahda*, 30 Jan. 1947.
57. *Al-Da'wa* (Cairo), 13 Feb. 1951.
58. *Sawt al-umma* (Cairo), 15 Oct. 1947; *al-Ikhwan al-muslimin* (Cairo), 18 Oct. 1947.
59. R. L. Speaight (Cairo) to the Secretariat (Jerusalem), 24 Oct. 1947, FO 141/1182/386/9/47, estimated that there was 'little sign of real enthusiasm for active service in Palestine among the mass of the Egyptian people'.
60. *Ibid.*; Tuck (Cairo) to Washington, 20 Dec. 1947, RG 59,890B.00/12-2047; same to same, 31 Jan. 1948, RG 59,883.00/1-3148; see also the evidence of Umar Bek, the Minister of the Interior and the Supreme Censor, during the trial of Nuqrashi's assassins, *al-Ahram*, 5 Sept. 1949.
61. Arif, p. 398; Sharif, Vol. II, pp. 73-74.
62. *Al-ikhwan al-muslimin*, 8 Oct. 1947; J. Bowker (Cairo) to London, 9 Oct. 1947; Sharif, Vol. II, p. 73; Arif, p. 398.
63. Carlson's report, p. 32, RG 59, 883.00/3-2948.
64. In fact, Sharif, Vol. II, pp. 73-79, even acknowledges the efficiency of the Government's efforts to block the Palestinian border.
65. Cited by Arif, p. 102. Also Subhi Yasin, *Harb al-'Isabat fi filastin* (Cairo, 1967), p. 166, confirms that only few Egyptians went to Qatna. A Memorandum by the

Arab Section of the Jewish Agency's Political Department (Jerusalem), 1 March, 1948, in G. Yogev (gen. ed.), *Political and Diplomatic Documents, Dec. 1947–May 1948* (Jerusalem, 1979), pp. 398–402, informs from 'authoritative Arab sources' that out of 700 Arab volunteers who crossed into Palestine during the last four days of February only 100 were Egyptians.

66. Carlson's third Memorandum to J. Evans (American Embassy, Cairo) enclosed in the Embassy's despatch to the State Department (Washington, DC), 23 Apr. 1948, RG 59, 883.00/4–2348; Abd al-Rahman Ali and Abdullah Mhanna, 'Min Dhikrayat 1947–48', *Shu'un Filastiniya*, May 1973, pp. 108–118; *al-Da'wa* (Cairo), 13 Feb. 1951.
67. Anwar al-Sadat, *Revolt on the Nile* (New-York, 1957), pp. 104–105; E. Be'eri, *ha-Kezuna ve ha-shilton ba olam ha aravi* (Tel-Aviv, 1966), pp. 40–41, 65, 67.
68. See, for example, Tuck's report on Sukkari's speech during the Ikhwan's annual meeting, 5 Sept. 1946, RG 59,883.00/9–546.
69. P. J. Vatikiotis, *Nasser and his Generation* (London, 1978), p. 88.
70. Muhammad Faisal Abd al-Mun'im, *Asrar 1948* (Cairo, 1968), pp. 190–198; Darwaza, p. 51.
71. Weekly Appreciation by Chapman Andrews (Cairo) to London, 28 Jan. 1948, FO 371/69190/J606(J22); Mitchell, p. 61.
72. Muhammad Hasan 'Uraibi, *Sira' al-fida'iyyin, al-fidaiyyun al-libiyyun fi harb filastin, 1948* (Tripoli, 1968), pp. 51, 58; Sharif, Vol. II, p. 81, Vol. III, pp. 132–133, 170–171; Muhammad Subayh, *Ayyam wa Ayyam* (Cairo, 1966), p. 298, tells us that Hakstap camp was first opened only as late as 20 Apr. 1948.
73. John R. Carlson [Avedis Arthur Derounian], *Mi Cair 'ad Damesek* (translated from English by Sh. Rosenfeld), (Jerusalem, 1952), p. 50.
74. Arif, pp. 329–330, 399; Mun'im, p. 270.
75. Mun'im, pp. 281–282. On Aziz's career, see Muhammad Abd al-Aziz al-Batashti, *Shuhadaina al-dubat fi hamlat filastin, 1918–1948* (Cairo, 1949), pp. 9–12; Sharif, Vol. III, pp. 137–147; Be'eri, p. 66.
76. Mun'im, p. 270, argues that every volunteering battalion had 400 volunteers, not all Egyptians. In the first battalion were, he says, 120 Tunisians. However, Aziz's personal diary, which is cited by Mun'im, p. 297, gives different figures. According to the diary Aziz's battalion had 804 people: 344 Egyptian volunteers, 297 Libyan volunteers, 45 Tunisians, and 118 regular Egyptian soldiers. 'Uraibi, p. 71 supports this version. He tells us that the major part of the first battalion was composed of non-Ikhwan volunteers, but was nicknamed 'the Ikhwan battalion', because several of its high officers were the Society's members. The Monthly Political Intelligence Summary of Libyan Affairs in Egypt, (Civil Affairs Branch, GHQ, Cairo), for April–June/Aug. 1948 (Issues no. 28–30), FO 141/1260/54/4–7/48, gives further support to the suggestion that Aziz's battalion contained a large number of Libyan volunteers.
77. Vatikiotis, p. 88.
78. Arif, p. 300; Carlson, pp. 39–43, 92–103, 137–141; Muhammad Kurd Ali, *al-Mudhakkirat* (Damascus, 1948), Vol. II, p. 532; See it also in its partial English translation by Khalil Tolah, *Memoirs of Muhammad Kurd Ali* (Washington, DC, 1954), p. 162.
79. Harris, p. 184.
80. R. Campbell (Cairo) to London, 28 Apr. 1948, FO 141/1246/1/269/48; Mamouth(?)'s Memorandum (Cairo), 6 May 1948, FO 141/1246/1/433/48 Tuck (Cairo) to Washington, DC, 20 Dec. 1947, RG 59,890B.00/12–2047; same to same, 26 April 1948, RG 59,867N.01/4–2648; Arif, pp. 340–341; Muhammad Faiyz al-Qasri, *Harb Filastin 'am 1948* (Cairo, 13 June 1961), Series of Military Studies, No. 16, p. 165.
81. Sadat, pp. 104–105; M. Naguib, *Egypt's Destiny* (London, 1955), p. 18.

82. *Al-Tali'a* (Cairo), March, 1975, pp. 134–145.
83. Sharif, Vol. II, pp. 102–108, Vol. III, pp. 138–143; Arif, pp. 400–402; 'Uraibi, pp. 109–111; Sluzki. Vol. III, pp. 1367–1368; Fathi, pp. 70–73.

The Arab States and Palestine

Aaron S. Klieman

The *locus standi* of Egypt, Jordan, Syria and Saudi Arabia in the Palestine conflict is taken for granted by contemporary observers who assume, mistakenly, that it derives from the military intervention of the Arab armies against Israel in 1948. Whereas the standing of Arab parties outside of Palestine was by no means always quite so clear and not open to doubt. Their claim to primary interest in the determination of Palestine's fate, moreover, is of earlier origin; it began a full decade earlier, in the period 1936–39. And it stemmed from Arab action of a definite diplomatic character rather than being established under the force of arms.

Exactly how and why the increased, direct involvement of the Arab states came about is therefore of historical and political importance. What is referred to here as the regionalisation of Palestine merits recall as a major turning-point in the modern, and tragic, history of Palestine, of Zionism and of the Middle East. For until 1936 the Palestine problem had been dealt with by the British mandatory power as an essentially local issue confined to the Arab and Jewish communities inside Palestine. After 1936, however, new political actors and interests intrude which, from our later perspective, only served to widen the sphere of the dispute; to complicate British and then later both American and international efforts at either resolving or moderating the conflict; and in this way to assure its perpetuation for at least another four decades.

Arab state involvement was a by-product of British policymaking in the years just prior to the Second World War and of the political struggle in 1937 over a proposal to have Palestine partitioned into independent Arab and Jewish states. That partition failed is due in no small measure to the influence brought to bear upon British leaders in London by the several Arab states, individually and in concert. The initiative came not so much from Great Britain as from the neighbouring Arab rulers. They shrewdly saw the British predicament in Palestine as a unique opportunity to gain influence with His Majesty's Government, as well as to assert their rival claims to Arab leadership. In the light of what has since befallen Palestinian Arabs, it is particularly noteworthy that the Arab diplomatic offensive was also encouraged by the local Palestinian leadership which thought to counter world Jewry's support of Zionism by appealing for help to other Arabs.

Though revolutionary in its impact this development took place gradually over the course of several years, marked by modest increments of Arab involvement and British acquiescence. Yet little has been written about the regionalisation process; and such references as do exist have not always been enlightened or accurate. To claim that 'one of the greatest mistakes ever made' by Britain was 'to induce' the Arab States to insinuate themselves into Anglo-Palestine relations implies that there had to have been a conscious decision at some point, which is as untrue as the opposite view that these States 'were ineffectual in their efforts to influence the course of British policy' during the 1930s.[1]

As a matter of fact the Arab countries were highly effective, even when acting competitively rather than jointly. They asserted their influence upon Whitehall in diverse and interesting ways, extracting such major concessions as were embodied in the 1939 White Paper and remaining a primary consideration throughout for British decision-makers. Likewise, the evidence now suggests that possibly as early as the autumn of 1936 the British Government was already losing control over the dynamic of regionalisation.

ESTABLISHING A PRECEDENT

On 9 October 1936 the monarchs of Iraq, Saudi Arabia and Transjordan issued a joint appeal to 'our sons the Arabs of Palestine' which read:

> We have been deeply pained by the present state of affairs in Palestine. For this reason we have agreed with our Brothers the Kings and the Amir [Abdullah, of Transjordan] to call upon you to resolve for peace in order to save further shedding of blood. In doing this, we rely on the good intentions of our friend Great Britain, who has declared that she will do justice. You must be confident that we will continue our efforts to assist you.

Its impact was immediate, because on the following day the Palestine Arab Higher Committee circulated a manifesto calling an end to the six-month strike which had virtually paralysed the country, which had cost the Palestinian Arab community heavily, in economic terms, and which had directly challenged British authority. For these very reasons the initiative of outside Arab personalities was greeted with relief by both the Arabs of Palestine and the local British administrators.

If the terse October statement inaugurated a chain of events in which the Arab countries were to play an increasingly prominent role, it also climaxed several months of political manoeuvering between these countries and England at one level, and on a second level among each other. In arguing for this starting-point a basic distinction is being made between non-governmental expressions of encouragement and support for the Palestinian cause in the past and what we are analysing here, i.e. the activities of Arab governments on a diplomatic plane and of Arab monarchs in their public, official capacities.

Regionalisation began with approaches by each Arab leader separately. While on a visit to England in June, 1936, Nuri as-Said, the Iraqi foreign minister, spoke with British officials about probable adverse reaction in his country were Jewish immigration allowed to continue unrestricted. Sitting restlessly across the Jordan, the Amir Abdullah sought to strengthen his ties with the Palestinians. He wrote personal messages to High Commissioner Sir Arthur Wauchope in Jerusalem on their behalf and sanctioned tribal demonstrations identifying Transjordan with their cause; on 26 July he summoned the Arab Higher Committee to Amman to probe for their minimum demands which, if met by Great Britain, could put an end to the general strike then in progress.[2] Meanwhile, from deep Arabia, King Abdul Aziz ibn Saud showed the first signs of active interest in the Palestinian cause, having consolidated his hold over most of the peninsula. Already in April he let it be known in London through the Saudi representative there that he stood ready to do anything possible, in conjunction with His Majesty's Government, to ameliorate the present troubles in the Holy Land.

Following consultation with the Colonial Office people, Assistant Under-Secretary of State for Foreign Affairs Sir Lancelot Oliphant replied:

> If King Ibn Saud is able to use his influence to persuade the Arabs to abandon this campaign of violence, he will indeed be doing a service, not only to His Majesty's Government, but to the Arabs themselves.[3]

Given this initial green light Ibn Saud made his next move in June. After reconsidering the matter, he felt it would be preferable that any action by him to influence the Palestinian leadership should not be undertaken alone but in conjunction with the King of Iraq and the Imam Yahya of Yemen. In dealing with London the Saudi monarch already exhibited that quality of prudence which would make his role throughout distinctive as well as effective. First, dynastic regional rivalries led him to pointedly exclude Abdullah, head of the Hashimites, in his call for collective measures, despite the latter's previous efforts in Palestine. Second, joint action relieved him of possible charges of personal ambition or of subservience to the British, while, on the other hand, he would always seek some prior confirmation of British intentions and support. Were he to risk his prestige on Britain's behalf, could he be assured of the full concurrence of His Majesty's Government? In this instance the insistence of Ibn Saud upon gaining British approval in advance did force an initial debate within the bureaucracy on whether to utilise the Arab rulers as a group rather than any single one of them.

One of the earliest memoranda on the subject, written by the Foreign Office's Eastern Department, is dated 20 June 1936 and is prefaced by Anthony Eden's confessing to an 'uneasy feeling' that the troubles in Palestine 'may affect unfavourably our relations' with various Arab countries.[4] In the body of the memorandum itself a first expression was given to what became with time a cardinal tenet of Foreign Office thinking and then of official Government policy: namely, that the Palestine problem 'is obviously not a temporary one and is considered by the Arabs not only in Palestine but all over the East to strike at the root of the future of the Arab people'.

Parkinson of the Colonial Office on 26 June wrote Oliphant that if Saudi Arabia, Iraq and the Yemen were to advise the Arabs of Palestine, with one voice, to put an end to the disorders, that would be 'all to the good and naturally we should welcome it'.[5] Still, at a time when relations between the two ministries were as yet free of rancour, Parkinson concluded deferentially, 'we are quite content to be guided by the Foreign Office as to the line to be taken'. The two men met the following day to further discuss whether or not a joint demarche by the Arabs ought to be encouraged. But their chief concern had nothing to do with the principle at stake or possible ramifications, only whether the Iraqis and the Saudis could be persuaded to use their good offices without imposing any preconditions upon Great Britain, especially on the sensitive issue of further Jewish immigration into Palestine.

Oliphant, reflecting the decision-maker's concern with only the more direct, tangible and immediate aspects of an issue, urged the desirability of answering the latest inquiry from Ibn Saud even before the next Cabinet meeting 'as otherwise Ibn Saud's friendly offer would have gone without an answer for something like 10 days'.[6] Consequently, he felt obliged to take independent action on behalf of the Foreign Office, but without Government approval. Inviting the Saudi Minister, Hafiz Wahbah, to his office, Oliphant told him on 3 July that His Majesty's Government 'appreciated to the full and gladly accepted' the offer of King Ibn Saud to take the lead in concerting joint action so as to secure a cessation of the Arab rising in Palestine.[7] Only afterwards, on the 9th, did the Baldwin Cabinet learn that Ibn Saud's offer had already been accepted on their behalf.

Even this procedural irregularity aroused no discussion, and certainly no misgivings. For the prevailing attitude is aptly captured by the number two man at the Foreign Office, Vansittart, who noted on 5 July:

> The desire of Iraq, Saudi Arabia and Egypt (*sic*) to help *us* (HMG) – with very little material – is indeed remarkable. Surely we shall not be unwise enough to let this disposition slip.[8]

Incredulity and a sense of extremely good fortune at having cultivated the Arab leaders to such a point where they were eager to help extricate Britain from her current embarrassment in Palestine summarises British attitudes in the earliest phase of regionalisation.

But in the next series of moves Wahbah delivered a message on 13 July from his sovereign in which Ibn Saud hoped Britain would agree, 'as a concession to the three Arab Kings who were their friends',[9] to suspend

Jewish immigration temporarily. While the Eastern Department favoured such a step, this time the Cabinet objected, being unprepared to make any pronouncement to that effect until the disorders had ceased; and Eden was instructed to inform the Saudi envoy accordingly. However, this rebuff was to be softened by thanking the monarch for his offer; 'the time would no doubt come when His Majesty's Government would be glad to avail themselves of the offer.'[10] For the moment though, the posing of preconditions seemed to have eliminated this British alternative of breaking the Palestine impasse through a plea to the Palestinians from the several Arab monarchs led by Ibn Saud.

But just then the idea was reactivated by Iraq whose turn had now come to play 'honest broker'. In the course of a general discussion with a member of the British Embassy in Baghdad on 13 July, the Iraqi Premier, Yusuf Yassin, brought up the question of Palestine. Suspicion of Ibn Saud's motives compelled him to ask for information on precisely how the Saudi initiative had come about. He then produced a memorandum in Arabic and English, setting out briefly the lines on which Iraq thought joint Arab action might yet be possible and on which Yassin wished to have Britain's reaction.[11] Although the Iraqi memorandum suggested suspension of Zionist immigration as the quickest method of ending the disturbances, there was nothing exceptional in this after previous Palestinian and Saudi overtures. More audacious, however, was the suggestion that it would be in the British interest were Palestine to be placed in 'closer contact than at present' with the neighbouring Arab countries. This draft, to be signed by Iraq and Saudi Arabia, ended by expressing belief that a satisfactory conclusion would be reached 'having regard to the spirit of friendship which inspires the Arab peoples' together with 'the conciliatory and sympathetic policy' habitually followed by Great Britain in her relations with the Arabs.

As part of this Iraqi diplomatic offensive, Nuri as-Said planned to visit Jerusalem in August while *en route* to Europe. Asked for his approval, High Commissioner Wauchope gave Nuri his consent on the clear understanding that he was to speak to the Palestinians as an Arab and not in his capacity as Foreign Minister of Iraq. Nuri's apparent success in putting himself forward as a mediator prompted a frantic exchange between Wauchope and his superiors in London. As William Ormsby-Gore, the Secretary of State for the Colonies, reminded him on 25 August, by their earlier encouragement of Ibn Saud the Government had not implied that any initial success would automatically earn him the right to make subsequent representations. Now, here was Nuri whose memorandum could easily be interpreted as admission by His Majesty's Government that Iraq could properly intervene in the affairs of Palestine; as the Colonial Secretary indicated, this would be 'most embarrassing'.[12] London for this reason deemed Nuri's proposal inappropriate and wished his role to remain that of a distinguished Arab on friendly terms with both parties, England and the Palestinians, and not that of a representative of a foreign government.

At this important juncture, it was Wauchope's local considerations which tipped the scale. From his point of view the offer by Nuri as-Said was a way of ending the deadlock and of restoring his own shaken authority. Consequently, he had difficulty in grasping some of the distinctions being made in London. Such is the Arab mentality, he wrote in a secret and 'most immediate' reply on 26 August to Ormsby-Gore's message, that it would be impossible for Nuri to intervene in his private and not in his official capacity; Arabs were incapable of understanding such semantic refinements. Besides, it could only be as Foreign Minister that Nuri's representations would carry any real weight with the Palestinians. Wauchope himself objected to what appeared to be the only other alternative for pacifying the country, martial law. On these grounds the High Commissioner urged reconsideration of Nuri's proposals, more so as he could see little danger in accepting such informal mediation. His final argument took the form of a warning: if the hopes which Ibn Saud and Nuri had aroused were to be dashed by Britain refusing to permit Iraqi mediation, this would engender widespread Arab disappointment and suspicion.

Wauchope's urgent plea had its effect, eliciting a reply from the Colonial Secretary that same day. He was prepared to accept the advice of his representative in Jerusalem and approve Nuri's mission. But still, formal mediation by a foreign government remained inadmissible in itself; not so much for the precedent it would establish as because of the difficulties it created for Britain with Ibn Saud and the other Arab rulers, each of whom judged himself to be the sole candidate qualified for the role of peacemaker in Palestine. Modifications made in Nuri's memorandum by the Colonial Office centred on strictly limiting his authority and on expressly deleting any reference to an ongoing voice to be had by Iraq in British policymaking toward Palestine.

When the Cabinet next discussed the issue on 2 September matters had changed somewhat. Jerusalem reported that Nuri as-Said's mission had been a failure. The Mufti remained unmoved by his arguments; and the acts of violence continued unabated. Although Wauchope desperately required a solution and had therefore reached a point of being willing to make concessions to the Arabs, including even on the central issue of immigration, the Government at home could not possibly entertain such Arab terms. Instead, there developed a noticeable shift toward renewed firmness. Law and order had to be restored. No decision would be made at present about temporary suspension of immigration. A division of troops was to be despatched to Palestine. And at an appropriate moment martial law would be imposed.[13]

The joint appeal issued on 9 October 1936 is thus a compromise by both sides, England and the Arab States. Britain gave her final consent to the initiative because, like Wauchope, there was no joy in martial law, and because the Arab effort was undertaken jointly among her several regional allies without any lasting formal British commitment. For much the same reasons Iraq, Saudi Arabia and Transjordan did issue their appeal, seeing it as a splendid opening in which, nevertheless, no Arab leader could gain a unilateral and exclusive advantage. Abdullah had feared being excluded entirely by his rivals to the north and south; Ibn Saud's suspicions of Nuri as trying to grab the limelight for himself led the Arab monarch to frustrate any such one-sided Iraqi success; while Nuri could interpret even a joint communique as the product of his initiative and ceaseless effort. In short, each Arab leader, for his own reasons, consented to share the prestige of having interceded with Britain and of having rescued the Palestinians in their time of distress.

Although unappreciated at the time, the October communique represented a number of not insignificant shifts: (a) from informal to formal intervention, (b) from individual action to a collective, united Arab front characterised internally by disunity, (c) from acting solely to end the general strike to an enduring and residual Arab obligation to intervene at will thereafter, and (d) from British opposition to any such Arab role to its tacit acceptance. Together, these shifts resulted in the progressive regionalisation of Palestine until it became, and has remained for many years, the core issue of Middle Eastern affairs.

SEPARATE ROADS TO ARAB INFLUENCE

In terms of politics during the 1936 to 1939 period, what were the considerations behind the Arab States taking up the Palestinian cause with England? One set of motives they at least shared in common. Italy's conquest of Abyssinia had a profound influence upon the Arab world, suggesting that Britain and France were vulnerable to pressure. By the same token, acquisition of political independence required that its privileges and limitations be fully tested. Further, the Palestine situation begged for some new factor or idea to help get it off centre, to break the intolerable deadlock. Lastly, intervention had a nuisance value for the Arab States in making Britain more amenable to changes in the separate bilateral relations with each State as a compensation for its support or assistance on Palestine.

Beyond these common factors, however, each Arab State – and in the context of the 1930s it is already hard to divorce these from their individual rulers – entered the Palestine struggle for its own particular motives. Having secured their thrones at home, the Arab leaders were already then embarking upon an era of competition for regional power and influence in the name of Arab unity, with each contender feeling he could capitalise upon and manipulate the Palestine problem to his own advantage. And while it is important, therefore, to assess the comparative strengths and stratagems of the Arab States individually, the main point is that despite their diversity they were able, as a bloc, to meaningfully influence the British policymaking process.

1. Transjordan In staking out his claim the Amir Abdullah could really only play two cards – dependency and proximity. Compared to his Iraqi and Saudi rivals, he was in the weakest position to influence London, since, without formal sovereignty, Transjordan lacked diplomatic representation. Indeed, being part of the Palestine mandate only further accentuated his complete dependence upon British goodwill, which he could scarcely afford to forfeit. Moreover, differences with the Palestinian Arab leader and Mufti of Jerusalem, Haj Amin al-Husayni, ensured that he, Abdullah, could not act as spokesman for the Palestinians so long as the Mufti remained in power.

Nevertheless, within these extremely narrow bounds of initiative, and in contradistinction to his Arab rivals, Abdullah sought to exert whatever influence he could muster not in England but indirectly through the British Administration and the British High Commissioner in Jerusalem. Realising his impotence in London but also the proximity of Transjordan to Palestine, Abdullah from 1936 to 1939 argued the grave implications of Arab unrest across the Jordan for his kingdom.

A constant of Abdullah's statecraft since 1921 had always been to wrest greater freedom for himself and possibly full sovereignty for his kingdom, which everyone regarded as 'a parasite state' and which even he referred to as 'this wilderness of Transjordania'. In May 1935, for instance, his newspaper, *Alif-Ba*, called for a halt to exaggerated ambitions of pan-Arabism, criticising Ibn Saud by name, and instead promoted the goal of uniting Syria, Palestine and Transjordan under Abdullah.[14] These objectives dominate Abdullah's identification with Palestine both before 1939 and after. They explain his willingness to intercede with the Palestinians in 1936 and to maintain discreet yet frequent contact with Zionists. They account as well for the tacit endorsement which he gave to the partition plan in 1937, since it would have made him an indirect beneficiary of union between Transjordan and an Arab Palestine. But the failure of partition also marks the decline of Abdullah, as he was quickly overshadowed by Arab leaders and countries of greater importance for Great Britain.

Nevertheless, Abdullah made one more attempt before the war to link his destiny to Palestine. As he had intimated in July 1937:

> whether or not the union of Trans-Jordan with those parts of Palestine to which the Commission referred is brought about, I must press for the rights of Trans-Jordan proposed by the Commission.[15]

Not giving up easily, once an end had been put to partition, the Amir narrowed his interests, devoting himself in contacts with London primarily to strengthening his position in Transjordan proper. Thus while his representative to the Round Table conference of Arab and Jewish delegations was in London in early 1939 to assist the Palestinians, in a series of private talks with British officials he gained several concessions aiming at greater independence for his kingdom.

Yet nothing could hide his basic dependence. At the time of the partition controversy so vulnerable was the Amir that Ibn Saud's rejection of the plan because Abdullah stood to gain from it evoked British displeasure — not with Ibn Saud but with Abdullah. Finding himself isolated, by 1939 the Hashimite ruler could merely discredit his rivals, advising the British, for example, that 'as the Egyptian and other Delegates are unaware of the true conditions in Palestine, they should not be relied upon in solving the dilemma'.[16] Sulking in Amman, he continued to promote himself and to bide his time, waiting for a more favourable opportunity, such as the one which arose finally in 1948 and led to his unilateral declaration of control over the West Bank of Palestine in April 1950.

2. *Iraq* The balance-sheet of Iraqi interests and influence with England differs substantially from that of its southern neighbour, Transjordan. Although the formidable figure of Nuri as-Said dominates the period, Iraqi considerations were as much national as personal. Dynastic or sentimental concerns had little if any weight, whereas economic and political interests were central. Saudi and Transjordanian efforts made a point of stressing the bond with Great Britain, in contrast with the Iraqi tendency to flaunt independence by taking steps which were uncoordinated with London.

During the 1930s ties were increasingly developed with Palestine, making the latter Iraq's window to the Mediterranean. A new automobile road cut across the desert from Baghdad; Iraqi oil revenues depended heavily upon the Kirkuk–Haifa pipeline; and by a commercial agreement concluded in December, 1936, Haifa harbour was made a free zone for Iraqi goods. Commercial interests therefore demanded a stable Palestine and that its final allocation be made either to Iraq or to someone acceptable to Baghdad.

Domestically, Palestine afforded a succession of Iraqi politicians the opportunity to issue strong nationalist declarations on behalf of the Palestinians in order to bolster their position at home. Thus in the case of Iraq, Palestine served to externalise domestic tensions and power rivalries while at the same time providing a chance for Iraq to promote herself in regional politics. But, by the same token, the governmental instability already plaguing Iraq became a definite liability in her attempt to play a consistent role in Palestine.

For these reasons the tendency during this period was for Iraqi diplomacy to be assertive toward Britain and on occasion even hostile. Following the successful October appeal, for example, the Iraqi Government allegedly had sought to consult other Arabs with a view toward adopting a common policy *vis-à-vis* His Majesty's Government, a step with rather ominous possible implications for Britain. Just how embarrassing and irritating the Iraqi approach could be, due to its failure to consult London first, is illustrated by Iraq's position on partition.

Only two days after publication of the Palestine Royal Commission report in July 1937, the Iraqi Premier, Hikmat Sulayman, informed the British Ambassador, Sir Archibald Clark-Kerr, that he was obliged to protest about the new British policy in order to satisfy local opinion which was in sympathy with the Arabs of Palestine. More important, Sulayman told the British diplomat quite frankly that his Government 'would feel it to be their duty to bring about concerted action by Moslem countries, members of the League of Nations, to put pressure on His Majesty's Government to reconsider their decision'.[17] True to their word, the Iraqi Cabinet had a formal protest delivered to the Foreign Office in July against the proposed partitioning of Palestine, as a result of which Ormsby-Gore, of all people, had to go before Parliament and criticise Iraq in order to repudiate the charge that the Foreign Office had encouraged Iraq as a way of torpedoing partition at the outset.[18]

Rejecting the alternative of maintaining discreet silence, in September of 1937, the new Iraqi Government of Jamil al-Midfai continued the hard line of his predecessors. A telegram was sent to the League of Nations sharply condemning British policy, in which one interesting passage insisted that having intervened earlier to end the general strike the Iraqi Government had 'thereby accepted the gravest moral responsibility towards the Arabs of Palestine and pledged itself to continue its efforts to assist them ...'[19]

Blatant Iraqi attempts at self-aggrandisement through Palestine did much to weaken Baghdad's influence with London, as did the tendency to overstate its case. For example, Dr Naji al-Asil, the Iraqi Foreign Minister, suggested in 1937 that the only solution was establishment of a confederation of three states – Iraq, Transjordan and Palestine – with the capital at Baghdad. His British listener had to make it clear that Iraq could entertain no such hope.[20] More than anyone else, though, Nuri as-Said, through his abundant energy, bluff and gambling ability, did succeed in projecting Iraq onto the Palestine scene. Yet eventually these traits caught up with him, making Nuri personally suspect with the British. For one thing they quickly came to regard him as an 'incorrigible intriguer', making unwarranted statements, misrepresenting positions and views of others and always submitting extravagant demands. Thus Nuri's being urgently summoned home during the London conferences of 1939 was greeted with relief by his British hosts, who felt his attitude during the discussions had been 'rather unhelpful throughout'. Because of such tactics, based upon confrontation, the Arab initiative toward England had for some time now slipped away from Iraq and toward Saudi Arabia.

3. Saudi Arabia Analysis of the Saudi influence upon regionalisation indicates that the desert kingdom enjoyed more advantages and suffered from fewer disadvantages than any of the other Arab state actors pressuring Britain on the Palestine issue. Contrary to the view often held of Arabia as primitive, British documents suggest that throughout 1936-39 Ibn Saud waged by far the most sophisticated, and hence successful campaign to influence both the British Government and the Palestine problem.

Like Transjordan, the foundation of Saudi diplomacy rested on personality; but whereas Abdullah was regarded as a weak figure, Ibn Saud enjoyed the highest reputation throughout Whitehall. The king was regarded as a trusted friend of England whose counsel would always be welcome. In October 1936, Foreign Secretary Eden noted on a file: 'I would be content to say "Thank you" to Ibn Saud. (He has behaved very well)';[21] a month later Eden sent a message of assurance that any representations which Ibn Saud wished to make 'at any time' on Palestine would be 'most carefully considered'[22] by London. Such receptivity gave the Saudi monarch a special standing on Palestine long before the Round Table in 1939 formally acknowledged the status of the Arabs as a whole.

Ibn Saud benefited from other assets as well. Expansion of his control over the Arabian Peninsula placed him in close contact with neighbours in whose affairs England continued to be intimately concerned: from Iraq and Transjordan to Kuwait and the Arabian littoral to the Red Sea. An alienated Saudi ruler had to be feared for the damage he might do to British interests in the area. Respect, on the other hand, derived from his guardianship of the Muslim holy places. Given British sensitivities, his ability to project for Englishmen the image of speaking for millions of Muslim faithful beyond the Arab world, and especially in India, only further enhanced the personal prestige of Ibn Saud. Two additional assets were a competent group of men in his service, such as his son Faysal and Hafiz Wahbah in London, and the fact that George Rendel, influential head of the Eastern Department of the Foreign Office, was tremendously impressed by Ibn Saud and often cited the above considerations in arguing for certain changes in the Palestine policy.[23]

What insured maximum use of these assets, however, is the style of Ibn Saud's diplomacy, which appealed so much to the worried British officials. Where the Iraqi Government sought to exploit the sensitivities of the British public and policymakers on Palestine by frontal assault, Ibn Saud took the high road of quiet diplomacy. If emotional appeals and critical statements issued forth from Baghdad, the British came to expect, and appreciate, the measured tones in which messages reached London from Jiddah. While Iraq adopted tactics expected of a belligerent in pressuring Britain, the image consciously projected of Saudi Arabia was that of a friend and ally. Objectively, both brands of persuasion worked – Iraqi fulmination as well as Saudi deference – in guiding British policy and thinking that much closer to that of the Arabs. But of the two diplomatic styles contrasted here, the British obviously preferred Ibn Saud's approach, were comforted by it and upon occasion even duped by it. And the wily monarch certainly took pains to give the impression throughout of consulting the Foreign Office, of acting only in the best interests of Great Britain and as her devoted servant.

Toward the end of 1936 Ibn Saud was instrumental in persuading the Palestinians to end their boycott of the royal commission and to present their case before it. Such candidness, the Saudi Minister in London was told by Rendel, had been praised by London as entirely in keeping with the 'friendly and straightforward manner in which Ibn Saud had dealt with His Majesty's Government from the first in regard to this Palestinian question'.[24] In Jerusalem Wauchope concluded for future reference how 'the influence and authority of Ibn Saud may well prove most helpful to us to prevent any further disturbances occurring after the decisions of HMG are made known'.[25] British dependence upon Ibn Saud and, through him, the Arabs to get them out of difficult situations in Palestine would continue to grow steadily.

In a long note on partition written on 6 September 1937 Ibn Saud gave full expression to the subtleties of his diplomacy. After setting forth the reasons for his disappointment, he wrote:

> In spite of the above and in spite of the understanding between the Arab Governments to act in conformity with each other ... we did not wish to increase the many difficulties with which the British Government is faced, by protesting publicly against the partition of Palestine, or declaring our condemnation or disapproval of it, but were content to state our remarks and express our views to our friend, the British Government directly, in a private manner, in the belief that it will favourably accept what we have expressed in all frankness and sincerity ...[26]

This single, albeit long, sentence explains why Ibn Saud's style proved so effective and was calculated to bring results.

In short, having consolidated his authority, by 1936 King Ibn Saud was ready to play an active role in regional politics, of which Palestine had by then seemingly become the chief issue. His position, prestige and style gave him the superior advantage over his other Arab rivals, although he, too, showed early traces of judging Palestinian aspects first and foremost in terms of self-interest. Thus his opposition to partition – 'a paroxysm of fury', as described by one British official – owed as much to concern lest it deprive him of Aqaba and Ma'an, coveted territory at the southern tip of Palestine and destined for Transjordan according to the partition recommendation, as to genuine defence of the Palestinian Arabs.

4. Egypt Of the individual Middle Eastern countries, Egypt was the one most deeply affected by the events of 1936–39. For by the end of this period her entire foreign orientation and self-identity had undergone a profound change, specifically in the direction of closer involvement with both the Palestine issue and, as a result, the politics of the Arab world. Brief comparison of her position in 1936 and again in 1939 highlights the transformation for Egypt.

In 1936 an article written by the Arab thinker Sati' al-Husri appeared in a Baghdad newspaper, refuting the thesis of Taha Husayn on behalf of Egyptian separatism and insisting, instead, that nature had endowed Egypt with all the qualities — size, population, geographical location — which made it incumbent upon her to assume longstanding leadership of the Arab nationalist movement.[27] Despite this debate among Arab intellectuals, however, at the government level Egypt remained detached from Arab affairs, showing little interest in developments beyond her borders and focusing upon her bilateral relations with Great Britain. Thus at the time of the Arab initiative late in 1936 the Egyptian Premier, Mustafa Nahas, felt it would be better in the circumstances for the King of Egypt not to join in the declaration by the Arab rulers.[28] In general the British Embassy in Cairo took the view during the general strike that the Egyptian Government were unlikely to go further than making informal representations to London in favour of the Palestinian Arabs.[29]

But events quickly induced Egypt, almost against her will, to act. While preoccupation with finalising the Anglo-Egyptian treaty had distracted Egyptians from the spectacle of recent Palestinian affairs, the successful conclusion of these negotiations in 1936 now freed her to consider other issues. Once British concern for the overriding strategic importance of the Suez Canal and Egypt added to her weight with London, it became all the more difficult for Cairo to resist the temptation to use this influence both upon England and upon the other Arab States. Palestine provided the perfect opportunity.

Sir Miles Lampson, Britain's Ambassador at Cairo, was quick to note the change. Until the end of 1936 Lampson had been insisting how Egypt 'both geographically and psychologically is much isolated from its neighbours, and its sympathy for the Arab world has always had to be artificially stimulated'.[30] But at the height of the partition controversy he reversed his stand, consciously seeking thereafter to point out the close link between Egypt, Palestine, the Arab region and British global strategy.[31] Whereas George Rendel had helped to thrust Saudi Arabia onto the partition scales, Lampson, for good measure, introduced the Egyptian factor.

By 1939, although a latecomer to the Palestine issue, Egypt came nearer to being at the centre of Arab activities. Just prior to the Round Table talks the Arab delegations met in Cairo before proceeding to London. At a banquet in their honour the Egyptian Premier chose to dwell on the significance of this reunion of Arab representatives in the capital of the Kingdom of Egypt; invoking glorious memories of the past and gratitude at the opportunity given Egypt to collaborate with the Arab countries.[32] Acceptance of the invitation to attend the conference reflects this decision and, from our perspective, represents the prologue to Egypt's subsequent leadership of the Arab struggle against Israel.

The 1939 period itself ended with the Egyptian Premier making a public announcement to the press: 'As regards Palestine and in view of the fact that the British Government has not accepted the demands of the ... Arab countries communicated in their name ... all these Governments cannot recommend the inhabitants of Palestine to collaborate with the British authorities on the basis of the project of the British Government.'[33] Arab 'demands' and sanction of Palestinian resistance – hardly an adequate compensation, one might say, to Britain for having enhanced Egypt's prestige and influence throughout the Arab world, or the kind of support London had counted upon in appeasing the Arab States by means of Palestine.

Why, then, did Britain, with all the influence at her command, permit Arab involvement to go quite so far?

BRITISH DEFENSIVENESS

Two basically variant interpretations attempt to account for Britain's role in the regionalisation of Palestine. At one extreme is the conviction that responsible British leaders wilfully encouraged larger Arab participation, beginning with the initial phase in 1936 and continuing through the 1939 White Paper decision. At the other extreme are those who argued that the British Government had not invited any such outside involvement but merely accommodated themselves to Arab wishes.

Representing the first school is the Zionist leader, Chaim Weizmann, himself a participant in these events. Looking back early in 1939, he told Chamberlain and the British:

> I shall not comment on the advantages or disadvantages or on the implications which the appearance of representatives of the neighbouring States may have. I know the British Government has weighed it up very carefully, and it is not for me, at this critical time to criticise them.[34]

Still, he believed, 'I think His Majesty's Government is fully aware of both sides of this particular implication.' Many others took it for granted that if the Arab States dared to assert themselves it could only be with British encouragement and consent. On the other hand, a British spokesman insisted before the Permanent Mandates Commission of the League of Nations in September, 1937, that 'intervention had been solely and entirely on the initiative of the Rulers themselves'.[35] Or consider, for instance, Foreign Office instructions earlier, in November 1936, to the Ambassador in Baghdad, which informed him that 'HMG clearly cannot agree to any foreign statesmen negotiating between them and Palestine Arabs' because it would be liable to 'mis-interpretation and might place HMG in (an) invidious position'.[36] Both extreme views share at least two assumptions: (1) that there was, as Weizmann simply took for granted, a conscious decision one way or the other; and (2) that the power of decision rested solely with Great Britain.

Yet sensitivity for the fallibility of decision-makers and a healthy disrespect for hard and fast dichotomies prompt suggesting here a third interpretation. In the context of 1936, when the Arab States first appear as an interested, or concerned, party, British leaders approved the joint appeal because it enabled Britain to extricate herself from an awkward, momentary situation in Palestine. Consequently, as George Rendel argued, 'we do not want to give any ground for the assumption that the Arab rulers acted at our invitation or on our behalf'; nevertheless, the fact remained that 'owing to their intervention, we may have been got out of a very nasty mess'.[37]

So preoccupied were Rendel and his associates with the immediate situation, so narrow and concrete their perspective that none of them could have easily paid attention to the long-term results stemming from their tolerant position in 1936. Thereafter, however, Arab involvement took on a dynamic and a life of its own, with 1936 events serving as the precedent. It would be well to remember, in this connection, that precedents take hold only if the options they offer are seized upon subsequently by the potential actors. As a corollary to this third, intermediate view, therefore, what happened after 1936 had less to do with strictly British wishes or decisions and owes much more to the ability and to the willingness of the Arab leaders themselves. Given the chance, they seized and exploited it to the fullest, making regionalisation an unanticipated policy outcome from the standpoint of Great Britain.

Then, and after 1936 as well, a number of attempts were made at rationalising what had happened. On 4 November 1936 William Ormsby-Gore made a statement before the House of Commons which, because of its importance, merits being quoted in full. In reply to a question, he sought to explain the appeal by the Arab States as follows:

> No application whatever was made to any Arab rulers either by His Majesty's Government or by the High Commissioner for Palestine, for assistance or advice concerning Palestine.

Certain Arab rulers, however,

> spontaneously intimated to His Majesty's Government through the diplomatic channel their willingness to use their influence with the Arabs of Palestine in the interests of peace and were informed ... that His Majesty's Government would raise no objection to the Arab rulers addressing an appeal to the Arabs of Palestine to cease the strike ... provided that the appeal was unconditional.

Lest there be misunderstanding, the Colonial Secretary added for emphasis,

> No understanding or promises either explicit or implied were given by His

Majesty's Government and it was made quite clear to the rulers concerned that His Majesty's Government were not prepared to enter into any kind of commitments whatever.[38]

In short, the dominant British view in 1936 held that the Government, although able to raise objections, had no cause to do so since the Arabs fully understood there would not be any bargaining or concessions.

Yet already then a few voices were raised, primarily inside the Colonial Office, in warning that externalising her Palestine problem could not be beneficial for Britain. We find, for example, John Shuckburgh arguing in September 1936, against using the Arab leaders. 'If we were to take the initiative in appealing to the Arab Kings on this occasion', he prophesied, 'this would be regarded as recognition by us of the right of foreign Arab Sovereigns to intervene in the affairs of Palestine.'[39] Furthermore, he cautioned, 'the case would be cited as a precedent, and it was difficult to see how far we might be carried if we once accepted the principle of external Arab intervention'. Speaking after Shuckburgh, the Minister of Labour, Ernest Brown, uttered words which are appropriate in understanding policy processes in general and both regionalisation and the partition policy. 'We must take no responsibility whatever for opening a door when we did not in the least know what was behind it.' That the Colonial Office was not heeded by the Government is but another indication of the general defeat experienced by that Ministry during the entire Palestine debate, since its support for partition also proved unsuccessful.

By 1937, however, the fact that the 1936 initiative, implying continuous Arab association, had been a major British concession in itself, was becoming more readily obvious, at least to outside observers. M. Orts, Chairman of the Permanent Mandates Commission, proved an extremely outspoken critic of Britain's having even tolerated Arab intervention. In his reading of events, as soon as intervention by the Arab Princes in the internal affairs of Palestine had been permitted, and recognised more or less as legitimate, the situation had been completely transformed. 'From that time forward, what could rightly be considered as a local problem had become the center of a vast international problem.'[40] The Arab intervention in 1936 M. Orts called 'a first step' in a direction in which 'fresh difficulties and obstacles to the solution of the problem were almost bound to be encountered'. Had it been some other country under British sovereignty or protectorate, and not Palestine, he stated critically, such intervention would surely have been rejected.

Increasingly on the defensive in the face of outside criticism, and having to justify even to themselves a precedent which was proving a rather mixed blessing, British policymakers devised several explanations. Some justified participation by the Arab States as a form of redressing the balance. For them, it was only fair that if the Zionists and the Jewish settlement in Palestine could be supported by world Jewry then the

Palestinians should be able to rely upon the Arab world, especially those countries which by virtue of their proximity might be affected by decisions on Palestine's future. This became the argument of symmetry.

The more predominant view, however, accepted the Arab stand not in terms of justice but as politically wise. On the one hand, the Arab States after 1936 could be counted upon to play a statesmanlike role, acting as a moderating influence upon the extremist Palestinians and, when deemed expedient, mediating between them and Great Britain. On the other hand, receptiveness to Arab feelings came to be also justified as both necessary and unavoidable. Malcolm MacDonald utilised both points when favouring invitations to the Arab States to participate in the 1939 Round Table talks, citing three advantages by this gesture. First, in the long run any satisfactory solution depended upon Palestine being joined in a federation with neighbouring countries. Second, the Arab Princes would exercise their moderating influence in the forthcoming negotiations. And third, the Arabs outside Palestine were already discussing the entire issue among themselves and with Britain informally, so 'it was as well to recognise openly their interest in the matter'.[41] The need to appease the Arabs as war approached of course only strengthened the argument of necessity.

The London conferences in 1939, closing out the early phase of regionalisation, do indeed testify to singular Arab success in playing upon British sensitivities. The Arab delegations figured prominently during the formal sessions, and the heady experience of being courted by a Great Power as a solid bloc of Arab States clearly foreshadowed the future creation of the Arab League. But the Arab representatives were that much more influential behind the scenes at London. They made it impossible for Britain to accept or reject proposed Palestinian delegations 'unless we were recommended to do so by the neighbouring Arab countries'.[42] More private talks were held by the Colonial Secretary with the Egyptian, Iraqi and Saudi heads of delegations than with the Palestinians, the original aggrieved party. And whenever such informal conversations took place the Arab diplomats were eminently successful in gently counselling Britain to make further concessions in her proposed policy on the chance it would then be acceptable to the Palestinians.

As the conference progressed, however, British calculations were upset. Ormsby-Gore's successor at the Colonial Office, Malcolm MacDonald, realised belatedly that instead of moderating the Palestinians the Arab States were actually endorsing their uncompromising attitude. Relating one such setback to the Cabinet, the Colonial Secretary admitted that the Arab delegates 'had not adopted a very helpful line'.[43] The British thus found themselves the unwitting tool of Arab considerations, reversing the traditional relationship. The Cabinet was informed that 'under strong pressure from the neighbouring Arab States, we had introduced into our scheme some points which we should have preferred to have omitted';[44]

once again MacDonald served as the bearer of bad tidings. But by then it had become too late to arrest the process of regionalisation, a process driven by the twin motors of Arab opportunism and British anxiety.

Not the least of the parties affected were the Palestinians themselves who, as the period ended, offered 'profound thanks' to the Arab countries and governments. In a manifesto issued at the abrupt termination of the Round Table talks, the Arab Higher Committee observed:

> The reason for this marvellous support is to be found in the friendly mutual relations between Palestine and those kingdoms who now believe that the Palestine question is one concerning the Arabs and the Moslems as a whole. They are prepared to fight in its cause as they would fight in their own. The Palestine cause has acquired these new forces which will undoubtedly pave the way to complete and speedy victory.[45]

The victory, however, has been neither complete nor speedy.

Larger Arab intervention, although a notable success for the several Arab States, led to a diminution of the Palestinians as an independent actor and to subordination of their interests. Writing after the shock of the 1948 war, one prominent Palestinian delivered a stinging indictment of the Arab States, since 'in the face of the enemy the Arabs were not a state, but petty states; groups, not a nation; each fearing and anxiously watching the other and intriguing against it'. What concerned them most and guided their policy, Musa Alami charged, 'was not to win the war and save Palestine from the enemy, but what would happen after the struggle, who would be predominant in Palestine, or annex it to themselves, and how they could achieve their own ambitions'.[46] But it is only really since 1967 that Palestinian disillusionment with the role of the Arab States has come to the surface in inter-Arab relations, with the Palestinians becoming a factor in the domestic politics of the Arab countries. Regionalisation, in effect, has come full circle.

NOTES

1. The first view is by Arthur Koestler, *Promise and Fulfilment* (London, 1949), p. 52, while the second is offered by Malcolm Kerr in his *Regional Arab Politics and the Conflict with Israel*. The Rand Corporation, Memorandum RM-5966-FF (October 1969), p. 32.
2. Abdullah's account of his early efforts is in *My Memoirs Completed (al-Takmilah)* (Washington, 1954), pp. 89–93.
3. FO 371/20021/E 3783.
4. FO 371/20021/E 3642.
5. FO 371/20021/E 4108.
6. FO 371/20021/E 3982.
7. FO 371/20021/E 4109.
8. FO 371/20021/E 4109. File E 4301 has the minutes of Cab. 51(36) of 9 July 1936.
9. FO 371/20022/E 4627.

10. CAB 23/85/Cab. 52(36) of 15 July 1936.
11. FO 371/20022/E 4621.
12. The exchanges with Wauchope were reprinted as a Cabinet paper, C.P. 227(36) on 27 August and are in CAB 24/264.
13. CAB 23/85. Cab. 56(36) of 2 September 1936.
14. Quoted in *Yalkut Ha-Mizrach Ha-Tichon*, No. 4, Jerusalem (June 1935), pp. 13–14.
15. C.O. 733/350. file 75718/2, with Abdullah's letter of 25 July to Wauchope.
16. Translation of Abdullah's letter to High Commissioner MacMichael, undated, but clearly at the time of the London Conferences. C.O. 733/406. file 75872.
17. Clark-Kerr to London (10 July 1937), in FO 371/20808/E 3919.
18. Both the Iraqi letter and British criticism of it are in FO 371/20809/E 4150.
19. The Iraqi telegram is in League of Nations document C.321 M.216. 1937. VI.
20. Rendel's report of the Iraqi proposals during his visit to Baghdad on 19 February 1937 and his reply, in FO 371/20805/E 1428.
21. 20 October 1936. FO 371/20027, file E 6600.
22. 6 November 1936. FO 371/20028, file E 6745.
23. Thus Rendel on 12 April 1937: 'I am convinced that the whole of that influence and prestige will inevitably be used against us if Ibn Saud regards our Palestine policy as unjust to the Arab cause.' C.O. 733/348, file 7550/70.
24. Rendel minute of 9 December 1936. FO 371/20029/E 7669.
25. Wauchope – Colonial Office, letter of 12 January 1937. C.O. 733/320. file 7550/27.
26. CAB 24/273. C.P. 281(37) of 19 November 1937, p. 13.
27. Al-Husri, *'Daur Misr fil-nahda al-qawmiyyah al-arabiyya'*, quoted in Sylvia G. Haim (ed.), *Arab Nationalism. An Anthology* (Berkeley and Los Angeles, 1964), p. 50.
28. FO 371/20026/E 6240.
29. Lampson to Eden, 12 August 1936. FO 371/20023, file 5207.
30. Lampson to Eden, (confidential), 12 August 1936. FO 371/20023.
31. Lampson insisted his object was to warn London, 'you must be obliged to call off immigration if you want to keep the friendship of the Arab world. The longer you delay that no doubt painful decision, the less value you will get from making it.' Lampson to Halifax, 6 December 1938, in CAB 24/281. C.P. 293(38).
32. Lampson to Halifax, 20 January 1939. FO 371/23221, file E 754.
33. Lampson cable of 18 May 1939. FO 371/23235/E673.
34. In his opening statement at the Round Table negotiations on 8 February 1939. FO 371/23223. file E 1058.
35. League of Nations, Minutes of the Thirty-Second (Extraordinary) Session, p. 89.
36. Telegram of 28 November 1936. C.O. 733/320. file 7550/27.
37. Rendel note to Sir L. Oliphant. 13 October 1936. FO 371/20027/E 6501.
38. In FO 371/20028. file E 6958.
39. C.O. 733/314. file 75528/44, Part II, with minutes of the Cabinet discussion on 11 September 1936.
40. Minutes of the Thirty-Second (Extraordinary) Session, p. 86, *passim*.
41. Extract of Cabinet conclusions 52(38) of 2 November 1938. FO 371/21865. file E 6471.
42. MacDonald, in his report to the Cabinet on 18 January 1939. CAB 23/97. Cab. 1(39).
43. CAB 25/97. Cab. 7(39) of 15 February 1939.
44. FO 371/23234/E 3147. Extract of Cabinet conclusions, 24(39) of 16 April 1939.
45. Consul MacKereth (Damascus). despatch No. 53 of 29 March 1939, with a copy of the Palestinian statement. FO 371/23232. file E 2472.
46. Musa Alami, 'The Lesson of Palestine', in the *Middle East Journal*, Vol. 3, No. 4 (October 1949), p. 385.

The Anglo-American Commission of Inquiry on Palestine (1945–46): The Zionist Reaction Reconsidered

Joseph Heller

INTRODUCTION

The end of the Second World War found the Zionists at a cross-roads. On the one hand, they were faced with the shattering consequences of the Holocaust which extinguished their hopes for preparing a Jewish State for the great reservoir of Eastern European Jewry. In addition to that, the Damoclean sword of the 1939 White Paper was still hanging over their heads with its ominous articles concerning limited immigration and the establishment of a Palestinian Arab state. On the other hand, the Holocaust was their best justification for Zionism, being the best proof that if anti-Semitism could reach such catastrophic proportions, the Jews could no longer rely upon the Gentiles, but must enhance their efforts to bring about a Jewish state.

A clash therefore between Britain and the Zionist movement, who only a decade before were on the best of terms (enabling the Zionists to increase their numbers in Palestine up to 554,000 by 1945), was just around the corner. No matter which Government was in power in England, Labour or Conservative, the clash was bound to come, since now the Zionists were neither prepared to agree to the 1,500 monthly limit for immigrants fixed by the White Paper, nor were they ready to wait for another delay in fulfilment of their long-drawn dream of a Jewish state. Most important of all, they could now rely not only on themselves as in the past, but on the assistance of the great mass of American Jewry, and on the thousands of remnants of Jewish refugees which they succeeded in concentrating in the American zones of occupation in Germany, Austria and Italy.

However, if for the first time in the history of Palestine, a British Government decided to call on the United States Government to assist it in finding a solution to the long-festering Jewish and Palestinian issues, it was not because of Zionist pressure, least of all from the United States. Rather, it was a decision influenced by the considerably weakened position in which Britain found herself as a result of the war. Her overall weakness, especially in economic and financial matters, which endangered her political and strategic status both as an empire and as a world power, necessitated American support more than ever before in British peace-time history.

I

Zionists have generally seen the Anglo-American Commission of Inquiry as an intended hindrance to them. Weizmann, Shertok and Eban saw British procrastination as an attempt to get British support against them.

Indeed, the very failure to implement its recommendations, specifically the British refusal to permit the entry of 100,000 refugees, according to Eban, enabled the Zionists to keep their strongest and vital card, and Bevin became Israel's George III.[1]

Britain's motive, it was alleged, was clear, according to Yigal Allon, then Commander of the Haganah shock troops, the Palmach. Faced with the Yishuv's struggle in Palestine, supported by world Jewry, Britain was forced to look to Washington for help.[2]

Even more uncompromising, Menachem Begin, Commander of the Irgun saw the Commission as redundant from the start. Bevin's attitude, in any case, had made him, according to the Stern Group, 'our agent meriting a statue in his memory'. Had Bevin in fact accepted the proposals of the Commission it would have dealt a greater blow against the underground than any number of arrests and executions.[3]

Was this image justified? I shall attempt to show that the Commission's record as a complete and utter failure was an exaggerated one, because Zionists overestimated the American identification with Bevin's policies, and ignored Washington's sympathy for their own ideas. They too easily assumed that Truman, by collaborating in the Joint Commission, had fallen into Bevin's trap.

Their attitude had already hardened before the public announcement of the Commission on 13 November 1945. The Zionist leadership had reason to believe that the British had made up their minds against free immigration and a Jewish State. David Ben-Gurion, Chairman of the Jewish Agency Executive, and Moshe Sneh, Head of the Haganah National Command, therefore agreed to co-operate with the Irgun and the Freedom Fighters of Israel (the Sternists), the first act of joint resistance being the blowing up of 153 bridges on 1 November 1945.[4] Thus by 13 November, the official establishment of the Commission, the Zionists were already in a militant state.

Here, by contrast, it might be worth mentioning that the Arabs, and in particular the Palestine Arabs, initially opposed the Commission because of the participation of the Americans and because of Truman's pro-Zionist statement. But they eventually gave evidence for tactical reasons rather than out of any spirit of compromise.[5]

Zionist misunderstanding can now be seen more clearly in the light of the British and American Archives, and more emphasis might now be put on Arab attitudes than was done at the time.

The central questions, then, are: Why was Britain so keen on a joint Commission, instead of a purely British one, for example, on the lines of the Peel Commission of 1937? Why did the Americans want to get involved, albeit in co-operation with a friendly power, in an area not particularly in their sphere of influence, when there was such a fundamental difference between them on the Jewish and Palestine questions?

It now seems clear that although differences could not be ignored or underestimated, the need to find some solution was urgent enough to overcome the gulf separating the two powers. Furthermore, in the aftermath of the Second World War, Britain felt too weak to deal with the Middle East by herself.

As in other issues Truman seemed to cut through Roosevelt's ambiguity. Writing to Churchill and Attlee in July and August he was prompted by the Earl G. Harrison mission to examine the conditions of Jewish refugees in occupied Germany. Harrison's findings were influenced by Zionist officials, and he condemned the American military authorities for the appalling conditions of the recently liberated refugees and recommended their immediate transfer to Palestine.[6] Truman's motive for supporting this had doubtlessly been humanitarian rather than political, but it nonetheless associated him with the Zionists' viewpoint. Yet clearly, though Truman favoured the immediate entry of 100,000 Jews, he did not go so far as to consent to the establishment of a Jewish State. Since 1938, and with the exception of the Cabinet partition proposal of 1943–44, this had in any case been unthinkable from the British point of view; Bevin had done little but accept the foreign policy establishment consensus that Zionism, if it won the day, would set the whole Middle East and India on fire. But by establishing the Joint Commission he surprised, (even enraged), his subordinates in London and the Middle East, since they were convinced, like the Arabs, that the Americans were entirely pro-Zionist, and therefore no valuable contribution could be made by them to the solution of the Palestine problem. Bevin on the other hand was confident that the Americans, once they shared responsibility through the Committee, could come round to accept the British point of view. But a few days later he expressed the fear that Zionist propaganda in New York had destroyed what a few weeks before had looked to him as a reasonable atmosphere in which Britain could get Jews and Arabs together. In many ways the idea of the Commission for Bevin was only a prelude to an Arab-Jewish-British Conference on Palestine. In a letter to Halifax he accused the Americans of being 'thoroughly dishonest' and added: 'To play on racial feelings for the purpose of winning an election is to make a farce of their insistence on free election in other countries'.[7]

II

Bevin himself first brought up the idea of a Joint Commission in the Cabinet meeting of 4 October 1945. Halifax, formerly foreign secretary, and then Ambassador to Washington, was worried about the effect of Zionist pressure, particularly important because of the Jewish vote, manifested in widespread support in Congress, and as James F. Byrnes admitted, in view of the impending election for the Mayoralty of New York. Failing the immediate possibility of United Nations intervention, and of United States reluctance to take responsibility solely on herself, the best alternative was to persuade her to share it with Britain.

All this was in the background of the possible collapse of British policy. The pressure was particularly acute because of the deteriorating condition of the Jewish refugees, the eruption of hostilities in Palestine, and the uncertainty caused by the changeover from the Mandate system to a Trusteeship of an entirely new kind.

Britain, lacking confidence in herself at this crucial juncture for Palestine, turned to the United States for help. Nonetheless, Bevin had come to accept that the Joint Commission should examine the plight of Jewish refugees in Europe and indeed consider how many of them should go to Palestine, or elsewhere.[8]

The most forceful criticism of the plan came from the Colonial Office, less influenced by American considerations, but Bevin indeed had the final say.[9]

Yet, whilst Britain hoped to draw the United States through the Commission into shared responsibility, Washington's idea was merely to influence Britain in favour of Zionism. The British had seriously underestimated Truman's commitment in this direction, relying too much on the line of continuity from Roosevelt's caution, and saw the role of the Commission as correcting the 'improper' conclusions of Harrison's report.

For the Americans, Palestine had to be the focus as the main target for the rehabilitation of Jewish refugees, or there would be no Joint Commission at all. Attlee finally accepted this in his meeting with Truman, seeing it as a tactical compromise rather than a major concession, since actual participation in the Commission would force the Americans to realize that there was an Arab side as well as a Jewish one.[10]

The Zionists also misinterpreted Truman's attitude and both Silver, Wise and Weizmann in America and Ben-Gurion in Palestine took their cue from Bevin. For them the Commission could never be neutral.[11]

Belief in such neutrality could be found only amongst the moderates of Aliya Hadasha and Ichud, and the ultra-orthodox of Agudat Israel. Nonetheless, the Zionists would have to face the question of their political attitude to the Commission.

The members of the Commission, six British and six American, announced on 10 December 1945, were, with co-chairmen from both groups: Sir John Singleton, a High Court Judge, co-chairman; W. F. Crick, Adviser to the Midland Bank; R. H. S. Crossman, then an activist left-wing Labour back-bencher; Sir Frederic Leggett, previously Bevin's

Deputy Under-Secretary at the Ministry of Labour during the war; R. E. Manningham-Buller, a back-bench Conservative M.P.; and Lord Morrison, a Labour peer. The American members included the co-chairman Judge Joseph C. Hutcheson of the Texas High Court; Frank Aydelotte, Professor of History at Princeton; Frank W. Buxton, editor of the *Boston Herald*; Bartley Crum, a Democratic Senator, James G. MacDonald, formerly League of Nations High Commissioner for Refugees, and the former American Ambassador to India, William Phillips.[12]

III

The Jewish Agency Executive could not at first agree on whether to give evidence to the Commission. Abba Hillel Silver, the prominent American Zionist leader, together with Moshe Sneh, became the most implacable opponents. Ben-Gurion suggested that bodies outside the Agency rather than the Agency itself might give evidence. Only one member of the Agency Executive, Werner D. Senator, a member of Ichud and representative of the non-Zionists, was unhesitatingly in favour of giving evidence.[13]

But, argued Nahum Goldmann, supported by Moshe Shertok, America's participation was a real factor which might prove to be crucial for Zionism. Shertok emphasized that Zionism ought not to boycott it because the Commission was to be the focus of the diplomatic campaign on Palestine and the Jewish question. Above all, he did not share the view that Zionism was strong enough to avoid the use of diplomacy. A policy of boycott and violent action without a parallel diplomatic struggle was a luxury which Zionism could ill afford, unlike the Arabs or the Indians. Zionism was still in its transitory period, in the midst of the process of the gathering-in of the exiles and the reconstruction of the Jewish people. It should therefore try and win the sympathy of the Commission. Furthermore, Zionism was facing a severe struggle in view of the new British, indeed United Nations, policy to replace the Mandate by a Trusteeship which would eliminate Zionism as a political force.[14]

Though not sharing Sneh's position of complete rejection of the Commission, Ben-Gurion believed that if the Jewish Agency was right in its assumption that Zionism would be defeated by the Commission then it was better to boycott it. His main fear was that the Commission would sanction the abolition of the Mandate with its Zionist articles. He was also worried because, whilst the Arabs were united, the Jews were divided into Zionists, non-Zionists and anti-Zionists.

However, Ben-Gurion's line was already defeated in his own party by a large majority (16:2) on 10 December. Two days later the Zionist Small Action Committee voted. Unlike the undecided vote of the Executive, the vote was clear-cut: 16 in favour of appearance and 11 against.[15]

Little did the Zionists know that the Commission's future was in jeopardy in view of the mounting violence in Palestine. Luckily, the Cabinet subordinated its law and order measures to its attempts to win over American support for its Palestine policy through the Commission.[16] Consequently, plans for general search for arms had to be delayed until the Commission had completed its work, otherwise power would have been thrown into the hands of the extremists.

IV

The Zionist protest against the Commission began in America, when after protest from the British members, the work of the Commission was begun. Wise and Silver, the foremost American Zionist leaders, had already condemned it on 30 October and after Bevin's announcement it was again denounced by the great majority of the American Zionist Emergency Council (AZEC).[17]

After a debate as to where its work should start from, the Commission began its hearings on 7 January 1946 in Washington. The Zionists, like their Arab opponents, were given full opportunity to present their case. Earl G. Harrison and Joseph Schwartz, the Director of the Joint Distribution Committee in Europe, gave 'excellent' reports from the Zionist viewpoint, both emphasizing the critical situation of the refugees. Reinhold Niebuhr, the famous theologian, gave the 'best' analysis of the Zionist idea. Economic experts such as Walter Lowdermilk explained how the absorptive capacity of Palestine could be increased from 100,000 acres to 750,000 at the cost of 200 million dollars. Others like Robert Nathan and Oscar Gass pointed out that Palestine could absorb another 600,000 to 1,200,000 people.[18]

On the whole the Zionists were not worried by the presentation of the Arab case or by anti-Zionist Jews. Of the pro-Arab witnesses Frank Notestein alone caused the Zionists some anxiety. Notestein, Professor of Demography at Princeton, refuted Nathan's claim that a Jewish majority in Palestine was feasible by 1950. Notestein argued that the Jews would never be able to obtain a majority and that the country would not be able to feed a large population. The 'territorialist' I.N. Steinberg argued in favour of settling the Jews in Australia instead of Palestine, and confused the Commission, as did Peter Bergson of the Committee for the Freedom of the Nation, with his idea of a Hebrew Nation as distinct from the Jewish one. Lessing Rosenwald, of the notoriously anti-Zionist American Council for Judaism, seemed ineffective.[19]

The proceedings in Washington gave encouragement to the Zionists. Of the six Americans, three, Buxton, Crum and MacDonald seemed fervently pro-Zionist, whilst amongst the British Crossman looked promising. His enthusiasm was generated by Zionists like David Horowitz, of the Agency's Political Department, who could conjure up for him the image of the resistance fighters of Europe.[20]

Such was the tide of optimism after these initial proceedings that Silver, who had just refused to appear before the Commission to leave himself room for manoeuvre, should it prove inimical to Zionism, now changed his mind. In the view of the British observers, however, it was the strength of the Arab case that had really been established.[21]

At this juncture a major shift in the Zionist position took place, originating from the Agency's representative in Washington Eliahu Epstein (later Elath). He suggested to Shertok that partition of Western Palestine be substituted for the Biltmore plan which had claimed the entire area. They had more chance of becoming a majority in a partitioned State, as the Jews constituted only one-third of the population and, although the Americans (and certainly the British) would not yet countenance a Jewish State, yet they might favour immigration and settlement in the area.[22]

Epstein's dramatic shift was made with regard to key changes in the attitudes and relationships of the Great Powers. The Zionists would have to move quickly, as hostility between the United States and the Soviet Union was growing, and Russia might now halt the flow of Jewish immigrants, making it even less likely that the Jews would achieve a majority in Palestine. The case might be argued however for a partitioned State. Britain for her part might be seduced by the new Jewish State offering her military bases as she had in Transjordan.

It is not yet clear whether Epstein was the first to suggest partition or whether it was Goldmann's or Shertok's idea. It certainly was favoured by Weizmann and even Ben-Gurion, though in secret. They envisaged the Jewish share as the area allotted to the Jews by the Peel Commission minus the Arab triangle, but with the addition of the Negev. Less than this would be tantamount to political suicide.[23] It was not however until the Black Sabbath on 29 June 1946 and the King David Hotel incident that the Jewish Agency was officially to accept the partition plan.

V

The London hearings of the Commission began on 25 January 1946, again with none of the Zionist witnesses appearing in the name of the Jewish Agency.

The general policy amongst the Zionists was that the hearings did not advance the Zionist cause. The only substantial witness in their favour seemed to be Leo Amery, a life-long Zionist, who had held the Secretaryship of State for India, amongst other Cabinet posts. He suggested partition with the Peel area, without the Western Galilee but with the Negev. The former Zionist and High Commissioner Viscount Samuel, and Leonard Stein, President of the Anglo-Jewish Association, both opposed a Jewish State. Bevin himself was particularly impressed by the Arab viewpoint as put forward by General Edward Spears and he dismissed Smuts' mention of the Balfour Declaration. 'It was a unilateral declaration and did not take into account the Arabs. It was really a power politics declaration.'[24]

Nor did the proceedings appear to have influenced the members of the Commission in the Zionists' favour. Even the pro-Zionist members favoured only political autonomy with Jewish control of immigration and economic union with Lebanon, Syria, and Transjordan. Crossman particularly was in a 'confused and exasperated' state. He felt the Zionists had made a 'serious tactical mistake' in pushing for a Jewish state: first with their attempt to create a Jewish rather than an Arab majority, and second because of the double loyalty problems which a Jewish state might engender for the Diaspora Jews and because of the impetus the establishment of the state would give to anti-Semitism.

The Zionists thought the Commission would be swayed by the visit to Palestine. Yet Weizmann, even if he could see the Commission recommending partition, remained pessimistic: 'HMG will say they need six Divisions to carry that through and will ask the USA to send some. USA will refuse and HMG will be delighted for excuse to do nothing, and the Yishuv will then lose patience.' This prediction, which proved almost correct, left Weizmann 'very gloomy and bitter'. A few days later he wrote: 'I really don't know what to expect of them [the Commission], the best is to expect nothing.'[25]

Before the Commission visited the Middle East, it was due to investigate the conditions of the Jewish refugees in Europe. The members eventually visited Germany, Austria, Italy, Switzerland and Greece, but the Russians only allowed them into Poland and Czechoslovakia.

Independent investigations by UNRRA and the American army made it clear that many camp dwellers wished to emigrate to Palestine, although attempts by the Jewish Agency such as the despatch of Gideon Ruffer (later Rafael) to ensure Zionist loyalty, had the effect opposite to that intended on some of the Commission members, and indeed encouraged the British to emphasize the evidence to the contrary.

When members of the Commission did in fact see the camps, as was the case with Leggett and Crum in Germany, they were appalled, and suggested the emigration of 200,000 over the next few years. For his pains Crum was rebuked by Singleton and threatened resignation.[26]

But to the Jewish Agency too few of the camps had been seen by too few of the members of the Commission, and suspecting British intervention, they got Judge Simon Rifkind, Eisenhower's advisor for Jewish affairs, to demand immediate evacuation of the camps and the transfer of their occupants to Palestine, a demand rejected by the Commission. It would doubtless recommend a transfer of the whole problem to the United Nations, where Zionism would get a first-class burial.[27] Yet, although the Zionists thought that the full impact of the camps had not really been felt, there was support from

Crossman and Leggett and Hutcheson for Crum's evacuation plan.

The crucial argument however was bound to take place in Palestine. Shertok had to defend the Agency's case before the Elected Assembly of the Yishuv on 13 February 1946. The Agency itself would still not appear before the Commission, nonetheless individuals and groups had to present some sort of evidence. It was true that the grant of independence to Transjordan at a time when the Jewish nation was treated like a beggar was a 'serious blow' but despite the Arabs the 1,500 monthly quota had been renewed, and the United States was now directly involved.[28]

VI

Shertok was able to hint at partition, but he was not yet able to make a clear statement in favour of it, so undivided Palestine (according to the Biltmore Resolution of 1942) still had to be the basis of the united Zionist front that he insisted should be presented to the Commission. Both Aliya Hadasha and Hashomer Hatzair refused to comply.[29]

Ben-Gurion had meanwhile been making some rapid tactical adjustments in his position because of his perception of an increasingly anti-Jewish Soviet attitude. He argued that the claim for a Jewish State and the demand that the Powers proclaim it should now be dropped, and that the Executive should press the Commission for: (a) the immigration of a million Jews in the minimum of time and with the assistance of the Great Powers; (b) the granting to the Jewish Agency of control over immigration, settlement and development. These two conditions were bound to bring about a Jewish majority and a Jewish State.

Shertok could not see how they could get one million immigrants to come to Palestine within the next two years. Five to ten years was a more realistic time span, for unlike the Greeks in 1922 the Jews were not faced with the desperate dilemma of massacre or flight. In any case 200,000 rather than two million was the likely number of potential immigrants, for he doubted whether the oriental Jews would be willing to come. Playing the numbers game was unsavoury to Ben-Gurion and his group of 'idealists' (Sneh, Fishman, Schmorak, and Joseph). For them the Bible was a surer guide to the righteousness of their cause, although even Ben-Gurion had to take tactical considerations into account. He saw the first million as a political rather than a statistical concept. His real fear was that Iraq and Russia would not let the Jews out, an anxiety not lessened by the Soviet attempt to propagate the Birobidjan Jewish autonomous region.[30]

The Russian hostility to Zionism was detected by a British observer, who saw Russia posing as the great Moslem Power, supporting a United Nations rather than a British solution to the Palestine question. In any case they claimed there was no Jewish problem in areas under their influence. Hence their rejection of the Commission's request to examine the condition of the Jews in Hungary, in Rumania, and in Bulgaria.[31]

VII

Much as they might welcome the visit of the Commission to Palestine, consideration by the Commission of the views of the Jewish communities in the rest of the Arab Middle East was quite another thing from the Zionist point of view. In the Arab capitals, the Rabbis and the notables, the traditional leaders of the community, in which Zionists were generally a minority, had an awkward time choosing between Government and Zionist pressures. Hence, minorities like the Maronites and the Assyrians were often more outspokenly pro-Zionist than the Jews themselves.[32]

Weizmann, the first Zionist leader to give evidence before the Commission in Jerusalem, appeared moderate in his view that the 100,000 could not arrive in such a short span as one year, but to the British authorities in Palestine he had lost much of his authority there. Yet there were others, like Ben-Gurion and Shertok, who suggested partition in camera, and indeed some members of the Commission were presented with a detailed partition map (see below). The Commission however remained unimpressed.[33]

The hearings in Palestine turned, as they had in London and Washington, into a verbal battleground between the Zionists and the Arabs. Neither side appeared to compromise, at least in public. The Zionists claimed that Palestine had already been divided in 1921–22 by cutting off Transjordan. But the Jewish Agency knew all too well that this could not be a sufficient answer. Hence the argument that economically Western Palestine was able to absorb several million Jews without expelling even one single Arab. Furthermore, inside the future Jewish State the Arabs were promised full and equal rights as individuals, followed by an alliance of friendship with the neighbouring Arab States. The Jewish Agency did not recognise the Palestine Arabs as a separate nation. Not unlike the Pan-Arabists, they claimed that the Arabs constituted one nation, who had sufficient territories in the Middle East.

If this was the kind of policy the Zionists adopted towards the Arabs, why, one may ask, did the Jewish Agency make so much of the Arab collaboration with the Axis Powers before and during the Second World War, or place such emphasis on the tottering and dangerous position of the Jewish minorities in the Arab world? The reply was that this was justified after the murder of more than 100 Jews in Tripoli in November 1945 and the notorious Baghdad pogrom of 1941, coupled with the similar fate of the Assyrians, Kurds and Maronites. The idea was to impress the Commission that no minority, Jewish or otherwise, and least of all Palestine Jewry, could live under any Arab regime.[34]

Indeed, the Arab press was full of indications of uncompromising enmity to Zionism. The Arab leadership in Palestine, and outside, made it quite clear that if a Zionist solution was recommended to the Commission, they would resort to violence and, Auni Abd al-Hadi threatened, with the assistance of the other Arab States. Palestine Jews would do better to give themselves up to the Arab majority, who had no religious or racial enmity towards them. Jamal Husseini, the foremost Palestine Arab leader in the Mufti's absence, did not lag behind Auni's declaration of war. He stated to the Commission that since Britain and America had failed to solve the Palestine problem, it would be better if the British were to evacuate Palestine, to be followed by a military showdown between the Jews and the Arabs. Other Arab politicians of the neighbouring countries, from Feisal of Saudi Arabia to Bourgibah of Tunisia, were not far behind in their threats.

It was only on the surface that the Jewish Agency failed to take the Arab threats seriously. In practice increasing efforts were being made by the Haganah to improve its capability to withstand Arab attack. Although Shertok admitted that the immigration of the 100,000 could lead to bloodshed, Ben-Gurion himself told the Commission that the Jews could look after themselves if assaulted by Palestine Arabs, for conflict was only temporary. Their confidence seemed justified for a number of reasons. The military weakness of the Arab States, not to mention the Palestine Arabs, was well known. The Jewish Agency was convinced that the Arab States had no interest in getting themselves involved in the Palestine question, because this might result in confrontation with Britain and America. Furthermore, Egypt was busy demanding the evacuation of the British Army, its natural interest being in the Sudan and Libya. Iraq was preoccupied fighting the Kurds, and was completely dependent on the British army. Syria and Lebanon had no army at all. Saudi Arabia had no common frontier with Palestine, and being in conflict with Transjordan it was unreasonable to imagine that she could send troops to Palestine.

In short, the Jewish Agency envisaged only a repetition of the 1936–39 infiltration of 'gangs' from the neighbouring countries. The Palestine Arabs would be unlikely to repeat their former revolt after learning a hard lesson both militarily and economically. The Jews could themselves take care of the small 'gangs', and there was no need for the half-million American soldiers which Truman had mentioned at Potsdam. A few air-force squadrons would be sufficient to watch the borders. Sneh claimed in his memorandum on the Jewish Resistance: 'Never has the dependence of the independent Arab States on Britain, on her favour and assistance, been greater than it is now. The pro-Soviet blackmail of the Arab States must therefore be regarded with suspicion – it is but a new and revised edition of their pro-fascist blackmail in Golden Age of the Rome-Berlin Axis.'[35]

Once it had proved that Arab military might was imaginary, the Jewish Agency thought it only natural to demand the establishment of a Jewish State through the initiative of the Great Powers. Both the Jewish question and the Palestine problem were international issues, and had nothing to do with the Arab world. Zionism had been internationally recognized by the Balfour Declaration and the ratification of the Mandate although that

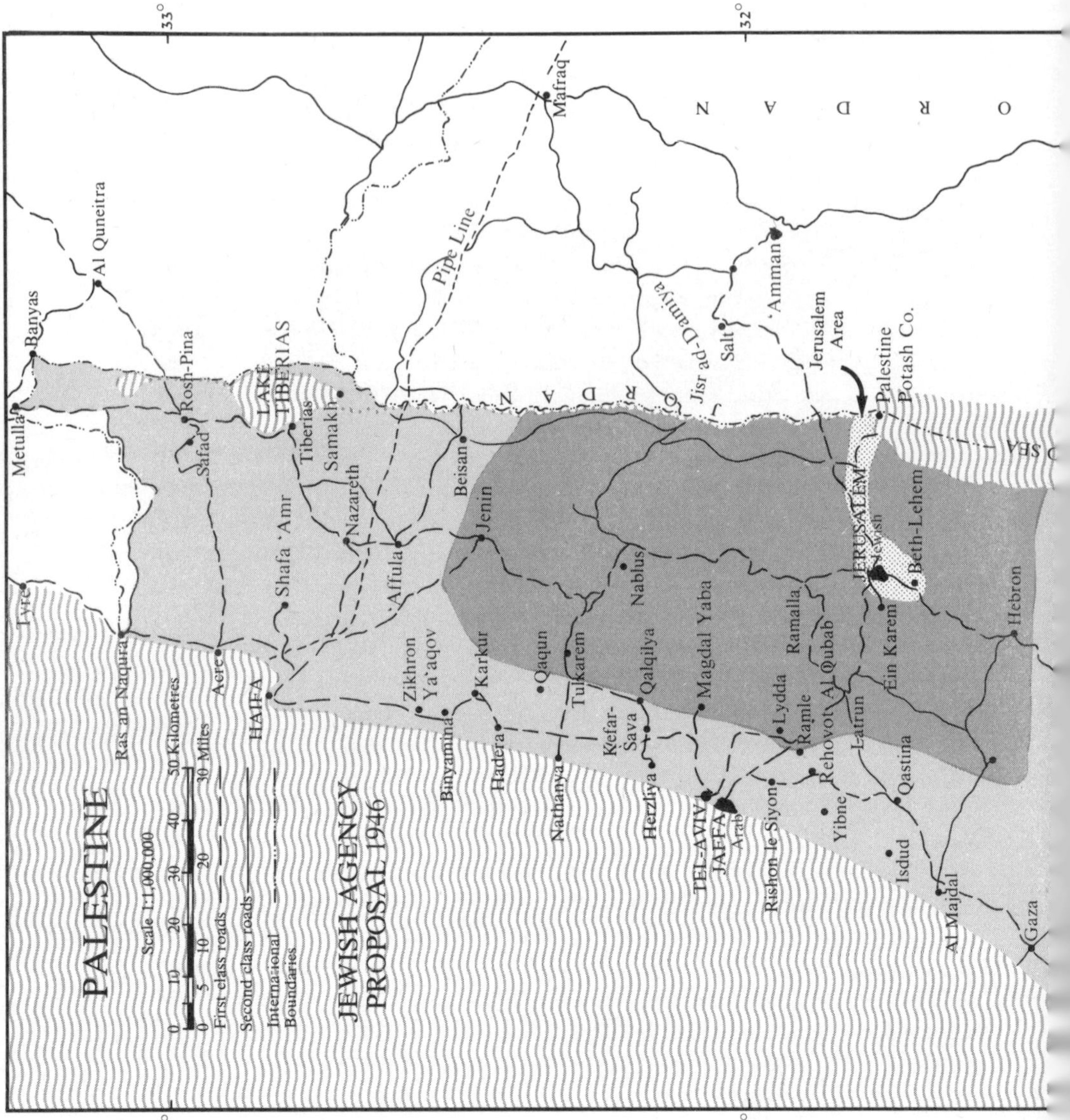
PALESTINE
Scale 1:1,000,000
0 10 20 30 40 50 Kilometres
0 5 10 20 30 Miles
First class roads
Second class roads
Interna-tional Boundaries
JEWISH AGENCY PROPOSAL 1946
33°
32°
Tyre
Metulla
Banyas
Al Quneitra
Rosh-Pina
Safad
LAKE TIBERIAS
Tiberias
Samakh
Ras an Naqura
Acre
HAIFA
Shafa 'Amr
Nazareth
Affula
Beisan
Jenin
Zikhron Ya'aqov
Binyamina
Karkur
Hadera
Qaqun
Nathanya
Tulkarem
Kefar-Sava
Qalqilya
Herzliya
Nablus
Magdal Yaba
TEL-AVIV
JAFFA
Arab
Lydda
Ramle
Rishon le Siyon
Rehovot
Al Qubab
Ramalla
Latrun
Yibne
Qastina
Isdud
Al Majdal
Gaza
Ein Karem
JERUSALEM
Jewish
Beth-Lehem
Hebron
Jerusalem Area
Palestine Potash Co.
Pipe Line
Mafraq
Jisr ad-Damiya
Salt
'Amman
JORDAN
SEA

THE ANGLO-AMERICAN COMMISSION 149

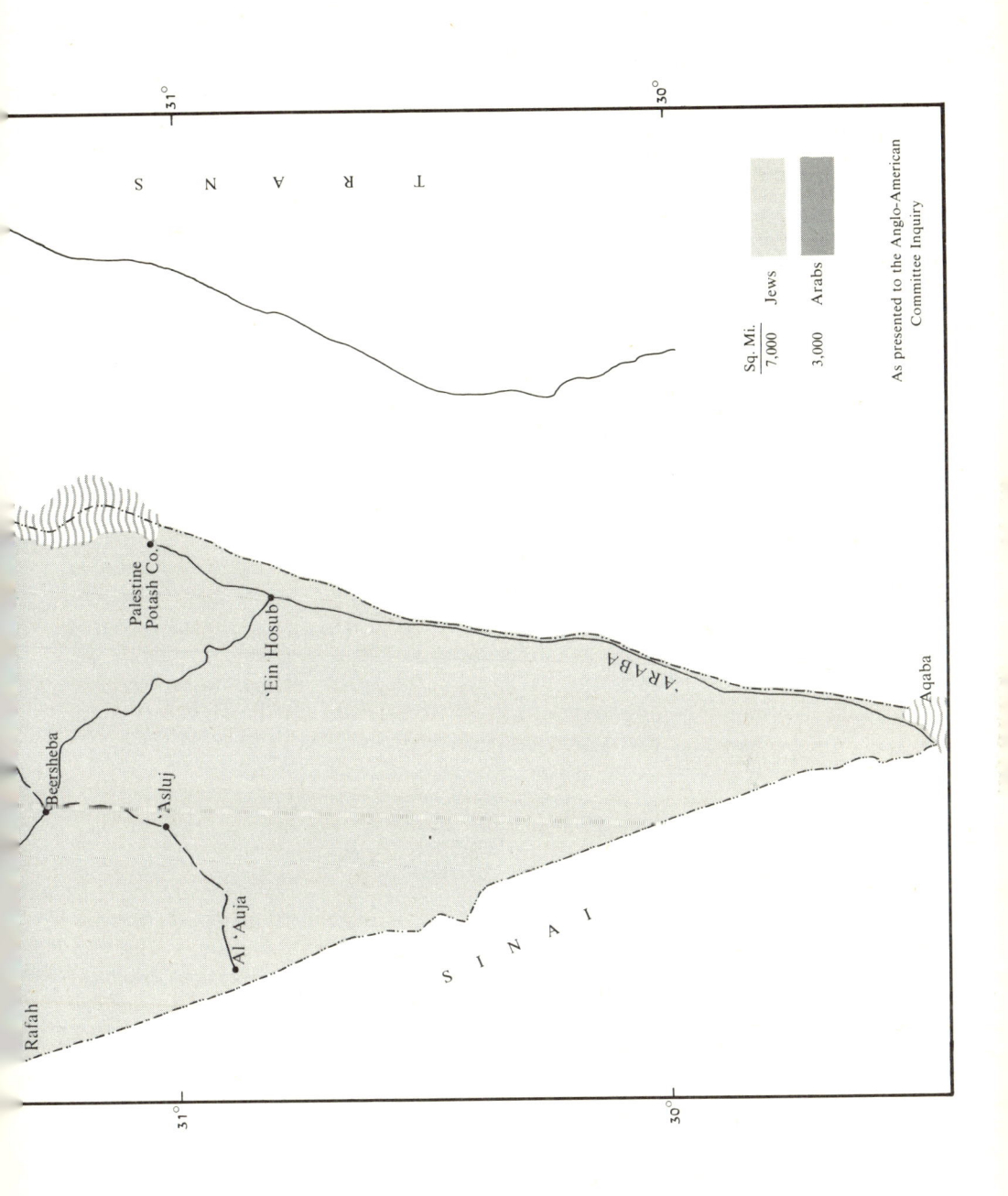

Sq. Mi.	
7,000	Jews
3,000	Arabs

As presented to the Anglo-American Committee Inquiry

had now failed but the Jewish claim for Palestine had existed long before 1917. Above all, the tragic fate of the Jewish people was the most powerful argument for the Jewish State.[36]

Yet, while demonstrating a great deal of self-confidence in its public stance, the Jewish Agency felt considerably disturbed as to what could be expected from the Commission. Shertok called upon the Executive to seriously contemplate the possibility of partition emerging from the Report, whilst Ben-Gurion stressed that Biltmore must be kept as a tactical line. It would be disastrous if the Agency were to initiate a partition plan. Zionism had better prepare itself for the renewal of the Jewish Resistance, since the British government might reject the Commission's proposals.

Contrary to its public arguments, the Zionists were very concerned with Arab opposition because of the growing Arab birth-rate and Arab immigration into Palestine and the mounting difficulties in buying land because of internal Arab terror and the high prices. Ben-Gurion was frightened of sudden changes in the area, especially the possibility that the United Nations might impose a trusteeship on Palestine excluding the Zionist articles of the Mandate (4, 11, 12). This distrust of the United Nations led him to the conclusion that only a State would solve these issues not in ten years ('God forbid') but in two years.

Ben-Gurion however found it difficult to agree to partition without a *quid pro quo*, such as the annexation to the Jewish State of some unoccupied areas of Transjordan in return for the Arab Triangle. In view of the complaint made by some Zionists that the Agency's tactics were confusing, he was ready to suggest this plan as the official Zionist programme.[37] Divided as the Zionists were concerning the right tactics, all were agreed that at this stage this debate was academic, in view of the fact that all the cards were still in the hands of the Commission.

VII

On 26 March the Commission left for Lausanne to compose its final report. At this stage three members out of twelve – Buxton, Crum and MacDonald – could be considered as convinced Zionists, whilst Crossman was still uncertain. In this situation the chances of a Zionist solution were not very great. A suspicion existed in Zionist circles that the Commission might adopt the British intention of outlawing the Jewish Agency and the Haganah as an *imperium in imperio*.[38]

In view of this deep division in the Commission, the Zionists were not agreed whether two reports would be better than one. The moderates preferred one report, believing that a minority Zionist report could have only a demonstrative value. So a special committee, headed by Shertok and Goldmann, went to Switzerland in an attempt to influence the Commission's discussions. They soon realized that the American co-chairman, Judge Hutcheson, who had hitherto doubted whether the Jews were a nation at all, now rejected the Arab solution. Significantly, his visit to Syria and Lebanon had convinced him that Jews could not live under Arab rule. Moreover, he now supported an immigration of 100,000 in 1946, and further immigration to be decided according to the potentialities of the country. He rejected partition because it would create two bi-national states in view of the mixed character of the population. Rather he preferred one bi-national state in an undivided country, probably under Magnes' and Hashomer Hatzair's influence. Legally speaking the Zionists were right and sooner or later they would win. The White Paper was unjust and the Land Laws must be abolished. The Zionists regarded this apparent change of Hutcheson's as a breakthrough in their favour.[39]

Sir John Singleton, the British co-chairman, was amazed that his American colleague had 'betrayed' him. Their relationship worsened a great deal. Singleton was obviously indignant because Hutcheson carried with him the rest of the non-committed American members (Phillips and Aydelotte). Manningham-Buller, who shared Singleton's views, argued that the Balfour Declaration had already been fulfilled and that now an Arab State must be established in Palestine. Hutcheson replied that Jews should not be submitted to Arab rule. The majority of the British members called for the abolition of the Jewish Agency and the Haganah. Palestine, they added, should be under a United Nations Trusteeship. But now Leggett followed Crossman, and Manningham-Buller's suggestion was defeated. The turning point was so sharp and astonishing that the Zionists were afraid Hutcheson might again change his views. MacDonald telegraphed to the White House to encourage Hutcheson in his new attitude.[40]

Thus by mid-April 1946 the Commission was so divided that there was a danger of its ending up with two or even three reports. Four Americans were against either a Jewish or an Arab State, but in favour of unconditional entry of the 100,000 refugees to Palestine, with a reaffirmation of the Mandate to include further Jewish immigration. Three British members agreed that there should be neither a Jewish nor an Arab State, but that the 100,000 should enter slowly on condition that the illegal armies disband. A third group, consisting of one Englishman and two Americans, Crossman, Crum and Buxton, were in favour of partition, if no unanimity could be achieved.

At this stage, Morrison, Leggett and Crossman were convinced that it would be disastrous if no consensus were achieved. They were adamant in their belief that the entry of the 100,000 should not be made conditional on disbandment of the illegal organizations, since it might weaken Weizmann, strengthen the extremists and enrage American opinion to the extent of enlisting Truman again behind Zionism. They finally managed to gain unity by including 'a full and objective' factual statement about the illegal organizations and by drafting Recommendation No. 10, which was interpreted by Whitehall as implying that the immigration of the 100,000 was conditional on disarmament.

No less objectionable to the British dissenters was Singleton's and Manningham-Buller's claim that Hutcheson's line implied war with the Arabs, unless the United States offered military assistance. To Crossman this seemed an irrelevant factor, being based on expediency rather than on justice. The American members, claimed Crossman, were on guard lest the British try to involve the United States in a military adventure in the Middle East. 'This stress, therefore, on the need for American military assistance aroused their keenest suspicions that the whole Committee had been framed for this express point of view. They argued, not unreasonably, that the Committee's job was to establish facts and to recommend a just solution and that they were not in a position to commit the President to active intervention.' Furthermore, Crossman, writing to Hector McNeil, Parliamentary Under-Secretary for Foreign Affairs, claimed that he did not underrate the Arab point of view, since he and the rest of the Commission favoured the establishment of an Arab self-governing community on the lines of the Jewish community to replace 'the present set of charming degenerates.'

Crossman was sure that the British members made no sacrifice whatsoever of British interests. He felt that the Commission did justice by offering a compromise. Whilst rejecting the pro-Arab policy of the Foreign Office they also disposed of the Jewish claim for a state, pointing to the Jewish failure to face up to the Arab problem, and to Jewish terrorism.[41]

There were other pressures for producing one report. The Montreux-based Zionist committee advised the pro-Zionist members of the Commission to favour one report since otherwise Hutcheson might retreat to his previous position. Both the British and the American governments also recommended one report, apparently after Singleton and Harold Beeley, the British Secretary, had visited London, and Philip Noel-Baker, the Minister of State at the Foreign Office, had visited Lausanne.[42]

Arthur Lourie, a senior Zionist diplomat, could now write from Montreux that Zionism was coming true. Senior American officers responsible for Displaced Persons (D.P.s) had been called from Germany to Lausanne to testify about how long it would take to evacuate the camps. Their reply, which startled the British, was that it could be done in one month. In vain did the British attempt a last minute manoeuvre by demanding that the number of immigrants should be limited by the housing situation, the Zionist Achilles' heel.[43]

At this critical stage, the Zionists attempted a dramatic coup in order to achieve partition. For this purpose they called Weizmann from the cold to intervene with the British government, in order to point out a new opportunity to solve the Palestine question.

The coup had its origins in a sensational report from Eliahu Sasson, the

Head of the Arab section in the Agency, claiming that there was little objection to partition on the part of the Arab States provided the Powers would agree. Both King Abdullah and Ali Maher, the Egyptian Prime Minister, had stated that partition was acceptable. For the first time since the appointment of the Commission, Weizmann could see 'a glimmer of light' at the end of the long tunnel. Unfortunately, there was nothing real in the proposal in view of the overwhelming opposition to Zionism in the British establishment and in the Arab States.[44]

Again, at the last minute Singleton tried to make the 100,000 immigration conditional upon the consent of the Arab States, with further immigration to be decided by the United Nations, but this failed owing to his complete isolation amongst the British members. Leaking the Report to the Zionists before its publication, Buxton, Crum and MacDonald told the Zionists that now they had a great opportunity and advised asking the President for help.[45] Indeed, the great opportunity was there, but for how long?

VIII

Although the Report of the Commission, signed on 20 April 1946 and formally issued on 30 April, did not try to suggest a new long-term solution to the Palestine and the Jewish questions, it was bold enough to make some revolutionary recommendations for short-term policies. The Commission, unlike the Peel Commission of 1937, was unable to reach a final decision on the constitutional aspect, because of the division amongst its members. Indeed, the United Nations Special Commission on Palestine (UNSCOP) was bound to return to the partition idea first raised by a purely British Commission a decade earlier. The Anglo-American consensus on Palestine and the Jewish question was too frail to arrive at a bold decision such as partition.

Yet even the short-term recommendations constituted a major Zionist victory. However, it is also understandable why the Zionists were basically disappointed. In the post-Holocaust period they lived in a Messianic mood, i.e. unless their solution to the Jewish question was accepted their opportunity would be lost for ever, as they confessed more than once. How could they then accept the Commission's No. 1 Recommendation which said that Palestine could not possibly solve the problem of the Jewish remnant in Europe?

The Commission had accepted nonetheless that the majority of the Jewish refugees regarded Palestine as their home. They had then in Recommendation No. 2 favoured the immediate immigration of 100,000 Jews from Europe, out of 391,000 Jewish refugees.[46]

Again, the Agency found further ground for objection in Recommendation No. 3 that neither a Jewish nor an Arab state should be established and that world peace would be disturbed if any independent state or states were established. Neither could it digest Recommendation No. 4, that it was necessary to continue the existing mandate until the end of the present animosity and a new trusteeship agreement. Similarly objectionable was Recommendation No. 5 which stated that the raising of the standard of living of the Arab community was essential for an understanding between the two nations. The Jewish Agency believed the conflict was basically a political one. Instead the Commission should have mentioned the economic improvement amongst the Palestine Arabs resulting from Jewish settlement.[47]

Recommendation No. 6 was more acceptable. This stated that until the Palestine question was dealt with at the United Nations the Mandatory Power must ensure Jewish immigration without injuring the Arabs. Recommendation No. 7 suggested that the Land Laws of 1940 should be abrogated but new laws to defend the Arab peasant should be introduced. Was not the Commission following here the British contention that Palestine was overpopulated? As far as the Jewish Agency was concerned this was nothing but a myth, since the country was underdeveloped and a 'Physiocratic approach' was unhelpful, and in any case the Jews owned only 7 per cent of the country's land. Nor was the Agency very happy when, in Recommendation No. 8 the Commission, though appreciative of the Agency's development plans, stated that these plans were conditional on peace prevailing in the area. This, claimed the Agency, was an invitation to the Arabs to start trouble. How could the Commission possibly come up with such a condition, whilst the Arab States boycotted Jewish industrial production? Neither was Recommendation No. 9 to the Agency's taste, since it condemned the Jewish education system as chauvinistic. The Zionist reply was that the idea behind this proposal was to limit the Jewish autonomy in education. Indeed, moderate Zionists like Weizmann and Magnes agreed with the Commission's view on this point.[48]

It is hardly surprising that Ben-Gurion disliked the Report, pressing as he was for a Jewish State. Shertok tried his best to persuade him that Zionism profited ('the wolf was satisfied and the lamb was still alive'). Harry Sacher, a prominent British Zionist and Weizmann's life-long friend, warned that Ben-Gurion's reaction was disastrous, and no better Report could have been anticipated. It would be better to accept the Report and meanwhile delay the Zionist long-term solution. Although he still feared crisis, Ben-Gurion finally admitted that his view was perhaps incorrect, and that it was incumbent upon Zionism to come to an understanding with Britain.

Sneh however, surprised by the Report, viewed it as an Arab defeat, so until the British actually accepted it, and in view of Arab pressure, it constituted a 'great danger'. But Weizmann was satisfied it aided the Zionist campaign whether fulfilled or not. Arab pressures could be countered by American Zionism. Most of the 100,000 could be brought and sheltered within one year, and within five years the Jewish State could materialize.[49]

Sneh's pessimism proved justified with the British rejection of the Report on 1 May 1946. And Britain's attitude to the illegal armies proved harder than expected. Some Zionists thought Attlee had meant only the Irgun and the Sternists, but as Hall indicated to Crossman in a stormy meeting, he regarded the Haganah too as responsible for the terror.[50]

Paradoxically, it has been claimed, the British rejection saved Zionism from the most serious crisis in its history, and 'achieved' greater unity in the Zionist movement. Weizmann, following Crossman, had stated at a meeting of the London Zionist executive before the rejection that it was the time to end the terror and finish off both the Irgun and the Sternists. Now it was clear that there would have to be a renewal of Jewish Resistance activities with intensified diplomacy, particularly in America. Israel Eldad, the Sternist ideologue, later admitted that it was a great miracle that Bevin saved the Yishuv from civil war.[51]

Attlee's statement threw Weizmann himself into a state of shock: 'I am absolutely bewildered ... I feel deeply distressed'. A few hours before he had experienced the greatest elation after a year of crisis. If they did not allow the 100,000 to go to Palestine, he warned Attlee, Britain would be confronted with terror.[52]

There was little to be salvaged from Britain. Churchill, now in opposition, persistently evaded the Zionists, proclaiming that the conflict between Jacob and Esau would go on for a very long time, and Tom Williams, the Minister of Agriculture and a former Zionist, justified Attlee's statement when approached. Furthermore, at the Labour Party Conference at Bournemouth on 12 June 1946, Bevin made it clear that if the Report's recommendations were implemented, another division and a further £200 million would be required.[53]

In their despair some Zionists demanded an uncompromising reply to the British questionnaire, but again it was decided it should be diplomatic (16 June 1946). More dramatic was a parallel decision to renew the Jewish Resistance on the lines of 1 November 1945. On 17 June the Palmach destroyed the bridges connecting Palestine with the neighbouring countries. As Shertok explained to his colleagues it was necessary to buttress Zionist diplomatic pressure in America and to save the Commission's Zionist recommendations. Also, the Jewish refugees were packing their bags since the publication of the Report.[54]

Yet tactics and diplomacy triumphed over the sense of anger and despair at least in the American scene, where Goldmann argued they ought to push for the 100,000, and ultimately accept partition rather than Biltmore in order to avoid the ominous Trusteeship. But in the Yishuv as before Zionist differences were reduced to a minimum. The only opponents of diplomacy-cum-resistance were, as anticipated, the minority: Hashomer Hatzair, the leftist bi-nationalists and Aliya Hadasha and Ichud. Yaacov Hazan of Hashomer Hatzair warned that the British were preparing for counter-attack. Shlomo Kaplansky, the Director of the Haifa Technical College, warned that Britain even in decline could still break Palestine Jewry.[55]

IX

How accurate was the Zionist assessment of Britain's policy? We are now in a better position to answer this in the light of the recently opened British official archives. Generally speaking the Zionist perception of British policy was only partially correct. The Zionist assumption that Britain's 'fear' of the Arab reaction to the Report, and the need to follow an 'appeasement' policy, engendered the official rejection of the Report, was correct. But neither was it quite as Crossman presented it: 'Why should HMG make less justice with more divisions when it is possible to make more justice with less divisions?'[56] Whitehall clearly believed the opposite. Although British military intelligence greatly exaggerated the strength of the Haganah, a view recently submitted to the Commission itself by General D'Arcy, G.O.C. Palestine, this led neither D'Arcy nor the Chiefs of Staff to the conclusion that Jewish military potential needed more British divisions than the Arab military nuisance value. British strategists did not wish as yet to give up their bases in Egypt, Iraq's oil or for that matter the oil terminal to Haifa. The crux of the matter was that neither the military nor the political establishment considered Palestine as detached geopolitically from the rest of the Middle East. Given this frame of mind, deeply rooted in Britain's policy-making elite for the preceding decade, the Zionists had only little hope of playing on their own nuisance value.[57]

Moreover, the fact that the Commission did not suggest a Jewish State did not change Britain's unfavourable attitude. For Britain the Commission's support for Jewish immigration was bad enough. After all the Arabs regarded immigration (as indeed did the Zionists) as a stepping-stone for a Jewish State.

It is clear that those moderate Zionists who believed that Britain could be persuaded to change the course of its Palestine policy were entirely wrong. These moderates established their hopes on the pro-Zionist recommendations of the Commission and on Truman's aid, which they believed would eventually convince Britain. Equally wrong however were the extremist-Zionists, who thought that the British Government could be convinced by a show of strength.

In fact the British Government itself was greatly surprised by the Report. The majority of the British members of the Commission, with the aid of Harold Beeley, were doing their best to bring the American members over to the British point of view. Just before leaving the country, Beeley had in Jerusalem already expressed some fear that the

Commission's Report might be far removed from Britain's policy. Beeley was apprehensive lest lack of coordination between the two governments over simultaneous publication of both the Report and the statement of policy, would lead to a complete failure to achieve common policy with America over Palestine: 'It would lead to a situation in which HMG would be confronted with the alternatives of submitting to the pressures of American public opinion or deliberately confronting it: if that were to happen the Committee would have lost its *raison d'être* as a means of a better understanding of the Palestine problem'. The only way to overcome this dilemma that Beeley could see was to enlist the War Department, possibly more effective than the State Department, to accept the British view on Palestine. But future events were to prove that public opinion was a more effective factor than both War and State Departments put together.

Nevertheless, to Whitehall the situation did not look so fragile as to Beeley. The consensus amongst the Foreign, War and Colonial Offices was that it was indeed possible to enlist American agreement to steps against the Haganah and the Jewish Agency alongside a 'reasonable' scale of immigration. But nonetheless, Britain should be prepared to fulfil such recommendations even without American support.[58]

Beeley, generally quite influential in the Foreign Office, was not alone in thinking that the predominantly Zionist American public opinion could be defeated. Neville Butler, Head of the American Department, thought that this was conceivable (a) if the oil pressure group in America could be effectively used against Zionism; (b) if Britain explained that they could not implement large scale immigration recommendations without the sanction of the United Nations, in view of the pledge which had been given to the Arabs in the 1939 White Paper. Moreover, there were no outstanding American personalities in the Commission, and therefore it was not an American 'show', hence the rejection of its recommendations would not be regarded as a national insult.[59]

Similarly, one of the most influential experts on Palestine at the Colonial Office, Sir Douglas Harris, had thought it unlikely that the Commission would repeat the 'sweeping' suggestion which Truman had made concerning the 100,000. Before the publication of the Report he saw little likelihood of any interim solution satisfying either Jews or Arabs, and he was inclined to favour a permanent solution through the United Nations, although the probability of agreement between both sides was remote. 'A difficult and dangerous operation is inevitable and the more speedily it can be accomplished the better chance will the patient have of recovery.'[60]

Once the Commission's Report became known to the public it aroused a considerable amount of emotional reaction on the already greatly agitated Arab side. As usual the Arab point of view was brought home with great zeal by the British diplomatic representatives in the Middle

East. According to Grafftey-Smith, the Minister in Jedda, forever alarming the Foreign Office on forthcoming ominous Arab reactions, the Report was 'disastrous' to Anglo-Arab relations. Apart from its failure to point to an end to immigration, the recommendation to move the 100,000 was a 'bombshell' for them. Here was yet another erosion of the White Paper of 1939, the Arab 'Charter'. Similarly, he was critical of the Commission's futile attempt to solve the conflict by reviving the 'old fallacy' that economic benefit should stifle Arab national sentiment.

Terrence Shone, the Minister to Syria and Lebanon, did not lag behind in forecasting 'intense and uncompromising' opposition in the Levant states, adding a plausible prediction that the Soviets would do all they could to exploit the situation to the detriment of both Britain and America. Nor was the reaction from the Cairo and Baghdad Embassies, and from the Viceroy in India, of different nature. The leitmotif was that the Report was offensive to the Arabs and a victory for the Zionists and for the Americans. At the time of negotiating the revised Treaties with Egypt and Iraq, the Report could only aggravate the situation.[61]

The Colonial Office took a more balanced view. Though not underrating the intense Arab dislike for the Report, they thought the initial reaction was bound to be vocal but ultimately would depend on Anglo-American unanimity and the degree of determination shown in its implementation. No less significant was the Colonial Office assessment that even if the Jewish leadership preached moderation, which they doubted, it was an open question whether they would be listened to. The local Arabs might resort to violence, but considering the fact that they were greatly dependent on the Arab States, the Colonial Office was doubtful whether the latter would back the use of force by the Palestine Arabs. Paradoxically, however, they concluded that the Report could be implemented only by Arab-Jewish cooperation, hinting at the 'considerable' influence the Report might have on moderate opinion on both sides.[62]

The first reaction in the Foreign Office was rather positive, but only on the junior level. Wikeley, who had to brief Bevin on the Report, thought it could be implemented although the Arabs would hate it. The Arab threats should not be taken too seriously since they were too frightened of Russia to turn against Britain. Jews must be disarmed, as well as the Arabs. Yet for this purpose American military assistance was needed.[63]

This view, however, as Wikeley anticipated, carried little weight. When the Cabinet Defence Committee came to deal with the Report on 24 April 1946 there was little enthusiasm for it. Bevin, though he feared Arab reactions, still felt that it would be difficult to avoid its acceptance. Its unanimity was for him an 'augury of cooperation by the United States Government in solving the problems of Palestine.' Naively Bevin believed that he could gain American military support for the suppression of the Jewish illegal organizations as a condition for Britain's agreement for the immigration of the 100,000. Otherwise these immigrants might join the ranks of the illegal organizations.

Attlee took a less favourable view of the Report than Bevin. He was irritated by the fact that Palestine was alone considered as a destination for the Jewish refugees. Contrary to Bevin, he found only little ground in the Report to suggest that Britain could expect American cooperation in solving the Palestine question. Believing that the implementation of the Report would aggravate the situation in Palestine, he suggested that it 'was time that others helped to share it with us'. He correctly assessed that pressure rather than support for the British point of view was to be expected from the United States.

Following the High Commissioner's advice, Hall too did not sound optimistic. Replying to complaints by some members of the Defence Committee about the heavy burden of the Palestine Mandate, the Colonial Secretary said that only by obtaining a new Trusteeship agreement which would be taken over by another country or countries was it possible to get rid of the present responsibilities.

But this was only wishful thinking. In reality, as Field-Marshal Alanbrooke, the C.I.G.S., explained, with the concurrence of the rest of the Committee, Palestine could be the last foothold Britain might have in the region in view of the uncertainty of the position in Egypt. He further stressed the 'very great' importance of Middle Eastern oil resources which made Palestine strategically indispensable.[64]

Before the Cabinet itself came to deal with the Report, a special Ad Hoc Official Committee was established to assess its value. Headed by Sir Norman Brook, Joint Secretary to the Cabinet, it included the well-known experts from the Foreign and Colonial Offices, and representatives from the War and India Offices and the Treasury. Thus its composition assured the rejection of the Report. The Committee was horrified by the 100,000 immigration recommendation, pointing out that never before had so many immigrants been admitted to Palestine in one year (the maximum had been 64,137 in 1935). They were particularly annoyed that the Commission had ignored the absolute objection by the Arabs to Jewish immigration. Still, they envisaged the possibility of conceding on the question, although with the proviso of a fully shared responsibility with the United States.

The Ad Hoc Committee shared the views of the British Representatives in the Middle East that the Palestine Arabs were not interested in social and economic betterment, which they would regard as a bribe, but rather in retaining Palestine as an Arab country. Following the usual pattern of thought they noted that although the Commission did not make disarmament a condition for the execution of the Report, yet in Recommendation No. 10 an invitation was made to the British Government to suppress terrorism, both Arab and Jewish.

They took a pessimistic view of the reaction of the Palestine Arabs, and could find little comfort in the possibility of American military support, for the Palestine Arab's martyrs would gain the support of the Arab and Moslem world.

Whilst the Committee preferred the view of the British Representatives on Arab extremism, rejecting the more hopeful view of the High Commissioner, they adopted the latter's assumption of a violent Jewish reaction, summarizing that the Report would satisfy no one and lead to aggressive reactions from both sides.

In conclusion the Ad Hoc Committee suggested that the British Government consider two alternatives: either to invite the United States to participate in the implementation of the Report, or to place the Palestine question before the Security Council of the United Nations. But they did not believe that the United States would agree to active participation. Hence they decided to recommend the Cabinet to make an early reference to the United Nations for two reasons: (1) In the event of the implementation of the Report either the Arab States or Russia would refer the Palestine issue to the United Nations. It would be better if the British Government did so before committing themselves to the Commission's Recommendation. (2) The Government had already undertaken, in Bevin's speech on 13 November 1945, to bring an agreed solution before the United Nations.[65]

The next day, 27 April 1946, Bevin tried to explain the British Government's view to Byrnes, the American Secretary of State, whilst both of them were attending the Foreign Ministers' Conference in Paris, overlooking the fact that Palestine policy had become the domain of the White House rather than that of the Department of State. Typical of the British misunderstanding of this basic tenet of American politics was Bevin's plea to Byrnes on 28 April that the United States Government should not make any statement about the Report without consulting Britain. As usual Halifax, the Ambassador, who more than once warned the Foreign Office as to the immense influence of Zionism in the United States, was unable to correct this distorted image.[66]

It was Bevin himself however who, more than his subordinates at Whitehall, understood the importance of trying to obtain direct American participation in Palestine politics. This was his view in the Defence Committee of 24 April and he repeated it to the Cabinet on 29 April, although the Ad Hoc Committee recommended the contrary. Reminding the Cabinet of his opposition to the immediate transference of the Palestine issue to the Security Council, Bevin explained that 'this would be regarded as a confession of failure and would have unfortunate effects on other aspects of our foreign policy'. Again, Bevin still refused to believe that the United States Government would not eventually grasp that the fulfilment of the Zionist demands or part of them was impractical. Bevin miscalculated his ability to persuade the American Government not to issue any statement of policy following the publication of the Report.

Surprisingly, Bevin dissociated himself from the British Representatives in the Middle East who predicted violent Arab reactions to the Report: 'We should not be unduly alarmed by some initial clamour from the Arab States.'

Agreeing with Bevin, Hall said that only if the Americans were unwilling to help should Britain refer the issue to the United Nations. In any event, as pointed out by Alanbrooke and Hugh Dalton, the Chancellor of the Exchequer, further military and financial commitments should be taken into account. On this and on the need to suppress terrorism, there was a general agreement in the Cabinet. In addition the Cabinet backed the idea of asking for alleviation of America's immigration laws to allow more Jewish refugees into America.

Although the tendency in the Cabinet was to accept Bevin's line of pursuing a joint policy with America, some Ministers were still preoccupied with the possibility that Russia would not tolerate its exclusion from handling the Palestine problem. Nonetheless, it would be better to obtain in advance a common policy with the Americans in the event of the Palestine issue being referred to the Security Council. In conclusion, Bevin's opinion remained predominant in the Cabinet, and a final attempt to bring the Americans to Britain's point of view was to be made.[67]

However, Britain soon found out that it was far easier to convince the Conservative opposition and the Dominion Prime Ministers than to persuade the Americans. Even Smuts, despite confessing that his sympathy lay with the Zionists, admitted that the problem was insoluble and approved Britain's policy. Speaking to the Dominion Prime Ministers Attlee stressed the point that the Report would lead to a storm on both sides. The Zionists committed to Biltmore could not accept it. The Commission's recommendations that the 'legitimate national aspiration' of both sides could be realized was rejected by Attlee as impractical, as had been proved in India, Ireland and South Africa.[68]

As before, the British Cabinet and Bevin in particular expected too much of the Americans. On the same day, 30 April 1946, Halifax reported that Truman was shortly to issue a statement of policy that was far removed from Britain's views, not mentioning the need to suppress the illegal organizations and going so far as to announce his great relief at the 100,000 Recommendation and that, in effect, the Report amounted to the abrogation of the White Paper. As if that was not enough Byrnes informed Bevin the next day that the United States could not endorse a policy which would involve them in further military commitments.[69] Bevin replied with a stiff letter to Byrnes in which he condemned the unilateral American declaration. He went so far as to hint that this was bound to encourage acts of murder by Jewish terrorists. He warned that this was a position which the British people could tolerate no longer: 'If the United States does not accept the implications regarding the need for disarming illegal armies before immigration, a situation which will endanger the security of the Middle East is likely to arise.'[70]

Following Truman's bombshell the Cabinet assembled for the second time in forty-eight hours in an attempt to reassess the situation. Now Attlee emphasized that they would have to issue an entirely different statement from that previously intended. Nevertheless, a complete break with the United States over Palestine was unthinkable.[71]

Again, Halifax was trying hard to bring home to the Foreign Office that the demand for the 100,000 had captured the American public mind. Apart from the fact the Government's objection to the 100,000 was a 'slight' to America's prestige, he doubted whether the latter would agree to Britain's present policy. Halifax therefore recommended placing the issue before the United Nations General Assembly in the coming September or at a specially convened meeting. Since the Arab States or Russia were bound to sooner or later, Halifax preferred that Britain herself should come forward as 'the appellant rather than the defendant in the dock'. However, since the Foreign Office did not yet have any clear idea as to the solution to recommend to the United Nations, especially a policy which ensured Palestine as a British strategic base, Halifax's suggestion was rejected.[72]

Truman's statement had indeed wrecked Britain's Palestine policy. On 8 May 1946 however, the President offered to initiate joint consultations with both Jews and Arabs. He said that after they had received the views of both sides the British and the American Governments could determine their common attitude to the Report as a whole. They would not, however make any approaches before the 20th May in order not to prejudice the Egyptian negotiations.[73]

This time it was Attlee who reacted with unwarranted enthusiasm to Truman's new move. On 9 May he told the Cabinet that it was a 'further admission by the United States Government of some share of responsibility in the Palestine problem'. While realizing that Truman did not refer to any financial or military assistance, he hoped to raise these points later on. Probably Attlee relied on Bevin's suggestion to Byrnes on the previous day that before undertaking consultations with both sides, a study of the Report by experts should be initiated by the Governments.[74]

Indeed, on 20 May Bevin, convinced that Britain was nearing a breakthrough, confidentially told the Cabinet that the Americans 'now seemed to be willing to remove this question from the realm of propaganda and to study its implications on a business-like footing.'[75]

The new American move was a much needed fillip to Britain's policy in view of the alarming reports, especially from the Ambassador in Baghdad, that the economic and social policy initiated in the London Middle Eastern Conference of September 1945 was doomed to failure. Since then, however, strategic considerations proved to be of far more importance than economic and social ones.[76]

Thus the Morrison (Brook)-Grady Committee was established, in effect making it clear that the Anglo-American Committee of Inquiry had failed in view of the failure of the two Governments to agree on the basic principles of Palestine policy, or even on a compromise.

X

Was the compromise offered by the Anglo-American Commission of Inquiry a practical solution, or was it only a middle-of-the-road formula which merely reflected the need for agreement amongst a group of people who had been chosen at random to deal with a highly complicated issue of which they had little prior knowledge?

Crossman perhaps proves the exception. He was sufficiently aware to realise in advance that the British Government would be lukewarm over the compromise, because of the heavy military commitment. Yet he attempted to base his case on other factors.

Primarily, the implementation of the Report would contribute towards the return to power of the moderates headed by Weizmann, who had surrendered the leadership to Ben-Gurion as a result of the White Paper policy. Hence the strength of the terrorists and the demand for a Jewish State. By nullifying the White Paper and allowing 100,000 Jews to enter Palestine, Crossman hoped that Jewish opinion around the world could be split between moderates interested only in saving European Jewry and the continued growth of the National Home, and the extremists who were 'exploiting humanitarian feelings for achieving totalitarian political ambitions'.

Crossman grossly overrated the strength of the moderate Zionists when he expected them to retain authority. Yet with the rest of the Commission's members he doubted whether the Jewish Agency would be able to absorb the 100,000 in view of the looming economic crisis. Consequently, it would have to collaborate with Britain in every possible way, including the suppression of terrorism. Here again Crossman had high hopes of the moderates headed by Weizmann and Kaplan, the Agency's treasurer.

Crossman indeed believed that the Report might defuse the Arab-Jewish conflict since it accepted the grievances of both sides, so far as the disparity in the standard of living was concerned. Hence the recommendation regarding the need for cooperation with the neighbouring Arab countries.

But what Crossman was really worried about was the long-term consequences of the Report's Recommendations. At least twenty-five years, if not fifty, were demanded for the fulfilment of these Recommendations. But neither the Mandate nor Trusteeship could continue for such a long time since both sides were in fact ready for independence. This bleak future led Crossman to the inevitable conclusion that the only solution could be partition in a matter of five years. At the present moment Crossman felt that partition involved too big a risk since it would have to be imposed by force, but given time, the Foreign Secretary might be able to force both sides to rethink along more realistic lines.

Again, although Crossman had listened to Arab evidence he obviously underrated the uncompromising extremism presented by the various Arab witnesses. Rather, he was impressed by the Jewish readiness to agree to partition.

After the official attack on the British members of the Commission complaining that the Report was a sell-out to the Americans, Crossman was not taken aback, but remained strongly convinced that it was just. Since he was preoccupied with the Jewish rather than with the Arab case, believing that a full confrontation with the Jews would be worse than the one with Ireland after the First World War, he and Leggett thought that to make the entry of the 100,000 conditional on disarmament, might be extremely dangerous since it might leave the Jews defenseless *vis-à-vis* possible Arab attack. He told the Government that the immigration of the 100,000 would not cost them a great deal. Here was an opportunity to bring back the moderates into the saddle.[77]

The other four members of the Commission had different views from those of Crossman and Leggett, but they too failed to convince the Government. Singleton tried to convince Attlee that the Report was not necessarily a sell-out to the Americans. The Report had emphasized that Palestine was not a Jewish State, the private armies were declared illegal, and after the admission of the 100,000 immigration was to be conducted on a new basis: the well-being of the country as a whole. Singleton felt that it was essential to obtain the consent of the American Government for these three conclusions. He fully supported the view that the Jewish Agency must accept it as a whole. He also believed that the Report removed the Arab fear of Jewish economic domination. The Commission, added Singleton, favoured a bi-national State, but had left the question of a constitution for the future.

Lord Morrison, who, at Lausanne, a month earlier, had sided with Crossman in an attempt to prevent the break-up of the Commission, now sided with the British Government. He castigated the Zionists for adopting only those parts of the Report which fitted into their own policy. He believed that Zionism succeeded in Palestine because it used the methods of the Hitler Youth Movement, and in the United States because of its unscrupulous use of anti-British propaganda.

Crick felt joint action with America was plausible, but on anti-Zionist lines: the special status of the Jewish Agency should be abolished and the Jewish refugee question should be solved by the United Nations. Subject to strategic considerations, the Americans should simply be told that if they did not come forward actively in support of Britain's Palestine burden, she would surrender the Mandate to the United Nations.

Manningham-Buller also saw the Jewish Agency as the chief stumbling block to Arab-Jewish cooperation. Clipping its wings through disarmament would restore power to the British Administration. Unlike Crossman, Manningham-Buller regarded partition as a dangerous solution which might lead to serious trouble.

So the British Government was supported by four out of the six members appointed by the Government. Those four, had, in Lausanne and after, the support of two American members, Aydelotte and Phillips. On the other hand two British members, Crossman and Leggett, and the rest of the American members opposed the Government. All the British members including Crossman feared it would bring Russia in, and warned against joint Trusteeship with America.

Attlee had expressed his disappointment with the Report with regard to immigration. In particular, Singleton, much as he sympathized with the British position, apologized that the Report could not directly attack the Jewish Agency or the Haganah, since that would have split the Commission. He felt that any proposal to abolish the Agency would have led to open war in Palestine.[78]

The Anglo-American Report was indeed a compromise between its members, but, although it rejected the Zionist demand for a state, it sounded pro-Zionist to the British Government. The Arabs, who had long before rejected any kind of compromise, reacted with a mixture of anger and despair to what they regarded as a major Zionist victory. They however laid the blame at the door of America rather than Britain. Meeting in Lebanon, at Bloudan on June 1946, the Council of the Arab League rejected Jamal Husseini's suggestion of establishing an Arab army to conquer Palestine and suppress the Jews. But they admitted that in the coming military confrontation they could not prevent volunteers from joining their brothers in Palestine. This indeed was a secret decision, as was the one which approved a cooling down of relations with both Britain and the United States in the event of the implementation of the Report.[79]

XI

It is difficult, however, to say whether the Report offered a practical solution, because it was never implemented. Undoubtedly it would have demanded a heavy military commitment. But would the later Morrison (Brook)-Grady solution have required fewer divisions? In fact none of these plans was practical, as the reaction of both sides proved. What was practical was the partition plan recommended by Crossman, Crum and MacDonald; and a handful of Arab statesmen like Abdullah, and British soldiers of the magnitude of John Glubb and Brigadier Clayton, were ready to give their support. Indeed, a year later, in view of the bankruptcy of Britain's Palestine policy, the United Nations Special Committee on Palestine (UNSCOP) returned to partition as more practical than all other solutions. To be sure, even if the majority of the Anglo-American Commission had accepted the idea of partition, there is no doubt that Britain would have rejected it, probably against Truman's view.

Faced with the choice of supporting either the Zionists or the Arabs, Britain made her decision. Obviously, it was an expedient one. The Labour Government accepted without murmur the deeply rooted concepts of the military and the officials of the Foreign and Colonial Offices that the Arab case was a stronger one. In these circumstances the failure of the Anglo-American Commission of Inquiry was inevitable, as was the alternative policy of the British Government.

Yet Bevin was hardly George III, since the Jews had yet to deal with a far more ruthless enemy than the British, the Arabs. Guided by his advisers, Bevin never thought of winning a 'major victory' over the Jewish Agency by a compromise of 50,000 immigration, instead of 100,000 as Dalton suggested,[80] and some Zionists feared.

The Anglo-American Commission of Inquiry demonstrated the failure of Britain and the United States to give the Palestine issue a top priority on the world agenda. Rather, Palestine was treated as a nuisance, a second-rate problem, which did not warrant a top-level agreement between the two Powers. Alternatively, one can argue that such an understanding was never possible between them, and the reference to the United Nations was inevitable. The last thirty years has proved their failure too. The problem still remained one for the Great Powers to solve.

NOTES

1. C. Weizmann, *Trial and Error* (London, 1949), p. 554. M. Sharett (Shertok), *On the Threshold of Statehood* (Tel-Aviv, 1958), p. 14. (In Hebrew). A. Eban, '1939–1949: Tragedy and Triumph', in *Chaim Weizmann: A Biography by Several Hands*, eds. M. Weisgal and J. Carmichael (London, 1962), p. 311. Sir I. Berlin, *Zionist Politics in Wartime Washington: A Fragment of Personal Reminiscence* (Jerusalem, 1972), p. 65.
2. Y. Allon, *A History of the Palmach* (Tel-Aviv, 1965), p. 142. (In Hebrew).
3. M. Begin, *The Revolt* (London, 1951). I. Eldad, *Maaser Rishon* (Tel-Aviv, 1963), pp. 196–97. (In Hebrew).
4. Y. Slutsky, *The History of the Haganah*, Vol. III (Tel-Aviv, 1972), pt. 2, pp. 816 ff. (In Hebrew). N. Yalin-More, *The Fighters for the Freedom of Israel* (Jerusalem, 1974). (In Hebrew).
5. The Arabs believed that the appointment of the Commission meant the suppression of the White Paper of 1939. FO/141//1021//129//143/45. It was suggested that the Arabs should be reminded that the King-Crane Committee of 1919 had been in their favour. Howe to Martin, 28.12.45. Secret. FO/371/45388/E9564.
6. Y. Bauer, *Flight and Rescue: BRICHAH* (New York, 1970), pp. 76 ff. H. S. Truman, *Years of Trial and Hope* (New York, 1956), pp. 141 ff.
7. Minute by Sir Walter Smart, the Oriental Minister in Cairo and the *éminence grise* of

THE ANGLO-AMERICAN COMMISSION 167

the British elite in the Middle East. 6.11.45. FO/141/1021/129/33/45. FO to Washington, 12.10.45. No. 1267. Most Immediate. Top Secret. FO/371/45380. M. J. Cohen, 'The Genesis of the Anglo-American Committee on Palestine, November 1945: A Case Study in the Assertion of American Hegemony', *The Historical Journal*, 22, 1 (1979), pp. 185–207.
8. Extract from the Cabinet Conclusions. 38(45).4.10.45. FO/371/45381/E7956/G.
9. Memorandum by G. H. Hall, the Colonial Secretary, n.d. Top Secret. *Ibid.*
10. *Foreign Relations of the United States* (FRUS), Vol. VII (Washington, 1969), pp. 774 ff. P.(M)(45) 2. Meeting Cabinet Palestine Committee Minutes 10.10.45. Report by the Lord President of the Council FO/371/45381/E7637/G. Top Secret. C.M(45) 40th Conclusions. Extract from Cabinet Meeting 11.10.45. FO/733/461/75872. Pt. IV. Note by R. G. Howe, Head of the Foreign Office Middle East Department, to the Colonial Secretary. FO/371/45380/E7479/G.Halifax to FO, 19.10.45. tel. No. 6964. Immediate. Top Secret. *Ibid.* Extract from Cabinet Conclusions, 52(45).13.11.45. FO/371/45380/E797.
11. D. Ben-Gurion, *Reply to Bevin* (London, 1945). Report on Weizmann's Talk with the President, 4.12.45. S25/7497. C(entral) Z(ionist) A(rchives).
12. In Whitehall it was felt that by giving their consent to the inclusion of MacDonald, well-known for his pro-Zionist views, they were not paying too high a price. Howe to Martin, 28.12.45. FO/371/45388/E9564.
13. Small Zionist Actions Committee, 11.12.45. S5/363. CZA. Senator was soon to resign. Cf. his letter of resignation in *Commentary* (October, 1946), pp. 384–6.
14. Small Zionist Actions Committee, 12.12.45. *op. cit.*
15. Mapai Archives, Bet-Berl. Israel.
16. C.M. (46) 1st Conclusions. 1.1.46. CAB/128/5. Halifax to FO, 13.1.46 No. 306. FO/371/52504.
17. AZEC. Meeting of the Executive Committee, 14.11, 26.11.30.11, 7.12.45. Z5/1206 CZA.
18. D. Horowitz, *A State in the Making* (New York, 1952), pp. 63 ff. Comay to Gering, 19.2.46. S25/1568. CZA. The Foreign Office feared that the Jewish organizations in America would prejudice the Commission: cf. Minute by Beeley FO/371/45389/E9828, and *ibid.*/9914.
19. All the evidence given to the Commission, including the cross-examination, but only a few memoranda, are conveniently assembled in: A. Carlebach *The Anglo-American Commission of Inquiry on Palestine* (Tel-Aviv, 1946). (In Hebrew). The English originals and other vast material are deposited in the CZA.
20. R. Crossman, *Palestine Mission* (London, 1947), pp. 35–41.
21. Kaplan to the Executive of the Jewish Agency, 10.2.46. Protocol CZA.
22. Epstein to Shertok, 25.1.46. Personal S25/451. CZA Meeting of the Committee of Eight (Jewish Agency Political Committee in America), 21.1.46. S53/2031. *Ibid.*
23. *Ibid.* And Goldmann to Shertok, 20.2.46. Strictly Confidential Z6/Package 18/File 15. CZA. The British were aware of the Zionist shift towards partition e.g. Memorandum on the Present State of Jewish Affairs in the United States by A. H. Tandy, 25.2.46. FO/371/52568/E2198/14/31. Halifax thought the Zionists overplayed their testimony. Halifax to FO, 13.1.46 No. 306. FO/371/52504. Rundall to Tandy, 15.1.46. FO/371/52508/E954.
24. *Baffy: The Diaries of Blanch Dugdale, 1936–1947*, ed. N. A. Rose (Vallentine, Mitchell, London, 1973), pp. 229–30. On the Foreign Office bias cf. Beeley's enthusiasm over Thomas Reid's testimony. FO/371/52507/E771. Manningham-Buller assured Bevin on 22.1.46 that 'so far ... things have gone pretty well'. *Ibid.* E838. Bevin's remark FO/371/52509/E1413.
25. *Baffy*, op.cit. 27.1.46. Weizmann to Major Hay, 5.2.46 Weizmann Archives. Crossman, pp. 168–69. J. Kimche to E. Braudo, 2.2.46. S25/6450. CZA. Comay to Gering, 19.2.46. *op. cit.*

26. Y. Bauer, pp. 201 ff. Ruffer to Shertok, 24.12.45., 6–15.2.46. S25/3342; S25/7566. Singleton and Manningham-Buller represented official British views. Cf. FO/371/57689/E839. (Minutes of the Refugee Department, 9–15. 1.46.)
27. On Rifkind's views: Jewish Agency Executive Session, 3.3.46. CZA.
28. The Yishuv Elected Assembly (Assefat Hanivcharim) 4th session, 12–13. 2.46. J1/7223. CZA. Bevin to Hall, 12.1.46. Secret. FO/371/52504/E513. Creech Jones to Bevin, 23.1.46. Top Secret. FO/371/5207/E879. Dixon to Attlee, 26.1.46. *Ibid.*
29. Rosenblueth to Shertok, 19.2.46. S25/6490. CZA. Small Zionist Actions Committee, 28.2.46. S25/352. *Ibid.* Bernhard to Shertok, 8.2.46. S25/6463. *Ibid.* Crossman met Yaari, the leader of Hashomer Hatzair, and Georg Landauer of Aliya Hadasha. Crossman, pp. 148–49.
30. Jewish Agency Executive Sessions, 24. 2.46; 27.2.46. CZA.
31. Roberts (Moscow) to FO, 14.1.46. No. 26 FO/371/52506. Same to same, 15.1.46. No. 29. Same to same, 8.2.46. No. 69 (quoting *New Times* attack on the Commission FO/371/52509. Minute by H. T. Morgan, 26.2.46. FO/371/52512/E2085.
32. Boaz to Atara (from Baghdad), 16–31.3.46. S25/6412. CZA. A. Z. Eshkoli to E. Sasson, 13.3.46. S25/6411. *Ibid.* B. Crum, *Behind the Silken Curtain* (New York, 1947), pp. 156–58; 267–70. Stonehewer-Bird to FO, 2.4.46. No. 116. FO/371/25214/E343.
33. Weizmann was assisted by Stein in preparing his speech. Weizmann to Stein 14.2.46. Weizmann Archives. Weizmann to Shertok, 11.3.46. *Ibid.* Jewish Agency Executive Session, 10.3.46. CZA. *The Jewish Case before the Anglo-American Committee of Inquiry on Palestine, Statements and Memoranda* (Jerusalem, 1946), pp. 52, 643. Crossman, *Palestine Mission*, pp. 123 ff. id. *A Nation Reborn* (London, 1960), pp. 23–24. High Commissioner to the Colonial Secretary, 2.4.46. No. 537A. Secret FO/371/52514. Crum, p. 65. The Jewish map left the area of Jenin-Nablus-Hebron-Lydda out of the Jewish State. The area Jerusalem-Bethlehem-Kalia was to be an international zone. S25/7162. CZA.
34. *The Jewish Case op. cit.* pp. 301–3. Zionism and the Arab World, *Ibid.* p. 349. Note on the Arabs in the War, *Ibid.* pp. 360–71. Memorandum on the position of the Jewish Communities in Oriental Countries. *Ibid.* 372–91. Anti-Jewish Riots in Tripolitania, *Ibid.* pp. 392–406. Paper on the Situation of Iraqi Jewry, *Ibid.* pp. 407–10.
35. The Jewish Resistance Movement. Memorandum submitted to the Anglo-American Commission, 25.3.46, FO/733/463//75872/138/7.
36. *The Jewish Case*, pp. 263–303.
37. Jewish Agency Executive Session, 24.3.46. CZA.
38. Crum, pp. 223–25. Crossman, p. 164.
39. D. Horowitz, *A State in the Making*, pp. 110–11. Talk with Goldmann from London, 31.3.46. Z6/Package 18/File 1. On Hutcheson's role cf. Halifax to FO, 23.4.46. No. 2069. Most Immediate FO/371/52516. Minute by Beeley *Ibid.* 28.4. *Baayot* (Problems), Ichud's organ published by M. Buber (July 1947), pp. 211–12.
40. MacDonald to the President, 5.4.46. (from M. Weisgal) Z6/Package 18/File. Lourie's letters, 11.4.46, *Ibid.* Crum, p. 269.
41. Crossman to McNeil, 22.4.46. FO/371/52524/E4469.
42. B. Joseph in the Jewish Agency Executive Session, 12.5.46; 2.6.46. Horowitz, p. 118. E. Monroe, 'Bevin's "Arab Policy" ', *St. Antony's Papers* (1961), p. 29.
43. Lourie's letters, 11.4.46. Z6/Package 18/Files. CZA. Halifax to FO, 23.4.46. No. 2069. Most Immediate, FO/371/52516.
44. Weizmann to Churchill, 14.4.46. Weizmann Archives. Weizmann to Smuts 14.4.46. *Ibid.* Weizmann to Attlee, 16.4.46. *Ibid.* Weizmann to Locker, 16.4.46. *Ibid.* Weizmann to Bevin, 16.4.46. *Ibid.* Sasson to Joseph, 12.4.46. Z5/1083. CZA.
45. Lourie's letters, 21.4.46. Confidential. Z6/Package 18/File 1. CZA. Crossman confused the Zionists as to his exact views. Shertok to the Executive, 19.6.46. CZA.

THE ANGLO-AMERICAN COMMISSION 169

46. The Report is included in Cmd. 6808. For refugees statistics see Appendix III. Ch. 2 Paragraph 19. The Agency estimate was higher: 505,450. S25/3342. CZA.
47. The Peel Report and the Woodhead Commission had acknowledged the Zionist contribution for Arab betterment, as did the Survey prepared by the Administration for the Commission's guidance: *A Survey for Palestine. Prepared in December 1945 and January 1946 for the information of the Anglo-American Committee for Palestine.* (Jerusalem, Government Printing Office, 1946), Ch. 16 p. 23 paragraph 182.
48. Weizmann to Magnes, 8.5.46. Weizmann Archives.
49. Minutes of Meeting held at 77, Gt. Russell St. 29.4.46; 30.4.46 Secret. Z4/10,380. CZA. Jewish Agency Executive Sessions. 30.4.46; 1.5.46; 20.6.46.
50. Jewish Agency Executive Sessions, 5.5.46; 12.5.46; 19.5.46. CZA.
51. Crossman, *Palestine Mission.* 176–87. Weizmann to the Executive, 1.5.46. Eldad, *Maaser Rishon op. cit.* AZEC (American Zionist Emergency Council). Meeting of the Executive, 3.5.46; 9.5.46. *op. cit.* Z5/1172 CZA. Akzin to Goldmann, 6.5.46. *Ibid.*
52. Weizmann to Magnes, 8.5.46. Weizmann Archives. Weizmann to Attlee, 13.5.46. *Ibid.*
53. Meetings held at 77, Gt. Russell St. 13.5.46; 15–16.5.46; 21.5.46; 23.5.46; 23.5.46; 31.5.46. *op. cit.* CZA. The British press saw the debate over the Report as a new version of the Arab-Jewish conflict. Particularly unfriendly was the Daily Telegraph. R. S. Churchill, *The Sinews of Peace, Post-War Speeches by W. S. Churchill* (London, 1948), p. 125. Gordon to Goldmann, 8.5.46 Z6/Package 2/File 3. CZA.
54. Small Zionist Actions Committee, 23.6.46. S5/355 CZA.
55. *Ibid.* AZEC. Meeting of the Executive, 13.5.46. *op. cit.*
56. Horowitz, pp. 128–29. B. Crum, *op. cit.*
57. C.O.S. (46) 77th Meeting. 15.5.46. Top Secret FO/371/52525/E4774/G. D'Arcy had been misunderstood by the Commission members, and by the Zionists, because he was not permitted to speak about anything beyond the purely military.
58. Beeley to Baxter, 25.3.46. Secret and Personal. FO/371/52514/E3057/G. Memorandum by the Joint Chiefs of Staff to the State-War-Navy Coordinating Committee, 21.6.46. Top Secret. FRUS, 1946. Vol. VII. Record of a Meeting held at the FO, 6.4.46. FO/371/5254/E3057.
59. N. Butler, The United States and the Palestine Report, 26.4.46. FO/371/52520/E4013.
60. Memorandum by Sir D. Harris, 21.3.46. Procedure in Connection with Palestine Policy Top Secret FO/371/52514/E3057/G.
61. Grafftey-Smith to FO, 23.4.46. No. 159. Most Immediate. Top Secret and Personal FO/371/52516. Shone to FO, 23.4.46. No. 365. Top Secret and Personal. *Ibid.* Stonehewer-Bird to FO, 25.4.46. No. 330. Most Immediate. Top Secret. *Ibid.* Same to same, 25.4.46. No. 339. Most Immediate. Top Secret. *Ibid.* Viceroy to the Secretary of State for India, 23.4.46. Ext. 2880 *Ibid.* Campbell to FO, 25.4.46. No. 734. Important. *Ibid.*
62. The Secretary of State for the Colonies to the High Commissioner, 24.4.46. Most Immediate. Top Secret. Personal. No. 666. *Ibid.*
63. Report of the Anglo-American Committee of Inquiry. Notes for the Secretary of State's discussion with the Defence Committee. Comment. First Impressions by T. Wikeley, 23.4.46. FO/371/52517/E3840/G.
64. Extract from D.O.(46) 14th Meeting, 24.4.46. Palestine (D.O.(46)61). FO/371/E3839/G.
65. C.P. (46) 173. Top Secret. 26.4.46. Palestine. Appointment, Terms of Reference and Constitution of the Committee. Draft of the Ad Hoc Official Committee. FO/371/52517/E3943. Extract from Cabinet Conclusions. 37(46). 24.4.46. *Ibid.* E3838/G.
66. U.K. Delegation to Foreign Ministers' Conference (Paris) to FO, 27.4.46, No. 7. Top Secret. Immediate, *Ibid.* Bevin to Byrnes, 28.4.46. Secret and Personal. *Ibid.* E3815/

G. Halifax to FO, 24.4.46. Top Secret and Personal No. 2712. *Ibid*. For details on some division in the State Department of FRUS, Vol. VII. pp. 597–99.
67. C.M. 38(46) 29.4.46. CAB/128/5.
68. P.M.M.(46)8th Meeting of Prime Ministers (U.K., Australia, New Zealand, South Africa), 30.4.46. Top Secret. FO/371/52520/E4061614/G.
69. Halifax to FO, 30.4.46. No. 2742. Most Immediate. FO/371/52519/U.K. Delegation at Paris (Bevin) to FO, 1.5.46. Most Immediate FO/371/52519. Acheson, the Acting Under-Secretary, and Henderson, the Head of the Near East and Africa Division, tried to prevent Truman's statement, but failed because of White House intervention. Halifax to FO, 7.5.46. Immediate and Secret. FO/371/52521.
70. U.K. Delegation to the Conference of Foreign Ministers (Paris) to the FO, 1.5.46. No. 30 Secret. FO/371/52519. Cf. F. Williams, *A Prime Minister Remembers* (London, 1961) pp. 193–95. id. *Nothing So Strange* (London, 1970) p. 249.
71. Cabinet Conclusions. 39(46).1.5.46. Palestine Report. FO/371/52520.
72. Halifax to FO, 4.5.46. No. 2858. Secret. Minutes Beeley, Baxter and Ward. FO/371/52521. FO to Halifax, 18.6.46. No. 825. *Ibid*.
73. FO to U.K. Delegation to the Foreign Ministers Conference (for Bevin), 8.5.46. No. 153. Most Immediate and Top Secret (Truman's message). FO/371/52522/E4305/G. Bevin to Attlee, 9.5.46. *Ibid*./4318/G.
74. Extract from Cabinet Conclusions 44(46)9.5.46 FO/371/52523/E 4346/G.
75. Extract from Cabinet Conclusions. 50(46)20.5.46. FO/371/52525/E775/G.
76. Stonehewer Bird to FO, 10.5.46. No. 390. FO/371/52523.
77. Crossman to McNeil, 22.4.46. Notes on Palestine Report of the Anglo-American Committee. FO/371/52524/E 4469. Points (by Crossman) for McNeil, n.d. 9.5.46. *Ibid*. Minute by Beeley. Cf. his *Paiestine Mission* and *A Nation Reborn* to the P.R.O. contemporary evidence which is more reliable apart from quotations from his diary.
78. Note of a Meeting held at No. 10 Downing St., on 14 May 1946, at which the Prime Minister and the Secretary of State for the Colonies met the Members of the Anglo-American Committee. FO/371/5254/E 4514. A strong plea in favour of abolishing the Agency was made by Crick in a letter to Bevin, 26.4.46. Secret. FO/371/52519/E 3961. It was supported by Sir D. Harris, but doubted by J. M. Martin. *Ibid*. Minutes.
79. Bloudan Resolutions in: *Behind the Curtain* (Tel-Aviv, Maarachot, 1954) pp. 12, 41 (no author).
80. H. Dalton, *High Tide and After, Memoirs 1931–45* (London, 1962), p. 150.

Husni al-Barazi on Arab Nationalism in Palestine

Allen H. Podet

Late in 1945, the stalemate between the United States and Great Britain over what to do about the Jewish refugee problem led President Truman and Prime Minister Attlee to create the joint Anglo-American Committee of Inquiry, whose terms of reference included surveying the refugee problem in Europe and the situation in the Near East.

The Committee convened in Washington and held hearings in the Department of State. Both Zionist and Arab Nationalist views were ably represented, and witnesses also submitted written memoranda.[1]

The central problem soon emerged: although the seams in the Jewish positions were clear enough, the Arab position appeared to be rigid and monolithic. That position was presented with minor variations by many Muslim and Christian Arabs, as well as others:

1. Jewish immigration to Palestine was to be terminated. All Arab or pro-Arab witnesses agreed on this point.
2. Sales of land to Jews or to persons acting for them were to be prohibited in any part of Palestine. Nearly all supported this demand as well.
3. The Grand Mufti, Hajj Amin al-Husayni, who was barred from Palestine by the British because of his close ties to Hitler, was to be readmitted to the country and returned to the Muslim Arabs as their leader. A majority, including of course all the Husaynis, supported this demand with varying degrees of fervour.
4. An independent Arab state was to be established in Palestine, with the result that there would never be an independent Jewish or Christian entity there. Although many witnesses supported this proposal formally, it was clear from the oral testimony that most witnesses looked upon it as somewhat unrealistic.

These four demands were heard in all the places that Arab public testimony was taken.[2]

In the early spring of 1946, however, one secret meeting or a series took place in Jerusalem between the former Prime Minister of Syria and members of the Commission.

Husni al-Barazi, born in 1883 in Hama, was a lawyer and politician. He had been Governor of Alexandretta, Superintendant in the Ministry of Justice, Minister of the Interior, Minister of Education, and Prime

Minister from April 1942 to January 1943. He was to remain an important figure in Syrian politics.[3]

His secret testimony consisted of five main parts: a general perspective, his credentials, how political realities operated in the geographic region, a proposal which included a legitimized or recognized Jewish state, and a means by which the British and Americans could retain certain controls of military significance.[4]

At about the same time, two members of the Anglo-American Committee of Inquiry were keeping private diaries which should be considered together with al-Barazi's proposals. These were the American Chairman of the Committee, the Hon. Joseph P. Hutcheson of the Fifth Federal District Court at Houston, and Professor James Grover McDonald, President of the American Foreign Policy Association.[5]

Judge Hutcheson made a fact-finding journey to Damascus and Beirut ending 21 March 1946, in which he found some small evidence of Arab-Jewish cooperation, mainly in the Haifa area. But on the whole he and his colleague were impressed with the 'denunciations of Zionism' and the 'apparently solid opposition to it'. This accorded with the information then supplied by the Foreign Office and State Department personnel who were attached to the Committee.

Dr McDonald, however, recorded different information. He was the former High Commissioner for Refugees under the League of Nations, and by 1945 was perhaps the most prominent refugee expert in America. According to his diary, an audience was granted him on 21 March 1946 with the Maronite Archbishop (Ignatz Moubarak) and with the Maronite Patriarch. In that interview it was made clear that Zionism was considered the creative force in Palestine, and that the Christian Arabs of Lebanon had no fear of it. Rather, they stood in dread of the 'latent fanaticism' of the Muslims. This was essentially confirmed by the Archbishop Abdullah al-Khouri, the Patriarchal Vicar.

Hutcheson's observations and reports reflected the virtually unanimous opinion of the American and British diplomatic field services. But it is contradicted both by the al-Barazi proposals and by the McDonald diary. If bodies of Arabs existed both on the nationalist political side[6] and on the Christian religious side who were prepared to deviate from the mainstream Arab nationalist prositions, then there may indeed have been room for manoeuvring between Zionists and Arab nationalists.

The proposals of the Committee itself, embodied in its report of April 1946, were a delicately balanced set of compromises which presumed that such manoeuvring was a possibility. But for entirely other reasons the proposals were never carried out and the region was further impelled towards war.

I

Al-Barazi's Testimony

Le problème palestinien, à mon avis, est étroitement lié aux problèmes des autres pays du Levant. La Palestine étant, le coeur et même la plaque tournante, des Pays Arabes. C'est à ce titre que je tiens à témoigner devant votre Commission.

Les troubles qui ont, depuis 20 ans, agité ce Pays, berceaux des 3 religions, l'inquiétude qui plane sur cette Terre Sainte, sont la cause primordiale

1° de la marche lente, indécisive de nos Pays vers le progrès
2° de l'instabilité politique de ce Moyen-Orient qui semble en marge de la civilisation
3° de sa faiblesse sociale et de sa pauvreté économique.

Une souffrance aigue me ronge le coeur en constatant cet état arriéré, alors qu'un désir ardent m'insite à voir nos Pays, par rapport à leur passé glorieux, jouer leur rôle véritable dans tous les domaines de l'activité humaine. Puissent les Dieux vous inspirer, Vous qui nous êtes venus de si loin et après de longs séjours ci et là, à travers le monde, la juste solution à nos problèmes ardus qui préocupèrent les esprits durant tant d'années. Les yeux de l'univers vous épient. Et je considère le hasard, qui m'a fait venir à Jerusalem pour des raisons de santé, heureux, car il me permet de témoigner devant vous.

Tout d'abord permettez-moi de mettre de côté toutes sortes de réserves afin de donner libre-cours à ma pensée. J'ai à coeur de crier certaines vérités, de dénoncer certaines gens et d'accuser certain Etats. Je tiens à parler franchement car contrairement à ce que vous avez écouté, ou lu dans les journaux, je suis convaincu qu'il vous incombe de trouver la solution à ce problème Palestinien, si épineux. Vous avez, à mes yeux, la lourde charge d'éclaircir les différents aspects de ce problème à vos gouvernements, auprès de qui vous jouissez d'un grand prestige, et qui devront mettre fin à toutes ces complications.

Nous avons assez des détours diplomatiques.

Nous voulons une marche directe vers le but.

Bien que je sois un lutteur acharné pour la liberté et pour la démocratie, je me permets de vous demander de mettre de côté, et pour un court moment, ces principes qui vous sont sacrés comme ils me le sont à moi-même. C'est que nous devrons nous placer sur un plan spécial en examinant la situation de nos Pays afin d'approfondir l'étude et de notre mentalité et des différents cas où nous nous trouvons aussi bien, en Syrie, au Liban, en Transjordanie qu'en Palestine. Je n'hésite pas à vous insinuer même de ne croire personne de ceux qui témoignent devant vous. La plupart sont des extrèmistes ou à la recherche d'une renommée; d'autres tiennent à affermir leur autorité aux yeux de leur public; certains se trouvent sous une pression. Doutez même de mon témoignage, si mon exposé vous semblera fait pour m'illustrer ou dans un but intéressé.

Ayant participé aux différentes phases de la vie politique de ces 3 Pays depuis 35 ans; ayant été à la fois ministre plusieures fois et déporté politique, j'ai également présidé le gouvernement Syrien en 1942–43 aux moments critiques de cette dernière guerre. Je crois pouvoir me flatter d'avoir organisé POCP pour assurer le ravitaillement de tous ceux qui vivaient dans nos Pays et surtout d'avoir préparé l'Indépendance Syrienne en luttant contre les Français si attachés alors au maintien du Mandat, malgré la volonté des Syriens. N'enviant personne, n'obéissant à aucun mobile intéressé, je tiens ici à défendre les véritables intérêts de ces Pays qui ont tant souffert du revers des évènements et du temps. Telle est mon attitude.

J'eus souhaité cet entretien dans une séance publique pour marquer un acte de courage. Mais, dans nos Pays, hélàs! Ceux qui déclarent leurs opinions ouvertement, et dans le cas où ces opinions déplaisent aux leaders, sont menacés. Malgré cela, si vous me donnez la garantie de mettre en exécution la solution proposée pour résoudre nos problèmes, il me sera particulièrement heureux, d'en être le prix. Je suis même disposé à aller à Londres et à Washington, pour plaider cette cause, si vous le jugez nécessaire. Là je tiens à reprocher à l'Angleterre sa mauvaise habitude d'abandonner en mi-chemin les gens et même les états, qu'elle engage dans une voie; de se retirer comme un cheveu de la patte de pain, et en belle dame, quand ses intérêts lui commandent de se retirer. Ce procédé devient une maladie contagieuse, et de plus en plus en vogue. L'Amérique en serat-elle atteinte?

Je reconnais ici, avec une amertume pénible que les Arabes ont perdu, aussi bien en Palestine qu'en Syrie, des occasions précieuses qui leur ont été offertes, pour résoudre leurs problèmes.

En Palestine	– en 1922: l'Assemblée Législative en 1939: le Livre Blanc
En Syrie	– 1919: le traité Fayçal-Clemenceau. (La rencontre Fayçal-Weizmann, Fayçal désirait l'unité des Pays Arabes; les Juifs y seront admis). En 1926: l'accord De Jouvenel; en 1928 la Constituante Syrienne et les six Articles. A ces différentes occasions, auxquelles j'ai participé, j'ai essayé de convaincre nos collègues, qui sont maintenant des Meneurs, de les saisir. Mais en vain.
En 1932	– l'Union de l'Irak et de la Syrie.

Ces différentes occasions furent perdues par les leaders qui ne visaient qu'à assurer des ambitions personnelles; qui forment dans tous les Etats

Arabes comme une sorte de Société Collective. Ils exploitent un peuple courageux mais naif et dont je tiens à analyser la mentalité devant vous.

1° D'abord nous souffrons de l'ignorance des masses. S'il est vrai que la vie universitaire prend de plus en plus de l'ampleur, elle laisse beaucoup à desirer encore: le côté scientifique étant negligé: nous avons surtout des demi-instruits.

2° L'éducation sociale et Politique est inexistante. Les partis politiques, en grand nombre, divisent les habitants. Ils n'ont pas de programmes. La lutte entre eux est dure et à ne plus finir. Les buts de cette lutte sont d'ordre personnel surtout. La Presse est dans un état lamentable. Un tel journaliste, agent nazi il y a 2 ans, ayant passé en Allemagne la période 1941–45, rentre maintenant, est devenu nationaliste d'aujourdhui.

Tous les journalistes reçoivent des soldes énormes du gouvernement qui semble les encourager dans la mauvaise voie. L'opinion publique est mal formée. Nous avons été toujours un champ favorable aux différentes propagandes. Du début de la guerre la propagande Nazie agissait sur les Arabes dont les leaders étaient en leur faveur. Actuellement tous se rangent du côté de la démocratie. Cependant ils se préparent à tendre la main à la Russie. Celle-ci mène, dans nos Pays, une propagande active. Il faut donc de votre part des mesures fermes et énergiques dans la solution, quelle qu'elle soit, aux problèmes de ces Pays. Car il faut, à tout prix, trouver la solution juste et saine à ces problèmes.

3° La Sécurité à l'intérieur laisse beaucoup à désirer. Inquiétude générale, le prestige des gouvernements est tout à fait ébranlé.

4° Un fanatisme absolu règne chez nous. Les Chrétiens, les Musulmans aussi bien que les Juifs sont des fanatiques acharnés. Les uns constituent un danger aux autres. A tout moment on fait intervenir le prétexte fameux de la protection des minorités.

Les leaders qui sont des démagogues, exploitent un peuple dont je viens de vous exposer la mentalité : ils exercent une autorité absolue sur la foule qu'ils dominent par ce qu'ils l'avaient engagée dans les différentes luttes dans les domaines passifs. Cette sorte d'activité plaît aux Arabes. Maintenant qu'il faut être positif, qu'il faut agir, il y a déséquilibre. La vie est anormale chez nous : on cherche à donner satisfaction aux chefs de quartier ; les ministres et députés interviennent auprès des différents services, pour appuyer un tel criminel ou un tel fauteur de trouble. C'est pour celà que la sécurité n'est pas assurée. La stabilité manque. Un malaise général inquiète tout le monde. La démagogie est une note agréable aux gouverneurs et aux gouvernés. Les leaders en sont responsables. Il faut ici une Cours de Justice telle celle de Nurembourg pour punir les responsables. Telle est la situation. J'en trace le tableau avec une amertume pénible. Obéissant à mon coeur, je ne dirai que des louanges de mes compatriotes. Mais il faut dire la vérité ; il faut soigner la plaie dont nous souffrons. J'aborde la difficulté en déclarant la situation telle qu'elle est afin d'y trouver la remède.

L'Amérique et l'Angleterre sont appelées à apporter ce remède. (1) Elles ont lutté pour sauver la liberté du monde contre la barbarie Nazie; (2) leurs intérêts sont liés aux nôtres; (3) elles ont fait face à de pareilles difficultés dans leurs propres pays. Si elles se décident à résoudre le problème, il faut qu'elles imposent l'audace et la fermeté dans leurs plans et les accompagner toujours de prudence et de souplesse dans l'exécution.

Ceci m'est d'autant plus blessant à dire que je me sens responsable de cet état de choses avec tous les autres chefs qui ont, en leurs mains, les intérêts et l'avenir du peuple. Pour éviter ces malheurs, il était et est de mon avis que nous passions de l'attitude passive, à l'organisation des questions d'ordre intérieur; à l'orientation du peuple vers une activité bienfaisante. C'est à cause de cet état de choses déplorable que je vous ai proposé, tout à l'heure, de mettre de côté les beaux principes de liberté et de démocratie. Un tel peuple ne semble pas bien préparé encore à digérer ces principes. Nos chambres reflètent la souveraineté des nombres: et la masse, chez nous, n'est pas encore à l'hauteur. En verité ce sont les antichambres qui dirigent chez nous. La France en est, pour une large part, responsable. Elle a mal accompli son devoir. Ses agents, dans notre pays ont empli leurs poches à nos dépens. Ils ont assuré leurs intérêts propres en négligeant ceux de leur Pays et en manquant à leur devoir. C'est pour celà que je constate nécessaire votre intervention par des mesures énergiques et fermes. Celles-ci permettent d'obtenir les résultats les plus considérables par des moyens peut-être désagréables mais surs. Tournons le dos aux beaux principes démocratiques pour atteindre leurs buts utiles. Un rameur habile gagne le but en lui tournant le dos. Ces résultats nous les obtiendrons si, comme je vous le disais tout à l'heure, l'Amérique et l'Angleterre consentaient à se mêler, une fois pour toutes et énergiquement, de la solution à nos problèmes. Elle orientera le peuple vers ses buts, son idéal. Ce sera pour son bien. Il est de notre intérêt comme du votre, que nos pays s'organisent, deviennent forts, pour constituer un front solide, capable de résister aux visées russes dont nous ressentons le danger.

Je ne vous cacherai pas que j'eus souhaité ne voir aucun sioniste dans notre chère Palestine. Si les leaders palestiniens avaient profité des occasions perdues, ils n'auraient pas eu maintenant, en face d'eux, tant de complications. Je désire voir la Palestine entièrement en nos mains. Mais les Juifs sont là. Je ne peux nier leur existence, leur travail. Sans conteste ils ont fait de la Palestine un pays avancé par rapport aux autres régions. Je reconnais donc les faits. Mieux encore je tiens à les exploiter afin de profiter des avantages que nous procure leur existence ici.

Ainsi je propose l'union dans les états du Levant, la Syrie, le Liban, la Transjordanie et la Palestine, pour ne former qu'un royaume, avec un des Hachémites comme roi. Mettre de côté la question religieuse pour que le sens de la Patrie occupe la place de la religion dans les coeurs du peuple qui vivra dans cet état futur. S'il semble difficile de réaliser d'emblée cette fusion, je propose la constitution, toujours dans la Grande Syrie, de 3 états:

1. l'Etat Chrétien au Petit Liban
2. l'Etat Musulman en Syrie, au Grand Liban, en Transjordanie, avec une partie de la Palestine
3. l'Etat Juif dans les régions occupées par les Juifs plus certaines autres régions. A ces répartitions présidera une commission de techniciens.

Beyrouth sera un port international. Jérusalem une ville sainte internationale. Les 3 états formeront une Fédération, et sous le contrôle Anglo-Americain, ils travailleront pour le bien de la Fédération. Le temps saura rapprocher les uns des autres. La paix rétablie, dans ces régions, unira les coeurs et ainsi, vous aurez accompli une oeuvre humaine qui ajoutera à vos mérites, un mérite inoubliable pour le bien de cette Terre Sainte, que dis-je pour l'humanité. Plus de revendications de droits sauf celui de voir les 3 états ne former qu'un seul où le sens de la Patrie a occupé la place de la religion dans les coeurs de tous.

N'hésitez pas, Messieurs, à avoir de l'audace pour être réalistes.

Les dossiers, les archives ne peuvent jamais résoudre les difficultés comme le feraient l'énergie et la fermeté.

II

The Hutcheson Diary (extracts)

Our committee, Morrison, McDonald and I, left Friday, March 15th. Since all of the members will have seen Jewish settlements, in Palestine, I shall not say more about the ones we visited than to comment briefly on the Pica settlement, which is one of, if not, the oldest in Palestine where the great wine presses are. We found a thriving village there built on a lovely hill top with vine land around it and one of the largest wine presses and cellars I have ever seen. Inquiry developed a first class condition for the colony and the best of relation with Arab neighbors, many of whom work for them. This Pica settlement is not a communal settlement at all, but is based on the idea of individual interest except of course that the wine presses and vaults are owned collectively and there is naturally a general closeness of community life.

At Haifa, whose Mayor is a Jew with an Arab as Assistant Mayor, a reception was given us by the assistant director, where we met many of the local people and discussed conditions generally with them. ... [Haifa] has a mixed Jewish and Arab population and they seem to be getting along fairly well. ...

The Saturday night and Sunday we spent at Damascus were full days ...

On every hand we were met with denunciations of Zionism, the statement of the firmest determination to resist it to the utmost, and to go to war if necessary to do so, and were met with an apparently solid opposition to it, a Jewish delegation even presenting us a paper supporting the Syrian opposition.

We saw the great mosque, the tomb of Saladin, and the museum which contained a wonderful collection of statues and figures taken from a Roman tomb in Palmyra done in the most exquisite Roman style in the period of the Second century. We also saw set up in the museum an old Jewish synagogue with some paintings on it of the Second century, discovered by a Yale exploration party, and I couldn't help being amused that the finest thing in the museum was this unique synagogue containing paintings and decorations unlike that in any other synagogue known.

We left Syria Monday morning, driving over the Anti-Lebanon and the Lebanon Mountains, a part of it in a driving snow storm which nearly obscured our vision and shortly after we passed blocked the road. Because of this storm for a part of our journey we did not have the magnificent views afforded by this drive, but for at least two-thirds of the way we did. ...

At Lebanon, where we arrived at 5:30, the night and the following day were very full of dinners, interviews, hearings, at all of which with unanimity we heard that the Lebanese feared Zionism, that with its program of bringing all the Jews that wanted to come into Palestine, that with its determination to take the land by force if necessary, it would then surge into Lebanon and seize Lebanon, and they assured us that the Arab World was at one in its determination to crush these movements out. Protesting that they had no objection to Jews as such and could live with them and would live with them, they kept insisting that the Zionist program with its importation of hundreds of thousands of Europeans to capture Palestine and take it away from the Arabs, its rightful owner, was a menace not only to Palestine but to the Arab world. They assured us that they would not permit it to persist. In general they declared that what they wanted was for the British Government to withdraw and leave the matter to be settled by Arabs and Jews, but some of the more thoughtful ones among them realized that this would be a mistake and that British withdrawal would have to be considerably delayed.

There was an interesting paper presented in Damascus on the economic aspects of the matter. The head of the Chamber of Commerce and the Merchants Association stated that all of the economy of Palestine was false because, based not upon realities but upon an effort to import Jews, it was creating abnormal positions which were bound to react disastrously on Palestine and the whole Arab world.

In both countries there was a great show of religious dignitaries and functionaries, Christian and Moslem all united against Zionism.

At the last hearing we had in Beirut, an archbishop, representing the Maronites, the largest Christian Congregation in Lebanon, some 600,000 people, appeared for them as did the archbishop for the Druzes and the Greek and the other churches, including one little fellow for the protestant churches. On questioning, I gathered that these protestant churches were mostly Presbyterian. Our Baptist and Methodist brothers don't seem to be strongly seated there.

The sum of what we learned from the governments in both places and the witnesses they presented to us was violent opposition to Zionism, a determination to resist it at all costs, and an unwillingness to concede the immigration of one single Jew. In short, the White Paper was the least they would take. I made a speech pointing out the difficulties in the situation created by the facts of history including the last 25 years of it, and calling for a sympathetic and helpful attitude in settling this tremendous problem. Their reply was, 'It is no problem of ours'. 'We had no part in the European tragedy'. I found an adherence to the Mufti and a demand for his return to Palestine. My arguments that his associations had impaired his authority, did not seem to register much. While I would say we did not learn anything new, we certainly confirmed the truth of the fact that the governments and the people generally of Syria and Lebanon are opposed to Zionism, and while no doubt there are some exceptions to it, the exceptions are so small as to be almost negligible.

The President at the dinner at his house took us into his private office and engaged us in a long and earnest conversation against Zionism and for a decision favoring the Arab side. We listened respectfully, asked him some questions, including one from McDonald as to what he would propose, with the typical answer, 'There is only one thing to propose. Give Palestine her independence and stop Jewish immigration.'...

To sum up the trip, I would say that it was a most delightful one from a scenic standpoint and perhaps it was worth while for us to put in our appearance to those governments as they seemed very much pleased to see us and Wadsworth seemed to think it was the thing for us to do, but from the standpoint of learning anything new, I would say that we learned nothing new except that we had visible confirmation of what we had heard everywhere from Arab citizens, that the Arabs all were united in their opposition to Zionism and their determination that it must come to an end.

Jerusalem, March 21st   J.C.H. Jr.

III

The McDonald Diary (extracts)

INTERVIEWS IN BEIRUT, THURSDAY, MARCH TWENTY-FIRST (1946)

Archbishop Ignatz Moubarak and the Patriarch

We found Archbishop Moubarak in his office in a large boys' school. He is a funny little man, about 4'8" and nearly as round as he is tall, looking exactly like Punch, constantly smiling and very fluent in his excellent French.

He answered readily my question about the attitude of the Maronites and the Lebanese toward Zionism in Palestine. Expressing his pleasure at our visit, he at once launched into a vigorous statement of his views, which can be summarized as follows:

1. Zionism has been the creative force in Palestine, transforming an arid and neglected country into a blooming, prosperous and modern one. The Jews have thus made a contribution not only to Palestine but to the Near East. Both on the soil and in industry, Jewish science, money, and most important of all – hard work have been brought to this part of the world and will, if permitted, fructify this whole area.

2. The Arab leaders, especially the political and religious ones, are reactionary in their program. They fan the latent fanaticism in their people for personal and political ends.

3. The Lebanese officials who spoke to us the two days previous were not expressing the real feelings of the people. Instead, for personal reasons and a feeling of cowardice, these men are betraying their people. The Lebanese, – especially the Christian Lebanese, are not anti-Zionist. They do not fear the Jews. They fear rather the latent fanaticism of the Moslems. An Arab Palestine would be a danger to all Christians in the East.

4. As to the president of the republic, who the Archbishop said was his personal friend and whom he had been largely responsible for placing in office by persuading the Lebanese Christians to support the government's anti-French policy, is a nice man but weak and fearful. The Archbishop even called him a poltroon.

5. The Archbishop added, go and see the Patriarch. He is the head of the Maronite community. He will speak for himself.

6. Without my referring at all to the Gerold Frank story, the Archbishop said: 'I gave an interview day before yesterday on this whole matter to an American correspondent, and in order that the whole world might know of it, I signed the interview.'

7. I asked the Archbishop if he was afraid to be so frank. He replied: 'I have never known fear, not even when I was a small child.'

Leaving the Archbishop, we drove directly up the mountain to the residence of the Patriarch, Monsignor Anthony Peter Arida. It was on a commanding site overlooking Beirut and the sea. We were received at once by associates of the Patriarch, taken into the throne room, where within a minute or two the Patriarch himself appeared through a side door. He greeted us warmly, sat on the throne, placed me on his right and Stinespring on his left.

His Beatitude expressed a very strong sympathy for and a desire to support the work of Zionism and of the Jews in Palestine. He spoke of their creative contributions, their rescue of the land from the desert and the swamp. He referred to Weizman as his friend. He denied staunchly that the Lebanese people were anti-Jewish. Instead, he said they were fearful of Moslem fanaticism and were particularly fearful of the effects on the Christians in the East of an Arab state in Palestine ...

Archbishop Abdulla El-Khouri

On the way out of the palace, we were urged to visit the Vicar of the Patriarch, Archbishop Abdulla El-Khouri. Unlike the Patriarch, who is rather tall and noble in appearance, the Archbishop resembled somewhat Moubarak, though he had more dignity.

The substance of the statement by Archbishop Abdulla El-Khouri was not unlike that of Archbishop Moubarak but was couched in less categorical terms. He developed, however, more fully than did either Moubarak or the Patriarch the reasons for Maronite fear of Moslem domination. ...

NOTES

1. The source material is in the original negotiations and reports now at the Department of State, Foreign Affairs Document Reference Center (FADRC), Files of the Anglo-American Committee of Inquiry, Lot 8, Box 1109, stored at Suitland, Maryland, hereafter cited as Lot 8, Box 1109.
2. See Richard Howard Stafford Crossman, *Palestine Mission* (New York: Macmillan, 1946), p. 21. Bartley Cavanaugh Crum, *Behind the Silken Curtain* (New York: Simon and Schuster, 1947), p. 20 ff. Anglo-American Committee of Inquiry, *Hearings*, First Transcripts (Washington: Ward and Paul, 1946), 7 Vols, Vol. 6. For a summary by a Committee-member, R. H. Crossman, *A Nation Reborn: A Personal Report on the Roles Played by Weizmann, Bevin and Ben-Gurion in the Story of Israel* (New York: Athenium, 1960), p. 79.
3. Or al-Barazi. See *Man hum fi al-'alam al-arabi*, Vol. 1, Syria, 1961. Husni b. Sulayman al-Barazi: Born in llama, 1893. Graduated from the Law Institute in Constantinople. Listed as an Agronomist at Hama in 1919. In 1926, he was Minister of the Interior, Minister of Education, and Administrator of Homs. He was arrested in that year as a political dissident. In 1928 he was elected Deputy for Hama, and in 1934 again became Minister of Education. In 1936 he was Administrator of Alexandretta, and in 1942-43 President of the Council of Ministers. He returned to being Minister of the Interior in

1943, and in 1949 became Administrator for Northern Syria. Al-Barazi was elected Deputy for Hama in 1950, and was arrested in 1953 as a political dissident. He was a founder of the periodical *An-Nasr* in 1954, and travelled in Turkey and Lebanon in 1955–56. He retired to Lebanon, where he died early in 1975. For further information on al-Barazi's political role and philosophy, see Patrick Seale, *The Struggle for Syria: A Study of Postwar Arab Politics* (London, 1965), and Gordon H. Torrey, *Syrian Politics and the Military, 1945–1958* (Colombus, Ohio, 1969). Many thanks to Mr George N. Atiyeh, Head, Near East Section, Orientalia Division, Department of Research, the Library of Congress for his kind assistance. Al-Barazi's testimony is in 'Confidential Memorandum of Husni El-Barazi, Former Prime Minister of Syria'. Manuscript, 16 Jerusalem, March 1946. In the files of the Anglo-American Committee of Inquiry, Lot 8, Box 1109, p. 4 ff.

4. The editing is mine. The original runs to 16 closely written pages in a fairly difficult hand and is rather given to the use of personal abbreviations.
5. For Hutcheson, Lot 8, Box 1109. His former private secretary denies any knowledge of this diary or of any longer one of which it was perhaps a part. His family is similarly unaware. The citations are from Joseph P. Hutcheson, Diary, Notes on the Journey to *Damascus and Beirut*. Typed original dated Jerusalem, 21 March 1946, p. 1. For McDonald, James Grover McDonald, *Diary, Interviews in Beirut, Thursday, March 21st* (1946). Typed original, Lot 8, Box 1109. Secret, recently declassified. P. 1. McDonald notes that Professor Stinespring, a confirmed anti-Zionist, was with him.
6. See the testimony of witness no. 4 of 15, His Excellency Muzahim Pachachi, ex-Minister in Baghdad, 16–17 March 1946, p. 8, filed in the Foreign Office AACI file by Harold Beeley.

'Withdrawal Without Recommendations': Britain's Decision to Relinquish the Palestine Mandate, 1947

Amitzur Ilan

When the Labour Party came to power in Britain in the summer of 1945, almost every possible course leading towards a settlement in Palestine seemed to have been tried, and tried in vain. Labour members of Churchill's wartime coalition cabinet had shared in a determined attempt to enact one solution – partition – only to see it founder in a mounting storm of Arab-Jewish rivalry and suspicion. Every conceivable course that was in British eyes equitable encountered active resistance from either or both the Arabs and the Jews.

Enforcement of a solution against such opposition was not ruled out, if it was thought that some such scheme would in the long run pacify Palestine. But it was not always clear which of the two rivals it was safer to antagonise. No pacification scheme offered promise. So the 1939 White Paper remained in force because no alternative policy looked feasible, though since 1941 no British government had ever tried to enact its main clause – the constitutional clause.[1] Britain's basic dilemma was constant: Which of the two rival peoples should be allowed to dominate the whole or part of Palestine? And if partitioned, where should the frontiers be drawn?

Nevertheless, the Labour Government espoused a new course. Instead of stating categorically what the 'final' solution would be (most cabinet members now favoured partition, though not the Foreign or the Prime Minister), it plumped for provincial autonomy.[2] This scheme envisaged joint UN-British supervision of an arrangement whereby each community would get a measure of self-government in the areas in which its members formed a majority. The central government would remain British and the hope was that 'instruments of government' would gradually develop with Arab, Jewish and British members. The City of Jerusalem was to be a third 'province' enjoying a special status. The attempt was reminiscent of the early days of the mandate for it left the ultimate government of Palestine for future discussion.

This plan took care of Britain's strategic and economic interests as well. A provincial autonomy regime promised free use of Palestine as a British base for some time – a use that might later be extended through 'treaty rights' obtained from whoever became sovereign in the end.

The scheme left the question of who would eventually rule Palestine open. But since it contained restrictions on Jewish immigration (the rate of which was to be determined by the country's 'absorptive capacity', the local political situation and the verdict of a UN arbitration), the character of the future government (or the boundaries, if the end-result was to be partition) depended on the length of the interim period, and the political facts that each of the parties would prove able to create. In any event, to British eyes the scheme looked like a departure from the White Paper. Land purchase, for instance, was to be decided by each 'province's' government.

But as was to be expected few liked the scheme. Neither Jew nor Arab saw in it even a minimal satisfaction of their aspirations. Nor had it the approval of the United States government, upon whose goodwill Britain now so largely depended.

In fact America, which at times came close to accepting the British scheme, was responsible until the end of 1946 for the lack of any serious attempt to implement provincial autonomy. President Truman's 'inconsistent', yet persistent, demand for the immediate immigration to Palestine of some 100,000 Jewish displaced persons, gradually wore the British down. Consequently, Anglo-American committees and teams of experts could often agree on a policy, but their respective heads of state could not. Eventually, the British realised that America was not going 'to share responsibility' with them – and at the same time was unlikely to stop criticising their policy, owing to Zionist domestic pressure at home. Simultaneously, Zionist impatience was leading to an ugly British-Jewish struggle in Palestine, including massive and embarrassing illegal immigration. Gradually, the British public grew sick and tired of these daily events, and the Parliamentary opposition blamed the government for an absence of policy. Towards the beginning of 1947 one 'last' attempt to bring about a settlement was therefore tried.

In February 1947, Labour announced that the problem would be transferred to the United Nations 'without recommendations'. At the time, this was seen as of a piece with their practical difficulties, and as indicating a political will to relinquish the Mandate. But the British documents now available show a different picture. The public announcements were merely to serve as yet another warning to Arabs, Jews and Americans, while the British government, during the rest of 1947, would seek a breakthrough at 'one minute before twelve'. The aim of this paper is to describe these attempts, and to show just how and where they failed.

THE PREPARATIONS FOR THE 'FINAL' ATTEMPT TO SETTLE THE ISSUE –
NOVEMBER 1946 TILL JANUARY 1947

In fact, the 'last' attempt that began to take shape in November 1946 was not so much an attempt to settle the Arab-Jewish dispute inside Palestine, as to reconcile Britain's foreign relations with its defence problems. On the one hand, it was impossible to ignore the pro-Zionist pressure in America which now supported partition, on the other – the Arab opposition to any furthering of Zionist aspirations was permanent. On the goodwill of neighbouring Arab states, and of the wider circle of Moslem populations around them, hung much of Labour's pattern for foreign relations and defence. It seemed essential to enact in Palestine some scheme that would in the first place win acquiescence from both these outside parties, without necessarily securing the approval of both the communities in Palestine. The Foreign and Defence Departments, not the Colonial Office, dominated the debate.

One reason for this domination was Foreign Secretary Ernest Bevin's influence in the cabinet, another the weakness of Arthur Creech Jones, the Colonial Secretary. For while, in Prime Minister Clement Attlee's words, Bevin 'kept the Cabinet *au fait* with foreign affairs to an extent which could have astonished earlier cabinets', Attlee had a poor opinion of Creech Jones's judgement.[3] Swept into the Palestine turbulence through Truman's personal intervention, Attlee usually fully backed Bevin, whatever Creech Jones might think.

British ministers therefore told the Arabs and Jews that the future of Palestine depended on the outcome of a new and 'last' round of talks, and that this would be held in London at the end of January. Within the cabinet, there was still confidence that Britain had the means to enact a policy lacking all round consent. For instance, Attlee and Bevin jointly held that if America was kept content, and if the more 'moderate' Arab rulers, as well as some 'moderate' Zionist leaders, were brought to agree to some formula, it was not essential to obtain formal approval from the Arab Higher Committee or from the Jewish Agency Executive.[4] The formula envisaged included a variant of provincial autonomy, but also the immigration of 100,000 Jews.

In fact, these 'last talks' were no more than the resumption of an earlier round, adjourned in October, in which neither the Jews nor the Arabs had been properly represented. The Cabinet now took steps to correct that fault. It approved a release of Palestinian Jewish leaders, who had been detained, or sought by the police, since the massive arrests of June 29. It also decided to wait until the 22nd Zionist Congress elected a new Executive, hopefully more moderate than the last.[5] British diplomats in Cairo managed to dissuade the exiled Mufti from heading the Higher Committee delegation, thus paving the way for the participation of Palestinian Arabs who had been absent from the September talks.[6] Moreover, since it was 'obvious' that no Arab delegation would agree officially to sit at the same table as the Jews, the pattern of the 1939 St James talks, in which two simultaneous conferences were held, was once again adopted.

During the lull, a British attempt was also made to resuscitate understanding with America. For since 4 October Anglo-American relations over Palestine had been in a state of crisis. On that date Truman, under pressure of electoral stress, and having misinterpreted the adjournment of the first round of talks, ignored a British plea from Attlee, and published a strongly pro-Zionist statement. He now rejected one variant of provincial autonomy to which his own experts had agreed in July (the so-called Morrison-Grady scheme), and came out in favour of the establishment of a Jewish state 'in part of Palestine'.[7] At the time, Attlee and Bevin were convinced that in their negotiation with the Zionists, the latter were close to submission; Truman's statement forced them to eat their words.[8]

Persuading America not to intervene was tried at a high level. During the months of November and December 1946, Lord Inverchapel, the British Ambassador in Washington, was busy explaining the situation to top State Department officials. Bevin joined in when he travelled to New York to attend the first UN General Assembly, when he also met President Truman and the arch-militant American Zionist leader, Abba Hillel Silver.[9]

But the results were not encouraging. Inverchapel could extract only evasive replies, and Truman told Bevin that given a Republican Congress, the Zionist lobby was not going to make life easy for a Democratic President.[10] A typical comment came from Acting Secretary of State Dean Acheson: the United States, he said, did not necessarily insist on partition. It merely wanted a solution 'holding the smallest promise of trouble'.[11] This poor fodder caused Attlee to tell his colleagues bitterly to 'dispel any illusion of anything useful coming from the American side'.[12]

Nor did the preparatory negotiations with the Jews and Arabs augur well. During the lull the views of both sides had hardened, owing to the new composition of their delegations. The Arab Higher Committee made it clear to Britain that they would not countenance any demand for less than the establishment of an Arab state in the whole of Palestine, plus a complete stoppage of Jewish immigration. On learning this, Azzam Pasha, Secretary General of the Arab League, though reputed to be a 'moderating influence', declined to come to London, excusing himself on grounds of ill-health.[13]

As for the Zionists, contrary to British expectations, not Dr Weizmann's 'moderates', but Ben-Gurion's and Silver's 'militants' won the day at the Zionist Congress. Consequently, they went back upon the Executive decision of the previous August that had allowed them to negotiate partition, were the British government to propose it. Nonetheless, some Zionists strove to return to the old line, though definitely no more. Ben-Gurion himself scarcely waited for the ink to dry on the resolutions. Early in January he was in London, hoping to hear from Creech Jones that this time the British would propose partition. The battle, Ben-Gurion hoped, would be over boundaries, not principle. He also hoped to dissuade the British from making the talks with the Zionists an official affair.

On the first point, he was told nothing definite. Creech Jones himself was for the moment a pro-partitionist, but the Cabinet had not yet discussed the subject. But on the second point Ben-Gurion won. The talks were to be held 'privately and secretly', and the Jewish Agency alone was to represent the Jewish side.[14] These arrangements were *post factum* approved by the Zionist Executive.

A DECISION AND A CHANGE OF MIND – DISCUSSIONS IN CABINET BETWEEN 15 JANUARY AND 6 FEBRUARY 1947

Towards the middle of January, the subject was to come before the Cabinet. But Attlee and Bevin discussed it first. They did not hope for much from the conference. According to Bevin, the Cabinet must consider in advance 'what to do in the event of a breakdown'. He foresaw two alternative courses. Either Britain could 'divest herself of all further responsibility', and ask the United Nations to take the burden, or it could 'impose a solution ... against an active resistance of either the Jews or the Arabs or both'. Either way, it was unavoidable that the UN would discuss it. Bevin preferred to try the second course, but he insisted on publishing the other alternative, for he held that 'communication of our intention ... might have a pacifying effect on Palestine'.[15]

The new line was, therefore, deliberately to engineer a crisis, in the hope that under the stress of a limited timetable and fear of the unknown, both sides, as well as the Americans, would soften their attitudes. The Arabs would fear total Zionist domination of Palestine with American backing; the Jews might fear 'another holocaust'; while the Americans might fear either Soviet penetration into the Palestine vacuum, or an American involvement entailing the use of American troops. Bevin seemed ready to use a version of the East-West 'brinkmanship' that was taking place in the rapidly developing Cold War. The trouble was that once he and his emissaries began to speak of quitting Palestine 'without recommendations',[16] his brinkmanship looked phoney. He needed to prove that the threat was genuine (and the threat gradually 'helped to materialise itself').

According to a British undertaking of April 1946, Palestine had in any event to come before the United Nations. It was at the time believed that Britain and America would be able to work out a complete proposal for the Assembly. But since Anglo-American disagreement continued throughout the summer and fall of 1946, reference to UN was deferred till the 1947 Assembly.[17] The new element now added was 'reference without recommendations', which meant that someone else must propose the solution.

By January 1947, Attlee and Bevin no longer wished to prolong the period in which Britain was to act as caretaker for provincial autonomy. Instead, they sought an interim period as short as was practically possible. Yet they felt that a few years at least of direct British rule were needed if Britain wanted an orderly departure. What was more, the Chiefs of Staff attached major importance to keeping Palestine in view of the need to evacuate Egypt and India.[18] Bevin prepared his proposal to the Cabinet along these lines.

He proposed that the interim period for the duration of provincial autonomy should be not longer than five years. Subsequently, power would be transferred to the UN; meanwhile the local inhabitants would gradually receive more and more share in the government. During the first two years of his scheme, the 100,000 Jews would be allowed to enter, but thereafter there would be no more Jewish immigration unless the UN or the Arabs or both agreed to it. Meanwhile, there would develop a pattern of government which, by parliamentary means, would lead to the formation of local government, obviously to be dominated by the Arab majority. Another step toward this arrangement would be the abolition of the Jewish Agency, with its special international status; the right to represent the Jewish community being granted to representatives of the Palestine Jews alone.[19]

Bevin pinned his hopes on acceptance of these proposals by the neighbouring Arab states. He expected them to understand that the single big dose of Jewish immigration needed to comfort America, and to serve as a bait for the Zionists, was a sacrifice worth making, in return for the opportunity to achieve Arab domination with British assistance.[20] His experts assured him moreover that provincial autonomy was the only scheme which had a chance of gaining a two-thirds majority vote in the General Assembly.[21]

The atmosphere during the Cabinet reassessment of Britain's Palestine policy reveals the extent of British perplexity. For between mid-January and mid-February, the policy-makers changed their minds no less than three times. First they overwhelmingly declined Bevin's proposals, preferring Creech Jones's solution – an attempt to enact partition. Less than two weeks later they switched to Bevin's new version of provincial autonomy, only once again to change their minds and decide, a week later, to refer the issue to the United Nations 'without recommendations'. But even when they had taken this decision, they were told by Bevin that it was merely a tactical *démarche*, his aim being to force the parties to reconsider their positions.

On 15 January and again on the 22, the Cabinet discussed its attitude towards the impending London talks; before that, a preliminary consultation took place in the Cabinet Defence Committee, with the three Chiefs of Staff.[22] During those meetings, an appreciation by the Palestine High Commissioner, Sir Alan Cunningham, made an impression on most of those present.[23] As an administrator as well as a renowned military man, Cunningham was of the opinion that 'the question whether any particular solution is administratively satisfying (in Palestine) was always relegated to the background'. For the Jews and the Arabs focused on achieving 'full political freedom' before all else. Since he believed that enactment of partition might in practice involve 'only local rioting in the main towns' and not a general uprising, a loss of territory for the two rivals would be 'balanced by the fullest political freedom'.

Arguments advanced by the man on the spot impressed even the military. The Chief of the Air Staff, Lord Tedder, thought that 'if one of the communities had to be antagonised, it was preferable that a solution be found which did not involve the continuing hostility of the Arabs', but was ready to waive his objection to partition, if no such 'antagonism' threatened. The Minister of Defence, A. V. Alexander, likewise reasoned that partition was preferable if there were no opposition to it. But if it came to a choice between antagonising Arabs or Jews, there was 'no doubt' that it would be 'more disadvantageous to us to incur the continuous hostility of the Arab states'.[24]

In general, the British troop disposals were as follows: no reserve was immediately available, unless taken from sensitive areas such as Trieste or Germany. But it was reckoned that no such reserves would be needed in the event of a mere general Jewish uprising. Only if an uprising of the Arab states occurred, or if both the Jews and the Arabs rebelled, would an extra one or more divisions of first-line troops be required in Palestine and its vicinity.[25] Temporarily, therefore, the High Commissioner's appreciation disarmed Bevin and the Chiefs of Staff, and created a strange conglomeration of pro-partitionists in the cabinet, concentrated around Creech Jones.

Bevin tried in vain to warn the cabinet of the danger of 'losing British influence' in the 'vast area between Greece and India', and to point out that the real difficulty was not acceptance of partition in principle, but drawing its boundaries.[26] For a while he remained the only voice in the cabinet against it. But he got enough support from the Prime Minister to obtain suspension of the final decision until matters were clarified at the conferences that were to begin on January 27.[27]

As the talks with the Arabs and the Jews got into their stride an atmosphere of uncertainty began to spread in the cabinet. Creech Jones, spurred on by the rank and file, set out to prepare yet another partition scheme.[28] Though his confidence was shaken by lack of support from Attlee and Bevin, this drawback was nothing compared with the practical difficulties of delimiting the frontiers.[29] Meanwhile, the positions of the Jews and the Arabs at the two simultaneous conferences were so wide apart that no definite scheme emerged at all.

Creech Jones's declared aim was to produce a scheme that would not only be 'the only practical course', and one 'with an element of finality', but also one that would 'do maximum possible justice to both communities'. But within days he found that it would be impossible to 'increase the viability' of the Arab state, satisfy the demands of the Chiefs of Staff for various strategic 'enclaves', and at the same time satisfy even the most 'moderate' Zionists. He could not make up his mind whether to connect the 'international entity' of Jerusalem to the coast of the Mediterranean, because to do so tampered with the southern frontiers of the Jewish state, which might or might not include Jaffa.

The result of his exertions typified his hesitation. He produced not one map but two. In the first, the Jewish state was to include the northern Huleh salient, but was to end at Jaffa. In the second, it was to include various Jewish towns south of Jaffa, but to lose the whole of Galilee. The total area that he allotted to the Jewish state was about 1,190 square miles – one third less than had been suggested in the 1937 partition proposal. Second thoughts now cast doubt on Cunningham's optimistic appreciation that the Arabs might accept a 'good' partition; instead it seemed as if Creech Jones's scheme was going to embroil Britain in the worst of all possible events, namely a total clash with both the Arabs and the Jews.

His confidence evaporated, and he decided to go to Canossa. On 5 February he added his signature to Bevin's on a memorandum ruling out partition, and proposing the scheme that Bevin wanted.[30] At a cabinet meeting of 7 February, he admitted his error, blaming the High Commissioner for spreading 'misleading' ideas. His *volte face* at once wrecked the pro-partition coalition; only the Minister of Defence complained about the shortage of the interim period in Bevin's scheme. The new proposal was stencilled with lightening speed and distributed to the Arabs, the Jews and the Americans.[31]

THE BREAKDOWN OF THE LONDON TALKS AND BEVIN'S TACTICS THEREAFTER

The partition fiasco in the cabinet restored Bevin's full control of Palestine affairs. He now decided to accelerate the proceedings and requested the Jews and the Arabs to give their answers within a few days. He made it clear to them that his proposal was not a basis for new negotiations, but a 'final' one. If they declined it, they must be ready to see the issue referred to the UN 'without British recommendations'.

The decision whether to enforce Bevin's scheme or not now depended mainly on the Arab response. The Jews feared such a consequence, but the Arabs did them a favour and failed to grasp the situation. The Higher Committee dominated the Arab side, and its head, the Mufti's cousin Jamal Husaini, rejected the British proposal in a language that left no doubt about the chances of further British persuasion. Representatives of Arab states, notably Fadil Jamali of Iraq and Faris al-Khuri of Syria, followed his lead. Unable to swallow the immigration of an extra 100,000 Jews, they called Bevin's scheme 'a surrender to Zionism', indicating that they were unable to contemplate a compromise, 'because there is no compromise between right and wrong'.[32]

The Jewish Agency too replied that it could not possibly accept Bevin's latest proposal. 'The scheme', said Moshe Shertok (Sharet), head of the Agency's Political Department, 'moved further in the direction of the White Paper than the Morrison-Grady scheme, which we have already declined'.[33] Within a few days, therefore, the two conferences came to an end.

Nevertheless, the Zionists were anxious not to close all doors to further negotiation. Their intelligence experts openly spoke of an evil British device 'to finish now what they had begun on June 29'.[34] They wrongly interpreted a letter, sent to their Jerusalem headquarters from the Palestine government's Chief Secretary on 4 February, asking whether they would co-operate in arresting 'dissident' terrorists, and they saw confirmation of their suspicion when British families were evacuated from Palestine. They feared that the failure of the talks, coupled with new Jewish terrorist attacks, might be used as a pretext for breaking the Jewish quasi-government and its military arm, the *Hagana*. In his diary, Ben-Gurion feared 'troubles, very soon'.[35]

Without direct consultation with his colleagues in Jerusalem, Ben-Gurion therefore decided to seek further 'private' talks with British ministers. He appears to have reckoned, as was common among Agency experts on foreign affairs, that the British warning to quit Palestine was an empty threat, 'aimed at blackmailing America'[36], and that it was unthinkable that Britain would jettison her strategic interest there. He also feared Bevin's fury, and is on record as telling American colleagues that 'Bevin will not imitate Hitler's furnaces, but short of this will do anything ...'.[37] He therefore continued, even after officially rejecting Bevin's scheme, to seek meetings and to send memoranda to Bevin and Creech Jones, illustrating the great advantages that Britain might get from an alliance with a future Jewish state.[38] But when he realised that those ministers were not interested in such ideas, and when rumours of a 'crucial' cabinet meeting, called for 14 February, had reached him, he decided to change course, and tactically to give up the demand for Jewish statehood. This he did at a meeting with a member of the cabinet, William Jowitt, which had been arranged late on the night of February 13, through a notable British Jew, Sir Simon Marks.[39]

At this eleventh hour, Ben-Gurion acted in total defiance of the Zionist Congress resolution – a thing that only a leader of his standing could dare do. Temporarily giving up the state idea, he was ready to put up with the resumption 'of the conditions existing before the enactment of the White Paper'. In fact he was ready for less. If the 100,000 were allowed to immigrate (as was laid down in Bevin's scheme) and if the land laws were abolished, the Jewish Agency might be satisfied, and might co-operate with the government in putting down Jewish terrorism.[40] Lord Jowitt was sure the ice had been broken, and joyfully told Ben Gurion that 'we have met just in time'. But this assertion merely showed that Jowitt did not know Bevin's mind.

When the cabinet met on the morning of 14 February, Bevin astonished his colleagues by refusing to hear any new proposals. Ministers like Jowitt, or Strachey, who attended specially to advocate acceptance of Ben-Gurion's latest proposals, were met with determined opposition not only from him, but from Attlee and Creech Jones. The last three were now convinced that an announcement about reference to the UN must be made before any further negotiation. This, Bevin said, 'was the only way to bring the parties into a more reasonable frame of mind'. But he assured his colleagues that 'submission to the UN would not involve immediate surrender of the Mandate'.[41] As a result of a plea from the new American Secretary of State, George Marshall, he even agreed not to indicate when and how the matter should be submitted to the UN. The public was simply told, on 14 February, as was the House of Commons, on the 18th, that reference to the UN was the result of the failure of the London talks.[42]

In fact Marshall's quick response[43] struck Bevin as a good omen. He had already learned from Inverchapel that Truman was now on bad terms with the Zionists, and that the State Department had received his scheme with modified enthusiasm.[44] He nevertheless believed that for the sake of his own parliamentary position, the Americans must be publicly denounced for their 'destructive' role in the Palestine affair so far. His speech in the Commons on 25 February was not – as it is sometimes described – an 'emotional outburst' which 'unwittingly' revealed the main reason for the decision to abandon the Mandate. His exasperated assault on Truman, for 'setting everything back time and again' and for making his country's foreign relations 'subject to local elections', and his lament that 'if only they had waited to ask us what we were doing', were all calculated assault – first and foremost to repulse some bitter attacks from the Parliamentary Opposition at home,[45] and secondly, to scold America. For if the Zionists could be brought to reduce their demands, the Americans must at all cost refrain from repeating 'acts of sabotage' such as that carried out by Truman on 4 October 1946.

In his cable to Lord Inverchapel, sent two days after his speech, Bevin explained:

> It was necessary to show the House of Commons how we have striven for American co-operation and how the attitude of United States has ... complicated our problem. But even now I have not given up hope of arriving at a settlement without recourse to the United Nations. The Colonial Secretary is still in contact with representatives of the Jewish Agency. On the Arab side I have received the Emir Saud ... I am personally convinced that the Arabs would eventually acquiesce in the entry of 100,000 Jewish immigrants ... if we

could give them satisfactory assurances about the future. I intend to raise it with Marshall in Moscow.[46]

Bevin's speech won cheers from both sides of the House, and it impressed the British press as well.[47] In America, by contrast, Secretary of State Marshall failed to get 'the message', and was greatly embarrassed by it. The American public and press were hostile to it.[48]

In accordance with Bevin's new tactics, attempts to reach a settlement before or without recourse to the UN continued through March. British officials in Cairo and in other Arab capitals discussed Palestine with the heads of the Arab League and rulers in an attempt to gain favour for the British aims at the coming League meeting,[49] but in forestalling these moves, Jamal Husaini swiftly toured some Arab capitals, managing to turn opinion his way. Consequently, the League 'preferred consideration by the UN on a settlement negotiated otherwise'.[50] The 'contacts with the Jewish Agency', to which Bevin had referred in his letter to Inverchapel, amounted only to a few secret meetings between himself, Creech Jones, Nahum Goldmann and Berl Locker, two 'moderate' members of the Zionist Executive, at the time in London. But it was soon realised that these last not only were now without much influence or knowledge of Ben-Gurion's recent moves with Jowitt,[51] but that Bevin's threat to abolish the Jewish Agency made them particularly suspicious of his aims. For they would then be the first to lose their standing.[52]

Finally, Bevin broke no ice during his prolonged stay in Moscow. Marshall, with whom he hoped to reach an understanding during the Foreign Ministers' meeting, was still sore about Bevin's attack on Truman, partly because he had come to office 'without any expertise in Near-Eastern affairs'.[53] He saw Britain's 'withdrawal intentions' from various countries in the area as all of a piece. He connected reference of Palestine to the UN with Britain's intention to relinquish her strategic responsibility for Greece and Turkey – an issue which had at that very time been under discussion in his absence between his deputy, Acheson, the White House and Congress. To him the whole phenomenon emanated from a growing 'domination of Britain's foreign policy by the left-wing group in the Labour Party'. He therefore refused to discuss any Middle Eastern issues with Bevin, pending clarification back in Washington.[54] He is on record as fearing being 'left to hold the bag'.[55]

Another reason for the quick evaporation of Bevin's hopes was the failure of a massive anti-terrorist operation, which, after many delays, the British government decided to carry out alone. For a long time it had hoped that the Agency and the *Vaad Leumi* would agree to co-operate, but adamant opposition from merely two executive members caused the whole executive to shelve a scheme whereby élite *Hagana* units would work hand in hand with the British police.[56] Late in February acts of terrorism grew uglier; the Chiefs of Staff accordingly pressed the government 'once for all to stop appeasing the Yishuv'.[57] The High Commissioner hoped for a degree of co-operation from the Jewish public in extraditing terrorists, but he too was disappointed. A green light to the army and police to act alone was given on 2 March, but martial law enacted in various areas of the country for two full weeks achieved poor results. A mere 24 terrorists were caught; meanwhile acts of terrorism continued despite the curfew. On 20 March the cabinet was informed of the 'disappointing results', and the High Commissioner declined to recommend any further imposition of martial law. Simultaneously, intelligence reports announced growing illegal immigration, and from European legations came news of failure to persuade governments to stop immigrants at ports of embarkation. It became clear that the detention camps built in Cyprus would soon be full up.[58] Everything pointed to the military inability to cope with the kind of war that the Zionists, however disunited, were launching. The difficulties were not purely military; they were the result of a delicate compounding of military and political events.

THE BRITISH DILEMMA ABOUT REFERENCE TO THE UNITED NATIONS

Meanwhile, Britain could not altogether abandon her public undertaking to refer the issue to the UN. On 3 March, she requested UN Secretary General Trygve Lie to place Palestine on the agenda of the regular autumn General Assembly. This, however, left six months to that date, and at first it looked as if there was no hurry in tackling the problem of who would make the necessary recommendations. It was clear that, according to Bevin's line and cabinet decision, Britain would not recommend a solution.[59]

But the failure to settle things secretly with the Arabs and Jews soon made the dilemma acute. When Britain and America sat down to consider it, there were three choices, all of them fraught with danger. The first was to sneak the creation of a committee through the UN Trusteeship Council. Lie was quite ready to assist this endeavour but British legal experts doubted whether this course was consistent with the UN Charter.[60] The second was to get the Security Council to do the job. But both parties feared that in view of East-West tension on the southern borders of Russia, the Soviets might veto the composition of any committee that did not include themselves. Sir Alexander Cadogan, Britain's delegate to the UN, predicted that the Soviets would be keen to 'instal troops on the banks of Jordan', and ships in the Mediterranean to supply them.[61] The third course was to convene a special UN Assembly, a practice never tested before. The US and Lie detested this choice, arguing that it was a bad precedent, that it would drain the organisation's budget, and that it was a mistake, perhaps impossible, to confine an Assembly to a single issue. For the British, by contrast, the third was the best of three bad choices, provided that the Assembly undertook no 'discussion on the substance' of the matter.⁶² For if that happened, they might find themselves in the opposite camp not only to the Arabs but the Soviet Union.

But the most searching British dilemma, in which no power could help, was what to tell the Assembly of Britain's intentions. Would Britain abide by any UN recommendation? Would she be ready to participate in its implementation? Cadogan pointed out that if Britain said that she would not, the Assembly might refuse to take the issue seriously, and might cold-shoulder some active British proposal. On the other hand, if Britain agreed in advance to abide by any UN recommendation, other UN members, including the United States, might reckon that any burden, including implementation of partition, might fall on them. Bevin (in Moscow) consulted his Foreign Office colleagues in London, and the topic eventually reached the Cabinet in his absence. The Prime Minister there stipulated that 'at the Assembly we seek settlement, not judgement', and that no definite obligation must be given to implement any recommendation that the UN might make. When the matter reached the Assembly, Cadogan was at one point pressed by the Indian delegate to make Britain's view clear; he replied that 'personally' he 'could not imagine Britain carrying into effect the policy which she does not approve'.⁶³

On 31 March all the permanent members of the Security Council agreed to put Palestine on the agenda of a special Assembly. They also canvassed the approvals that would be required to gain the requisite majority. On 2 April Cadogan officially requested the meeting, and the Assembly opened on 28 April.

When it opened, the British had not lost hope that things would eventually turn out as they wanted. They based this conviction on the implicit assumption that the Russians could only side with the opponents of Zionism.⁶⁴ While such a Russian attitude was bad enough, in that it endangered full British understanding with the Arabs, it comforted them in other ways. For instance, it ensured the lack of two-thirds majority for more pro-Zionist resolutions, such as one for partition. It seemed almost safe to predict that the end-result of the process would be either a more pro-Arab compromise (and one close to Bevin's scheme) or else no conclusion at all.

From the point of view of pure procedure the special Assembly was an Anglo-American success. The two delegations acted in concert and managed to defeat all attempts to divert the proceedings from the single item tabled by Cadogan.⁶⁵ Soviet Russia, which first went some way hand in hand with the Arab states, later recognised that this course would lose the battle; so, suddenly, either by design, or, more likely, after study of the UN chess-board by a high-ranking élite, she unexpectedly changed course. For the first time she broke the Soviet taboo against supporting Zionism, and by so doing wrecked British hopes. True, the Soviets failed to bring about a 'discussion of the substance' or to get themselves included on the Special Investigation Committee (UNSCOP) which was formed.[66] But on 14 May, the last day of the debate, they launched a campaign that was in the end to frustrate Bevin's United Nations tactics.

On that date, the Soviet ceased to speak vaguely of 'immediately granting independence to Palestine', and instead became specific. If a binational state was 'impracticable', said the young head of their delegation, Andrey Gromyko, then there must be partition, and two separate states should be established. He amazed the Assembly when he used orthodox Zionist arguments to support the 'historical rights of both the Arabs and the Jews in Palestine'. Jewish Agency observers called the event 'a miracle', and Soviet diplomats had their hands full persuading the Arab rulers that Gromyko was merely over-playing his hand.[67]

There is some evidence that at this juncture Russia was not yet convinced of the value of its line, and that its initial aim was more modest – that it intended only 'to play both ends against the middle', as the Director of the State Department's UN Office, Dean Rusk described it.[68] For when, for example, Ben-Gurion was rushed to New York in the second week of May, 'to take advantage of the Slavic intention to get Britain out of Palestine',[69] he made little progress at a meeting with Gromyko. The latter was taken aback by Ben-Gurion's stark proposal for formal relations between the Zionist movement and Moscow; he even refrained from repeating his partition idea. His only advice to the Zionists was to concentrate their efforts on ousting Britain which was against Ben-Gurion's own policy just recently.[70] But now Ben-Gurion agreed to it and acted accordingly when, on 4 July, he spoke before UNSCOP.[71]

But thereafter, Soviet diplomacy got deeper into Palestine affairs, and into supporting partition. As early as March, and later – in July – Soviet diplomats visited Palestine, under the guise of registering Armenians for repatriation. On both occasions they witnessed some of Britain's unfortunate attempts to quell terrorism, and were no doubt impressed.[72] Activities increased in Soviet legations all over the Middle East, and UNSCOP members got the impression that a solution that might obtain a two-thirds majority in the next UN Assembly would not necessarily be the solution Britain wanted.

THE BRITISH NEGLECT OF UNSCOP

Abstention from making 'recommendations' for the future of Palestine had given Britain some diplomatic advantages. In the first place, it had increased a feeling of 'responsibility' in the United States and other UN members. It also made them, or at least the Western powers among them, more prone to see that Britain herself had vested interests, not just 'obligations' in Palestine; and that these interests must be considered, if a measure of subsequent British co-operation was desired. After all, the simplest and smoothest way to implement any solution was to use the machinery and experience of the then British Palestine administration. Moreover a British withdrawal prior to implementation of any potential scheme so horrified the United States, that its policy-makers refused to speculate on such a possibility.

But Britain's formula was also self-defeating. In the first place it prevented Britain from influencing decision-making at the United Nations. When, for instance, at the April–May special Assembly, the Soviets demanded that the Palestinian Arabs (that is, the representatives of the Higher Committee) should be heard, British diplomats could only quietly advise the Arab states not to insist on this, because of the official position thereby automatically granted to the Jewish Agency. (Two Soviet allies, Poland and Czechoslovakia, advocated just this.) But the Arab states, now baffled, could not lag behind the Soviets, with the result that a hearing (though eventually only before the Assembly First Committee) was granted to both communities.[73]

But where Britain's abstention had really disastrous results was in UNSCOP. In fact neglect of UNSCOP, emanating from the conviction that partition would never be adopted by anyone who really wanted a solution, was greater than the circumstances called for. Tired British officials and diplomats seemed almost bent on enjoying the respite just bought, and thankful to forget Palestine for several weeks. When the committee intended to leave New York, the Palestine Desk-Officer at the Foreign Office, Harold Beeley (who was also member of Britain's UN Delegation), advised that 'as far as he could judge ... it should not be necessary to send any senior officers to give guidance to the Committee'. In his opinion the young Liaison Officer to whom the Palestine administration had allotted this task, Donald M. C. MacGillivray, was enough.[74] In July, a Foreign Office circular to various British Middle Eastern legations advised them that it saw 'no point in conversation prior to the publication of UNSCOP report'.[75] Further, British diplomats refused to persuade the Arab states and the Arab Higher Committee not to boycott UNSCOP altogether. Sir Lawrence Grafftey-Smith, the British Minister in Saudi Arabia, wrote that the Soviet attempt to persuade the Arabs to appear before UNSCOP was 'another reason why right-minded Arabs should boycott it'.[76] The British retained this line despite constant warning from Sir Abdur Rahman, the Moslem Indian member of UNSCOP, that the boycott would have 'disastrous results' for the Arabs.[77]

UNSCOP members were far from pro-British at the start. Its two Moslem members were pro-Arab, and two of its Latin-Americans pro-Zionist.[78] The rest, including the two Commonwealth representatives, were an unknown quantity. And, in contrast to the position at the previous year's Anglo-American Committee of Inquiry, UNSCOP secretaries were no longer the friendly occupants of the Palestine Desks in the Foreign Office and State Department; instead, they were a multinational group of UN officials, whose chief interest was not guidance to the Committee, but smooth procedure.

But the strongest influence on UNSCOP's unpredictable conclusions was the scene in Palestine itself. UNSCOP reached Palestine in mid-June, and spent the rest of the month touring the country while it waited for the Arabs to change their minds. During weeks in which the shock of first impression is strong, the Jews took full advantage of the situation, ready, in the words of a hostile American Consul-General, Robert Macattee, to 'fête Committee members individually and collectively *ad nauseam*'. When the hearing began, with the Arabs absent, 'the Jews had no opposition ... and the Agency had given more than half the time granted to all witnesses ... what else could one ask?'[79]

And yet, until after mid-July, British observers continued to predict that a 'key group of five members', i.e. Sweden, Peru, the Netherlands, Canada and Australia, 'were not impressed by the Zionist arguments'. They whispered that Chairman Sandstrom was in fact deeply interested in 'some form of trusteeship' and 'in the elimination of the Jewish Agency'.[80]

A 'key group' with such views may have existed and, together with the two Moslems, assured a majority of non-Zionists in the Committee. But the calculation did not necessarily imply rejection of partition. For circumstances were such that UNSCOP members inevitably gained the impression that the main difficulties in Palestine were not between Jews and Arabs, but between Jews and the British government. During their stay, illegal immigration and Jewish terrorism reached their zenith. On 19 July the *Exodus*, carrying some 4,553 Jewish Displaced Persons, was turned back from Haifa, this time not to Cyprus but to Europe. Echoes of the immigrants' struggle, and their subsequent refusal to disembark in France, followed the Committee's visit to the DP's camps in Europe. On the very date of the deportation, the Palestine government's Chief Secretary, Sir Henry Gurney, gave 'excellent but badly timed' evidence to the Committee. Events at the coast stole his thunder.[81] Ten days later, as a terrorist reprisal for the execution of their members at a British prison (for whom UNSCOP tried in vain to gain amnesty),[82] two British NCO's were hanged by the terrorist IZL organisation. In consequence, and much to the British government's horror, anti-Semitic riots occurred in some of Britain's northern cities.[83]

Towards the end of UNSCOP's stay in Palestine, reports from MacGillivray at last began to shake the confidence in the Foreign Office. Now the reports were alarming. On 25 July he wrote that UNSCOP's relations with the Palestine administration were tense, and at the same time Sandstrom intimated to the High Commissioner that although 'having started as a federalist', he had now come to the conclusion 'that any form of central government would not work'. He therefore espoused partition and the whole 'key group' followed him.[84]

Equally alarming were reports from Amman that in defiance of Arab solidarity and British instructions, King Abdullah had told Committee members that he might favour partition. A short hearing arranged at the last minute for members of the Arab League in Soffar, Lebanon, and held between 22 and 24 July, did not alter the impression.[85] For the presence of Jamal Husaini there once again prevented representatives of the Arab states from contributing anything but 'extremism'.[86]

Nevertheless, full alarm never reached top echelons in London. Early in August, when UNSCOP was already in Geneva, an urgent Foreign-Colonial Offices meeting was held at a lower level, and a decision was taken 'to write a paper about it'.[87] Beeley himself, recalling how callous he had been in June, rushed to the Geneva hotel where the Committee was considering its report, and at the last moment attempted to win their interest to the scheme, proposed to the Cabinet by Creech Jones last February. But his request failed to gain attention, because 'it had not been included in the material that the British government provided in May'. The Committee also decided 'to refuse any additional oral information from the Mandatory power'.[88]

And so UNSCOP's report, signed on 31 August, although not unanimous, unequivocally recommended the end of the British Mandate as quickly as possible. In addition, a substantial majority of seven members[89] recommended partition in a form that, in Bevin's words, was 'so manifestly unjust to the Arabs that it is difficult to see how we can reconcile it with our conscience.'[90] Conscience apart, it was clear that although most Zionists might agree to the scheme, any attempt to impose it on the Arabs would involve serious conflict with the whole Arab world.

THE BRITISH POSITION AT THE REGULAR UN ASSEMBLY

The UNSCOP majority proposal included the formation in Palestine of no less than seven separate areas, six of which touched at geometrical points. Three of them were to form a Jewish state, and these three formed the biggest share of the country, including the Negev down to the Red Sea. Another three were to form the Arab state, including most of the hill country. The seventh area was to be a *corpus separatum* around the city of Jerusalem, and to remain an international entity. The whole geographical complex was to enjoy 'economic unity'. An UNSCOP minority proposal, supported by Yugoslavia and the two Moslem members, suggested a federal state with Jewish autonomy. This scheme was in essence rather close to Bevin's scheme, for the complicated bicameral constitution in the last account gave the domination of the country's future to the Arabs.

Now Britain, however embarrassed by the results, could not turn the clock back. The UN Assembly was due to open in a few days; the question was what to say there? Bevin remained convinced that the only course was firm refusal to implement any scheme, except one 'sufficient to produce a solution which His Majesty's Government would feel justified in accepting responsibility for'.[91] During the cabinet meeting of 20 September,[92] a pro-Zionist minister (but one of whose judgement Attlee thought poorly[93]) said that 'it might well be that in the course of the ... Assembly, neither the Majority nor the Minority plan would be accepted, and something approaching the scheme suggested in 1946 would be approved'. But it was not certain that even then Britain would be able to enforce the solution. For at this point the Chiefs of Staff, who had gone a long way since their argument of the previous January, injected a dose of pessimism. They now no longer insisted on keeping Palestine, because of developments in the Cold War. They reckoned Britain unable to pay the price (in troops) of staying in Palestine, and instead, planned a run-down of her army there.[94]

There was one last hope. Maybe the United Nations would eventually come close to Britain's view about the only practicable solution — and one which British and UN troops together would implement. The cabinet therefore agreed to tell the Assembly that Britain 'would not be able to give effect to any scheme unacceptable to both the Arabs and the Jews and that in any other event, the UN would have to find another implementing authority. The prime responsibility for the implementation of such a solution would in any event be transferred to the UN.'[95] A high-ranking British delegation, lunching at the State Department, told Marshall of this conclusion,[96] and a day later Creech Jones told it to the UN Assembly's *ad hoc* Committee on Palestine. Britain's Palestine policy grew more and more like that of a ship which had stopped its engines but hoped to drift on the desired course, whereas in fact the current was taking it farther and farther out to sea.

In the beginning it seemed that the British tactics would work, at least as far as America was concerned. The American UN delegation, although in principle favouring the majority scheme, did nothing. But this deadlock lasted only until the Soviets decided to step in with new and clear support for it. Now the American delegation did something unexpected; it turned to cooperation with Russia.

That such a possibility was not foreseen by the Foreign Office is shown by their refusal to discuss Palestine with the Americans at the secret conference known as the Pentagon Talks, and held between mid-October and early November.[97] In these talks, which were prepared during the whole summer, top British and American military and political experts discussed the coordination of their strategies in no less than twelve Middle-Eastern and African countries. Britain, however, bound by her 'no-recommendation' canon, insisted that Palestine was 'a thing apart'. Therefore, although it was agreed that the developments there would 'have important bearing on any endeavours toward Anglo-American cooperation', it 'should not be debated'.[98]

The United States, which now inherited some of Britain's Palestine perplexities, only gradually came to favour partition. During the summer, various schemes of an entirely different nature were aired at the State Department.[99] When, however, UNSCOP published its report, Marshall decided not to expose the United States to criticism (such as he had recently heard much of at the Inter-American Conference at Rio de Janeiro) about disregard for international organisations.[100] In his speech before the Assembly, on 17 September, he 'highly commended' UNSCOP's work,[101] and simultaneously reinforced his country's UN delegation with pro-partitionists like Mrs Roosevelt, General Hilldring and the republican John Foster Dulles.[102] But until mid-October, he himself made little effort to help partition get off the ground. Then, on 13 October, after the Soviet delegate at the *ad hoc* Committee, Semion K. Tsarapkin, had made an unequivocal statement supporting the majority proposal, Marshall began to be bombarded with advisory opinion to take up the challenge. This time it did not come from pro-Zionist circles, but from various quarters of his own department. 'The United States', advised Fraser Wilkins, the Palestine Desk Officer (and it was against his own superior's opinion, that of Loy Henderson), 'must take the lead in lining up votes for partition (sic) at the Assembly'.[103] 'There is only one course', wrote Robert McClintock, an expert on UN Affairs, '... firmly to support the majority plan and see it passed at the Assembly',[104] and so on.

On 21 October, therefore, the US delegation began to act according to a new strategy, aimed at co-operating with the Soviets in passing partition through the Assembly, and at the same time, trying not to harm Western defence interests in the Middle East. One way to achieve it was to try and reduce the interim period proposed by the majority, so reducing the time available for Soviet penetration manoeuvres. Another was to 'perfect' the geographical frontiers in some way more acceptable to Britain and to the Arabs. The Negev, for instance, which the majority allotted to the Jewish state, was planned to be ceded to the Arabs. Finally, an attempt was made to eliminate the participation of any Big Power, save Britain, from practical implementation of the partition scheme.[105] This line was of course contrary to the British concept of the circumstances in which Britain still might play some role in implementing a solution.

News of the American approach enraged Bevin. He intimated to American diplomats that this course was in his opinion hopeless. For 'if the Americans were really concerned about keeping the Russians out ... why didn't they abandon their support for partition?'[106] Meanwhile, members of the British delegation in New York tried to persuade some Arab delegations to announce acceptance of the UNSCOP minority proposal. Beeley had actually been openly advising various Arab delegations in this vein. But the latter preferred to keep such tactics to the last moment (when it proved too late). Meanwhile they preferred to make war noises. Azzam Pasha declared that 'partition means war', and Egypt and Syria moved troops nearer to Palestine's borders.[107]

THE IMPACT OF THE AMERICAN-SOVIET COOPERATION AT THE ASSEMBLY ON THE FINAL BRITISH DECISION TO WITHDRAW

Even at this late stage, there was no British decision, or even full government awareness that the Palestine game was up. Hypothetically, it is possible to imagine further British exertions to convince the US and the UN how vain it was to seek a settlement of which they themselves did not approve. But it soon became evident that with the wholly unexpected cooperation between Russia and America, Bevin's UN policy had been manoeuvred into a blind alley. To understand this point, a few words about the Assembly's procedure are called for.

Until Tsarapkin's speech of 13 October, the British government and its UN delegation believed that given the Cold War, American-Soviet cooperation was untenable. Consequently, they counted on American awareness that in the Assembly, a solid block of over one third of the members would vote against partition, come what might. It was in this spirit also that the Assembly, on 23 September, delegated the preparation of a resolution in line with the UNSCOP report to an *ad hoc* Committee, consisting of representatives of all 57 Assembly members. It was hoped that since there were two sets of proposals, that Committee might work out some proposal less objectionable than the majority scheme.[108] Indeed, no less than 17 new proposals were soon put up before the Committee Chairman. On 21 October, therefore, this Chairman split his Committee into three Sub-Committees, which for a moment seemed to give a chance for the emergence of a compromise. The task of preparing a resolution for the plenary was equally delegated to Sub-Committee 1, which was to prepare it according to the majority scheme; Sub-Committee 2, which was to do the same to the minority one, and Sub-Committee 3, consisting of the Chairman and his two deputies, which was to reconcile the two conclusions.[109]

But this procedure failed to lead to 'conciliation'. Members were allowed to opt for transfer from one Sub-Committee to another, and eventually each Sub-Committee consisted of supporters of one scheme only. All the Arab and Moslem countries, for instance, had become members of Sub-Committee 2, and *vice versa*. When, therefore, the *ad hoc* plenary Committee reassembled, it was faced with two incompatible resolutions, one reproducing the Arab position, in a scheme more uncompromising than the UNSCOP minority proposal, and the other pro-Zionist, similar to the one proposed by the UNSCOP majority. Of course, the conciliatory work of Sub-Committee 3 was void.[110]

An additional ill-omen for Britain was the efficient co-operation between Russia and America in the most important of Sub-Committee 1's 'Working Groups'. The two delegations worked along with the Canadian and the Guatemalan, and during the first week of November reached full agreement in regard to the method and details of the implementation of partition. Meanwhile, the chances of Anglo-American agreement faded as the United States delegates failed to obtain a simple majority inside Sub-Committee 1, for ceding the Negev to the Arab state. The dramatic last-minute visit to the White House by the ageing Dr Weizmann was in the circumstances hardly necessary to cancel the American initiative. The US delegation was, in any event, in Truman's words, standing as 'a useless minority' in Sub-Committee 1.[111]

At this point the British decided to give in. They did not wait until the *ad hoc* Committee vote of 25 November, in favour of partition, or until the Zionists, with the unofficial, yet indispensable assistance of the United States, managed, on 29 November, to obtain a two-thirds majority in the General Assembly.[112] For them all was over the moment it became clear that the Americans and the Soviets had decided to make a deal.

THE BRITISH WITHDRAWAL DECISION

Already after the Cabinet's 20 September meeting, thought was dedicated to the possibility of withdrawing the British army and administration from Palestine. Yet not until the second half of October, that is, after Tsarapkin's statement, were the Chiefs of Staff requested to plan the military part of the withdrawal. A week later, on Attlee's instruction, an inter-departmental committee was formed, headed by a veteran Colonial Office official, now serving as a Cabinet Secretary, S. E. V. Luke. It had to plan the evacuation from Palestine of the civil administration. But when it first met, on 31 October, it was told to await further developments at the UN. It began its work in the second week of November.[113]

It appears that the die was cast when, on 6 November, Cadogan heard, from the Canadian member of Sub-Committee 1's 'Working Group', of the progress made there between the Americans and the Russians. For later that night Hector MacNeil, Minister of State at the Foreign Office and the senior member of the British delegation, cabled Bevin that there was no longer much point in suspending a British announcement about a timetable for evacuation.[114]

The issue was discussed in cabinet on 11 November, 'in the light of the latest developments ... at the General Assembly'. The Cabinet agreed to authorise Attlee, Bevin, Creech Jones and Alexander, without further resort to the cabinet, to decide about the exact time and form of the British withdrawal announcement. It was also agreed that the deadline for ending British withdrawal would be 1 August 1948.[115] Two days later, Cadogan read a statement to this effect before Sub-Committee 1, adding that British troops would not be available for enforcement of any policy unacceptable to both sides.

At this point military planning quickened. On 14 November, General Sir John Crocker, Commander in Chief of the British Middle Eastern forces, flew to Jerusalem to seek with Cunningham an agreed solution on the general lines for evacuation; after a lengthy conference at Government House 'matters where military and civil plans overlapped ... were cleared'.[116] The detailed scheme was then flown through Cairo to London, where the Chiefs of Staff approved it on the 21st and the Luke Committee on the 27th. The Cabinet itself did not review the withdrawal scheme before the General Assembly voted on the partition scheme.

When it met to discuss it, on 4 December, its members were exhausted and humiliated by the whole affair. No opposition was encountered, and it accepted that from now on the guiding principles should be to save as much as possible of British blood and resources. Consequently it decided that no UN implementing body should be allowed to enter Palestine until a short time before the final withdrawal. After Bevin had assured it that members of the Arab League undertook 'not to make trouble while we are still in charge', it was decided that such agreement merited continuation, as long as possible, of the restriction on Jewish immigration.[118] It accordingly approved a procedure, whereby, with the exception of Jerusalem, the area held by the British army and civil administration would gradually shrink to a hard core around the port and refineries of Haifa. Evacuation of equipment would start immediately, but because of the short notice, some 150,000 tons, worth many millions of pounds, would have to be abandoned or destroyed. The troops would be evacuated to Libya and the Suez Canal-Zone, first-line units getting priority. Once an area was evacuated, it should not be re-occupied, so as to create the minimum possible 'friction' with the Arabs and the Jews.[119]

All these steps were taken in an atmosphere of mixed indignation and relief. Bevin was still telling his men 'to watch carefully and report to me at once' any development hinting at an Arab wish for British arbitration between themselves and the UN.[120] But on the eve of the debate of 12 December in the House of Commons it was whispered that Foreign Office advisers were 'having a difficult time finding something for Bevin to say' at the debate.[121]

NOTES

1. The one single attempt to implement the constitutional clause was made by Lord Lloyd, then Colonial Secretary, early in 1941. See my (Hebrew) 'The Shelving of the Constitutional Steps of the White Paper' (in) *Hatzionut*, Tel Aviv, Vol. VI, 1980.
2. The 'Cantonisation' idea was first proposed by Archer Cust, a member of the Palestine administration in 1936, but was never seriously considered by any government before Labour.
3. Notes on Cabinets. The Attlee Papers, Churchill College, Cambridge. Attlee wrote that Creech Jones 'was hardly strong for the position' and that 'despite much hard work and devotion he ... [did] not have a real grip of the Colonial Office' and that he 'contributed nothing to Cabinet'. Not one word of criticism is there about Bevin.
4. Bevin to Attlee, 12.1.47, FO 371/61761, E 74.

5. Cab 128/6, 94(46)4, and 99(46)3.
6. FO 371/61747, E 885. As a collaborator with the Nazis, public opinion and perhaps the British courts too, would not tolerate him on British soil.
7. For some new light on this affair see the Eban Ayers Diary, Harry S. Truman Library (henceforth HSTL), Independence, Missouri. See also FO 371/52560, E 9967.
8. Cab 128/6, 94(46)4, and 99(46)3.
9. *Ibid.* See also report in 867N.01/11-2246, US National Archives (henceforth USNA) Washington DC; Silver's Political Diary, The Temple, Cleveland, Ohio; J. M. Proskauer, *A Segment of My Life*, New York 1949, pp. 244-5.
10. FO 371/61764, E 221; FO 371/61763, E 670.
11. FO 371/61764, E743; Foreign Relations of the United States, 1947, Vol. V (henceforth – FRUS) pp. 1008-11.
12. FO 371/61765, E 1174.
13. FO 371/61747, E 981.
14. Minutes of the Jewish Agency Executive, Jerusalem (henceforth – JA), 29 December, 11 and 17 January, The Central Zionist Archives (henceforth – CZA). Ben-Gurion Diary, Sde Boker (henceforth – BG). See also FO 371/61762, E 261 and E 300.
15. Bevin to Attlee, 12.1.47, FO 371/61761, E 74.
16. Such warning is first recorded during Bevin's and Inverchapel's talks with American Jewish leaders in November. See note 9, above.
17. Cf. Cab 129/16, pp. 209-13.
18. According to an appreciation, prepared by the Chiefs of Staff early in January 1947, Palestine was now to become a chief 'base for mobile forces which must be ready to meet any emergency in the Middle East', and 'an area for deployment of greater forces' in the event of a clash with Russia. FO 371/61763, E 463; Cab 128/11, p. 7; Minutes by Beeley, CO 537/17871.
19. 'Palestine', Memorandum by the Secretary of State for Foreign Affairs, 14.1.47, Cab 129/16, CP(47)30; Cab 128/9, 18(47)2.
20. Advocating his scheme in Cabinet, Bevin said that Britain 'would be justified to bring the scheme into operation on her own authority ... or with the United Nations backing'. Cab 128/9, 18(47)2.
21. 'Palestine, Reference to the United Nations', Memorandum by the Secretary of State for Foreign Affairs, 13.1.47, Cab 129/16, CP(47)28.
22. Cab 128/9, 6(47)2, 3, 4,; Cab 128/11, pp. 7, 11-18, 20-2.
23. 'The Weakness of the Provincial Autonomy Plan' and 'A Note by the High Commissioner', two memoranda of 8 and 14 January, Annexed to Cab 129/16, CP(47)31.
24. Cab 128/11, p. 7; See also FO 371/61763, E 463.
25. *Ibid.*
26. Cab 129/16, p. 225.
27. Talks with the Jewish Agency actually began on 29 January.
28. 'Palestine, Future Policy', Memorandum by the Secretary of State for the Colonies, 16.1.47, Cab 128/11, pp. 11-18; Cab 129/16, CP(47)32.
29. For drafts and Minutes concerning Creech Jones's scheme see the Arthur Creech Jones Papers, Rhodes House, Oxford, Box 31.
30. 'Palestine' ... 6.2.47, Cab 129/16, CP(47)49.
31. Cab 129/16, pp. 327-30; FO 371/61748, E 1231; FRUS, pp. 1033-5.
32. FO 371/61747, E 986; FO 371/61748, E 1386.
33. 'Private and Informal Talks', reports from London in the Zionist Archives, New York (henceforth – ZANY). Other sources from which the conference was studied were: CO 733/464/75872/127, Cab 129/17, pp. 58-61 and FO 371/61746-61749, *passim*.

34. JA, 17, 19, 28 Jan., and 5, 6 Feb. 1947.
35. BG, 5, 6 Feb. But Cf. also FO 371/61765, E 1210.
36. Ben-Gurion to Weizmann, 28.10.46, the Weizmann Archives, Rehovoth. Note also Zaslany's talk with members of the US legation in Cairo, 867N.01/2–2447, USNA. The Zionist fears quickly developed into panic and spread to the United States. Marshall himself made representation in that regard to the British Embassy in Washington, and that made Creech Jones instruct Cunningham to tell the Jerusalem Agency headquarters that no such evil was contemplated. Security Meetings, Minute of 5.2.47, The Cunningham Papers (henceforth – Cunningham), St Antony's College, Oxford, Box IV.
37. Minutes of the Executive of the American Zionist Emergency Council, 25.7.46, ZANY.
38. Ben-Gurion to Bevin, 11 and 14 Feb., FO 371/61900; See also an unsigned report in 'Private and Informal ...', *ibid*.
39. *Ibid*. Other sources about the Ben-Gurion–Jowitt affair are: CO 537/233 and Cab 128/9, 22(47)2. But the formula proposed to Jowitt was not new. Two months earlier Ben-Gurion told a world conference of his own Party (Mapai-Ichud) that Britain must be 'given a choice' between a 'proper conduct of the Mandate and a Jewish state'. Archives of the Israel Labour Party, Zofit.
40. *Ibid*.
41. Cab 128/9, 22(47)2. See also Cab 129/17, CP(47)59.
42. *The Times*, 15.2.47; *Hansard*, Vol. 433, cols. 989–93.
43. At the same time Marshall requested an increase in the rate of Jewish immigration from 1,500 to 4,000 per month during the interim, but the British Cabinet did not accept this.
44. Cab 128/9, 23(47)3; FRUS pp. 1037–9.
45. On 31 Jan. Churchill told the House of Commons that the flare-up of terrorism in Palestine 'could have been avoided' and asked 'how should we have got through the latest (War) if we had allowed our will-power to relax in this way?' *Hansard*, Commons, Vol. 432, cols. 1343–50.
46. Bevin to Inverchapel, 27.2.47, FO 371/61768, E 1832.
47. *The Times*, 26.2.47.
48. For Marshall's reaction see below. For a typical American press reaction see Walter Lippmann's 'Bevin's Scapegoat', *NYT*, 26.2.47.
49. FO 371/61769, E 1918; FO 371/61768, E 1832; *al-difa'*, 19.3.47.
50. *Ibid*. See also Weekly Intelligence Report, FO 371/61769, E 2049.
51. Ben-Gurion declined to report to his Executive about his meeting with Jowitt, the reasons for which are not difficult to understand. Even in an intimate letter to his wife he only told her he had 'a late night meeting with Lord Jowitt, the content of which I cannot tell'. BG 15 Feb. 1947.
52. JA 14 March 1847. See also in 867N.01/3–147, USNA.
53. Clark M. Clifford, interview to the *American Heritage*, April 1977.
54. The result of the Washington assessment was, of course, the so-called Truman Doctrine, launched on 12 March.
55. FRUS, pp. 511–20.
56. Cab 129/17, CP(47)95; JA 7.2.47; Cunningham, 5.2.47, Box IV, File 2.
57. For instance at the Cabinet Defence Committee, WO 32/10260.
58. Cab 129/17, CP(47)95; Cunningham, 5, 7, 14 Feb. and 21 March, *ibid*.
59. FO 371/61769, E 1786.
60. FO 371/61767, E 1481 and FO 371/61679, E 1786. See also Henderson to Acheson, 867N.01/3–1847, USNA.
61. Appreciation by Cadogan, 24.2.47, FO 371/61768, E 1676. Also in FO 371/61676, *passim*.
62. FO 371/61768, E 1210 and E 1677.

63. Cab 128/9, 41(47)2; Cab 129/18, pp. 309–12; FO 371/61771, E 2738, and UN A/AC 13/82.
64. For such an appraisal by the British Ambassador in Moscow (Peterson) see CO 733/463/75872/140, and one by an American colleague in FRUS 1946, pp. 720–1.
65. Marshall to Truman, 16.5.47, FRUS pp. 1085–7; FO 371/61756, E 5489. The only point of disagreement had been a resolution condemning Jewish terrorism and illegal immigration, which in consequence was dropped.
66. A Soviet intention, to base the Committee membership on the Security Trusteeship and Economic and Social Councils was defeated. Only three 'Slavic' members were elected to serve among the eleven 'neutrals' – Australia, Canada, Czechoslovakia, Guatemala, India, Iran, the Netherlands, Peru, Sweden, Uruguay and Yugoslavia – that composed UNSCOP.
67. FO 371/61875, E 3245, and E 4898 and E 5752.
68. Rusk to Acheson, 27.5.47, FRUS pp. 1088–9.
69. JA, 11.5.47. In March, the Executive was delighted to learn that some Communist Parties in Eastern Europe no longer regarded Zionism as 'a tool in the hands of British Imperialism'. JA, 14.3.47.
70. JA, 22.5.47; Intelligence Report, FO 371/61900, E 4776.
71. UNSCOP, Vol. III, pp. 48–69.
72. FO 371/61861, E 285; Cunningham, Box II File 2.
73. Report by Beeley, FO 371/61780, E 5047. The confinement of the hearing to the First Committee was the result of American pressure behind the scenes. The Zionists subsequently managed to extend their achievement at the autumn regular Assembly. See 93.03/2269/5 at the Israel State Archives, Jerusalem.
74. FO 371/61777, E 4112.
75. FO 371/61780, E 5001. Also typical was the absence of any discussion of major Palestine issues in Cabinet between 29 April and 20 Sept. 1947.
76. FO 371/61875, E 5139.
77. FO 371/61875, E 5662 and E 5752. See also 501 BB Palestine/7–2147, USNA.
78. J. G. Granados of Guatemala and E. R. Fabrigat of Uruguay were deeply offended by an unsuccessful British manoeuvre at the UN, to disqualify their inclusion in UNSCOP, and by the successful British attempt to prevent the selection of Granados as Chairman. See: FO 371/61777, E 4043; FO 371/61778, E 4169 and FO 371/61779, E 4726. See also J. G. Granados, *The Birth of Israel*, NY 1950, ch. 2.
79. Macattee to Merriam, 501 BB Palestine/7–2147, USNA.
80. *Ibid.* Sabnstrom was in fact not completely unknown to the Zionists, and upon becoming candidate for UNSCOP he was briefed by the Jewish Agency through a Zionist friend, Dr Hugo Valentine of Uppsala.
81. Cunningham, Box II, File 1; FO 371/61876, E 6848. Granados, *ibid.* ch. 17.
82. L. Larry Leonard, *The United Nations and Palestine*, NY 1949, p. 633.
83. Almost at his wits' end, Creech Jones cabled Cunningham demanding 'extraordinary measures', but was calmly answered that 'the services have already made use of all measures under the Defence Regulations ... except blowing Houses' which in the Jewish case would not be effective. Cunningham, 2 and 4 August, Box II, File 2.
84. FO 371/61875, E 5752 and E 6515; Leonard, *ibid*, p. 634; private reports sent to Rabbi Silver by I. L. ('Si') Kennan. The Silver Archives.
85. FO 371/61876, E 7242; Eliahu Sasson, *Baderech el Hashalom* (Hebrew – 'On the Road to Peace'), Tel Aviv 1978, pp. 391–3.
86. Cunningham, 2 August, Box II. Sassos, *ibid*; Granados, *ibid*, ch. 19; See also *Report to the General Assembly of the United Nations Special Committee on Palestine*, London 1947, pp. 11, 64.
87. FO 371/61877, E 7498.
88. *Report to the General Assembly ...*, *ibid*, p. 11; Leonard, *ibid*, p. 636; D. Horowitz.

Bishlichut Medinah Noledet (Hebrew) Tel Aviv 1951, p. 234; The author's interview with Harold Beeley, London, January 1973.
89. Canada, Czechoslovakia, Guatemala, the Netherlands, Peru, Sweden, Uruguay. The Australian delegate abstained.
90. 'Palestine', Memorandum by the Secretary of State for Foreign Affairs, 18.9.47, Cab 129/21, CP(47)259. A special meeting of the Zionist General Council in Zurich on 5 Sept. decided to accept the majority proposal.
91. The Foreign Secretary's memorandum, *ibid*.
92. Cab 128/10, 76(47)6.
93. It was Philip Noel-Baker. See the Attlee Papers, *ibid*. But Attlee himself told the Cabinet on 20 Sept. that 'salutary results might be produced by a clear announcement of His Majesty's Government's intention to relinquish the Mandate'. *Ibid*.
94. Summary of the Chiefs of Staff Conclusions, Cab 129/21, p. 121.
95. Cab 129/21, p. 46.
96. Marshall told Messrs Creech Jones, MacNeil and Inverchapel that he realised that the British were 'the victims of an impossible situation', but he 'refused to comment' on the wisdom of the British position now. FRUS, p. 1164.
97. The Pentagon Talks originated in Britain's continued disagreement with America over the deployment of British troops in Greece. For despite the Truman Doctrine, Britain intended to withdraw her forces. For the conference's proceedings see FRUS pp. 582–5, and FO 371/52560, E 9966.
98. Satterthwaite to Acheson and Webb, 11.3.49 (sic), the NEA Files, Lot 55 D/36, USNA.
99. Those schemes envisaged the internationalisation of Palestine under a UN Trusteeship regime, and confinement of the Jewish National Home to 'spiritual and cultural aspects only'. The chief advocates of those schemes were Loy Henderson, Chief of the Office of Near East and African Affairs, Robert McClintock, expert on UN affairs and Senator Warren Austin, the head of US UN delegation. See: 'Position File' 867N.01/7–747/LWH/GG, USNA. Also various memoranda from July throughout September in the McClintock File, USNA.
100. Memorandum by Marshall, undated, McClintock File. See also FRUS pp. 1147–51.
101. GA (plenary) II, Vol. I pp. 19–20.
102. The Clark M. Clifford Papers, Box 13, HSTL. The dismissal of pro-Arab professor Virginia Gildersleeve made the latter try to turn the affair into a public scandal.
103. Wilkins's correspondence with Mattison, 501 BB Palestine/10–2547, USNA; the author's interview with Wilkins, Washington, March 1978.
104. Memorandum by McClintock, FRUS, pp. 1188–92.
105. Marshall to Lovett, 23.10.47, FRUS pp. 1200–7.
106. Telegram from Austin, 501 BB Palestine/11–1147, USNA; FRUS pp. 1209–13. See also 'The Palestine Question at the Second Session of the General Assembly'. Memorandum by Harold Beeley, CO 537/2351/75872/154/13.
107. FRUS pp. 1909–12; FO 371/61883, E 9695, E 9727 and E 9757; see also Epstein to Klinov, 11.12.47, 93.03/148/9, Israel State Archives.
108. 'The Palestine Question at the Second ...', *ibid*.
109. GA II, Ad Hoc Committee, pp. 126–37.
110. 'The Palestine Question ...', *ibid*.
111. Memorandum by Matt. Connelly, the Acheson Papers (sic), HSTL, Box 27; 501 BB Palestine/11–1949, USNA; R. J. Donovan, *Conflict and Crisis*, NY 1977, pp. 326–8.
112. This affair is outside the scope of this paper.
113. Creech Jones–Cunningham exchange, 24 Oct. through 5 Nov. Cunningham, Box II, File 2.

114. CO 537/2351/75872/145; FRUS pp. 1244-6; Cunningham, a telegram of 9.11.47, *ibid*.
115. Cab 128/10, 86(47)2.
116. Cunningham, Box IV, File 4.
117. Cab 128/10, 93(47)1; 'Palestine', Memorandum by the Secretary of State for Foreign Affairs and the Secretary of State for the Colonies, 3.12.47, Cab 129/22, CP(47)320.
118. *Ibid*. See also intelligence report on the December Meeting of Arab League Committee by Sasson, 93.03/2267/16, Israel State Archives.
119. *Ibid*.
120. FO 371/61797, E 1193.
121. Michael Wright in conversation with US Ambassador Douglas, 867.01/12-1247, USNA.

Jewish Emigration and Soviet-Arab Relations, 1954–67

Yaacov Ro'i

In the late 1960s to early 1970s the Soviet Union frequently reiterated the tenet that the nature and extent of Jewish emigration from the USSR to Israel were inextricably linked with the 'Middle East crisis'. Although other factors besides the Middle East influenced Moscow's stand on this emigration, notably Soviet domestic considerations and Soviet relations with the West, particularly the USA, it can indeed be ascertained that the issue of Jewish emigration played a role in Soviet-Arab relations in this period.

The emigration of Soviet Jews to Israel before the Six Day War was on a very small scale and took place within the framework of what was called the 'reunification of families'. However, it was sufficient to enable the observer to discern certain trends and characteristics. Moreover, it was completely stopped on two occasions: at the outbreak of both the Sinai War in 1956 and the Six Day War nearly eleven years later – in both instances after a distinct increase. The fact that the process was terminated each time when hostilities erupted between Israel and its Arab neighbours surely indicates a link between Soviet policy on the 'reunification of families' and on the Arab-Israeli conflict.

The most serious Soviet work on Israel, Galina Nikitina's *The State of Israel*, also demonstrates this link. According to Nikitina, 'the practical implementation of Jewish immigration to Israel acquires an obvious political nature since it is first and foremost connected with the issue of Israeli-Arab relations.'[1] Nikitina also relates the question of immigration to Israel's military capacity: 'a special "plan for the militarization" of the State adopted in October 1953 was intended to raise the standard of the newly arrived immigrants' military training ... to encourage the immigration of youth of the 16–18 year age group in order to reinforce the human resources of the armed forces.'[2] The same author relies on Israeli sources for information that since 1952 Israel has conducted a selective immigration policy intended to augment the country's population precisely by attracting people under the age of 35.[3]

Although Nikitina makes no mention of or even indirect allusion to immigrants from the USSR to Israel, the significance she attributes to immigration is a sure indication of the connection in Soviet minds between immigration, on the one hand, and the Arab-Israeli conflict and

Israel's military capability on the other. In this context it is relevant to stress that in 1964–67, the very years when – according to Nikitina – Israel's policies and expansionist tendencies endangered peace and security in the Near and Middle East,[4] the USSR combined its increasing rapprochement with the Arab States with the permitting of Jewish emigration from its confines.

Of the numerous factors influencing Soviet policies on Jewish emigration in the period under discussion, this essay will examine the link between the Kremlin's position on this emigration and Jewish emigration from Eastern Europe, on the one hand, and its stand on the Arab-Israeli conflict, on the other. Our enquiry will do this not only by analysing the USSR's attitude to the two questions, but also by surveying Arab reactions to the Soviet position on Jewish emigration.

Early in 1954 the USSR adopted a stand which blatantly contradicted the one which it had advocated in 1947–48 when it had supported the establishment of Israel. Its motives, however, in first supporting Israel and then the Arabs were identical, i.e. to strengthen the party that was currently conducting the struggle against the West and to create a position of influence for the Soviet Union in the Middle East.

In the earlier period the USSR had demonstrated beyond any measure of doubt that it sought not only the ejection of the British from Palestine but, simultaneously, recognition of its own status as a power with a legitimate political interest in the region. This aspiration, however, had proved unrealistic, as the Soviet Union had been unable to provide evidence of any real political presence in the Middle East while the USA, Britain and France had clearly demonstrated their dominance of the area first in their control of the machinery set up to supervise the various cease-fires, armistice agreements and other arrangements imposed by the UN, and later – in 1950 – through the Tripartite Declaration.[5]

In 1954, on the other hand, the Soviet Union was able to prove a political presence in the area. At the Security Council debates on the Arab-Israeli conflict in January and March of that year Moscow twice used the veto to overrule Western-initiated draft resolutions (one concerning a dispute that arose in the Syrian-Israeli demilitarised zones, the other on the passage through the Suez Canal of Israeli vessels and cargoes going to and from Israeli ports). The USSR's behaviour was a result of the consolidation of its ties with Egypt and Syria, both vetoes being an open expression of the pro-Arab policy which reached a first peak in the new arms deals the Soviet bloc concluded with Arab states, notably the Czechoslovak-Egyptian deal that was announced in September 1955.

The Soviet Foreign Ministry's statement on Middle Eastern security that was published on 16 April 1955 (on the eve of the opening of the Afro-Asian Bandoeng Conference) clearly indicated that support of the

Arab states as such, not necessarily in the context of the Arab-Israeli conflict, was designed to promote Soviet goals in the Middle East. This first official statement devoted to this region noted the increasing tension in the area caused by the latest attempts to entice its component states into joining Western defense organisations (the reference was to the formation of the Baghdad Pact with Britain's official adherence early that month to the Turkey-Iraq-Pakistan axis). The statement also stressed the USSR's geographical proximity to the Middle East, insisting that this circumstance prevented the Soviet Union from standing idly by in face of attempts at foreign intervention in the region.[6]

The statement significantly made no mention of the Arab-Israeli conflict. In a second statement, however, issued in February 1956 – following a further Western diplomatic effort to strengthen the Western Powers' position in the area (the Eisenhower-Eden communiqué of 1 February) – the Soviet Government explicitly attributed Middle Eastern tension to this conflict. In this document, the Soviet Union rejected the Western Powers' assumption that they had the right either to act as they pleased to mitigate tension in the Middle East, especially since their interests contradicted those of the states of the region, or to make decisions concerning the settlement of the Arab-Israeli conflict without the participation of these states.[7]

These two statements clearly reveal the USSR's two claims regarding its own right to wield influence in the Middle East: geographical proximity and the coincidence of the main Soviet foreign policy objective – the struggle against Western imperialism – with the ambition of the states of the region to free themselves from dependence on the colonial powers. The second statement indicates, moreover, that Moscow had learned in the course of its contacts with the Arab States since early 1954 that control of the course of the Arab-Israeli conflict was a major key to influence in the area.

Despite Soviet identification with the Arabs and their stand on the conflict, publicised by Khrushchev himself in a speech at the Supreme Soviet in December 1955, the Soviet Union thus sought to consolidate its own position by making an explicit proposal to settle problems outstanding between the Arab States and Israel – within the United Nations or in collaboration with other States. In April 1956 the Soviet Government published its suggestions in yet another statement of its Foreign Ministry on the Middle East.[8]

Apparently out of a desire to play the role of mediator, the Soviet Union had already taken steps to maintain appearances of a balance in its policy toward Israel and the Arab States while, however, constantly consolidating its ties with the latter. Thus, for example, after the Egyptian Legation in Moscow and the Soviet Legation in Cairo were raised to embassy level (April 1954), a similar step was taken regarding the Israeli Legation in Moscow and the Soviet Legation in Tel Aviv (in August

1954). Similarly, the Soviets signed agreements with Israel and Egypt on the sale of oil to almost the same value: the oil deal with Israel was significantly cancelled immediately after the Sinai Campaign since oil was considered a strategic commodity of prime importance.

When we turn from considering the Soviet position on the Arab-Israeli conflict, which the Soviet Union saw as a key instrument for penetrating the Arab East in the mid-50s, to examining its policy on Jewish emigration, it seems that the USSR viewed the latter too as an important political means for increasing its influence on events in the region. The USSR realised that Jewish immigration to Israel in general, and from the Soviet Union in particular, was likely to be a significant means of pressure. As long as the gates were locked this means could not be used, but as soon as the USSR allowed Jews to leave, if only in small numbers, on the one hand Moscow raised the hope that emigration would be increased, and on the other threatened to stop it. In other words, as Soviet penetration into Egypt and Syria grew prior to the first arms deal, and even more so afterwards, the Soviet Union aimed at influencing Israel's actions concerning the Arab-Israeli conflict both to maintain the advantage which the Arabs had by virtue of Soviet aid and to prevent greater deterioration in the situation than Moscow considered desirable, i.e. one that would entail increased US involvement in the region.

In the period when the Soviet Union had supported the establishment of a Jewish state in Palestine and even demanded recognition of the Jews' right in principle to free immigration, it had constantly rejected the idea of Jewish emigration to Israel from its own confines in any framework.[9] This policy towards its Jews was an integral part of its general policy on emigration in both these and the following years. As distinct from the Stalin period, however, when the Soviet Union did not distinguish between the reunification of families and other emigration, there were indications in 1954–56 of a certain change in the Soviet position: as a result of the attempt to ease international tension, the USSR permitted limited movement from and to the West.[10] This included a thin trickle of emigration to Israel[11] despite Soviet rapprochement with the Arabs and the all-out support for the Arabs on everything concerning the conflict with Israel.

During the contacts established between the Soviet leadership and Western socialists as part and parcel of the post-Stalin relative liberalisation, the latter began to reveal interest in Jewish emigration from the USSR. In these talks Soviet officials mostly stated that as long as the state of inter-bloc conflict existed and Israel was linked with the opposing side, the USSR would not permit emigration to Israel.

Thus, for example, when a French Socialist delegation visiting Moscow in May 1956 raised the question of Jewish emigration before the Soviet leadership, Khrushchev replied that the USSR disapproved of Jewish emigration to Israel because that country depended on 'American reaction' which used Israel to carry out acts of espionage and provocation. At the same time, Khrushchev added, the Soviet Union hoped that the Cold War, which determined the Soviet attitude to Israel, would end. When that happened a change would occur in the policy on Jewish emigration.[12]

In a conversation with a group of 'progressive' Americans in July 1957 Khrushchev continued to make the inter-bloc conflict a pretext for the ban on Jewish emigration. He said that the Soviet authorities did not allow anyone to leave the Soviet Union. However, the time would come when every Russian or Jew would be permitted to leave the country, and then any Jew who wanted to go to Israel would be permitted to do so. Meanwhile, he argued, he did not want a Jew who went to visit his relatives to become a traitor to his country, for it was well known that American Intelligence had many times used Jews who had fled from their country, and this was harmful to the security of the Soviet Union.[13]

On this occasion, however, and apparently on this occasion alone, Khrushchev linked the Soviet Union's policy on emigration with the Arab-Israeli conflict. In this instance the First Secretary of the Soviet Communist Party significantly spoke not of the hundreds of Jews who had arrived in Israel from the USSR in the framework of the reunification of families, but of the many thousands of Polish repatriates from the USSR who had made their way to Israel.[14] Khrushchev noted that despite Soviet reservations about emigration, connected with the inter-bloc conflict and questions of the security of the Soviet Union itself, the USSR had permitted, in accordance with its repatriation agreement with Poland, many Jews with Polish citizenship to leave the Soviet Union for Poland, even though the Soviet authorities were well aware that a large number of them would go on to Israel. However, at the present time (mid-1957), Khrushchev continued, the USSR considered that Jews returning to Poland from the Soviet Union should not be allowed to go to Israel because the latter was conducting a policy of aggression towards the Arabs.

As has been said, this explicit statement by Khrushchev deviated from most of his comments on Jewish emigration made to Western figures. In a conversation with American ex-servicemen, including Jews, in May 1959, Khrushchev repeated the main points of the usual argument. He stressed again that in due course freedom of emigration from the Soviet Union would be granted to all desiring to leave, including Jews. He also reiterated an argument he had used when talking to the group of Americans above, that many Jews who had left the Soviet Union for Israel were requesting to return.[15]

In July 1960 Khrushchev was asked at a press conference in Vienna if the Soviet Government would permit people of Jewish origin to emigrate from the USSR in the framework of the reunification of families which applied to members of various peoples.[16] He replied:

We do not object to the reunification of any people if they desire it. The term reunification of families is, however, a fairly relative concept. Probably today, too, one can read many announcements in Viennese newspapers that a wealthy widow is looking for a husband or that a rich old man is looking for a young wife. But, talking seriously, our Foreign Ministry files contain no requests of people of Jewish nationality or other nationalities who would like to emigrate to Israel. On the contrary, we have many letters from Jews in Israel applying for permission to return from Israel to their native land, the Soviet Union.[17]

This statement by the Soviet leader was published in *Pravda* and merits two comments, in parentheses: first, besides the cynical attitude it revealed to the question of the reunification of families, Soviet citizens who wanted to leave the country applied not to the Foreign Ministry but to a department of the Ministry of the Interior.[18] It is therefore obvious that such applications were not to be found in the files of the Foreign Ministry. Second, when the Israeli Foreign Minister, Mrs Golda Meir, was questioned on this matter in the Knesset on 8 August 1960, she replied that over the past five years Israeli residents had sent 9,236 applications for reunification of families to their relatives in the Soviet Union, in response to the latter's request, each application concerning one family unit. Only a few of these people, she noted, had been able to join their families for, according to the replies of the Soviet Red Cross and Crescent Society, 'the Soviet institutions did not find sufficient reason to satisfy the request'.[19]

In early 1962 Khrushchev promised Raymond Schmittlein (a member of the French National Assembly and chairman of the France-USSR Friendship Association) that the Soviet policy on Jewish emigration from the Soviet Union would change. But in the summer of that year Schmittlein was informed, without any explanation, that the promised liberalisation in the field of emigration from the USSR would not be implemented and that it would be inapposite to raise this matter further.[20] Not only did the promises to increase Jewish emigration in this period come to nothing, but the so-called 'Zionist propaganda of lies' became the butt of an intensified campaign evidently directed at the Jewish reading public inside the country, i.e. potential emigrants to Israel. Many articles in Soviet newspapers and periodicals stressed that the living standard in Israel was low, taxation high and unemployment widespread. Much space was devoted to describing the absorption difficulties of immigrants, especially of those who did not know Hebrew, and in this context it was repeatedly noted that Yiddish would not help anybody adjust to Israeli life. The authors of the articles emphasised the lack of values of Israeli society; it was capitalist, did not care for its elderly and sick and discriminated against the Arab minority and the 'black Jews'. It was sometimes stated too that Israel was on the edge of economic and physical destruction because its policy was mainly one of aggression against its

Arab neighbours in accordance with the interests and directives of its American protector, even though Israel was only an alien and small island in the Arab East. These articles, some of which were written by Soviet Jews who had visited or lived for short periods in Israel, were aimed, in accordance with Khrushchev's much vaunted thesis, at exploding the illusions of Soviet Jews about the 'imaginary paradise of Israel' and at making it quite clear that the Soviet Union had not yet altered its policy of basic, traditional hostility to Jewish emigration.[21]

In the years 1964–67 there was a certain change in Soviet policy. In 1964 Soviet aid to a number of Arab countries increased, Khrushchev's visit to Egypt in May symbolising complete Soviet-Arab reconciliation after the crisis of 1959–61. That year saw the beginning of Soviet-Arab political coordination on the Arab-Israeli conflict which continued until May–June 1967 and also afterwards. However, at the same time the gates of the Soviet Union were opened a little – a reality which was given official sanction in a statement made by Kosygin on the reunification of families. This statement came at a time when Soviet support for the Arabs was being limelighted by the threats and warnings made to Israel by the Soviet delegate to the Security Council, Nikolai Fedorenko (in July–August and November 1966). Indeed, at the beginning of 1966, as at the beginning of 1956, the USSR sought, while maintaining its pro-Arab position, to take an active part in settling the Arab-Israeli conflict and in mediating between the two sides. Soviet diplomats in Israel, headed by Ambassador Dmitrii Chuvakhin, frequently referred to the Soviet Union's policy of peace and the application of the 'Tashkent spirit' to the Arab-Israeli conflict.[22]

Referring back to Kosygin's statement to a press conference in Paris on 3 December 1966, the *New York Times* quoted him as saying, 'If there are some families divided by the war who want to meet their relatives outside the USSR or even to leave the USSR, we shall do all in our power to help them. The way is open to them and will remain open to them and there is no problem.'[23] This statement, like Khrushchev's promise to Schmittlein, aroused hope in the West and throughout the Jewish world that a change in Soviet policy on Jewish emigration might be beginning. In particular, it aroused hope among Soviet Jews who read their Prime Minister's statement in the Soviet press[24] and were aware that a few Jews were actually leaving for Israel. Nonetheless, it very soon became clear that the Soviet Prime Minister's statement had led to no significant change in the amount of Jewish emigration from the USSR. Both the central and the provincial press began a new intensified smear campaign against Israel to deter potential emigrants. On 11 January 1967 the government paper *Izvestiia* attacked a number of tourists from Israel, among them a member of the Jewish Agency Executive, Eliahu Dobkin, for disseminating false propaganda among Soviet Jews to incite them to emigrate to Israel. *Izvestiia* explicitly linked these charges with the Israeli Embassy in

Moscow. Following this signal in the government newspaper, the newspapers of the Union Republics and local periodicals, especially in republics with large Jewish centres, launched a campaign describing the difficult situation in Israel and the disillusionment which those who desired to emigrate there could expect.[25] At the same time it became known in the West that Kosygin had failed to carry out his promise. Bertrand Russell wrote to the Soviet Prime Minister that letters had reached him proving that, despite the promises, people desiring to leave the Soviet Union were still being severely obstructed by Soviet officials. Tourists who returned from the Soviet Union also told about the systematic hindrance by the Soviet bureaucracy. Jews who came to OVIR offices in Moscow and Riga with copies of the Soviet newspapers in which Kosygin's statement on the reunification of families had appeared were told by officials that the family reunification programme had almost been completed, while the applications which had not yet been answered would be dealt with 'as before', that is before Kosygin's statement. In Chernovtsy the answers were formulated differently, but the practical implications were the same: those applying for exit permits were told there that instructions for carrying out Kosygin's promise had not yet been received and it was suggested to them that they return another time.[26]

Although the thin trickle of Jewish emigration from the USSR did not grow significantly in the months December 1966–June 1967, it did continue until stopped completely, as mentioned above, at the outbreak of the Six Day War,[27] just as the Jewish emigration of 1955–56 had been stopped with the Sinai Campaign. Although the official version given by Soviet leaders attributed the policy on Jewish emigration from the USSR to other factors (except for Khrushchev's statement of 1957), their actual policy thus indicated a link between their policy on this question and their position on the Arab-Israeli conflict and the developments connected with it. The dual policy of rapprochement between the USSR and the Arab states in the years discussed, on the one hand, and of permitting a small amount of Jewish emigration to Israel on the other, led to Arab reactions. An examination of these can illuminate an additional aspect of Soviet policy in the region, i.e. the use of Jewish emigration as a means of pressure not on Israel but on the Arab states, and give further confirmation of the link between the Soviet attitude to Arab-Israeli relations and its policy on Jewish emigration.

As stated above, there was a very small Jewish emigration from the USSR in the 1954–56 period. In 1956, however, a far more considerable emigration took place from Poland to which Arab leaders duly addressed themselves. Some actually complained about it to the Soviet leaders, who seemed to give serious consideration to the arguments of their new allies.[28]

The Arab interest in the emigration from Poland and the Soviet reaction were reflected in an article which appeared in the Cairo newspaper *al-Ahram*. It was noted that the Syrian President, Shukri al-Quwwatli, had devoted special attention to the intention of 20,000 Polish Jews to emigrate to Israel by permission of the Polish Government. Quwwatli had 'conducted a number of political contacts' and as a result had received a letter from Soviet Foreign Minister Dmitrii Shepilov which said:

> (1) The Government of the USSR in no way encourages any organized emigration from the Eastern Bloc to Israel, since such emigration is liable to increase disorder in the region and [the Soviet Union] is not interested in exacerbating the situation; (2) the Polish Government has permitted the emigration of several old people with relatives in Israel, but does not encourage and will not permit the emigration of any Polish Jew who is of military age or capable of technical work since the [Polish] state itself needs such people.

The Polish Government had sent a similar letter to the Secretariat of the Arab League.[29]

Shortly afterwards, Jews who had left the USSR for Poland in the framework of the Soviet-Polish repatriation agreement mentioned above began to join the emigration from Poland to Israel. It seems that as a result the pressure of the Arab states on the Soviet Union grew, although I have found no explicit expression of this in the Arab press (probably because the Arabs did not want to exacerbate their relations with the USSR). Western sources tended to see the delay suffered by repatriates in Poland before they were permitted to emigrate as the result of Egyptian pressure on the Soviet authorities.[30] In July 1957 Khrushchev may well have been hinting at Arab pressure to prevent the emigration of Jews who had returned to Poland under the repatriation agreement, when he told the American delegation of 'progressive' public figures that the Soviet Union had changed its positive position on this emigration because of Israel's aggressive policy towards the Arabs (see above, p. 214). However in this period the Soviet channels of communication continued to remain silent on this question. *Al-Ahram*, which reported Khrushchev's conversation with the American delegation, made no mention of the subject of emigration.[31]

In the first months of 1959, on the other hand, when relations between the Soviet Union and the UAR were strained,[32] Arab newspapers with various political tendencies, and in the first place *al-Ahram*, began a fierce campaign against the Soviet Union for permitting Jewish emigration from its confines. Every day for an entire week, beginning 14 February 1959, *al-Ahram* published long articles under banner headings intended to arouse Arab public opinion concerning 'the greatest danger threatening the Arab people at the present time', namely the immigration of large numbers of Jews from Eastern Europe to Israel.[33] The paper claimed that for nearly a year a programme to treble the Jewish population of Israel had been in secret preparation. The first stage in this programme, according to *al-Ahram*, was the immigration of hundreds of thousands of Jews from Eastern Europe, who had started to reach Israel in ever increasing numbers since September 1958. *Al-Ahram* explained that the programme had been revealed in a speech made by Ben-Gurion on 17 November 1958 in which he had stated that 'the immigration of East European Jewry is the miracle of the coming years'. *Al-Ahram* found proof of the existence of this secret programme, publicly disclosed by Ben-Gurion's supposed slip of the tongue, in the attack of the Israeli press on the Prime Minister for having broken the 'conspiracy of silence'.[34] As a result of the disclosure of the programme, *al-Ahram* said it had begun to follow what was happening with regard to this matter in the capitals of the world, and now (February 1959) the time had come to reveal the results of its research. According to *al-Ahram*, the primary aim of the programme was to strengthen the army for the purpose of territorial expansion. Even though at the present stage, the paper added, it was a question of immigration from Hungary, Poland, and, especially, Romania, 'Ben-Gurion clearly hinted that he has information suggesting that Russia for its part will agree to permit the emigration to Israel' of Jews living there, who so desire; the number of Jews in the Soviet Union, it was stressed, was three and a half million.[35]

Given the danger of this 'secret programme', *al-Ahram* wrote on the following day: 'The prevailing opinion in the Arab states now is that there is no need at all to keep silent about the immigration of three million Jews from Eastern Europe to Israel.' The immigration programme would not only prevent the Arab refugees from returning to their homes since 'others will take their place once and for all', but would also lead to further eviction of Arabs from their lands, even though the Soviet Union had denounced Israel several times for the eviction of a million Arabs in the past. Radio Moscow had repeated this denunciation in a broadcast of 13 February, stating that this eviction was the main cause of tension in the Middle East.[36] *Al-Ahram* stressed that the ambassadors should demand that the Soviet Union again prove its friendship to the Arab people by adopting a forceful position to stop the emigration from Eastern Europe.[37] The paper stressed that at this stage the emigration of a few Jews from the Soviet Union itself was also planned. 'Official Jewish sources in Vienna', *al-Ahram* wrote on 17 February 1959, had announced that they were 'expecting the Soviet Union to grant a number of Russian Jews permits to emigrate to Israel.' According to secret information 'it is clear that the Kremlin government is preparing to permit a restricted emigration of a few Russian Jews to Israel'. The source on which the Egyptian paper based its information had related, according to *al-Ahram*, that 'the intention of this limited emigration is to take stock of the reaction of the Arab states, since public opinion in the UAR is alive to the issue in consequence of the Jewish immigration from Romania'.[38] *Al-Ahram* continued that although the Soviet Government could argue that the motives for allowing this limited emigration were purely humanitarian, in order to assist the reunification of families whose members had been living apart for many years, this argument was also being put forward by the Romanian Government at a time when many thousands of Jews were leaving that country every month.[39]

The intensive campaign against Jewish emigration from Eastern Europe ceased without explanation after the appearance of a last long article in *al-Ahram* on 20 February 1959. From then onwards the Arab press published only brief items on the emigration, mostly of an informative nature without playing up the subject.[40]

An explanation for the sudden end to the Arab press campaign against Jewish emigration from Eastern Europe can be found in a speech made by the President of the UAR, Jamal Abd an-Nasir, on 21 February 1959, in which he stated that as he had no longer been able to tolerate the worsening of relations between the USSR and the UAR, he had sent a letter to Khrushchev. The reply to this letter, which covered ten pages, was received at midnight on 20 February and dealt with 'important and grave' matters. Nasir revealed that the Soviet letter, whose content he was unable to disclose, noted that 'as regards communism in the UAR, the Soviet Union had no desire to interfere in the internal affairs of the UAR.'.[41] It is reasonable to suppose that the Soviet letter also dealt directly or indirectly with the subject of Jewish emigration. It is possible that as a result of this exchange of letters Khrushchev promised not to interfere in the persecution of communists in the UAR, emphasising that this was an internal affair of the UAR, while Nasir agreed explicitly or implicitly to stop giving publicity to the Jewish emigration from the USSR and Eastern Europe, which was an internal affair of those countries. Thus, Khrushchev stated in an election speech on 24 February, with reference to the deterioration in relations with the UAR, that questions relating to the domestic policy of any country are the concern of the government and people of that country alone.[42]

The Eastern bloc, moreover, took pains to deny the charges of a large Jewish emigration from its confines. On 26 February 1959 *al-Ahram* published a statement according to which Romania admitted that small groups of Jews had indeed emigrated from it to Israel in the framework of the 'reunification of families', but, in the words of the Romanian authorities as quoted by *al-Ahram*, this fact had been exploited by Israel and international Zionism to 'create an incident' between Bucharest and Cairo. At the same time the Romanian Government promised, according to the same source, to stop any emigration programme beyond this limited framework.[43]

The Soviet Union explicitly denied in its press (*Izvestiia*, 21 February) and Arabic broadcasts (19 and 26 February 1959) any programme of large-scale emigration. On 1 March even the official Soviet news agency *TASS* published a special communiqué on the subject. The Soviet statement emphatically denied the information on emigration to Israel from the USSR which had been disseminated by 'certain newspapers in Beirut and Cairo on the basis of American sources'. *TASS* described these reports as 'lacking in foundation' and as a 'provocative and malicious lie', and the very question of Jewish emigration from the USSR to Israel as an invention of 'Washington and Tel-Aviv'.[44] *Al-Ahram*, which gave prominence to the official Soviet denial, ignored its own part in inflating the affair, emphasising the fact that the information was attributed to 'American sources'.[45]

A few weeks later, in mid-March 1959, Nasir again attacked the communists in the Arab world in general and in the UAR in particular, while on 16 March, in a speech to an official Iraqi delegation visiting the Soviet Union, Khrushchev renewed his attacks on the UAR. The question of Jewish emigration, however, was given no publicity. Nonetheless, in May when Khrushchev told the delegation of American ex-servicemen (see above, p. 214) that in due course freedom to leave the USSR would be granted to anyone who so desired, including Jews, *al-Ahram* stated that the USSR 'intended to allow Jews to emigrate, whenever they desired'.[46] Indeed, it seems that the question remained a factor in Soviet-Arab relations despite the silence maintained on it by the UAR communications media after the above polemic. *Al-Ahram* revealed a little of the renewed Arab activity when it published in July an exchange of letters between the Yemenite Imam Ahmad ibn Yahya and Khrushchev. In response to the Imam, who desired to examine how much truth there was in reports on Jewish emigration from the USSR and Eastern Europe, Khrushchev argued, as quoted in *al-Ahram*, that the information on collective emigration of Jews from the Soviet Union was false imperialist propaganda aimed at troubling Soviet-Arab relations. According to this source, Khrushchev stated:

> It is untenable that there is in the Soviet Union a group of Jews who desire to emigrate to Israel. On the contrary, applications are received from Jews in Israel who desire to return to the USSR. As to rumours concerning the emigration of Jews to Israel from our fraternal states [...] although the matter of entry and exit belongs to the prerogative of these independent states we have considered it necessary, in reference to your Majesty's wish, unofficially to inform the governments of the fraternal states of the apprehensions you expressed in your letter.[47]

These developments in 1959 occurred against a background of exacerbated relations between the UAR and the USSR. Consequently, some information indicating the extent and strength of Arab pressure on Moscow to prevent Jewish emigration and the sensitivity of the Soviet government to this pressure, to the point of announcing direct intervention on this question in the people's democracies, filtered through to the press.

In later years, with the increasing dependence of the Arab states, and in particular of the UAR, on the Soviet Union, it became inconvenient to give publicity to Arab displeasure with Jewish emigration from Eastern Europe. It is even possible that the Arab governments received convincing promises from the Soviet Union that there would be no Jewish emigration of significance[48] and that permitting Jewish 'reunification of families' did not entail any danger for the Arabs. In any case, the Arab press almost completely ignored Kosygin's statement of December 1966 which was made, as mentioned above, at a time when the Soviet Union was granting extensive military, economic, technical and political aid to the Arab states in general and Egypt and Syria in particular.[49] The question, however, continued to be a subject of clarification between the USSR and various Arab groupings. On 11 May 1967 a sharp exchange took place between a visiting Soviet parliamentary delegation in Lebanon and the Foreign Relations Committee of the Lebanese Parliament. A member of the Committee, Muhammad al-Barjawi of the Front of National Struggle, claimed that Israel had been strengthened by the Soviet Union's recognition of it and immigration from the Eastern bloc. To this the head of the Soviet delegation, Deputy Chairman of the Presidium of the USSR Supreme Soviet Kiril Iliashenko replied:

> The issue of immigration to Israel from the socialist countries has been exaggerated. True, we are a democratic state whose sons enjoy freedom of movement and emigration, and there are Jews who have emigrated from the Soviet Union to Israel, but now they are returning to the Soviet Union.[50]

It is noteworthy, in parentheses, that in the period 1969–71, when emigration to Israel from the USSR was renewed and indeed reached an unprecedented scale, the press of the pro-Soviet Arab states ignored this subject almost entirely. Only the press of states not aligned with the Soviet Union attacked the USSR for permitting Jewish emigration. It is most probable that in this period, too, Arab politicians attempted to exert their influence in order to close the gates of the USSR to Jewish emigration to Israel, but without great success. With the growth of public criticism of the Soviet Union in Egypt from early 1972, emigration to Israel from the Eastern bloc was again given publicity in the communications media of that country, but this subject is beyond the bounds of the present article and merits a separate paper.

*   *   *   *   *

Even though Soviet policy in the Middle East was by no means the sole factor determining Jewish emigration from the USSR and Eastern Europe to Israel in the 1954–67 period, Moscow's stand on the 'reunification of families' was *inter alia* subservient to considerations of its Middle Eastern goals, interests and constraints. This hypothesis is confirmed by several instances of Soviet linkage of immigration to Israel with the Arab-Israeli conflict and by the portrayal of immigration in Soviet publications as an inherent component of Israel's strategic planning and overall defence policy. It is likewise confirmed by the periodicity of the closing and opening of the gates of the Soviet Union for purposes of 'family reunification'.

An examination of the timing of the decline and increase in departures for Israel from the USSR in the years under discussion indeed corroborates this hypothesis. The gates were opened to Soviet Jews desiring to reunite with their families in Israel precisely when the conflict was being exacerbated, namely in the two or so years preceding first the Sinai Campaign and then the Six Day War. At first this presents difficulties, given the Soviet Union's unqualified public commitment to the Arab side in the conflict in both the mid-fifties and the mid-sixties. Yet it becomes clear when the Soviet constant strategic consideration of acquiring a position of mediator between the parties to the conflict is taken into account, for the achievement of this aim requires the possibility of applying pressure on both sides.

Throughout the period discussed, the USSR had no effective means of exerting influence on Israel in the framework of normal bilateral relations. The reunification of families programme and emigration from the People's Democracies were thus assigned the role of influencing Israel which, as the Soviet Union had known since Israel's establishment, attached great importance to immigration in general and immigration from Eastern Europe in particular. The oil contracts of the 1954-56 period, which followed a curve parallel to that of the reunification of families, were an excellent indication of the process of Soviet thinking, Moscow making no secret of its evaluation of oil as a strategic material.

Family reunification, moreover, had the advantage of serving as a means of pressure on the USSR's Arab ally, as a potential threat to strengthen the opposing side.[51] Indeed, the Arab states showed a marked sensitivity to this issue, although – significantly – their leverage in preventing Jewish emigration from the Soviet orbit was in inverse proportion to the measure of their dependence on Moscow: the greater the Arab dependence on the Soviet Union, the less consideration the latter gave to their demands to prevent emigration. Similarly, those Arabs who wrote from an anti-Soviet standpoint criticised the Soviet policy on Jewish emigration – or, to be more precise, on the reunification of families – arguing that this policy permitted too many Jews to leave and worked to the disadvantage of the Arabs in their conflict with Israel. By contrast, pro-Soviet Arab sources tended totally to ignore statements on the reunification of families and information about Jewish emigration to Israel.

Finally, as we have seen, the gates were locked to Jews desiring to leave when the USSR was convinced that it was powerless to influence the course of the Arab-Israeli conflict by means of Jewish emigration, notably with the eruption of actual fighting in October 1956 and June 1967. At this point Moscow had to relinquish hopes of becoming sole arbiter and replace them by attempts to prove its position of strength through attempts at cooperation with the USA.

NOTES

This article first appeared in Hebrew in *Behinot*, No. 5, Jerusalem–Tel Aviv, 1974. The author thanks the editors for their permission to publish this translation.

1. G. Nikitina, *Gosudarstvo Izrail'* (The State of Israel), Nauka, Moscow, 1968, p. 210. (An updated edition of the book appeared in English in 1973, but I have preferred to use the original Russian text.)
2. *Ibid.*, p. 174. Nikitina's information is based on Israel's *Government Yearbook*, 1962, pp. 32–3.
3. Nikitina, *op. cit.*, p. 213.
4. *Ibid.*, pp. 193–209.
5. For the Tripartite Declaration on Security in the Middle East, see Yaacov Ro'i, *From Encroachment to Involvement. A Documentary Study of Soviet Policy in the Middle East, 1945–73*, Jerusalem, Israel Universities Press, 1974, pp. 82–9.
6. *Ibid.*, pp. 135–40.
7. *Documents on International Affairs*, 1956, pp. 53–6. For the Eisenhower-Eden communiqué see *Middle Eastern Affairs*, Vol. 7, p. 102.
8. Ro'i, *op. cit.*, pp. 161–5.
9. The Soviet Union's opposition to the emigration of its Jews was declared for the benefit of the world at large by Gromyko at the UN as early as May 1947 – *UN General Assembly Official Records, 1st Special Session, 1st Committee*, 8 May 1947, and for the Soviet Jewish public that seemed to be having contrary illusions by the writer Il'ia Ehrenburg – *Pravda*, 21 Sept. 1948. Gromyko also, however, gave expression to Soviet acceptance in principle of the Jews' right to immigrate into the Jewish State – *UN Security Council, Official Records, 3rd Year, No. 58*, 16 April 1948.
10 A repatriation agreement was signed, for example, with Spain in 1956, while the issue of repatriation was of major importance in Moscow's relations with Federal Germany.
11. See announcement by Prime Minister Moshe Sharett – *Divrey ha-Knesset*, Vol. 17, p. 67, 15 Nov. 1954; also *New York Times*, 14 Aug. 1955.
12. L. Leneman, *La Tragédie des Juifs en URSS*, Desclée de Brouwer, Paris 1959, p. 226.
13. These 'progressives' were a group organised by the Committee for Promoting Enduring Peace and comprising public figures acceptable to both the American Left and Moscow, notably the Quaker Jerome Davis and General Hugh Hester. Accounts by Davis and Hester of their talks with Soviet leaders, including Khrushchev, appeared in *Daily Worker*, 15 Aug. 1957; *Jewish Chronicle*, 23 Aug. 1957; and *National Jewish Monthly*, March 1962.
14. Repatriation to Poland had begun in the wake of a verbal agreement that was finally given official form in an agreement signed on 25 March 1957 – *Vedomosti Verkhovnogo Soveta SSSR*, No. 16, 1957, p. 418. In the same month, reports were appearing in the West concerning difficulties encountered by Jewish repatriates from the USSR to Poland who wanted to emigrate to Israel. These difficulties were attributed to Soviet efforts to delay such emigration.

15. *Jewish Chronicle*, 15 May 1959.
16. A quiet repatriation had been going on since late 1959 in which approximately one thousand people were said to have been permitted to reunite with their families in the USA, Britain, Australia, Canada, Argentina and Sweden – *National Jewish Monthly*, March 1962.
17. *Pravda*, 9 July 1960.
18. The Department of Visas and Registration of Foreigners (OVIR) was responsible for issuing exit permits. When the All-Union Ministry of the Interior was replaced in 1960 by Ministries for Internal Affairs at the Union Republic level, OVIR was transferred to these new ministries. (In 1962 the Ministries for Internal Affairs were renamed Ministries for the Preservation of Public Order.)
19. *Divrey ha-Knesset*, Vol. 29, pp. 2101–2.
20. *Jewish Chronicle*, 9 Dec. 1966.
21. Numerous such articles had been appearing since early 1958. For articles from 1960, see *Evrei i evreiskii narod*, 1960–.
22. The agreement between India and Pakistan achieved in Tashkent in January 1966 with Soviet mediation seemed to endow the USSR with the role of arbitrator in protracted regional conflicts. Statements by Chuvakhin and members of his staff on the Soviet peace policy and its applicability to the Arab-Israeli conflict were printed in the Israeli press: *Kol Ha'Am*, 20 Feb. 1966; *Ha'Aretz*, 11 March and 9 Oct. 1966; and *La-Merhav*, 21 April 1966.
23. *New York Times*, 2 Jan. 1967. The *New York Times* version of this quotation differs from the one that appeared in *Le Monde* on 6 Dec. 1966. The fact that the *Le Monde* version appeared 3 days after the press conference and is identical with the modified version in the Soviet press (see n. 24) indicates that the *Le Monde* text was first approved by the relevant Soviet authorities.
24. A slightly watered-down version of Kosygin's statement appeared on 5 Dec. 1966 in *Pravda, Izvestiia* and *Komsomol'skaia pravda*.
25. E.g., *Sovetskaia Moldaviia*, 18 Jan. 1967; *Sovetskaia Litva*, 1 Feb. 1967; and *Dagestanskaia pravda*, 9 Feb. 1967. The *Sovetskaia Moldaviia* article, entitled ' "The Promised Land" Without Embellishment', described the scene in the OVIR office of the Moldavian SSR Ministry for the Preservation of Public Order: the clerk informed two Jews that their application to join their relatives in Israel had been granted. He informed them of the procedures they must undergo and then asked them if they knew what awaited them in Israel. He told them the story of two couples who had emigrated to Israel and recently returned to the USSR. They had discovered that the tales of Israeli tourists concerning the good life in Israel were fabrications based on instructions they had received before travelling not to tell the truth but simply to encourage people to emigrate to Israel. Indeed, the story of these two couples had led one family to renounce its plan of going to Israel. Others, on the other hand, said that what they had heard was propaganda which they refused to believe. 'What can we tell these people?', *Sovetskaia Mol'daviia* concluded. 'Go and see, taste the charms of Israel, but never say that we did not warn you, that we did not tell you beforehand.'
26. *Jewish Chronicle*, 27 Jan. 1967. For Russell's letter see *ibid.* 27 Feb. 1967. The same paper reported too on 3 March 1967 that the historian Aldo Garosci had written in the Italian socialist paper *Avanti* on 26 Feb. that 50,000 Jews had applied to emigrate in the wake of the Kosygin statement.
27. *Ma'ariv*, 20 June 1967; and a statement by Prime Minister Levi Eshkol in the Knesset on 27 Nov. 1967 – *Ha'Aretz*, 28 Nov. Although no emigration took place after June 1967, the Soviet authorities denied that it was in any way prohibited – *R. Moscow* in Swedish, 16 Dec. 1967/*BBC, Summary of World Broadcasts, Part I*, 20 Dec. 1967.
28. Arab protests against emigration from Eastern Europe first to Palestine and then to the State of Israel in 1947/1948 had been dealt with much more summarily – e.g., *UN General Assembly, Official Records, 3rd Session, Part I, 1st Committee*, 29 Nov. 1948.

29. *Al-Ahram*, 17 Sept. 1956.
30. *New York Times*, 15 March 1957. See also n. 14 above.
31. *Al-Ahram*, 3 Aug. 1957.
32. The landmarks of the deterioration of relations were: Nasser's Port Said speech of 23 Dec. 1958; Khrushchev's remarks on the UAR at the 21st CPSU Congress on 27 Jan. 1959; Nasser's Damascus speech of 15 March; Khrushchev's speech before the Iraqi Government delegation in Moscow the following day; and Nasser's reply on 20 March. The very establishment of the UAR – the United Arab Republic – comprising Egypt and Syria in early 1958 had strained relations between Moscow and Cairo. See Ro'i, *op. cit*, pp. 276–80 and 296–309.
33. The *Al-Ahram* headings read: on 14 Feb. 'The Great Danger', 15 Feb. 'The Arab States Will Not Be Silent', 16 Feb. 'Plan For Withstanding the Danger', 17 Feb. 'The Bells of Danger Are Ringing', 18 Feb. 'Israel Discloses Its Intentions', 19 Feb. 'Israel Makes Desperate Efforts in Moscow', 20 Feb. 'Prepare to Withstand New Danger'.
34. *Al-Ahram* referred in particular to an article by Zeev Katz in *Ha'Aretz*, 7 Dec. 1958, entitled 'East European Diplomatic Sources on Chances of Immigration from "Certain Countries" '. 'Spectacular public statements by Israeli public figures on "the redemption of Jews from certain countries" and all the noisy propaganda in the press on the subject of this immigration are not likely to benefit this cause' was the tenour of the reaction of East European diplomats in Israel as reported by Katz. 'As to the Prime Minister's statement about the "second miracle in our generation" in his speech during the Immigration Loan campaign a few days ago ... we consider that the reference is to the Soviet Union – the diplomats said.'
35. *Al-Ahram*, 14 Feb. 1959.
36. *Al-Ahram*, 15 Feb. 1959. On 18 Feb. *al-Ahram* wrote that the Israeli Foreign Minister had said in Chicago that Israel was prepared to pay reparations to those Arabs still in Israel so that they would emigrate and make room for the new immigrants.
37. *Al-Ahram*, 17 Feb. 1959.
38. *Al-Ahram*, 18 Feb. 1959.
39. *Ibid. Al-Ahram* wrote similarly on 19 Feb.
40. E.g., *al-Ahram*, 24 Feb. 1959. Nonetheless on 3 March the paper published a long account of an Arab League meeting at which League Secretary-General Abd al-Khaliq Hasunna presented 'a serious report' that: (1) Israel had received 50,000 Jews in the past six months and was expecting 100,000 more; (2) Israel was trying to collect a billion dollars in America to cover the expenses of this immigration; (3) Israel desired to form a million-strong army so as to force its will on the Arabs. Husunna noted that the emigration from Eastern Europe, which had recently assumed considerable dimensions, was the first such emigration since 1952; he also pointed out that Ben Gurion had declared the hope that the doors of the USSR would likewise be opened. Preparations for the urgent convention of the League to discuss immigration to Israel had been underway from 14 to 20 Feb. – *al-Ahram*, 15, 17 and 20 Feb. 1959.
41. *Al-Ahram*, 22 Feb. 1959.
42. *Izvestiia*, 25 Feb. 1959.
43. *Al-Ahram*, 26 Feb. 1959.
44. *Pravda*, 2 March 1959.
45. *Al-Ahram*, 2 March 1959.
46. 'Khrushchev said in a conversation with four American World War II veterans that the USSR intended to allow Jews to emigrate whenever they desired. One of the four ex-servicemen asked him the reason why the Soviet Union did not let Jews emigrate to Israel and other countries, and the Soviet Premier replied: "We are now moving toward the idea of allowing every citizen in the future to leave Russia at any time" ' – *al-Ahram*, 13 May 1959.
47. *Al-Ahram*, 13 July 1959.

48. It was reported, for example in 1963, that the USSR had promised the Government of Iraq that it would never permit Jews living on Soviet territory to emigrate to Israel – *Mideast Mirror*, 22 Nov. 1963.
49. Of the papers of the various Arab countries which I examined, the Jordanian *al-Manar* alone reported the Kosygin statement (on 4 Dec. 1966).
50. *Al-Anwar*, 12 May 1967. On the other hand, a Lebanese pro-Western source, *as-Safa'*, wrote that when a member of parliament of the Progressive Socialist Party asked one of the Soviet delegation about 'the secret idea behind the granting of permission to Jews from the socialist countries to go to Israel, the delegation member answered: to establish a communist state in the region.'
51. The issue of German repatriation from the USSR likewise operated as a means of leverage *vis-à-vis* the two Germanies. See George Ginsburgs, *Soviet Citizenship Law*, Leyden, 1968, pp. 250–3.

POSTSCRIPT TO NOTE 11

Jewish emigration figures from the USSR to Israel prior to June 1967 were:

1948–53	18
1954	53
1955	105
1956	753
1957–1963	968
1964	539
1965	1,444
1966	1,892
1967 (Jan–July)	1,162

The numbers in the righthand column represent Israeli visas issued for Soviet Jews. The discrepancy between visas issued and emigration is minimal. The figures have been published in Z. Alexander, 'Immigration to Israel from the USSR', *Israel Yearbook on Human Rights*, Tel Aviv, Vol. 7, 1977, pp. 268–335.

The Development of African-Israeli Relations to the Yom Kippur War: Nigeria as a Case Study

Ibrahim A. Gambari

In the aftermath of the Yom Kippur War, all the black African countries broke off diplomatic relations with Israel. Among the countries that took this action were Ethiopia, Kenya, Liberia (highly pro-western states), and Nigeria, which for many years after its independence walked a 'tightrope' policy for non-partisanship in the Middle-Eastern situation. What was responsible for this dramatic set-back for Israel, a country that was highly regarded by some African states and peoples for its achievements in nation-building, economic development, and modest but effective agricultural and military aid? Is the damage to African-Israeli relations temporary or permanent? What is the future of that relationship?

Nigeria has been used as a case study in the attempt to answer these questions for a number of reasons. First, Nigeria is the most populous country in Africa, estimated to have over 70 million people (i.e. one-fifth of the total population of Africa). Secondly, the country's natural resources, especially oil, and the quality of its national leadership are responsible for transforming it from a sleepy and shy country to a vigorous and potential giant in Africa. Thirdly, Nigeria is one of the most important members of the Organization of African Unity (OAU) which is increasingly becoming involved in the intricacies of Middle-Eastern diplomacy.

Nigeria's relationship with Israel and the Arabs was characterised by three conflicting pulls during the decade and a half following the country's independence. First, there was the Northern region's overt friendship and ties with the Arabs while the Southern regions developed friendly relations with Israel. Second, the South accepted loans and other economic aid from Israel but the North stoutly rejected them. Finally, the Northern government was openly partisan to the Arab cause while the federal government was attempting to follow a 'neutral' or non-partisan policy in the Middle East situation.

Hence, Nigeria did not speak with one voice on the Middle East problem in this period. Instead, there was a three-way division of policy and attitude toward the Arabs and Israel.

The Arabs relate to the Muslims in Nigeria largely through the Northern region and the Northern Peoples Congress which favoured a pro-Arab policy. On the other hand, Israel works closely with the Christian elements in the Western and Eastern regions of Nigeria and naturally encourages a policy favourable to it. The federal government attempts to pursue a middle, non-partisan policy.

There were three main reasons for this dis-united approach to the Arabs and Israel. First, Britain gave no consistent leadership on this issue before granting independence to Nigeria. Although British antipathy to Egypt under Nasser following the Suez crisis was well known, British officials in Nigeria did not discourage Northern leaders, who were then British subjects, from developing intimate contacts with Egypt and the Muslim world. Ever since Lugard established British rule in Northern Nigeria in 1900, successive British administrations have followed a 'hands-off' policy to Islam in that region. Indeed Christian missionary activities were checked while Islam grew and the traditional and modern rulers of that region of Nigeria were allowed to develop friendly relations with their Islamic brothers elsewhere in the world.

Secondly, the British policy of preserving the Islamic activities and culture of the North and its people contributed to the ideological separation of that region from the South of Nigeria. Hence while the North and its leaders continued to develop its historic trade and religious links with North Africa and other Arab lands, the South leaders and many of the peoples of that part of Nigeria embraced Western education and looked to the Western World for new ideas and principles of law and government.[1]

Thirdly, in the early to mid-1960s, Nigerian politics and constitutional arrangements were dominated by powerful regions, which enjoyed the political advantage of having had as Premiers two men who were leaders of the federal coalition government political parties (the Northern Peoples Congress – NPC, and the National Council of Nigeria and the Cameroons – NCNC). The Nigerian Prime Minister, Sir Abubakar Tafawa Balewa, who was not the leader of his own party, had the unenviable position of directing foreign policy on the issue of the Middle East with which his own party leader, Sir Ahmadu Bello, also Premier of the North, vigorously disagreed.

How then were the differences of policy and attitude manifested in Nigeria in the early period of Nigeria's independence? Influential Southern leaders such as Chief Awolowo, head of the third major Nigerian political party, detested Nasser's Egypt and the Arab world. He did not really consider Egypt an African country and accused Nasser of 'undisguised totalitarianism (at home) and territorial ambitions in Africa and the Muslim World'.[2] Chief Awolowo's deputy and main spokesman on foreign affairs, Anthony Enahoro, wanted the exclusion of Arab North African countries from discussions of, and meetings about, Pan-Africanism.[3]

The Premiers of the Southern regions of Nigeria visited Israel several times, established close ties with, and readily accepted loans and economic assistance from, that country.[4] Many educated Southern Nigerians admire Israel's phenomenal economic success[5] and would like to share the secrets of Israeli achievement. Sometimes the Premiers of the Southern regions were very partisan in their pro-Israeli positions.[6] For example, Dr Michael Okpara, Premier of the Eastern region, told an Israeli representative in Nigeria: 'I myself am almost an Israelite. I love and admire Israel.'[7] In general, however, the leaders of the Southern regions and their supporters accept the federal government's policy of remaining 'neutral' and non-partisan in the Middle East problem.

It was the Northern Premier, Sir Ahmadu Bello, and his government which totally rejected the federal government's policy and position. The Northern government denounced the loan agreement which the federal minister of Finance, Chief Okotie-Eboh, concluded with Israel in June 1960.[8] Under normal circumstances, there was hardly anything strange about a developing country's finance minister negotiating financial loans and economic aid from foreign governments. That was part of his job, and, in Chief Okotie-Eboh's case, he had done this several times before. Indeed, the Nigerian Six-Year Development Plan envisaged substantial external borrowing of up to half the L700 million proposed for the public sector by 1968.[9]

However, in an immediate reaction, the Northern Peoples Congress (the senior partner in the federal coalition government) condemned the federal government's financial deal with Israel.[10] The party not only called for the withdrawal of all negotiations with Israel but asked the federal government to withdraw recognition of the Israeli representative in Lagos. The party's spokesman, Raji Abdullahi, recalled the Northern Premier's statement rejecting all and any assistance from the Israeli government and explaining that 'when we [meaning the Northern region] want help, we know where to go for it'.[11]

The Prime Minister had to come to the aid of his finance minister and defended the federal government's attitude toward assistance from any country in the world including Israel. Sir Abubakar warned that the introduction of religion into politics 'will mean the end of happiness in Nigeria'.[12] In his view, the federal government intended to be friendly with all countries and would not be party to any dispute between Israel and the Arab world.[13] He said, however, that if any region was opposed to accepting particular loans from particular sources, it needed only to say no but it could not prevent the federal government from taking any such loans for the country as a whole.[14] This defence of the loan from Israel did not satisfy the NPC-controlled Northern government and it continued to express its opposition to the whole idea of relationship with Israel.[15] The Prime Minister, who was Vice President of the NPC, continued to maintain his government's stand on financial and other dealings with Israel.[16]

Alhaji Ahmadu Bello, the Northern Premier, never bothered to conceal his adverse attitude to Israel and sided his party and government with the Arab cause whenever there was an opportunity to do so. In a party for Mr Hamid, the United Arab Republic Ambassador to Nigeria, Alhaji Ahmadu Bello announced that his region and the UAR would take joint measures to come close together.[17] In reply to this announcement, the ambassador said that his country 'would give full support to her Muslim brothers in Northern Nigeria'.[18]

How then did the federal government, especially the NPC cabinet members and the Prime Minister, deputy leader of the party, maintain a 'neutral' policy in the Middle East dispute, even accepting an Israeli loan and economic assistance despite Alhaji Ahmadu Bello's views to the contrary? In the first place, to reject the loan negotiated by a senior member of the federal government would mean that the Prime Minister would be repudiating his own finance minister who was also the leader of the NCNC (National Council of Nigeria and the Cameroons) Parliamentary party in the federal coalition government. This might damage the coalition agreement and relationship at its early period of operation and weaken the show of national unity prior to independence. Secondly, the Southern regions wanted the Israeli loans and assistance and would vigorously oppose any efforts to block such economic aid. Furthermore, the federal government would then appear as the mouthpiece of the NPC and the Northern government while the Prime Minister himself would be little more than the errand boy of the Northern Premier, Alhaji Ahmadu Bello. This was not a view of his office and government which Sir Abubakar could easily swallow. It was for these reasons that the NPC members of the federal government backed the Prime Minister, rather than the leader of their party, Alhaji Ahmadu Bello, in the pursuit of the federal policy of non-partisanship in the Middle Eastern situation.

Naturally, Alhaji Ahmadu Bello was infuriated that he could not carry along with him on his anti-Israeli, pro-Arab policy, members of his own party who were in the federal cabinet. Nonetheless, he often went on tours of several Muslim countries where he made partisan statements on the Middle East which acutely embarrassed the federal government and antagonized Southern Nigerian leaders and newspaper editors. For example, on one of these tours, he was reported to have advocated a 'Commonwealth of Muslim States' to include Nigeria.[19] In a swift editorial response entitled 'No, Sir Ahmadu', the *Daily Times* reminded the Northern Premier that Nigeria is a secular state and that Nigerians do not wish to introduce religious groupings into African relations although the newspaper declared that it was not against the aim of universal brotherhood of Muslims.[20] *The Service*, a new organ of the Action Group, official Opposition party in the federal parliament, condemned Alhaji Ahmadu's utterance as repugnant and provocative which 'should be abandoned at once'.[21] The *Daily Express*, also sympathetic to the views of the AG, told Alhaji Bello that he was not the Prime Minister and that Nigeria is not a Muslim State.[22] The newspaper asked the Prime Minister to speak up on the issue which he did by assuring the nation that Alhaji Ahmadu's interest in Muslim brotherhood must not be construed to mean that Nigeria would join an Islamic Commonwealth of Nations.[23]

It did seem that when Alhaji Ahmadu Bello spoke for a Commonwealth of Muslim States, possibly including Nigeria, he often really had only the North in mind.[24] In the 1952–53 census (perhaps the least unreliable count to date), the North recorded 11,661,000 Muslims against only 558,000 Christians out of a total population for the region of 16,835,000. This overwhelming Muslim population of the North tended to buttress Alhaji Ahmadu Bello in his Pan-Islamic tours and pronouncements. Since the Northern Premier often thought about the rest of Nigeria in very negative terms rather than as positive factors to be considered in his own or his region's policies and views, Alhaji Bello probably dismissed the largely non-Muslim South from his mind when he made his pro-Arab and Islamic utterances.

Furthermore, from about 1963 on, the Northern Premier came to be identified more and more with the propagation of Islamic religion and theology at home. He defended his regional government's new laws against the drinking of alcohol by Muslims in Northern Nigeria by saying that as long as his party was in power, 'it will not legalize what God has forbidden'.[25] He also went on holy pilgrimages to Mecca, sometimes twice a year, in the company of prominent Northern leaders; and he personally undertook a series of 'Islamic conversion tours' to remote areas of his region where non-Muslims were predominant.[26] The World Muslim Congress apparently recognised Alhaji Ahmadu's role in Nigeria and abroad to propagate Islam by appointing him, in absentia, Vice President of the Organization.[27]

Hence, it is easy to see why he reacted angrily to renewed pressure and suggestions from Southern Nigeria that the country should establish an embassy in Israel by declaring defiantly: 'What is Israel? To my mind it does not exist and it never will exist. I don't know what it is.'[28] While this was a fervently held sentiment it was a strange remark from the leader of a party, the NPC, which was senior partner of the federal government that recognised Israel, received the Israeli ambassador in Lagos and accepted economic aid from Israel.

The acrimony of the Middle Eastern dispute seemed to be spreading to Nigeria despite the federal government's determination to prevent this. Indeed, when Golda Meier, then Foreign Minister of Israel, visited Nigeria in October 1964, there were demonstrations of support for the Palestinians and against Israeli policy by the All-Muslim Organization of Nigeria.[29] The federal government disapproved of the demonstration and the Ministry of Foreign Affairs emphasised that Nigeria was not interested in the Arab-Israeli feud and that the country's foreign policy was one of 'friendliness to both Israel and her Arab neighbours'.[30] The Ministry of Foreign Affairs was even more outraged by the attempt made by a group of Arab diplomats' wives to prevent Mrs Meier from giving a scheduled lecture to the National Council of Women Societies in Nigeria.[31] To add to the confusion of opinion and attitude, Dr Nnamdi Azikiwe, then ceremonial head of state of Nigeria, told visiting Mrs Meier that Israel was one of Nigeria's 'staunchest friends' notwithstanding the contrary views of the Northern region and its leader.

However, Dr Azikiwe's remarks may well have been prompted by the internal political disagreement which he was then having with the Northern leaders. He may also have been expressing the views of the Eastern region (his home region) and its leaders which were clearly supportive of Israel. For instance, Dr Michael Okpara, Premier of the Eastern region, gave a farewell party for the Israeli ambassador to Nigeria, Mr Hannah Yavor, in which he praised the cordial relationship between Eastern Nigeria and Israel.[32] Dr Okpara also warned against importing into Nigeria the bitterness of the Middle Eastern dispute.[33]

The two major Nigerian opinions on the Middle East became increasingly irreconcilable, like the situation of the Israelis and the Arabs themselves, and this was worsened by the deteriorating political relationships between the NPC and the NCNC federal coalition partners which spread to the Northern and Eastern regions they respectively controlled. The Publicity Secretary of the NCNC, Mr Amechi, who had the reputation of being the anti-NPC and anti-Northern region political trouble-shooter of his party, accused the Northern leader, Alhaji Ahmadu Bello, of trying to encourage the annexation of Nigeria to the Arab Empire.[34] Amechi further said that, 'by tracing his origin to the Arab World, [in the controversial 'I am an Arab' remark] the Northern Premier was giving a clear indication of his ambition to win political power in Nigeria and convert the country into an extended empire of the Arabs.'[35] In his reply, the Northern leader maintained his stand on Muslim unity adding that 'I'll stake my life for Islamic unity'.[36]

Therefore the Middle Eastern situation presented difficult problems for Nigeria's policy makers. Although the federal government's declared policy of non-partisanship in relation to the Arabs or Israelis enjoyed a broad consensus in Nigeria, the Northern leader and his government ignored this federal policy. It was not politically feasible for the Nigerian Prime Minister to force his own party leader, Sir Ahmadu Bello, who was also Premier of the largest region of Nigeria, to accept the federal government's policy. Hence, the federal policy on the Middle East applied to less than half of the country. Quite unlike many of his colleagues in other African states, the Prime Minister of Nigeria did not have the free hand in foreign policy questions which the constitution assigns to his federal government. That is why, instead of a united policy on the Middle

East situation, that conflict was highlighting, as well as contributing to, the disunity of Nigeria. This unhappy situation continued until the civilian regime was overthrown by a military coup d'etat in January of 1966.

When General Ironsi took office as head of the military government of Nigeria, there was no occasion for the Northern region to reassert its policy on the Middle East or for the East to respond to such a move. The country was far too preoccupied with internal matters. Moreover, had Ironsi succeeded in carrying out his Decree 34 which was designed to abolish the regions and centralise administrative and political authority in federal government's hands, the power of the North or any region to challenge federal policies in the Middle East and elsewhere would have been permanently removed or greatly reduced. However, it was Ironsi himself and his Decree 34 that were removed when Gowon came to power in July 1966, following the second military coup (or counter-coup).[37] This did not mean that the North was allowed to revive its pro-Arab policies, since party politics and open public or political pressures remained banned by the Gowon regime, which also broke up the North into six new states as part of a new twelve-state structure in Nigeria. Therefore federal policies of non-partisanship continued after Gowon's assumption of power.

Nonetheless, it was not the mere fact of the military overthrow of the civilian regime which brought about the centralisation of authority in foreign affairs. Gowon decreed the new twelve-state structure mainly to avoid the repetition of the previous situation whereby a weak central government was effectively challenged in several matters by powerful regions, and also to discourage the then Eastern region from seceding from the federation.[38] Once the Eastern region finally declared a secession as an independent state of 'Biafra', the federal government organised the country's armed forces, economy and administrative structure to fight, and later win, the war of national unity with the inevitable result of greater centralisation of power in Nigeria.

Nigeria then began to speak with one voice in foreign affairs in general and on the Middle East in particular. However, while it is conceivable that the basic policy of non-partisanship could have remained in effect, there were three main factors which made Nigeria become pro-Egypt and impatient with Israeli policy in the Middle East. First, there were the respective roles played by Egypt and Israel in the Nigerian Civil War. When the war began in Nigeria in 1967, Israel was not only sympathetic to the secessionists but gave some arms to the rebel regime while Egypt and the Arab states supported the federal side.[39] The victorious federal government did not forget the different roles played by the Arabs and Israelis in the Nigerian Civil War.

Secondly, Nigeria became increasingly frustrated with Israel's policy of continued occupation of Arab lands. For a country which had fought a bitter war to preserve its territorial integrity, Nigeria could no longer sympathise with Israel, which was violating other countries' territorial integrity. At the OAU Heads of State Meeting at Addis Ababa (Ethiopia) in 1973, General Gowon of Nigeria said so: 'It is an intolerable provocation that a part of Egypt, a member state of our Organization, should continue to remain under armed occupation since May 1967.'[40]

Thirdly, as a leading member of the OAU and Chairman of both the Ministerial Council and General Assembly of the Heads of Government of the OAU in 1973, Nigeria began to strongly articulate and spearhead those views which were almost unanimously held by the Organization. The resolutions on the Middle East at the OAU Summit meetings at Rabat, Morocco (June 1972) and Addis Ababa the following year clearly sympathised with the Arabs' positions and condemned Israeli policies.[41] Israel, of course, ignored the resolutions of both the OAU and the United Nations demanding its withdrawal from occupied Arab lands. General Gowon himself visited the Middle East, as a member of the OAU Special Mission to help bring about the settlement of the dispute in that area, and concluded with other members of the mission that, despite a reasonableness they found among the Arabs, Israel would not make any significant concessions.[42]

The Yom Kippur War of 1973 was as much a turning point for the parties to that war as it proved for Israeli relationships with Nigeria and other African countries. In quick succession, African states, including Nigeria, began to break diplomatic relationships with Israel. This action represented the abandonment of Nigeria's careful balancing act towards the parties in the Middle Eastern dispute and the taking of sides against Israel and in favour of Egypt and the Arabs.

It is very difficult to accurately assess the feelings of the Nigerian national elite on the breach of relations with Israel because the military government in Nigeria discourages open expression of dissenting opinion in the country. However, it is safe to assume that the Northern states of Nigeria (which have managed to retain a measure of cohesion since the old Northern region was broken into six new states, in 1967) feel a sense of satisfaction with the federal government's decision. In the view of the largely Muslim population, the breaking of diplomatic relations with Israel was long overdue. On the other hand, there is indeed a residual feeling of support for Israel in Nigeria. A newspaper in Southern Nigeria, *Nigerian Tribune*, sharply criticised the breach of diplomatic relations with Israel and tersely declared that 'the Middle East crisis is an Arab problem. It is not an African affair. It is not the business of the OAU'.[43]

However, this has become very much of a minority opinion in Nigeria. It is a far cry from the time when, as the influential journal, *West Africa* recalls, 'ministers in Southern Nigeria saw much to admire in the Jewish state'.[44] Quite apart from the respective roles that Egypt and Israel played in Nigeria's civil war, Israeli continued defiance of the resolutions of the United Nations and OAU on withdrawal from occupied Arab territories did little to preserve the previously enthusiastic attitude of Southern Nigerians to Israel.

There are three other reasons why it was relatively easy for Nigeria to break relations with Israel. First, as a Member of the Organization of Petroleum Exporting Countries (OPEC), Nigeria has worked closely with Arab countries such as Libya, Algeria, Kuwait and Saudi Arabia and the contact and highly satisfactory relations here may have had a spill-over effect on Nigeria's sympathy for the Arabs' position towards Israel. Secondly, with Nigeria's increasing oil revenue which jumped from N1,914 million in 1973 to N5,523 million the following year,[45] Nigeria now considers foreign monetary aid as marginal to its development. Hence, Israeli small scale loans and technical assistance are now far less significant to Nigeria than they seemed to be to the Southern regions in the 1960's. Indeed, whatever foreign technical assistance Nigeria may need in executing its development programmes, the country can now afford to pay to get it. Thirdly, the act of breaking diplomatic relations with Israel consisted in no more than asking the Israeli ambassador in Lagos to leave for home. Nigeria has no embassy in Israel and no ambassador to recall home.

The future of Nigerian-Israeli relations remains very uncertain, largely because the future of Nigeria's own political development is difficult to predict. If the military government continues to rule Nigeria, it is likely that the centralised control over foreign policy, rather than localised and divergent regional attitudes to the Middle Eastern conflict, will indeed endure. However, if there is a return to civilian government which is not strong enough to check the centrifugal forces in internal and external affairs, there may be a return to the situation of the early 1960s with regard to Nigerian relations to the Middle East. Of course, General Gowon has informed his country that he has indefinitely postponed the date 1976 which he earlier mentioned as the probable time for return to civilian rule. According to him, the civilian leaders who wanted power did not show signs that they had mended their divisive and parochial ways.[46] Nonetheless, there is a serious question and doubt as to whether and how long General Gowon can safely prevent legitimate civilian aspiration for power in a country like Nigeria which has a sophisticated intellectual class and a politically aware national elite.[47]

Now, if there were an Israeli withdrawal from all occupied Egyptian and other Arab territories in a general peace settlement which recognised the legitimate rights of both Israel and the Palestinians, there would be a good chance of a resumption of Israeli-Nigerian diplomatic and business relations. However, this is a very complex problem involving Arab nationalism, Zionism, bitterness from the prolonged conflict in that area as well as the interests of the Super-Powers and other great powers in the Middle East. Its resolution to the satisfaction of all concerned is very unlikely in the near future.

To what extent, then, is Nigeria's example of relations with the Arabs and Israel applicable to other African states? Unlike Nigeria, most African states are small and militarily very weak. They are therefore, far more sensitive to the idea of a powerful country like Israel, backed by the United States, conquering another state on African soil. It was at the point when Israel crossed to the Western bank of Suez into Egyptian territory within the geographic boundary of Africa during the last war, that many African states decided to act against Israel through the breach of diplomatic relations.

This action was made more palatable for some African states by the apparent promise made by the Arab states to extend their oil boycott weapon to punish the old enemies of the African countries: Southern Africa's racist and white minority regimes. There were also the diplomatic, financial and economic campaigns mounted by the Arab states, especially Libya's Qadafi, to move the African states away from Israel and towards the Arabs.

Those African states with large Muslim populations, such as Nigeria and the Sudan, will continue to find it difficult to develop warm relations with Israel, notwithstanding a possible resumption of formal diplomatic contact, until the Arabs express satisfaction with an over-all settlement in that area. However, with progress towards a settlement, concern for the reality of increasing price of Arab oil, decrease in the size and delivery of promised Arab monetary aid and the negative effect of withdrawn Israeli technical assistance, may lead many African states to reopen diplomatic relations with Israel.

Meanwhile, one thing has become very clear in the African-Israeli relationship. Africa may not be considered militarily important in Israeli strategic and political calculations, but the continent's diplomatic support, or at least neutrality, can be important to Israel. The Arabs clearly recognise the usefulness of African states' diplomatic support and the presence of Arafat at the last session of the United Nations General Assembly illustrates this. Israel can ill afford *permanent* diplomatic isolation from *all* the states of Africa – an entire continent which is contiguous to Israeli occupied and other territories.

NOTES

1. See James S. Coleman, *Nigeria: Background to Nationalism* (Berkeley and Los Angeles: University of California Press, 1963), pp. 91–6 and H. O. Davies, *Nigeria: Prospects for Democracy* (Weidenfeld and Nicolson, 1961), p. 92.
2. *Daily Times* (Nigeria's leading newspaper), 12 Sept. 1959.
3. Report of Speech made in the United States, *Daily Times*, 27 June 1960.
4. Claude S. Phillips, Jr., *The Development of Nigerian Foreign Policy* (Northwestern University Press, 1964), p. 82.
5. Frederick A. O. Schwarz, Jr., *Nigeria, The Tribes, The Nation, or The Race, The*

Politics of Independence (Cambridge, Mass.: MIT Press, 1965), pp. 233–4.
6. The Western Premier, Chief Akintola, told the Israelis 'You can be assured of our friendship and support at any place.' *Daily Times*, 10 Oct. 1961.
7. *West Africa*, 3 Nov. 1962.
8. *Daily Times*, 16 June 1960.
9. Douglass Anglin, 'Nigeria: Political Non-alignment and Economic Alignment,' *Journal of Modern African Studies*, Vol. 2, 2, 1964, p. 249.
10. *Daily Times*, 16 June 1960.
11. *Ibid.*
12. *Ibid.*, 17 June 1960.
13. *Ibid.*
14. *Ibid.*
15. *Ibid.*, 22 June 1960.
16. *Ibid.*, 23 June 1960.
17. *Daily Times*, 11 Aug. 1960.
18. *Ibid.*
19. *Ibid.*, 28 June 1961.
20. *Ibid.*
21. *The Service*, 1 July 1961, p. 7.
22. *Daily Express*, Editorial, 29 June 1961.
23. See Editorial, 'Prime Minister Clears the Air,' *Daily Times*, 12 July 1961.
24. Former federal minister, Nuhu Bamali, and the leader of the Northern Elements Progressive Union (an important political party in the North opposed to NPC policies), Aminu Kano, respectively confirmed this point to author in separate private interviews at Kaduna, 13 July 1972, and Lagos, 7 Aug. 1972.
25. See C. S. Whitaker, Jr., *The Politics of Tradition: Continuity and Change in Northern Nigeria, 1946–1966*, (Princeton, New Jersey: Princeton University Press, 1970), p. 349.
26. *Ibid.*
27. *Daily Times* report, 15 Jan. 1965.
28. *Daily Times*, 1 Sept. 1965.
29. *Ibid.*, 28 Oct. 1964.
30. *Ibid.*
31. *Ibid.*
32. *Morning Post*, 30 Jan. 1963.
33. *Ibid.*
34. *Daily Times*, 13 Aug. 1964.
35. *Ibid.*
36. *Ibid.*, 28 Aug. 1964.
37. See 'Gowon Abolishes Decree 34 and Reinstates a Federal System,' in A. H. M. Kirk-Greene, *Crisis and Conflict in Nigeria*, (London: Oxford University Press, 1971), Vol. 1, pp. 215–16.
38. Details of this can be found in S. K. Panter-Brick, *Nigerian Politics and Military Rule: Prelude to the Civil War*, (London: University of London, The Athlone Press, 1970).
39. See details in John de St Jorre, *The Brothers' War: Biafra and Nigeria*, (Boston: Houghton Mifflin Co., 1972), pp. 219–20.
40. 'Official Record of General Gowon's speech to the Organization of African Unity, 24 May 1973,' (Lagos, Nigeria: Ministry of External Affairs), p. 6.
41. See Susan A. Gitelson, 'The OAU Mission and the Middle East Conflict,' paper presented at the International Studies Association Convention, New York, March 1973 (version expected to be published in *International Organization*, XXVII, 3, 1973/74), p. 7.
42. *West Africa*, 15 Oct. 1973, p. 1443. Details of the mission's activities are given in Gitelson, *op. cit.*, pp. 11–12.

43. Report in *West Africa*, 26 Nov. 1973, p. 1681.
44. *Ibid.*, 15 Oct. 1973, p. 1443.
45. One Nigerian Naira (N1) is approximately equal to one and a half United States Dollar ($1.50). The figures are from General Gowon's Budget Broadcast, 31 March 1975 (Lagos: Ministry of Information) p. 9.
46. General Gowon, 'With Peace and Plenty', Independence Day Broadcast, 1 Oct. 1974, (Lagos: Ministry of Information), pp. 28–9.
47. Colin Legum, 'Nigeria is Struggling Over Control of Her Wealth', *New York Times*, 16 March 1975, p. E3.

Integration of Arabs in an Israeli Party: The Case of Mapam, 1948–54

Yael Yishai

It has been argued that political parties play a major role in resolving strains in society. Although the parties are not alone in performing this function, their contribution might play a crucial role in the internal cohesion of the society, especially in a new nation. The importance of the integrative function increases in a new state in view of the need to gain legitimacy, support and loyalty from all segments of the population. Israel, in its formative years, serves as an instructive case study in which the party's integrative function can be examined.

The Israeli political system is characterized by the multiplicity of its political parties, well-organized and ideologically oriented.[1] In contrast, Arab society in Israel (in the first years of its existence) was still in a pre-individualistic, kin-controlled stage of development. Correspondingly, the Arab 'parties' or alliance were 'little more than expressions of personal loyalty to a group of "natural" leaders, whose leadership is based on their economic status, local prestige and their position within a kinship group'.[2] The emergence of these 'parties' was encouraged by the leading Jewish party, Mapai, who gave organizational and financial support to the Arabs in exchange for an electoral alliance. Only one Jewish, Zionist party, Mapam (United Workers Party), considered the mobilization of the Arabs as party-members. This must be seen in the light of the fact that relations between Israel and her Arab neighbours were characterised by a state of war after 1948, and that circumstance had many implications for Israeli Arabs. Security became a major issue for Israeli society, and the assumption was constantly made that Israeli Arabs, in view of their cultural affinity with other neighbouring, belligerent Arab states, posed a security risk to the state. Consequently, the integration of the Arabs into the political, social and economic life of the state was impeded. Indeed, Israeli Arabs lived under a 'military government system'[3] which imposed restrictions upon their equal rights as full-fledged citizens.

Conversely, almost all Israeli parties tried to absorb the mass Jewish immigration which flooded the country in the first years of its existence and thus fulfilled the role of serving as integrating agents. In fact, the parties (the chief among them being Mapai) integrated various Jewish social and ethnic groups in a way that inhibited the establishment of ethnic-based parties. However, only Mapam considered the integration of the Arabs into its ranks as one of its primary functions, and that became a major issue of internal politics for Mapam. That no other Jewish political party in Israel struggled with the issue of integrating the Arabs at the time is revealing. This paper will analyse the development of Mapam's position on the full participation of Arabs in its party structure. Most of the studies available on the politics of Israeli Arabs deal with Arab motivation and possibilities for participation in Israeli politics.[4] Here we will examine the attitudes and forces prevailing in a *Jewish* party with respect to its role as a socialising agent in society.

Mapam, formed in January, 1948, was a merger of two major elements, Achdut Haavodah and Hashomer Hatzair. Achdut Haavodah[5] (The Unity of Labour) was formed in 1944. It was a former left wing of Mapai which held extreme views opposing the partition of Palestine. Hashomer Hatzair (The Young Watchman) was founded in 1946 and was originally a socialist youth movement which sought to combine Marxist theory with a collective way of life. Both parties were Zionist-Socialist and had strong kibbutz organizations affiliated with them. The two parties merged in order to become an influential political factor. Although both were in political opposition to the dominant party, Mapai, they were not 'anti-system parties'[6] since they shared the basic values of Zionism prevailing in the Jewish society. In the elections to the Constituent Assembly in January 1949, Mapam became the second largest party in the parliament (Knesset), gaining 14.7 per cent of the total vote.

However, it became clear very early that Mapam was united in name only. A short time after its emergence, Mapam had to deal with factional disputes that disrupted the party's internal processes and inhibited the effective performance of the party's functions, including the integrative one of resolving societal conflicts. The Arab problem was one of the most disputed issues.

Mapam took a special interest in the Arab population for historical and ideological reasons. This fact made it a potential political 'melting pot' for Arabs and Jews. However, Achdut Haavodah and Hashomer Hatzair held different and contradictory views on the Arab problem. The merger between the two parties was made on the assumption that the change in the political constellation brought about by the establishment of the state would be followed by a new reality which would make possible an ideological revision. That assumption proved to be wrong. It is suggested here that it was the inter-factional dispute in Mapam that prevented the party from fulfilling its function as an integrative force. The Arabs who might have been integrated into the party remained outside the Israeli political system. They had only two other alternatives: to join the Communist party which already included Arab members and was basically an anti-system party, or to organise Arab parties, differentiated from the main stream of Israeli society and thus functioning as disintegrative political bodies.

HISTORICAL POSITIONS OF ACHDUT HAAVODAH AND HASHOMER HATZAIR

Achdut Haavodah had clear-cut political positions concerning the solution of the *Jewish* problem. It was less explicit with regard to the Arab problem. The party opposed any proposal or political solution based on the partition of the country. On those grounds it rejected several plans to establish a minor Jewish state in Palestine. The party proclaimed the moral and historical rights of the Jewish people to settle in all parts of the land. However, the fact that the country (at least partially) was already settled by a hostile Arab population could not be disregarded. The party's leaders rejected the option (which was not supported by any Zionist leader) of dislodging the Arabs. Thus, a political formula was evolved which proposed building relationships with the Arabs on the basis of 'non-domination and non-subjugation'. Achdut Haavodah aimed for coexistence with the Arabs on the basis of '*mutual* acceptance and recognition of the liberties and independence of the Jewish and Arab nations'.[7] The party was not ready to translate this formula into reality by collaborating with the Arabs on the partisan level. Achdut Haavodah defined itself as a *Zionist* party (though not anti-Arab) and thus excluded a solution which would satisfy the needs of both nations. It concentrated on the problems of the Jewish people, neglecting those of the Arabs, without admitting that one was tied to the other.

Hashomer Hatzair was also a Zionist party, but with a different set of values. It advocated the establishment of a bi-national state, founded on the assumption that Palestine was a bi-national state by its very nature and could be a homeland for the returning Jewish people as well as the Arabs who already lived there. It held that the only feasible way to implement the Zionist objective (ingathering of exiles) was to form an alliance between the two nations in the framework of *one* independent, sovereign state. Hashomer Hatzair, like Achdut Haavodah, opposed the partition of the land, but not because the whole country was designated to be Jewish, but because there was no other alternative to settling peacefully in the land. However, it was not only the 'negative' argument (lack of alternative) but also the positive drive for solidarity on class-bases between the proletariat of the two nations that made the bi-national solution desirable for Hashomer Hatzair.[8] The party demanded an active Zionist policy aimed at building a bi-national form of government in order to ensure the uninterrupted development of both nations. Hashomer Hatzair's outlook was optimistic. It believed that the conflict between the Jews and the Arabs could be solved once the *people* of both nations would unite on the basis of socialist international solidarity. The struggle, it believed, was an unavoidable result of imperialistic intrigues. Achdut Haavodah was more pessimistic in viewing the struggle as inherent, stemming out of the clash between two claims for the same one land. Hashomer Hatzair tried to implement its policies by sponsoring a 'League for Jewish-Arab Rapprochement and Cooperation' (formed in 1939).[9] The party published a periodical in Arabic and was active politically in the Arab villages.

In 1947 both parties re-evaluated their former positions in view of the political changes which were due to take place upon the implementation of the U.N. decision and the termination of the British Mandate. Both parties still resented the partition of the land, but as Zionist parties could not resist the realistic chance to establish a sovereign, Jewish state. Both agreed on the need to replace the British during the transitional period and on the importance of international recognition. They were in accord on other major issues, but the Arab problem remained the major obstacle blocking the unification of the two parties since both already had a lot in common in terms of ideology and social structure.[10] In the negotiations that took place, the partners to the potential unification tried to reach a compromise that would enable them to bridge the ideological gap and reach a consensus that included the controversial Arab issue. Thus, 'a new formula was designed to which the parties were not bound in the past, albeit each of them could find in it a true expression of its ideological programs'.[11] The formula was based on 'equality, mutual aid, alliance with the working people and a common socialist front' or the coexistence of both nations on the basis of mutual consent and respect. These values were agreed upon by everyone. However, the party platform did not specify explicitly what the concrete forms of collaboration between Arabs and Jews would be. Neither did it bother itself with the war that was already being fought (although not declared officially) between the peoples of the two nations. The platform was ambiguous to the extent that it did not specify whether the Arabs would be full members of the Hebrew Labour Movement (Histadrut),[12] and potential membership for Arabs in the party was not even mentioned.

WAR OF INDEPENDENCE – RE-EVALUATION WITHIN A NEW CONSTELLATION

In May 1948, following the Declaration of Independence of the state of Israel, the formation of a new political constellation created the need for a re-evaluation of traditional positions. The flight of the Arabs was at its height. It seemed that Mapam's programme for building bridges between the Arabs and the Jews had vanished in the face of the turmoil of reality. The party was faced with three concrete problems relating to its Arab policy: what were to be its attitude (1) towards the flight of the Arabs, (2) towards the Arabs who remained in Israel, and (3) towards the Arab state which was to be formed in accordance with the U.N. decision. On each of these issues there was a gap between the two factions, since each faction returned to its traditional position. However, a consensus on these issues was a prerequisite for Mapam to be able to achieve an effective policy regarding the Arabs.

1. Hashomer Hatzair related the flight of the Arabs to the following factors: (1) the intrigues of the British, who were interested in creating a refugee problem which would enable them to return to Palestine as 'peace-makers', (2) Arab fear, (3) the pressures of an Arab leadership which promised the Arabs that they would return as winners, and (4) a Jewish policy that encouraged the flight of the Arabs for political and military reasons. Hashomer Hatzair denounced the flight of the Arabs on the basis of security and ideology. Accordingly, it was thought that the flight would aggravate Israel's security since the refugees were due to be 'bitter enemies for at least two generations'.[13] On the other hand, coexistence with the remaining Arab population was seen as enhancing the chances for peace between Israel and its neighbours. There was concern that the flight would create the image of a conqueror, as M. Yaari, Hashomer Hatzair leader suggested, 'If we shall conquer the whole land it will be said we are the most aggressive and dangerous party.'[14] Mapam was thus in an ambivalent position on matters of security, even though it had the image of being a peace-loving party. Despite the war and the bloodshed, the party's representatives in national political institutions proposed the recruiting of Arab ministers for the Provisional Government.[15] Moreover, the party (especially the Hashomer Hatzair faction) did not abandon its dream of a 'Greater Israel' which would include an independent Arab state, whose establishment would solve the Arab-Israeli conflict. According to this attitude, the flight of the Arabs was harmful in the long run and irrational in the short run. On the other hand, many leading party members held high positions in the Israeli armed forces, and their opinions and actions were much more militant than the party's declared policy. Mapam, as a member of the Provisional Government could not, due to the principle of 'collective responsibility', dissociate itself from the official line which had not opposed the flight of the Arabs. Thus, Mapam as a coalition party was bound to the decisions of the official Jewish political leadership. However, Hashomer Hatzair demanded that their army commanders obey the *party* and refrain from any act that would encourage the Arabs to leave.

Achdut Haavodah, the other faction, had different views on the flight of the Arabs. It believed that with fewer Arabs within Israel there would be less of a security issue, and the Arab problem would be solved more easily. Consequently, Achdut Haavodah advocated an approach of 'silent encouragement', leading the governmental policy on the flight of the Arabs. The atmosphere of war (and its unavoidable consequences) had, no doubt, encouraged a rigid attitude towards the Arabs. Achdut Haavodah members expressed their views explicitly: 'In times of war we should not bring in the Arabs ... each remaining house (in which the Arabs remained) who knows how much blood it will cost us.'[16] Although Achdut Haavodah also took part in the war activities its socialization patterns, which were basically pro-Arab, made its adjustment to the war conditions more difficult. Ideologically, Achdut Haavodah gave precedence to the needs of the Jewish people (including the Jewish refugees) and was willing to be engaged in a bitter war in order to secure what were defined as 'the Jewish rights'. According to Achdut Haavodah, the Arabs, by their animosity, undermined their own rights. 'He who fights against us endangers his rights', said Tabenkin, the leading Achdut Haavodah authority, adding 'if we shall not settle (on the Arab lands) we shall risk our own survival'.[17] It was disregarded that it was the *rights* claimed by the Arabs that were the focal point of the clash. Achdut Haavodah considered the return of the refugees as feasible only after the conclusion of a formal peace treaty between Israel and her Arab neighbours. Achdut Haavodah leaders made a distinction between moral attitudes and pragmatic calculations. Morally, they were not 'against' the Arabs. On the contrary, they wanted to foster international solidarity. However, the faction was not willing to give up what it considered to be the basic rights of the Jewish people for the sake of that solidarity. Since there was a basic contradiction between the rights of the two nations, one could not avoid making the choice, and for Achdut Haavodah that meant making Israel a Jewish state with a massive Jewish majority.

Mapam's official policy reflected the attitudes of Hashomer Hatzair. The party's political committee adopted decisions opposing the policy of encouraging the flight of the Arabs. Moreover, according to another decision, Mapam was supposed to propose that a governmental appeal be made to the Arabs asking them to stay in their homes.[18] The party was not united around these policies, but they were adopted on the basis of the majority principle.

2. Apparently, there was a consensus in Mapam on the orientation towards an Arab-Jewish agreement within the Israeli borders. The wish to 'build up a front striving to achieve peace and socialism' was common to the two factions. All Mapam's members considered the Arabs to be equal *citizens* and objected to any kind of discrimination. However, there was some gap between the humanistic-moral approach and actual political needs which were accompanied by human feelings. Mapam, despite its professed ideology, was part of the Jewish nation in Israel which was fighting for its existence. In this fight there were more than a few things of which to be critical. The war activities included the destruction of Arab villages by the military forces. Security needs were not compatible with the party's declared policies. As previously mentioned, there were many Mapam members among those holding high ranks in the army, and the party leaders were very concerned about the possible link between military actions and Mapam's image. 'Its moral and

political base is shaken', said a party leader.[19] Achdut Haavodah was less concerned, claiming that 'war has a logic and ethics of its own'. It demanded a moratorium on moral obligations until the end of the war and supported doing everything possible, including anti-Arab measures, in order to win.

Hashomer Hatzair was very extreme in demanding the application of strict moral rules of behaviour, even for army commanders (party members). It argued that morality had a universal value detached from time or space and its test was during war. Hashomer Hatzair demanded the use of disciplinary measures against the commanders whose actions were not compatible with the party policy. Achdut Haavodah objected categorically to this motion since it considered security issues to be 'out of bounds' for the party. The party's decisions were a compromise between the two conflicting attitudes of the factions. Mapam was thus inhibited from making a commitment to a clear policy.

3. Hashomer Hatzair believed that peace could be attained in the region by the establishment of a neighbouring Arab state, within the boundaries of former Palestine and attached in a federative form to the state of Israel through economic relationships. In the party platform, issued at the founding conference, there was an article referring to the future Arab state. Achdut Haavodah rejected this plan on the grounds that it abolished the historical dream of a 'whole Israel.' It had not lost hope that Israel, on the basis of historical rights, would gain (or rather regain) sovereignty over the whole, unpartitioned land, being able to offer the Arabs rights of citizenship without granting them national rights of self-determination.

In the provisional government one of Mapam's ministers proposed that a free Arab government in the Arab part of partitioned Palestine be set up.[20] Hashomer Hatzair believed that unless the national aspirations of the Arabs were realized, Israel's independence might be endangered. Conversely, Achdut Haavodah considered the potential Arab state both unrealistic and harmful. In contrast to Hashomer Hatzair demanding the initiation of efforts towards the establishment of the Arab state, Achdut Haavodah argued that an Arab state might impinge upon the Jewish historical rights and destiny.

THE INTERACTION BETWEEN MAPAM AND THE ARABS

Since Mapam (including Hashomer Hatzair) had a tradition of supporting the Arab cause, it could have become the first 'pro-system' party based on a bi-national membership and united in the recognition of the need for Arabs and Jews to live together in the same land. This possibility became the centre of a bitter, interfactional dispute in the party.

The relationships between Mapam and the Arab population in Israel were affected by two factors. (1) Mapam was a Zionist party, oriented towards a Jewish, national ideology. As such, it was difficult for Arabs to identify with its objectives. (2) Mapam did not compete very well with the two other major parties that attracted Arab affiliation, Mapai and Maki. Mapam could compete with Mapai's resources and with Maki's ideology only by offering the Arabs a unique reward, membership in a pro-system party, which could have the result of giving the Arabs a feeling of belonging, diminishing their feelings of alienation and exclusion.

While the War of Independence was being fought, the possibility of recruiting Arabs into the party was not even mentioned. Moreover, Mapam did not want to be the first Zionist party which included an Arab candidate on its list for the first election. Thus, Mapam supported (morally, financially and organisationally) an independent Arab list that failed to pass the 'blocking percent'.[21] The list received 2,812 votes (0.6 per cent of the total vote).[22]

After the elections (held in January 1949), it was proposed by A. Cohen, a leader of Hashomer Hatzair active in the Arab arena, that the party accept those Arabs who were active during the campaign. Those activists were to be 'the seed from which a large Arab membership in the party would grow'.[23] Hashomer Hatzair approved this motion and demanded its adoption, using moralistic, utilitarian and nationalistic arguments. (1) The moralistic argument – Mapam, in its platform, guaranteed equality to all citizens, the implication of this being that no one could be excluded from the party because of nationality. Moreover, as a traditional Arab-oriented party advocating a bi-national state, it would be immoral for Mapam not to accredit the Arabs with full membership in the party without restrictions. (2) The utilitarian argument – Mapam, as any other party in a democratic, political system, searched for electoral support which could be found in the Arab electorate. The admission of Arabs to the party could mean increased votes at the ballot box. This objective was not defined by the party in terms of sheer political interest, but as a mission to save the Arabs from the Communist party which was anti-system and anti-Zionist. Mapam was the only party, except for Maki, that considered recruiting the Arabs, even though Arabs voted for other parties, including the religious, Jewish ones.[24] (3) The nationalistic argument – Cooperation with the Arabs in the same party seemed to be a reasonable way of establishing a bridgehead to the fifty million Arabs surrounding Israel. The resolution of the conflict was regarded as a necessary, though not sufficient, condition for implementation of the Zionist idea. Thus, the idea of a 'territorial party'[25] (a term replacing bi-national state) was a product of the social revolution accompanying Jewish settlement in Israel.

Achdut Haavodah had a different version to the same arguments. (1) The moralistic argument – Achdut Haavodah did not repudiate the need to establish mutual, positive relationships with the Arabs. Morally, the Jews were under an obligation to bring progress and relief to the area and by means of modernisation to improve the lives of all people (Arabs included) in the region. Tabenkin, Achdut Haavodah leader, declared that he was willing to be the 'vanguard for changing the Arab nation, for implementation of agrarianism, industrialisation, education, etc.'[26] However, fulfilling this mission was not necessarily linked to admitting Arab members into the party, argued Achdut Haavodah. In fact, it would make the Arabs assimilate into a Jewish party and would hinder their progress as an autonomous group. Thus, the theme of Achdut Haavodah was 'equal but different'. The Arabs would have to do their own political job, organise in an Arab party that would maintain close ties with its counterpart Jewish party. 'He who thinks that the Arabs are not capable of maintaining an autonomous party doubts the value of equality', went the argument.[27] Therefore, for the sake of the Arabs it would be preferable to be separately organised. (2) The nationalistic argument – Integration of the Arabs into a Jewish party was viewed by Achdut Haavodah as a repudiation of the party's basic values which were centred in the Jewish people. The Arabs (including the Arab workers) were not partners to those objectives and did not share those values. By belonging to a different nation, the Arabs were excluded de facto from the Jewish consensus. 'Our destiny is Jewish,' said Tabenkin, who refused to replace a Jewish identity (meaning world Jewry) with a territorial one. Achdut Haavodah did not share the notion that social revolution, which might take place within the boundaries of the territory, was a sufficient condition for the solution of the Jewish problem. The faction defined the party's objectives in a manner emphasising Jewish interests, which were not compatible with those of the Arabs. Acceptance of Arabs into the party would result in the transformation of the party from a Zionist (though Socialist) party into a territorial one, devoid of clear national identification. The party was not only an 'organisation of opinion' but an organisation of sentiments as well. Arabs and Jews could share opinions but could hardly be partners to sentiments anchored in ethnic identifications. In addition, the party's function was not restricted to the *organisation* of opinion but also included such things as making a security policy. Achdut Haavodah leaders questioned whether having Arabs in the same party would impinge on the party's capacity to deal with delicate security issues.

Thus there were two clear policies concerning the integration of the Arabs into Mapam. One (Hashomer Hatzair) was in favour of full admittance of the Arabs as members on an equal basis; the other (Achdut Haavodah) was in favour of a separate Arab party, sponsored by Mapam and allied with it. Between these two positions there was a third one, forming an Arab section within Mapam.

Mapam approached a state of 'non-decision'. The issue was debated in the various party institutions with three pressures being brought to bear. Achdut Haavodah threatened to split the party if the Arabs were admitted. Hashomer Hatzair demanded the implementation of the principle of 'international solidarity'. The Arabs who were campaign activists in the elections to the Constituent Assembly demanded justice and equality. Their representative, Y. Hammis, said, 'We cannot understand the difficulties surrounding our acceptance into a party with whose ideas we are in absolute accord and with which we have been connected for years.'[28] The Arabs who were affiliated with Mapam were not willing to be second-class members, not enjoying full rights and sharing duties. They felt like double losers, neither having the benefits attached to affiliation with the government party, Mapai, nor being identified with the anti-Zionist party, Maki. Moreover, Mapam had not succeeded among the Arabs in the first elections and hoped to do better in the second ones. It was clear that the major incentive for an Arab to vote for Mapam was membership in a Jewish party, based on equality and comradeship.

THE COMPROMISE – 'TENDENCY' TOWARDS INTEGRATION

On 29 October 1949, the Mapam third council decided to set up an Arab *section* in the party, thus not granting the Arabs full membership. The representatives of the Arab section would have the right to participate in the party's political meetings. In addition, the party decided to have an Arab candidate on its list for the national elections to the second Knesset. Despite not having membership in the party, the Arab section was to be an integral part of Mapam's organizational framework. Although there was a founding rally to establish the Arab section in the party,[29] no further action followed. In February 1950, the Arab section notified the party that it had dissociated from Mapam because of the failure of the party to carry out its decisions.

Mapam spoke with two voices. On the one hand, an official party communique bitterly criticised the government policy which deprived the Arabs and discriminated against them in various social and political ways. On the other hand, Mapam was not strong enough to implement a decision, adopted by its own institutions, for setting up an Arab section in the party. Moreover, some of the kibbutzim affiliated with Mapam cultivated Arab lands, disregarding the request of the original landlords for ownership.

Achdut Haavodah, consistent in its position, saw no fault in the ambivalence and related it to the state of war which was not initiated by Israel. The Arab activists continued to press and even escalated their demands. Why, asked R. Bastouni, 'do we adopt only the Jewish national goals? As an Arab I am willing to fight for the ingathering of the exiles on condition the party would strive for the return of the Arab refugees'.[30] Bastouni insisted upon Mapam adopting a policy favouring Arab national liberation. The Arabs expected Mapam to fight for them in view of their inferior status as a deprived minority, and they rejected what seemed to be complicity, though silent, in the 'policy of deprivation'.

A party convention was convened for the purpose of bridging the gap between the factions and reorganizing the party's institutions and platform. The Arab problem became the focal point in that convention. The changes that had occurred in the political constellation and the social environment after 1948 had their effect on the distribution of opinions in Mapam, especially with respect to Arab integration. By mid-1951 it became evident that peace between Israel and her Arab neighbours was not to be expected in the near future. As a result the Israeli Arabs were no longer seen (as they had been in 1948) as a potential 'bridgehead' for peace with the larger Arab world but were a deprived minority, posing a security risk to the state. What was there in common between the peoples of the two nations that could have united them in one party, struggling to achieve common goals?

Hashomer Hatzair based its answer on a belief in socialism combined with Jewish nationalism. The 'socialist' part of the answer was simple. Both the Jews and the Arabs could secure their social needs through progressive, *Jewish*, socialist parties. The nationalist argument was more ambiguous. Hashomer Hatzair was a Zionist faction which advocated the integration of the Arabs into Israeli society which was a Jewish society. This included granting membership in the party to the Arabs.

Achdut Haavodah disagreed and blamed Hashomer Hatzair with trying to have its cake and eat it too, by demanding Arab integration into the party without making serious concessions on policies or institutional structures. Achdut Haavodah argued that Hashomer Hatzair recognised that the Arabs, being a minority, would have no chance to assert effective political influence on disputed questions and could certainly not influence the Jewish-Zionist character of the party, so their inclusion in the party would just be a sham. Nevertheless, Hashomer Hatzair regarded the integration of the Arabs into the party as the first step towards peace, based on the old dream of a bi-national state. For Hashomer Hatzair the ideological argument overruled the utilitarian one.

Achdut Haavodah's positions were also rooted in ideology, based on other issues. In 1951 it was more militant than in 1948, visualising Mapam as a 'security party'. Its members pressed for joining the coalition 'to share the responsibility' with regard to national security. Moreover, Mapam's orientation towards Russia and the Communist world was opposed by Achdut-Haavodah, who advocated 'neutralism' as an alternative. In contrast to Hashomer Hatzair's emphasis on socialism, it gave primacy to Zionism, concluding that 'as long as the Jewish nation is ex-territorialistic and has no possession of its land (meaning all Palestine), a Zionist party cannot be a territorial Jewish-Arab one'. The identification of Achdut Haavodah with world Jewry was more explicit in 1951 than in 1948, at the height of mass Jewish immigration to Israel. As for the Arabs, the faction still favoured an autonomous Arab-socialist party. Although it did not favour discrimination, Achdut Haavodah held that the Jews had unique rights in Israel which could not be shared with the Arabs. 'There is no Palestinian nation', said Tabenkin,[31] since there is an Arab nation in Syria, Egypt and Jordan. The Arabs form a single national entity, whereas the Jews have no national identity elsewhere. Israel was designated to be a land for the Jewish people, and that hard fact excluded a partisan, binational system, argued Achdut Haavodah. Nonetheless, the Arabs should enjoy equal rights as a minority in Israel.

In view of contradictory positions, Mapam again reached a stage of 'non-decision' with regard to the issue of Arab integration, despite the fact that intra-party power relations had shifted,[32] enabling Hashomer Hatzair to reach a decision by a majority. Thus a compromise was reached; it was decided to adopt a 'tendency' towards integration, meaning broadening cooperation with the party's Arab section and working *towards* a territorial party that would unite all workers.[33] Mapam made a commitment to struggle for the admittance of Arabs to the Histadrut as equal members. The intra-party conflict ended without winners or losers. The Arabs were not admitted into the party, but the spirit of the decision adopted by the convention hinted that this provision was only temporary. It was decided to enlarge the Arab department in the party and to allocate more resources (funds and manpower) to its activities. Thus, the party started moving towards the final stage of integration.

THE END OF THE 'TENDENCY'

The elections for the second Knesset took place in July 1951. Mapam lost four of the nineteen seats it held in the previous Knesset. Although the party placed an Arab on its list in a 'realistic' place, meaning having a real chance of election according to former election results, only about 4,000 Arabs out of a total of 86,000 voted for Mapam. Regardless of its tendency towards territorialisation, Mapam was seen as a Zionist party by the Arabs, and despite its social philosophy advocating 'international solidarity', it failed to secure the Arab vote.[34]

R. Bastouni embarrassed Mapam by making extreme demands, such as calling for public rallies to protest against the military government which applied to the Arabs and advocating the establishment of a friendship league between Israel and the Arab nations.[35] For an Arab these proposals were moderate. For a Jewish-Zionist party (especially one with an Achdut Haavodah faction) these demands were unreasonable. They were incompatible with government policy and with the struggle for survival in which Israel was engaged. Bastouni demanded that Mapam be active in Arab affairs on the national front and not restrict itself to the partisan arena.

Mapam reacted to these demands in its traditional manner. It decided in April 1952, after tedious deliberations, to set up a committee with the purpose of strengthening the relationships between the party and the Arab section.

In 1952 an event occurred that had a serious effect on Mapam and its policies. One of the party's leaders, M. Oren, was convicted as a spy and imprisoned by the Czechoslovakian government. Because of its communist orientation, Mapam was divided in its opinions concerning the trial. The majority believed in Oren's innocence, although one group saw the trial as a 'tragic mistake' and another group thought it was simply a manifestation of anti-semitism. Only a minority expressed an unquestioning solidarity with the Czech Communist regime and its procedures of justice. Part of the Arab section, headed by Knesset member, R. Bastouni, belonged to this group. In January 1953, the Arab section announced its support for the Republic of Czechoslovakia and vociferously demanded the 'internationalisation' of the party.

Hashomer Hatzair explained the radicalisation of the Arab section, part of which left the party in order to join Maki, as the result of the frustrations which grew out of the continuous delays in integrating the Arabs into the party. Following Hashomer Hatzair views, Mapam decided to make a concession and admit into the party about 600 Arab activists on an *individual* basis after one year of apprenticeship. Achdut Haavodah was unwilling to compromise. Tabenkin defined the proposal as 'hypocrisy and comedy' and charged that 'it excludes from the party those wishing to be in a Socialist-Jewish party.'[36] The fact that only 600 Arabs were to be admitted to the party was irrelevant since the dispute concerned the principle. Achdut Haavodah argued that it was impossible to hold both ends of the rope, to be Zionists and to admit Arab members, and that the damage (with regard to potential electoral gains and ideology) would be greater than the benefits derived from the integration of the Arabs into the party because it would cause the party to lose its Jewish identity and its Zionist orientation. Achdut Haavodah objected to any further deliberations on the issue, defining it as a 'critical level'[37] that, when passed, would bring about the split of the party.

In the summer of 1953 Hashomer Hatzair made another attempt to admit the Arabs into the party through the back door. In the organisational regulations set up by the party's secretariat (in August 1953) there was an article which permitted the mobilisation of each person willing to be a candidate and having been recommended by two veteran party members. This was the tribute paid by the party to the group of Arabs who had rejoined the party after affiliating with a small, leftist faction that dissented from the party because of the Prague trial. However, the implementation of these regulations was delayed due to Achdut Haavodah's veto, based on a threat to quit the party.

Israel's security position deteriorated in 1954. Arab infiltration into the country was followed by Israeli reprisals. It seemed that Israel was on the verge of another war (the war actually broke out two years later). This state of affairs had an effect on the attitudes of the factions towards the Arab problem within the party. Hashomer Hatzair's strategy was far more conciliatory than that of Achdut Haavodah. The majority opposed a militant security policy and continued efforts to transform Mapam into a 'bi-national party'. Achdut Haavodah did not relinquish its objections. However, that was not the only reason for the rift that developed in the party. The two factions disagreed on many other issues such as foreign policy orientation, attitudes toward participation in the government, social policy and organisational framework. The controversy around the issue of the integration of the Arabs into the party symbolised the different views that existed in Mapam on the eve of its split.

The party split in August 1954 after Achdut Haavodah refused to abolish a factional publication. One of the first measures taken by the remainder of the party, who still carried the name Mapam and who consisted mainly of former members of Hashomer Hatzair, was to admit Arabs into the party. They emphasised that they felt that this was the only key to the solution of the Arab-Israeli dispute, or if not the key, it would at least be an instrument to prevent war.

CONCLUSIONS

It has been suggested in the foregoing pages that ideological, political and psychological factors inhibited what might have been a smooth path for the integration of the Arabs into Israeli society through membership in a Jewish-Zionist party.

The ideological factors were rooted in historical attitudes that proved to be unbridgeable, despite the merger between the two factions. Ideology played a major role in forming the factions' policies and attitudes. Hashomer Hatzair professed 'international solidarity' as an integral part of the all-encompassing socialist, Marxist orientation. Achdut Haavodah placed the highest value on the uniqueness of Jewish nationalism. An adjustment based on tactical calculations could not erase the ideological gap. Integration of the Arabs into the party was made possible only after the values of Hashomer Hatzair had gained exclusive dominance.

Mapam's attitude to the Arab problem was political rather than ideological. The party did not employ majority rule in order to pass a decision which the minority strongly opposed. Mapam was not willing to pay the price of a split in order to fulfil the mission of integration. However, there were other political calculations, mainly based on electoral factors and linked with intra-party power relations.

Mapam could have attracted only the socialist Arabs. Their admission to the party would have had the effect of strengthening its left wing or Hashomer Hatzair, a result not desired by Achdut Haavodah. That faction was oriented towards Jewish ethnic minorities, especially among the new immigrants, who would not have joined an Arab-Jewish party because of psychological factors.

There were some economic interests involved in the various attitudes taken toward the Arabs. The kibbutz movement affiliated with Hashomer Hatzair, Hakibbutz Haartzi, could hardly implement its leaders' policy since it clashed with day-to-day interests. The kibbutzim cultivated Arab lands, and they were not enthusiastic about the party's attempts to organise groups of young Arab pioneers who would get their training on the kibbutz. The kibbutz movement affiliated with Achdut Haavodah was even more nationalistic, and it was not interested in improving relations with the Arabs. Its affiliation with Mapam just increased the conflict that ended with the split in the kibbutz movement.

The psychological factors were more elusive. It was only seldom mentioned (in private meetings) that many party members were 'contaminated with chauvinism' and still needed to acquire, by way of socialisation, a feeling of comradeship with the Arabs. A party resembling a small, primary group (especially Mapam which was rather small in size) was not the proper structure to achieve bi-national integration.

What were the motivations of Arabs to join Mapam? Being on the fringes of Israeli society, the Arabs felt alienated. They were attracted to Mapam because it was both an opposition and an establishment party. As an opposition party it criticised discriminatory policies. As an establishment party it shared the basic values of the Israeli political system. Mapam might have served as a modest starting-point for the integration of the Arab population into the institutional political system in those critical years in which Arab-Jewish relations in Israel crystallised. The insurmountable obstacles faced by Mapam prevented the realisation of this process and prevented the accommodation of some of the frustrations and grievances of the Arabs. Hence, Mapam failed to make a significant contribution not only to the solution of the Arab-Israeli conflict, but also to the integration of at least part of the Arab population into the Israeli political system.

NOTES

1. E. Gutmann, 'Some Observations on Politics and Parties in Israel', *Indian Quarterly* (17) 1961, pp. 1–27.
2. B. Akzin, 'The Role of Parties in Israeli Democracy', *Journal of Politics* (17) 1955, pp. 507–15.
3. Since 1948 until its formal termination in 1966. On the general condition of the Arabs see: O. Stendel, *The Minorities in Israel*, Jerusalem, Israel economist, 1973.
4. See the leading book on the Arabs in Israel: J. M. Landau, *The Arabs in Israel: A Political Study*, London, Oxford University Press, 1969, especially chapter 4.
5. This group united with another small, leftist party, Poalei-Zion, in 1946.
6. G. Sartori, 'European Political Parties: The Case of Polarized Pluralism' in J.

Lapalombara and M. Weiner, *Political Parties and Political Development*, Princeton, Princeton University Press, 1966.
7. Achdut Haavodah platform for the elections to Knesset Israel, July 1944.
8. See A. Cohen, *Israel and the Arab World*, London, W. H. Allen, 1970.
9. On the League see A. Cohen, *op. cit.*, especially pp. 300–7.
10. As was mentioned, both had strongholds in the kibbutz. Hakibbutz Hameuchad was affiliated to Achdut Haavodah and Hakibbutz Haartzi to Hashomer Hatzair.
11. Ben Aharon, Achdut Haavodah, in the party's centre meeting, 30 Oct. 1947. Mapam's archive.
12. Despite the orientation towards a bi-national state, Hashomer Hatzair did not sponsor the Arabs for admission into the Histadrut, which was Hebrew in ideology and organisation.
13. Hazan, Mapam's centre, 16 Sept. 1948. Mapam's archive.
14. Yaari, *ibid*, 15 Dec. 1948.
15. Mapam's centre, A Letter to the Activists, No. 5, 14 May 1948.
16. B. Marshak, Achdut Haavodah party centre, 16 Sept. 1948.
17. *Ibid*.
18. Mapam, political committee, 15 June 1948, *ibid*.
19. E. Peri, Mapam political committee, 26 May 1948, *ibid*.
20. M. Bentov in the Provisional Government, 1 Aug. 1948, in D. Ben Gurion, *The Restored State of Israel*, Tel-Aviv, Am-Oved, 1969, p. 250 (in Hebrew).
21. 1 per cent of the total eligible vote that has to be passed in order to win a mandate to the Knesset.
22. See Landau, *op. cit.*, p. 110.
23. Mapam, The Department of Arab Activity, Bulletin No. 5, 20 Feb. 1949.
24. See Akzin, *op. cit.* and Landau, *op. cit.*
25. Meaning a party which includes all people living in the territory as potential members.
26. Tabenkin, Mapam political committee, 18 Aug. 1949. Mapam's archive.
27. Bar-Yehuda, Mapam party secretariat, 19 July 1949, *ibid*.
28. From a letter written by A. Cohen to the political committee, 6 July 1949, private archive.
29. 18 Dec. 1949.
30. R. Bastouni, an Arab intellectual, was Mapam's Arab candidate to the second Knesset and its first Arab member.
31. Lebhinat Shlehutein, *Mibifnim*, 17 Feb. 1954.
32. Achdut Haavodah came out of the internal party elections as a minority faction, securing only 34 per cent of the vote.
33. Mapam's platform adopted at the second convention, Haifa, 6 June 1951.
34. Lanau notes that Mapam gained 5.6 per cent of the Arab vote in comparison to 0.2 per cent in the previous elections, *op. cit.*, p. 116.
35. Mapam, the central committee, 10 March 1952. Mapam's archive.
36. In the secretariat meeting of the Kibbutz Hameuchad, 7 April 1953, Archive Efaal.
37. See K. W. Deutch, *Politics and Government*, New York, Houghton Mifflin, 1970.